AT ISSUE:
POLITICS IN
THE WORLD ARENA

At Issue:
Politics in the World Arena

STEVEN L. SPIEGEL, Editor
University of California, Los Angeles

St. Martin's Press
New York

To the memory of my father

ACKNOWLEDGMENTS . . . .

p. 15: "Color in World Affairs," by Harold R. Isaacs. Reprinted by permission from *Foreign Affairs,* January 1968. Copyright is held by the Council on Foreign Relations, Inc., New York.

p. 27: "Ambush at Kamikaze Pass," by Tom Engelhardt. From *Bulletin of Concerned Asian Scholars,* Winter–Spring, 1971, pp. 65–84. Copyright © and permission by Tom Engelhardt.

p. 44: "Are the Poor Countries Getting Poorer?" by Theodore Caplow. Reprinted from *Foreign Policy* 3, Summer 1971. Copyright 1971 by National Affairs, Inc.

p. 55: "The Developing World—Should We Give a Damn?" by Robert Hunter. Reprinted by permission from *War/Peace Report,* April 1971, pp. 3–5.

Preface

This book is a response to the frustrations of teaching an undergraduate course in world politics and finding my students dissatisfied because few books I assigned seemed to address their needs and interests. I have sought here to fill the gap by dealing directly with the major political, economic, and social issues that are current in international affairs: among them, racial and ethnic conflict, the balance of power, the future possibilities of world order, and the crisis of foreign policy-making institutions. My aim has been to give the reader a sense of the complexities and dynamics of present-day world politics while also providing background on specific questions. Though the problems encountered by Americans in formulating and conducting foreign policy have not been stressed exclusively, I have generally oriented the volume to the dilemmas faced by the United States as we enter the post-Vietnam era. The book should therefore be useful for courses in American foreign policy as well as world politics.

The twenty-nine articles contained here were chosen after extensive investigation in the major journals and periodicals that are concerned with international affairs. Over three hundred individual manuscripts were examined, the most promising of which were assigned to an upper division seminar in the fall of 1971 and to a freshman seminar in the fall of 1972. The preferences and reactions of my students counted heavily in the final selection. Among the criteria were readability, the extent to which articles informed students and might be relevant to a variety of international problems, how well they represented a broad spectrum of ideological and national views, and how well they might withstand the constant change of events.

I am grateful to many who have provided needed advice and assistance through their reactions to the material presented here. My students have afforded me constant encouragement and made the project an exciting one. In particular, Kathleen Humphrey served as a judicious critic when the huge number of prospective articles seemed almost overwhelming. Karin Gomez and Robert Krueger contributed time, effort, and significant advice. I am also grateful for the enthusiastic response of St. Martin's Press to my proposed project. In particular, Jonathan Latimer served in the role of intellectual companion as well as editor; Judy Green and Jenny Lawrence skillfully guided the volume through production. The secretarial staff of the UCLA Political Science Department graciously accepted my entreaties that they meet unreasonable deadlines.

The subjects discussed in this volume represent some of the most important questions now before the statesmen of the world, and many of the articles present grim alternatives and disturbing analyses. On the other hand, humor or at least an appreciation of irony seems to me sometimes almost the only possible response to the vicissitudes of world politics, and I trust that an occasional touch of humor in this volume will not be mistaken for levity. Above all, I hope that the student's experience with the books will help to make the study of international politics both intellectually rewarding and enjoyable.

Steven L. Spiegel
Los Angeles
January, 1973

Contents

INTRODUCTION

The Post-Vietnam Era:
America Faces the World

As the United States seeks a new foreign policy in a changing world after Vietnam, it seems clear that the shibboleths of the 1950's and 1960's are inadequate, even irrelevant, to the urgent issues that will occupy nations and peoples in the years ahead. New perspectives are needed. Our purpose in this book is to identify the crucial developments in world politics with which an adjusted American foreign policy will have to deal—that is, to attempt to understand the international environment in which future foreign-policy decisions will have to be made.

We are not so much concerned here with examining the alternatives available to American leaders on specific policy questions: the developed versus the developing world; a Japanese versus European orientation; the Soviet Union versus China; neo-isolationism versus interventionism; economic diplomacy versus coercion; trade wars versus cooperation with allies. The articles presented here touch upon these topics because they represent the salient issues of present-day world politics; but our primary aim is to understand the forces underlying such issues as these so that we can reorient our thinking to meet future problems, arising from the conflicts of peoples, new kinds of alliances, changes in the balance of power, the crises of institutions, the rise and fall of leaders, and technological change.

For Americans a peculiar perspective shapes foreign-policy considerations—an underlying egalitarian assumption that seems to prevent due consideration of the importance of differences in race, religion, ethnic identification and economic status. It is ironic that our politicians, who have so readily perceived the effect of ethnic differences in voting patterns at home, have failed to take such differences into account when they have turned their attention to the international scene. National self-determination—our slogan in foreign affairs from the days of Woodrow Wilson to the present—is a concept we have applied mainly to European areas and defined in formalistic democratic terms without due consideration for local conditions. The impulse toward self-determination of subnational and transnational ethnic cultures outside the United States we have tended to disregard entirely. This fallacy and its effect on policy can be demonstrated by the 1971 upheaval in Pakistan. The United States government thought it could contribute to the amelioration of the dispute by maintaining influence with the West Pakistani government while avoiding dissension with Pakistan's international patron, China, before the President's trip to Peking. If the conflict had been perceived in social and ethnic rather than legalistic terms, the Nixon Administration would have recognized that Pakistan was finished as a viable state—regardless of great-power considerations—when, in March 1971, the West Pakistani army occupied what was to become Bangladesh and proceeded to rob, rape, and ravage the local population. How a problem is understood affects the policies one adopts to deal with it.

The experience of the United States in Vietnam poses a challenge to future American interventions and dramatic actions abroad. The trauma of defeat, of sending soldiers to fight and die for unclear goals, has brought into question the premises on which post-1945 American policy has been based. Even more fundamentally, Vietnam has shaken the confidence of Americans in their ability to discern the difference between right and wrong, between good and evil on the foreign scene. It has even challenged the applicability of that criterion. (The American *weltanschauung* has for decades been based on a view of world politics as a morality play, in which the U.S. and its allies play cowboy with the world's Indians.) There are those among both critics and supporters of the Vietnam war who now predict an increase in American isolationism as one of its outcomes. But such a perspective reflects the conditions and assumptions of a bygone era, for America today is too involved abroad economically, militarily, and politically to withdraw from the world arena. In the 1920's America could retreat from the world in the belief that she was insulating herself from corruption. But after Vietnam and the domestic crises of the sixties, the suspicion runs deep among Americans that the center of corruption lies at home; isolationism no longer offers the possibility of escape to an untainted and virtuous condition within our own borders.

Just as the Civil War of the 1860's brought Americans for the first time to a realization of internal tragedy and ended the prevailing belief in the inevitability of the freedom and unity of the Republic, so the Vietnam crisis of the 1960's ended the faith of many Americans in the moral and political superiority of this nation to other nations. Many now question the principles, morality, and propriety of past American actions abroad while others seek to defend America's global role at all cost. Both groups have implicitly supposed that once our faith in an American-led world order based on harmony and justice is undermined, the moral and intellectual framework of Americans' views about themselves and the rest of the world is bound to crumble. The failure thus far to bridge the gap between the total certainty of some and the abject disillusionment of others about the correctness of the American course represents one of the major challenges of the post-Vietnam era.

After 1945 the Cold War that was waged between capitalist and communist forces gave world politics a unifying theme and an ironic principle of order. The Eastern and Western blocs were engaged in intense rivalry, but this focus of hostility provided an organization and orientation for international affairs. So central was the ideological theme that it was reflected in the domestic politics of many leading countries: in McCarthyism and Stalinism in the United States and the Soviet

Union; Gaullism and Communism in France; the political division into two states of both Germany and China. More than any other single movement, McCarthyism in America reacted to the prevailing world theme in an effort to drive the bearers of evil from the hallowed homeland. In both the domestic and international arenas, predominant sections of the decision-making elite advocated a policy oriented to what was perceived as a pervasive Communist threat. In more moderate American quarters, a bipartisan foreign-policy consensus preserved the appearance of unity and perpetuated the faith in harmony, order, and the American conception of global justice.

But today Washington flirts with Peking, Bonn with Moscow, and Peking with Tokyo. A gradual recognition of global diversity has been forced upon Americans by the events of the sixties and early seventies. The superpower blocs have degenerated to hollow shells of their former strength, and new powers have arisen to challenge the primacy of the United States and the Soviet Union: China on ideological issues; Japan in economic matters; and a vaguely defined Europe as a potential third force. Concurrently with the decline of blocs and alliances, the level of hostility has declined among all of the great powers except for that between the Soviet Union and China. Interest in greater economic cooperation or competition and the fear of nuclear confrontation loom far larger in great-power calculations than ideological disputes. The frightening great-power crises represented by Berlin, Korea, Hungary, and ultimately Cuba have disappeared. They are replaced by hot and cold wars among smaller states which are now freer than ever before to concentrate on their own concerns. Headline-makers today are Arabs, Israelis, Indians, Pakistanis, Quebeckers, and Irishmen. Hijackings, terror campaigns, and political assassinations by men who are devoid of power in their own local areas have replaced capers at the global brink by leaders of the world's strongest states.

The polychromatic nature of the present period is similarly reflected in the changing themes of domestic politics. A world focused on ideology tended to ignore cultural differences between peoples; skin color, religion, or even form of government counted less than allegiance to a particular bloc or set of ideas. Today this unifying theme is gone, and the cultural and ethnic diversity of the world's population and the hostility of proximate groups seem paramount. In domestic as well as international politics, ethnic identification and differentiation are on the rise. In the United States, our changing politics and social mores reflect a country grown more knowledgeable about cultural divergence and less addicted to ideological consensus. Archie Bunker and Detective Shaft have risen on the graves of Yankee Doodle and Uncle Sam. In the Soviet Union the Jews, once lost in silent assimilation, suddenly have emerged as the most vocal of that nation's various peoples, while prominent scientists, artists, and writers encourage dissent by their defiance of the established Kremlin order. In Britain the government must face demands for Welsh, Scottish, and, most prominently, Irish autonomy, and the greater visibility of Asian immigrants engenders fear that remains a continuing theme of domestic politics. In France, Brittany challenges the concept of ethnic and national unity, while the North Africans residing in Paris are an uncomfortable Third World presence comparable to the South Asians in London.

The anthropological has thus replaced the ideological as the key contributor to present-day world tensions. National, racial, and ethnic conflicts occur between and within large states and small, while the world's Gullivers scramble for a concert of power and achieve a stalemate of forces. A stand-off rather than actual cooperation may be their fate, but at least the United States and the Soviet Union can hope to avoid the radiated Armageddon which each has the power to inflict on the other. Meanwhile, neither can avoid the effect of ethnic conflicts in either its domestic or international politics.

Even in the forties and fifties—although American doctrines relied on ideological (and to a lesser extent economic) explanations of the sources of conflict and instability—the real causes of tensions were often, and increasingly, based in social and ethnic conflicts between peoples who had been thrust together by the upheavals resulting from the breakup of the colonial order. This condition has existed in such diverse areas as the Middle East, Southern Africa, Cyprus, Nigeria, Sudan, and the Indian subcontinent. Ethnic differences lie at the heart of international and internal conflicts in Southeast Asia (Vietnamese versus Khmer versus Thai versus Chinese), in Latin America (Black versus Indian versus Mestizo versus White), and in the tribal conflicts of Africa that crisscross international boundaries. Indeed, the four major conflicts of the fifties and early sixties—over the two Germanies, Koreas, Vietnams and Chinas—were distinctive for their ideological basis. Each seemed to bear out the analysis of international politics which the American position presented. Especially after the Cuban Revolution, the ideological and economic basis of world instability seemed confirmed. The essential uniqueness of these conflicts went unnoticed.

Today ideological conflict, fought between parties of similar ethnic background but divergent political outlook, has become even less frequent. Blacks battle Whites in Africa; Bengalis battle Pakistanis in South Asia, and Israelis battle Arabs in the Middle East.[1] Though Vietnam represented the ultimate globalization of anti-Communism in American foreign policy, America entered the conflict just as this ideological criterion was becoming obviously inappropriate to both national security and international peace. One of the ironies of the Vietnamese conflict is that it was becoming most clearly an aberration rather than an embodiment of the norm of international politics just at the time when the Johnson Administration was conceiving of it as the model of American action elsewhere.

The difficulties which Americans face in attempting to integrate

altered international conditions into a new foreign policy are aggravated
by our penchant for recognizing only the rational and orderly while
ignoring the chaotic or irrational. American Administrations have
tended to view the world as being composed of abstract units which
could be fitted into neat scenarios in accordance with doctrines having
universal applicability. All states, it has been assumed, will act alike
in response to similar stimuli and can be deterred or defended on the
basis of the same kinds of goals that motivate Americans. In Vietnam
in 1965 the consequences of this assumption came to haunt the Johnson
Administration; it was naturally assumed that the North Vietnamese
would surrender in the South when faced with American bombing.
Indeed, it is conceivable that a society like our own, subjected to such
an attack, might have been forced to surrender; but the North Vietnamese, with a different culture, standard of living, and set of objectives
did not.

It is distinctive of the American approach to world affairs that
despite massive expenditures of men and materiel in the longest war
in American history, Americans know almost as little today about the
culture and history of Vietnam as they did before it all began. Calculations concerning bombing, pacification, and "Vietnamization" were
made in terms of abstractions, of "A affecting B," rather than in terms
of actual conditions and realities. Unlike Europeans, Americans have
little appreciation for differences in culture, and particularly those of
non-Western countries. The American myth of a "melting pot" has
inhibited this country's capacity to perceive differences in peoples
abroad. In a land where immigrants brought with them diverse cultures that were to be woven into one unit, the ability to perceive the
importance of distinctions among other countries was impeded. As a
consequence of this underlying assumption of the similarity of all
peoples, the nation's leaders could believe that they would be able to
transport their way of life to states of differing cultures and economic
and ideological backgrounds. The Johnsonian "Great Society" was presented as a viable domestic program within the United States; it was
somehow also perceived to be appropriate for the Vietnamese. In this
sense the American *weltanschauung* is strangely like the Marxian—a
kind of economic determinism which assumes the universal applicability
of its own principles.

This view of the similarity of all states facilitates an international-
ized Horatio Alger myth in which the notion that anyone who works
hard can rise from rags to riches is applied to countries abroad. Just
efficiency to be the principal requisites for advancement up the economic
as in the domestic scene Americans have considered perseverance and
ladder, we have tended to view weaker states as worthy of our friendship only if they could produce political order and increased economic
proficiency. Unlike the Marxist-Leninists, who have insisted on a com-

plex ideology, or the French who have had a preconceived notion of civilization, Americans have required of weaker nations only good work habits and democratic institutions as criteria for approval. But economic success is more easily measured than political or social accomplishments, and so economic measurements have taken precedence over more abstract considerations such as the level of democracy or of justice in a society. Taiwan and South Korea will serve as examples. And since democracy has proved for most countries difficult to achieve and even more difficult for us to assess, countries whose governments have cooperated with the American government have tended to be the ones chosen for American favor, even over those who have democratized. Hence Pakistan was favored over India, Brazil over Chile. Thus the American precept that "all men are created equal" led to the implicit belief that regardless of the diverse races and cultures, the differing locations and conditions of men, American activities abroad could be conducted according to a single, universal standard.

In the post-Vietnam era, it appears that the tendency of American politicians of both parties is toward a concentration on relations with great powers and a policy of leaving the troubled Third World to fend for itself as best it can. Emerging economic competition with European allies and Japan, and the prospects of improved relations with the Soviet Union and China, are likely to dominate American foreign policy throughout the 1970's. The great powers will concentrate on each other while Third World states continue to focus on their own concerns. Local tensions may intensify, but there will be less involvement, assistance, and interest from all major powers.

The technological framework within which policies are formulated will alter as well. Alvin Toffler warns that constant change creates, and is likely to continue to create at an accelerating pace, conditions for which present institutions are not prepared:

> To survive, to avert what we have termed future shock, the individual must become infinitely more adaptable and capable than ever before. He must search out totally new ways to anchor himself, for all the old roots—religion, nation, community, family, or profession—are now shaking under the hurricane impact of the accelerative thrust.[2]

American foreign policy will also be forced to take these conditions into account. Such topics as the population and pollution explosions and the energy crisis will probably become more central to the calculations of Americans in international affairs than they have been in the past. Under the pressure of these and other problems, Americans will be forced to examine the capacity of their institutions to cope with diversity and change. The magnitude of the difficulty is vividly suggested by James Thomson's account of the frustration of a member of the government opposed to the American role in the Vietnam conflict:

> To put it bluntly: at the heart of the Vietnam calamity is a group of

able, dedicated men who have been regularly and repeatedly wrong—and whose standing with their contemporaries, and more important, with history, depends, as they see it, on being proven right. These are not men who can be asked to extricate themselves from error.[3]

Not only governmental institutions but international institutions as well will affect the global society of the twenty-first century. The United Nations will have to be revived or it is not likely to play an effective role in an increasingly complex international environment. Multinational corporations—those semiprivate and semisovereign agencies which have become more and more influential in international affairs—probably will continue to grow in prominence. Finally, it remains to be seen whether leaders of the stature of Bismarck or Churchill will again emerge in international politics or whether conditions have become too complex to permit such widespread influence on the part of single individuals—even national leaders.

This book is divided into four parts. The first, *The Conflict of Peoples,* examines the nature and causes of current international conflicts—between great and small, rich and poor, satisfied and dissatisfied. The role of ethnic differences in motivating conflict is stressed, but the influence of economic gaps and great-power aims is considered as well.

The second part, *The Burden of the Strong,* concentrates on the relations and problems of the major powers. We try to assess the currently popular notion that somehow a "balance of power" can be reinstated between the world's strongest units, the United States, the Soviet Union, Europe, Japan, and China, similar to the concert of powers which existed in the nineteenth century. The articles assess relations between specific states, the nature and concept of the balance, and the role of armaments—especially nuclear weapons—in promoting or inhibiting that balance.

The third part, *The Crises of Institutions,* deals with the institutional problems that seem to plague political actors on all levels of global society. The European unity movement, the plight of the United Nations, and the impact of the multinational corporation are considered. We next focus on the nation-state itself, paying special attention to the American context. Some have argued that it is organizational constraints and bureaucratic procedures that cause governments to act in ways that are seemingly irrational. Others attribute the poor performance of states to their leaders, and we examine here the records of Charles deGaulle and Mao Tse-tung for possible lessons about the role of leaders in the future.

Finally, in the fourth part, *The Problems of the Future,* we turn to a consideration of the promise and pitfalls represented by technological development with special attention to population growth, the food supply, and the environment, and to the divergent effects of future conditions on the rich and poor. As new technologies developed, enabling men to come in closer contact through more efficient means of travel and communication, many hoped that a comparable increase in international understanding and cooperation would evolve. History, however, has moved in another direction, and men seem to have reacted to the growth of global communications by turning inward to their own local groups. The transistor thereby becomes a vehicle for whipping the masses to frenzied hatred, the jet an instrument for the delivery of destruction and a focus for terrorist activities outside the indigenous area of conflict.

It is ironic indeed that while the superpowers have been transfixed by the threat of nuclear weapons, the number of human beings killed as a consequence of local upheavals has increased at an accelerating rate. The atomic bombs dropped on Hiroshima and Nagasaki killed and wounded approximately 220,000 Japanese; but it is estimated that as many as three million were killed in the 1971 war to establish the independence of Bangladesh, more than two million in the unsuccessful effort to free Biafra. On the one hand, the great powers have become cautious in the face of a technology of ever greater destructiveness. On the other hand, weaker states and groups have attained an improved capacity to conduct traditional types of conflict despite the preferences of the strong for tranquility.

It is evident that the challenges to American foreign policy of the future will be severe. Yet it should also be apparent that our increasingly technological world offers new opportunities for cooperation as well as for conflict. Vietnam, through tragedy and torture, has taught Americans the lesson of difference: men and nations are not universally similar; they do not react to comparable objectives and needs. Our task in the years ahead is to apply what has been learned. This volume seeks to provide material for discussion and debate in the hope that a new American approach to the world will in fact emerge— one less devoted to ideological abstractions and simple contrasts between weakness and might or globalism and retreat, more inclined to recognize the differing conditions and to respect the distinct cultures in which the peoples of the world exist.

NOTES

1 Though South America might seem an exception to this generalization, the domestic conflict in Chile over the Marxist experiment is much less central to continental politics than is the growing concern about Brazilian domination. In an era when the appeal of Cuba's Castro has declined and even Peru's military government has nationalist aims, ideological themes are no longer primary.

2 Alvin Toffler, *Future Shock* (New York: Bantam Books, 1971), p. 35.

3 James C. Thomson, Jr., "How Could Vietnam Happen? An Autopsy," *The Atlantic*, April 1968, p. 51.

PART I

The Conflict of Peoples

The first part of this volume concentrates on the conflicts of peoples: disputes between nations or groups in close proximity who are thrust into a cauldron of contention by economic, ideological, social, or ethnic differences; disputes between the strong and weak powers of the world over divisions arising from their differing levels of strength and wealth. All of these articles focus on deeply held attitudes of hostility among peoples, but each has a different perspective on the origins of international contests.

The two articles in the first section of Part I develop the theme of the impact of national outlook and cultural divergence on the attitudes of particular groups toward their adversaries. Harold Isaacs in "Color in World Affairs" presents an overview of the role of race in international politics. He points out that when the vaguer concepts of ethnicity and tribalism are added to that of race, the perceived differences between people play a role in almost all conflicts in the world today. He thus presents us with a lesson: particular issues in dispute between national spokesmen may represent only the tip of an iceberg of underlying suspicions and antagonistic attitudes. These feelings of animosity are often far more important in understanding a particular conflict than the public discussions and diplomatic niceties in which the controversy may be couched.

Tom Engelhardt, in "Ambush at Kamikaze Pass," warns that estrangement between peoples may not consciously be recognized by the parties themselves. Many American readers may view Mr. Engelhardt's characterization with a sense of skepticism and be reluctant to accept the article's conclusions. But Engelhardt teaches an important lesson: enmity need not be conscious, for subliminal suspicion toward those who look or act different is a self-perpetuating incentive to conflict. Engelhardt demonstrates how American cinema has reflected and perpetuated the prevailing American view of other peoples. Though his article deals with the United States, it could conceivably have been applied to other countries as well. For example, the Russian fear of peoples both to the east and west, especially in their Germanic and Mongol manifestations, is an oft-recounted theme in Russian cinema. The Engelhardt article should serve to refine the appreciation of an American audience for its own unrealized prejudices.

If we introduce this part with a section on underlying ethnic conflicts, the second section concentrates on the more traditional and better-known gap between the have and have-not countries of the world. Theodore Caplow asks, "Are the poor countries getting poorer?" and proceeds to examine the ways in which the weaker states are developing, how the considerable gulf between them and the stronger states is being maintained, and the ways in which that gulf is actually widening. Given what Caplow considers to be a stable hierarchy of states in which the strong remain strong and the weak remain weak, Robert Hunter's question is essential: "Should we give a damn about the developing world?" Hunter reviews the various arguments for and against foreign aid in the wake of Vietnam and attempts to discern whether or not great-power assistance can be effective in relation to developing countries. He also investigates the real motives for American interest in such aid as against the sense of moral obligation to which it has so often been ascribed. Hunter's article, whether one agrees with his conclusion or not, sheds much light on the implications of what is likely to continue to be one of the central issues of world politics.

In the third section, Hans Morgenthau and Ronald Steel, in their respective articles, explore the political and the military roles of great powers (particularly the United States) in relation to smaller countries. Steel considers the ways in which U.S. involvement in weaker states is seen by the radical critics of American foreign policy to be demanded by the capitalist system itself. Steel's examination of the various arguments concerning the role of imperialism in world politics and the nature of American imperialism is extremely useful in weighing the nature and causes of the American role in world affairs. Hans Morgenthau deals more directly with the political and military choices and consequences involved in the options of American intervention in local disputes. Though he may not solve the problem, he does provide a framework for encouraging more coherent discussion of the question he poses, "To intervene or not to intervene?"

We conclude this part by focusing on the dynamics of revolution, a type of conflict which has been much discussed in the last several years in ideological and academic terms. Those who have been intrigued with the problems of revolution have had ample cases of both successful and failed efforts on which to base their studies and conclusions. Francis Hutchins' "On Winning and Losing by Revolution" reminds Americans that violence may be a legitimate part of a political process, that stability and law and order are not universally to be preferred when people feel oppressed. Hutchins places the subject of revolution in the context of conflicts among peoples and shows that the fate of a particular group may be seriously affected by its role in a national upheaval. The nature of a group's participation and the identity of the victors are likely to affect the future balance of ethnicity, as well as of ideology, within a specific polity.

The other selections in this last section provide examples of particular revolutions. They are diverse in terms of geography, relevant issues, and outcome. Robert Lamberg describes the Bolivian revolution which was planned by Cubans but failed from within. The next three articles deal with ongoing conflicts with constituent revolutionary elements. We have included here the epilogue to John McAlister, Jr., and Paul Mus's book, *The Vietnamese and Their Revolution*. This selection examines the dynamics of the revolutionary elements which have been at work in South Vietnam as the conflict for control of the country has continued. McAlister and Mus describe the role of cultural values in the revolutionary and yet traditional setting that is Vietnam; they give special attention to the contrary perspectives of urban and rural Vietnamese societies. In his review of the Arab–Israeli conflict, Shlomo Avineri focuses on Palestinian-Israeli discord. He claims: "The real conflict in the Middle East is not between the great powers, nor is it a conflict between imperialism and anticolonialism, or between rural Vietnamese societies. In his review of the Arab-Israeli conflict, between two movements for national liberation." In Avineri's view the conflict can be solved only if there is some resolution between the Palestinian Arabs themselves and Israel. Since his article was written before King Hussein of Jordan crushed the Palestinian guerrillas in September of 1970, Avineri may have underestimated the role which Hussein might play in some form of ultimate settlement, but he offers a very useful tableau of the major factors in this dispute. Conor Cruise O'Brien presents a commentary on the violence in Ireland. He begins by considering whether the situation in Northern Ireland is similar to that which existed in French Algeria, where the indigenous Algerians attempted (at last successfully) to oust the French government while the French *colons* identified with the mother country. O'Brien concludes that the Algerian model is not applicable to the Irish situation. The Protestants of Northern Ireland are proportionally a far larger number than the French in Algeria; they have lived in the area much longer; and consequently their fate has been entwined with Irish and English questions in a much more intricate manner than was the case in Algeria.

The Vietnamese revolution has been fought largely over ideological issues, while the conflicts in the Middle East and Ireland are characterized more prominently by ethnic and religious divisions. More clearly than most conflicts in the current period, these two struggles are between divergent peoples for the habitation of a particular territory, and this condition contributes to their intensity. All three conflicts, however, typify the localized and tension-ridden conditions of most present-day disputes. All three have resulted in far greater bloodshed and suffering than the abortive Bolivian revolution planned by Che Guevara.

Race and Ethnic Nationalism

1

Color in World Affairs

HAROLD R. ISAACS

Matters of race and color are not actually more important in world affairs now than they were, say, a generation ago; only the thrust and direction of their importance have changed. This has been, of course, quite a change. The world of the 1940s was still by and large a Western white-dominated world. The long-established patterns of white power and nonwhite non-power were still the generally accepted order of things. All the accompanying assumptions and mythologies about race and color were still mostly taken for granted, hardly as yet shaken even by the Japanese challenge to Western primacy in Asia or by the attempt of the Germans to make themselves masters of the master race. The world of these late 1960s is a world in which this white dominance no longer exists, certainly not in its old forms. The power system which supported it has crumbled. Its superstructure of beliefs about the superiority-inferiority patterns of races and cultures lies in pieces amid the ruins. While some people cling to chunks of the debris and stand defiantly in the door-openings of their shattered towers, most of us are stumbling blindly around trying to discern the new images, the new shapes and perspectives these changes have brought, to adjust to the painful rearrangement of identities and relationships which the new circumstances compel. This is now the pressing business of individuals, nations and whole societies, and in the cluster of matters with which they must deal, hardly any is more nettling and more difficult to handle than the matter of race, especially as symbolized by differences of physical feature and color of skin. Of all the elements involved in this wrenching rearrangement, race or color is surely one of the most visible, more important in some cases than in others but hardly in any case not important at all.

Taking it in perhaps its largest aspect, we begin with the fact that the entire cluster of some 70 new states carved out of the old empires since 1945 is made up of nonwhite peoples newly out from under the political, economic and psychological domination of white rulers. Our legacy from the fallen empires is a world now often seen as divided between the northern and southern hemispheres, between have-nations and have-not-nations, and in this picture all the haves, except the Japanese, are white, and the have-nots are all nonwhite, each bearing the heavy burden of the carryover of the past with its experience of subjection or of mastery. To the political and economic tensions and conflicts that divide the world along these hemispheric and class lines, race differences and the recent history of racial behavior by whites add their own special quality of greater explosiveness. Indeed, among those who feel these differences most strongly—usually the angriest nonwhite radicals or the most frightened white conservatives—many are prone to put the race issue at the front and center of all current and prospective world conflict. Their prime threat or prime fear is the approach of a series of racial confrontations leading to a universal race war that will drive the line of color across all the other fields of conflict that now criss-cross the globe. This is commonly foreseen as an apocalyptic collision between what Sukarno used to call the OLDEFO (old established forces) under the leadership of the United States and the Soviet Union brought together by their common whitism, and NEFO (new emerging forces) led by China, mobilizing behind it all the peoples of the Third World united by their nonwhitism and their shared hatred of all whites. It would come as a crushing and catastrophic fulfillment of the famous prediction of W. E. B. DuBois of nearly 70 years ago, that the problem of the twentieth century would be "the problem of the color line—the relation of the darker to the lighter men in Asia and Africa, in America, and the islands of the sea," bringing a terrible time of reckoning for the white man called to account for his sins.

This may seem an unnecessarily feverish view of a world whose prospects under the plainest light just now are lurid enough. But it will not do to dismiss it just because it is usually held in this form by racial extremists of one kind or another. This would be like dismissing as wholly implausible the notion that the United States would not have dropped on Germany the atom bomb it did drop on Japan, or speculation over the possible reasons having to do with race why a mercy airlift to rescue a handful of Europeans in the Congo was feasible while a mercy airlift to bring succor to thousands of dying Africans in Biafra is not. Even the most cogently argued explanations in both these matters could not entirely ignore their racial components. In any case, it takes only a slight jog of the kaleidoscope to produce a view of the future held by some quite sober citizens who believe that the necessary power arrangement to come—and possibly the ultimate nuclear showdown as well—must be a Russian-American combination against the Chinese, a prospect not as far removed from the race-war view as some of these sober citizens might want to insist it is.

But it is not necessary to be overcome by overheated visions of an oncoming race war to see that issues of race and color *are* in some degree almost universally present in the great issues and problems that dominate this hemispheric set of confrontations. These are in the main issues of resources and development, population and the shaping of the political institutions—more open or more closed—that will govern the great majority of men for the next long while. Wherever the racial element is added to national, class, religious, ethnic and tribal lines of cleavage, it brings its own peculiar accretion of greater glandular involvement and emotional violence to all the other elements of conflict in which we are now entangled.

II

Race or color does not often appear as the central or single most critical factor in conflicts affecting international relations. As an issue of identity or relationship it is more usually present as one element among many. There are, however, some countries and situations where color does in fact figure as the core issue making for both internal and external conflict. Of these the most obvious and most important is the Union of South Africa.

The maintenance of white power by brute force in southern Africa —taking in Rhodesia and South West Africa—probably supplies the main source in current reality for the vision of a world eventually engulfed in a race war. If the actualities of power in southern Africa and in black Africa have so far belied the frequent predictions of explosive racial conflict there, this hardly means that it will not come to pass at all. The chances for that depend on whether the whites of southern Africa do finally come to their senses before it is too late, or whether the black peoples of those countries will submit indefinitely to their condition of total subjection. There is no present sign of the first outcome and no basis for expecting the second. An ultimately bloody confrontation of black and white in South Africa, with all its possible, predictable or imaginable consequences in the rest of the world and especially in the United States, is by no means the least certain of all the grim possibilities that lie ahead for us all. It may be a nightmare of a prospect, but as so much of our recent history has shown, nightmares are a good deal more likely to come true than any of our sweeter dreams.

But it is not only the possibility of future eruption that counts in this measure of things. White power in southern Africa is right now probably the sharpest of all the wedges that separate the newly emergent nonwhites of the world from its whites. It continuously mobilizes the emotions, if not yet the effective action, of the new nonwhite nations, especially in Africa, which figure so prominently and yet so insecurely in the world's politics. It may very well be that the South African mote helps them not to see their own assorted beams with respect to racism or oppression of minorities, but the fact remains nevertheless that the survival and blatant exercise of white supremacy in South Africa keeps their own experience with white racism alive

and vivid. It provides them—and the communist powers who are happy
to be handed an additional weapon—with a set of issues and emotions
on which they can all join despite so much else that divides them.
Colonialism, often used to serve the same purpose, may indeed be a
dead horse—except, to be sure, in Angola and Mozambique—but there
is nothing dead about white power as it is wielded in southern Africa.
It has figured on the United Nations agenda every year since 1952.
Pushed by the nonwhite newcomers, often to the acute discomfort especially of the British and the Americans, U.N. majorities have repeatedly
denounced South African apartheid, pressed the South West Africa
issue, handed down detailed indictments of oppression of blacks and
Indians, and demanded international action to put down the South
African and Rhodesian white racists.

The dragging reluctance of Britain and the United States to join
in these indictments—much less to take the actions voted—has served
as a measure in the minds of many nonwhites (American as well as
others) of the value of the commitments which these governments
always make on the issues of equality and justice in general. Those
winds of change which blew away the British Empire have by now
largely also dissipated the sentimental-romantic fog that for a while
overhung Britain's relations with its ex-colonies. The influx of black
and brown immigrants from the Caribbean, India and Pakistan has
produced a full-fledged white backlash in England, complete with
riots, liberal dismay, civil rights legislation and restrictions on immigration. This new state of affairs was dramatically underlined when the
British Government recently reneged on its promise of an open door
for passport-holding Asian British subjects fleeing, ironically enough,
from black nationalism in Kenya. Britain's temporizing response to
white Rhodesian defiance has undoubtedly been due mainly to Britain's
post-imperial weakness, but African blacks and Asian browns could
quite reasonably interpret Britain's behavior as not so much weak as
white. In the case of the United States, the equivocation over white
racism in Africa helped to cancel out the flickering sympathy the United
States commanded at times during the last ten years or so for its own
turbulent and only half-successful effort to do away with the survivals
of white racism at home. Into this equation must also go the size and
weight of Anglo-American investments and strategic-military interests
in South Africa, not to speak of the demonstrated over-readiness of
American power to intervene forcibly elsewhere when its vital interests
were thought to be involved. The overall effect has been to reinforce
in a general way the communist, radical nationalist and radical racialist
views of Anglo-American realities.

III

Race or color is also a central or even governing factor in a number
of other places and situations which may have less weight in the balance of world affairs but can hardly be seen as negligible in the working
out of the next chapter of the human story.

Of these only Portugal's stubborn effort to keep power in its African colonies carries over what we might now call the old colonial pattern of things, although the Portuguese style of handling the color issue is several shades more ambiguous than that of its ex-counterparts elsewhere. Somewhat like the French colonialists, the Portuguese like to insist that they are a good deal more flexible in such matters, especially with nonwhites whom they coöpt as willing instruments of white power, whether in bed, in politics or in business. It is rather striking to note that the colonialists who have insisted most strongly on their paternalistic or racial flexibility as masters have tried the hardest or fought the longest and bloodiest wars to hold on to their colonies: the Dutch, the French and lastly now the Portuguese. On the political side, no enduring vitality appeared in the methods and institutions by which they gave some limited voice to their colonials in their own affairs. On the racial side, there is little to support the claims of greater humanity that have often been made for themselves by the French, Dutch and Portuguese colonialists as compared, say, to the British. The differences are more a matter of style than of substance. Taking it in its most literal aspect, much waits to be learned about these differences from a comparison of the experience of the varieties of Eurasians and Eurafricans produced out of some of these colonial relationships. None of it seems likely to put any higher gloss on the picture we already have of this past. It is a matter of some suggestive relevance to our present theme, however, that the nationalist movement in Angola is reportedly split between at least two groups, one of which is said to be led by blacks, the other by mulattoes.

The other examples that fall into this category are in quite a different way part of our legacy from the colonial era. They all arise from the effort to create nations out of the often disparate and mutually hostile population groups which made up the former colonies where, as the saying went, division generally made for easier ruling. These differences are usually regional, tribal and in highly varying degrees "ethnic" or "racial," two vaguely defined terms used, for lack of more precise definition, to mark out some blurry lines between distinctions and differences that are sometimes physical, sometimes cultural, often both. Almost every "new" nation—and not a few "old" ones—is now more or less painfully hung on this kind of centrifuge.

Probably the bloodiest of these new confrontations where the difference is most distinctly racial is going on in the Sudan. Here a civil war has been under way since 1962 between the predominantly lighter-skinned Arab rulers in the north and the black non-Moslem people of the south, a clash in which this difference plays a paramount role. Another example was the heavy bloodletting between the tall Hamitic Watusi and the short Negroid Bahutu that accompanied the creation of the two small states of Burundi and Ruanda. Other situations with similar elements exist in several West African countries, like Sierra Leone, Gambia, Liberia, where coastal "creoles" of varying degrees of racial mixture or foreign origin confront indigenous tribes in contests to hold or win power. There are north-south divisions in India which are divisions of culture and language but also, to no small extent, divisions between light-skinned northerners and dark-skinned southerners with strong feelings about their lightness and darkness. Some of our "new" situations are filled with "new" anomalies that in some cases have a strong racial cast, as in the encounter between European and Oriental Jews in Israel, Arabs and Berbers in the Maghreb, Hindus and Nagas in India's northeast, Hindus and Singhalese in Ceylon, the "black" Khmers and the "yellow" Vietnamese. Also on this list must appear the bizarre reproduction of older imperialist patterns by the neo-imperialist brown Indonesians in the imposition of their rule on the black Papuans in West New Guinea.

If we were to extend this catalogue from the more distinctly "racial" to the more vaguely "ethnic" or "tribal," it would obviously be possible to multiply examples almost indefinitely. In cases where the colonial boundaries have been retained as national boundaries, again without regard for population groups, conflict has been revived or ignited, both internally and across borders, between peoples whose physical or racial differences may be much less marked but between whom the ethnic or racial clash is hardly any less intense. Consider on this score Nigeria, the Congo, India in Assam and Nagaland, Indonesia in Borneo, the Ethiopian-Somali-Kenyan irredentisms, the high permeability of the frontiers of all the countries of the Indochina peninsula, to say nothing of the presence of this factor on both sides of the lines which arbitrarily divided North and South Korea and North and South Viet Nam, with rather notable effects on American and world affairs.

Nor can we entirely fail to mention here—despite the absence of the color factor as such—the long-vibrating hostility that separates such European tribes as the Czechs and Slovaks, Serbs and Croats, Flemands and Walloons, Welsh and Scots and English, Bretons and French, French and English Canadians, Spaniards and Basques, etc. The failure of so many political systems—national, imperial, international—to satisfy the identity needs of people in these many groups has led to the powerful resurgence of their feelings about their special separateness. Some of these tribal differences have been bloodying the world's fields for ages and we are plainly not done with them yet. However else they are caused and defined, almost all are rooted in or reinforced and rationalized by those physical and cultural differences which they themselves often see as "racial" or "ethnic" and which, despite all the mixing that has been done, manage somehow still to dominate so much of man's affairs.

There is, however, one group of "new" nations crippled by divisions of this kind which are in a peculiarly special way the most direct legacy from the colonial era. The largest and most internationally important of these is Malaysia, whose bi- or tri-racial character and consequent political and social fragility are mirrored in such smaller new states or microstates as Guyana, Trinidad and Tobago, Mauritius, Fiji (all former parts of the British Empire) and in Surinam, which is still a Dutch dependency. These are countries into which the colonial power deliberately imported working populations, either enlarging on older migrations or organizing new ones by large-scale contract labor, indenture or semi-indenture, in numbers large enough to become, in two or three generations, a significant minority, a plurality or even a majority of the entire local population.

In one territory where this took place, Hawaii, a political solution was ultimately found in statehood within the developing framework of a new and uniquely American pluralism. In other areas, the option has had to be for nationhood, generally with much less hopeful results. In the Caribbean this process began with the slaves brought from Africa, ultimately displacing the indigenous Amerindians with a predominantly black population. When slavery was abolished, the freed blacks largely abandoned the land for the towns. The colonial rulers then brought in shiploads of more docile laborers for their plantations, in the main drawn from some of the lowest strata of the peasantry in India. The result today, in Guyana, for example, is a society composed of nearly equal parts of black Afro-Guyanese and brown East Indian Guyanese, whose differences, mutual antipathies and conflicting interests have erupted in outbreaks of cruel violence as each group sought the uncertain prize of power in their rickety new national home.

Of considerably greater importance in world affairs, however, is Malaysia, a country of some eight million people at the tip of the Southeast Asian peninsula where the Indian Ocean meets the South China Sea at one of the world's major interoceanic crossroads. Here under the uncomfortably ill-fitting mantle of nationhood is a population made up of close to equal parts of Malays, who see themselves as the indigenous "sons of the soil," and Chinese, some of whose families have lived in the region for centuries but most of whom are products of the immigration begun in the last century when the British began to need workers more energetic than the pastorally inclined Malays. They also brought in workers from India for the rubber plantations, and Indians now comprise about 10 percent of the population. The bulk of the Malays remained poor farmers and fishermen while the Chinese came, in a generation or two, to control all sectors of the economy not dominated by the British. When the Japanese invaded in 1942, the Malays welcomed them and the Chinese resisted them, a difference that erupted in Chinese-Malay bloodletting just after the war ended. The communist-led uprising that kept the country in turmoil for about five years thereafter was a virtually all-Chinese movement. When the assorted Malay states and sultanates were put together for the first time in their history in 1957 as the new state of Malaya, the Malay princes and other leaders negotiated Malay political dominance with the willing British. The Chinese, most of them uncertain or ambivalent about their hitherto firm political ties to their homeland, now a communist power, found themselves insecurely relocated as second-class citizens, accepted as nationals of the new state only under certain limitations and restrictions.

When Malaya was enlarged to become Malaysia in 1963, taking in the predominantly Chinese city of Singapore and the North Borneo states of Sarawak and Sabah, the population also acquired sizeable minorities of Dayaks and other tribes who shared an immense lack of any affinity—racial, cultural or political—with either the Chinese or the Malays. The Borneo territory was brought in partly to offset the threat of an ethnic Chinese majority produced by the inclusion of Singapore. The mutual mistrust and hostility between Malays and Chinese forced the withdrawal of Singapore in 1965, with Singapore becoming an independent city-state on its own, leaving Malaysia still with a 40-percent Chinese minority. The cleavage between Chinese and Malays here is deeply cultural, having to do with history, language, religion, philosophy and style of life. These are accented all the more by the racial and physical differences, including color, which mark them off from each other and which provide, as always, the handiest and most explicit basis for expressed hostility between individuals. On some satisfactory resolution of this conflict depends the viability of the Malaysian nation and on this viability depends much that has to do with the bigger politics, the power alignments and positions, and the issues of war and peace among the larger powers whose interests meet or clash in that strategic corner of the world.

IV

Running far out beyond these small and localized blots of detail, changing color patterns are staining and rearranging the look of much larger areas of the new power-political map of the world. Besides the new and highly fluid patterns created by the north-south hemispheric view of the world to which we have already referred, there are also the triangular shapes created by that other hemispheric arrangement—East and West: the U.S.-Russian, Russian-Chinese and Chinese-U.S. cleavages. In each of these combinations and often spreading through and across all of them run the feelings that have to do with race and all the attitudes, fears, self-perceptions and mutual perceptions that go with it.

The Soviet Union has long had to deal with race and color problems in its effort to create a successful federation of many diverse peoples, including the many nonwhites who make up the populations of the Soviet east. The dominance of the Great Russians in Soviet affairs has often had a racial as well as national character. More recently the most visible outcropping of this kind in the Soviet Union has been the appearance of its own set of "yellow peril" fixations around its power conflict with China. The Russian-Chinese conflict has deep roots in the geography and history of these two huge continental powers. As in all such cases, mutual fears and hostilities are fed by racial differences which serve to reinforce or to rationalize politically dictated behavior. In recent years Russians have more and more openly expressed their feelings about Chinese in these terms. In conversations with Americans and Europeans, they frequently promote a common cause against the prospective Chinese threat in terms of a common "whiteness" united against Chinese "yellowness." They endow the latter with full-strength versions of all the most negative and fearsome stereotypes, bearing on numbers, limitless energy and endurance, fiendish cleverness and cruelty, deviousness and inscrutability. These are all images they already hold in common with other Westerners, especially Americans, who get them from the same sources, indeed, from the same historic experiences. That Russians also share other varieties of "white" attitudes and behavior patterns toward nonwhites is amply indicated by the testimony of African students in Russia who met with discrimination, hostility and violence at the hands of their Russian hosts and fellow students. Chinese students in Russia had similar experiences. However one might balance out the "facts" of these episodes, it is clear that some of this Russian "whiteness" is at least part of the story of the Russian failure to win allies and keep influential friends both in black Africa and yellow China.

In the case of China, its racial chauvinism has been a factor of great weight in communist Chinese political behavior, as it indeed has been in all of China's history. Chinese pride of place in the history and culture of the world is not always easily separable from pride of race in its most literal physical form. Chinese feeling about the inferiority of all non-Chinese is almost always expressed in physical terms; outsiders are often portrayed as animals or animal-like demons, or are otherwise denied the status of human beings. It took a good deal of Chinese self-pride to sustain these convictions of Chinese superiority during the last century or so of repeated humiliation at the hands of foreigners. Repairing this damage to the Chinese ego and restoring the Chinese sense of greatness to its fullest luster are among the prime purposes and driving motivations of the present communist leadership in China. Although racism, at least crude racism, is anathema in communist ideology (as it is in the American credo), the Chinese, like the Russians, play heavily on its themes. They do so mainly negatively, charging their foes with its evils. Peking's heavy-handed and largely unsuccessful efforts to whip up support for itself in Africa and in the Third World movements associated with Bandung, Cairo and Algiers were deeply—if informally—larded with racial arguments. In open propaganda the Third World formula became a code for "nonwhite world" counterposed to the white world of the United States and the Soviet Union. In their private manœuvring, it was specifically on racial grounds that the Chinese moved to keep Russia out of the councils of the Third World and to create an all-nonwhite international trade union movement which they could dominate.

The failures of this Chinese effort were, again, due to many causes: the actuality of Chinese weakness; the marked lack of enthusiasm among a great many Afro-Asians for Maoist extremism or for becoming tributaries to a new celestial empire; the counter-pulls of Western strength, resources, influence; or, often most powerfully of all, their own nationalism or their own values. But to judge from a variety of accounts, they also came about in part because the Chinese involved in these encounters could not help conveying their strong belief that, if Western

whites were not superior to Africans and others, the Chinese *were*. We
are far from through with Chinese chauvinism or with its racial component.

V

For the United States most of all—more than for any other nation,
new or old—the element of race and color has finally become a matter
of central and crucial concern. Its importance cannot be separately
assigned or portioned out between our internal or our external affairs.
In the fundamental sense that the role of the United States as a world
power will be determined by the nature and quality of the American
society, the United States itself has now become the principal arena of
our struggle to shape the future. In that arena the principal issue,
plainly put, is whether our partially opening society will open enough
to include Americans who are black on the same common and equal
basis as all others.

This is not to suggest that race and color did not figure importantly
in our foreign affairs before this. Until 25 years or so ago, white supremacy was a generally assumed and accepted state of affairs in the
United States as well as in Europe's empires. It did not begin to give
way seriously in the United States until it had clearly begun to give
way in the rest of the world. Up until that time, the notions of white
supremacy and superiority and the subordinate position of blacks and
other nonwhites in American society had been duly refracted in American affairs abroad. It showed up mainly in American relations with
Asia, where in the middle of the nineteenth century we joined Europe's freebooting imperialist system, acquiring our own "little brown
brothers" in the process. Our behavior in these affairs was marked by
that uniquely American combination of benevolence and rapacity, attraction and repulsion, virtue and cynicism which, for a great many
Chinese at least, became our special national hallmark. At home in the
United States in the same period we moved into an era of remarkable
bigotry and violence against nonwhites. This was in the post-Reconstruc-
tion decades when nominally freed blacks were driven into new and
even deeper pits of debasement. It was a period marked by the exclusion
acts aimed at the Chinese beginning in 1882 and then against the
Japanese, and not long thereafter similar restrictions on all further immigration from anywhere except Anglo-Saxon northern Europe. The
restrictions on Chinese and Japanese, including denial of the right to
citizenship by naturalization, were continued until as recently as 1946.
On the political side, we did not yield our extraterritorial position in
China—won for us by European armed conquest a century earlier—
until 1943. We are obviously not dealing here with matters of ancient
or remote history.

The direct role of racism in these relationships and its effect on
Asian-American relations during the last hundred years are almost always more or less consciously underplayed in American historical
accounts. But there it is, barely out of view beneath the surface of

most versions of our experience in the Philippines, where we were, to be sure, enormously benevolent, but where our soldiers sang about the monkeys who had no tails in Zamboanga. It is seen in the lynchings and other mob violence against Chinese in America; in the first anti-foreign boycott in China in 1905, which was directed specifically against U.S. maltreatment of Chinese there; in the practice of discrimination against Japanese in the United States and its effect on Japanese-American relations before and after the First World War and particularly in the negotiations at Versailles; and in the heavily race-tinted propaganda used by Japan against the United States before and during the Second World War.

Today this part of our past continues to dog us, mutedly in Japan just now, but quite explicitly in China, where communist propaganda against the United States makes heavy use of racial themes and images, not just because the Chinese are themselves racial chauvinists but because this kind of crude racism is no small part of what they had to take from us in the years of their weakness. It is still not easy for many Americans to understand that we are now simply getting quite a bit of our own thrown back at us, whether from China or Japan, from Latin America where the gringo syndrome carries its own special racial ingredient, or from Africa, in whose darkest experience of human enslavement we played such a prominent role.

But now the worms—and the wheels of history—have turned. The end of the system of white supremacy in the world, except in southern Africa, has forced the quickening of the end of white supremacy in the United States. The changes that have taken place in this country in the last twenty years have come about for many reasons and as the outcome of many slowly—oh, so slowly—converging forces and circumstances. But surely not the least of these was the sudden American need to deal as a great power with a world in which long-subordinate, submissive races had ceased to be subordinate or submissive. The racial facts of American life abruptly became vital to our success as leader, whether in pitting our claim of democratic freedom against the challenge of communist totalitarianism or in winning the trust, not to say the alliance, of the new nations. It is hardly necessary to belabor this point at this late hour in the proceedings. It does not require too much distortion by our enemies to depict our destructiveness in Viet Nam as a product of our disregard for nonwhite Asian lives. It does not require much imagination to guess how much more hopelessly untenable our position in Viet Nam would be if we were claiming to fight there for Vietnamese democratic freedom of choice with an army that was still as racially segregated as it was when we fought for democracy and freedom in World War II, and as it remained until harsh military necessity imposed battlefield integration in Korea in 1950.

Through the 1950s and early 1960s, these issues were dramatized by repeated incidents in the United States involving newly arrived black and brown diplomats from the newly independent nations, who were constantly being caught in the still-prevailing patterns of discrimination and exclusion in hotels, restaurants and other public places as well as in housing in New York, Washington and elsewhere. The embarrassed apologies to the diplomats involved and the exhortations addressed to recalcitrant white Americans about these episodes must fill a large file at the State Department and at the headquarters of the U. S. delegation to the United Nations. It is not far wrong to say that the desegregation of many of these places was largely won in the first instance because nobody could ever be sure any more that a reasonably well-dressed dark-skinned man who came seeking service was not the Ambassador from Ghana or India, an outcome that served only to deepen the humiliation and anger of dark-skinned men or women who happened to be just ordinary Americans who wanted that service too.

Much more dramatic was the turmoil set in motion by the Supreme Court decisions and the early racial clashes in the schools and universities, at the lunch counters, in terminals and other public places. The events of this period commanded the fascinated attention of a world that had never seen anything like it: the Negro rebellion launched by Martin Luther King's walkers in Montgomery in 1955; Federal soldiers and marshals enforcing compliance with the law on southern white racists at Little Rock, Tuscaloosa and elsewhere; the sit-in movement and the freedom rides; the civil rights laws finally pushed through a reluctant Congress; the climactic confrontation at Birmingham; and the tardy but unmistakable commitment of the Kennedy Administration in 1963 to see the issue through. All of this on balance offset the uglier scenes that even then were cast so widely on all the world's screens. There remained the image of a society finally moving to cope with some of its most deep-seated problems, and doing so more boldly and more openly than any other nation in a world where scarcely anyone was free to cast stones.

In the last five years, the picture has cruelly changed. Belief abroad in the relative virtue or morality and—perhaps even more decisive— even in the intelligence of American behavior as a world power has been largely shot away in Viet Nam. At home, the civil rights revolution, having cleared the barricades of legal segregation, came up against the much more difficult problem of achieving a decent existence freed of the shackles imposed by poverty, of overcoming the rot of our inner cities and the persistence of strong racial attitudes and behavior in large sections of the surrounding white population. Negro hopes of change raised by the swift victories of the civil rights revolution have given way to deep frustration that often seeks an outlet in bristling ultra-militancy and a profound skepticism about the society's good intentions. Hopes of many Negroes in the promises of integration have given way to despairing impulses toward some new kind of separation. For large numbers of white Americans, especially among the young, much of the same faith has been buried in the Viet Nam morass, while in other large sections of the population a nascent readiness to accept change in race relations has been obscured by the angry and fearful resurrection of old racial spectres spurred by outbreaks of violence in the ghettos. The crisis now wide open in American life is a concatenation of long-unsolved problems of poverty, the cities and race, each set formidable enough in itself but woven all together now in a single massive tangle of issues, demands and circumstances.

Of the three, the most critical is clearly race. To see that this is so, one has only to imagine what our present national condition and state of mind would be if our poor, especially in our city slums, were not so largely black. Without the problem of race, we would be facing demands of the kind this society has shown itself matchlessly able to confront and solve. It is the demand that we finally resolve the place of the black man in the American society that makes this the potentially mortal climax of an issue that has been with us since the founding of the Republic. It bears on what our society is and on what we say we think it is or want it to be—namely an open society offering freedom of choice and growth and well-being to all its citizens regardless of race, creed, color or national origin.

There has been no such society on earth and the American promise of it is in fact the unique substance of the American alternative to the claims of the communist totalitarians. It is the difference between the promise of our open society and the closed society of the communists that makes the world power struggle something more than a matter of deciding an issue of brute force. It can of course be argued that American power will impinge heavily on the world no matter what is done about the place of the black man in American society. This is no doubt so. But the proposition here is that the world power role and impact of an American society on its way to becoming an open, humane society for all its members is one thing. The role and impact of an American society moving toward new forms of racial separation in a garrison state will be quite another.

2

Ambush at Kamikaze Pass

TOM ENGELHARDT

"Westerns" may have been America's most versatile art form. For several generations of Americans, Westerns provided history lessons, entertainment and a general guide to the world. They created or re-created a flood of American heroes, filled popcorned weekends and overwhelmed untold imaginations. It's as difficult today to imagine movies without

them as to think of a luncheonette without Coca-Cola. In their folksy
way, they intruded on our minds. Unobtrusively they lent us a hand
in grinding a lens through which we could view the whole of the
non-white world. Their images were powerful; their structure was
satisfying; and at their heart lay one archetypal scene which went something like this:

> White canvas-covered wagons roll forward in a column. White men, on
> their horses, ride easily up and down the lines of wagons. Their arms
> hang loosely near their guns. The walls of the buttes rise high on either
> side. Cakey streaks of yellow, rusty red, dried brown enclose the sun's
> heat boiling up on all sides. The dust settles on their nostrils, they gag
> and look apprehensively towards the heights, hostile and distant. Who's
> there? Sullenly, they ride on.
>   Beyond the buttes, the wagon train moves centrally into the flat-
> lands, like a spear pointed at the sunset. The wagons circle. Fires are
> built; guards set. From within this warm and secure circle, at the center
> of the plains, the white-men (-cameras) stare out. There, in the enveloping
> darkness, on the peripheries of human existence, at dawn or dusk, hoot-
> ing and screeching, from nowhere, like maggots, swarming, naked, painted,
> burning and killing, for no reason, like animals, they would come. The
> men touch their gun handles and circle the wagons. From this strategically
> central position, with good cover, and better machines, today or tomor-
> row, or the morning after, they will simply mow them down. Wipe them
> out. Nothing human is involved. It's a matter of self-defense, no more.
> Extermination can be the only answer.

There are countless variations on this scene. Often the encircled
wagon train is replaced by the surrounded fort; yet only the shape of
the object has changed. The fort, like the wagon train, is the focus of
the film. Its residents are made known to us. Familiarly, we take in the
hate/respect struggle between the civilian scout and the garrison commander; the love relations between the commander's daughter and
the young first lieutenant who-has-yet-to-prove-himself; the comic routines of the general soldiery. From this central point in our consciousness, they sally forth to victory against unknown besiegers with
inexplicable customs, irrational desires, and an incomprehensible language (a mixture of pig-latin and pidgin Hollywood).

What does this sort of paradigm do to us? Mostly, it forces us to
flip history on its head. It makes the intruder exchange places in our
eyes with the intruded upon. (Who ever heard of a movie in which
the Indians wake up one morning to find that, at the periphery of
their existences, in their own country, there are new and aggressive
beings ready to make war on them, incomprehensible, unwilling to
share, out of murder and kill, etc.) It is the Indians, in these films, who
must invade, intrude, break in upon the circle—a circle which contains
all those whom the film has already certified as "human." No wonder
the viewer identifies with those in the circle, not with the Indians left
to patrol enigmatically the bluffs overlooking humanity. In essence, the
viewer is forced behind the barrel of a repeating rifle and it is from
that position, through its gun sights, that he receives a picture history

of Western colonialism and imperialism. Little wonder that he feels no sympathy for the enemy as they fall before his withering fire—within this cinematic structure, the opportunity for such sympathy simply ceases to exist.

Such an approach not only transforms invasion into an act of self-defense; it also prepares its audiences for the acceptance of genocide. The theory is simple enough: We may not always be right (there are stupid commanders, etc.), but we are human. By any standards (offered in the film), "they" are not. What, then, are they? They are animate, thus they are, if not human, in some sense animals. And, for animals facing a human onslaught, the options are limited. Certain of the least menacing among them can be retained as pets. As a hunter trains his dog, these can be trained to be scouts, tracking down those of their kind who try to escape or resist, to be porters, to be servants. Those not needed as pets (who are nonetheless domesticable) can be maintained on preserves. The rest, fit neither for house training nor for cages, must be wiped out.[1]

From the acceptance of such a framework flows the ability to accept as pleasurable, a relief, satisfying, the mass slaughter of the "non-human"—the killing, mowing down of the non-white, hundreds to a film and normally in the scene which barely precedes the positive resolution of the relationships among the whites. Anyone who thinks the body count is a creation of the recent Indochinese war should look at the movies he saw as a kid. It was the implicit rule of those films that no less than ten Indian (Japanese, Chinese . . . .) warriors should fall for each white, expendable secondary character.[2]

Just as the style and substance of the Indian wars was a prototype for many later American intrusions into the third world (particularly the campaigns in the Philippines and Indochina), so movies about those wars provided the prototype from which nearly every American movie about the third world derived. That these third world movies are pale reflections of the framework, outlook, and even conventions of the cowboy movie is easy enough to demonstrate. Just a few examples, chosen almost at random from the thirty or forty films I've caught on T.V. in the last few months. Pick your country: the Mexico of toothy Pancho Villan bandits, the North Africa of encircled Foreign Legionaires, the India of embattled British Lancers, or even South Africa. One would think treatment of South Africa might be rather special, have its own unique features. But Lo! We look up and already the Boers are trekking away, in (strange to say) wagons, and, yep, there's, no . . . let's see . . . Susan Hayward. Suddenly, from nowhere, the Zulus appear, hooting and howling, to surround the third-rate wagons of this third-rate movie. And here's that unique touch we've all been waiting for. It seems to be the singular quality of the Zulus that they have no horses and so must circle the wagon train on foot, yelling at the tops of their voices and brandishing their spears . . . but wait . . . from the distance . . . it's the Transvaal cavalry to the rescue. As they swoop down, one of the Boers leaps on a wagon seat, waving his hat with joy, and calls to his friend in the cavalry, "You've got 'em running,

Paul. Keep 'em running, Paul! Run 'em off the end of the earth!"
(*Untamed,* 1955)

Or switch to the Pacific. In any one of a hundred World War II
flicks, we see a subtle variation on the same encirclement imagery.
From the deck of our flagship, amidst the fleet corraled off the Okinawa
coast, we look through our binoculars. The horizon is empty; yet already the radar has picked them up. Somewhere beyond human sight,
unidentified flying objects. The sirens are howling, the men pouring
out of their bunks and helter-skelter into battle gear. At their guns,
they look grimly towards the empty sky: the young ensign too eager for
his first command, the swabby who got a date with that pretty Wave,
the medic whose wife just sent him a "Dear John" letter (he's slated to
die heroically). A speck on the horizon, faces tense, jokes fall away,
it's the Kamikaze! Half-man, half-machine, an incomprehensible human
torpedo bearing down from the peripheries of fanatical animate existence to pierce the armored defenses of the forces of Western democracy. The result? Serious damage to several ships, close calls on more,
several secondary characters dead, and an incredible number of Japanese
planes obliterated from the sky.[3]

That there is no feeling of loss at the obliteration of human tor-
pedoes is hardly surprising. Even in those brief moments when you
"meet" the enemy, movies like this make it immaculately clear that
he is not only strange, barbarous, hostile and dangerous, but has little
regard for his own life. Throwing himself on the Gatling guns of the
British with only spear in hand, or on the ack-ack guns of the Americans
with only bomb in portal, he is not acting out of any human emotion.
It is not a desire to defend his home, his friends, or his freedom. It has
no rational (i.e. "human") explanation. It is not even "bravery" as we
in the West know it (though similar acts by whites are portrayed
heroically). Rather, it is something innate, fanatical, perverse—an inexplicable desire for death, disorder and destruction.

When the enemy speaks a little English, he often explains this
himself. Take, for instance, the captured Japanese officer in *Halls of
Montezuma* (1950). The plot is already far advanced. On an island in
the Pacific, hours before the big attack, Marines are pinned down by
Japanese mortars whose position they cannot locate. Yet if they do not
locate them, the attack will fail. The Japanese officer obstinately refuses
to help them. Richard Widmark pleads with him, appealing to his
life force. "You have a future—to rebuild Japan—to live for . . ." But
the officer replies: "Captain, you seem to have forgotten, my people
for centuries have thought not of living well but dying well. Have you
not studied our Judo, our science . . . We always take the obvious and
reverse it. Death is the basis of our strength." Suddenly a mortar shell
explodes above the bunker. Everybody ducks. Rafters fall; dust billows;
slowly the air clears; a shocked voice yells out: "My God, the Jap's
committed Hari Kari!" Fortunately the idiot gave it all away. He reminded the Americans of the quirks in the non-white mind. As any
schoolboy should have known, Orientals think backwards. The Japs put
their rockets on the front slope of the mountain, not the protected rear

slopes as an American would have done. The attack, to the tune of the Marine Hymn, moves forward, preparing to wipe the Japs off the face of the island.

If, in print, such simple idiocy makes you laugh, it probably didn't when you saw the film; nor is it in any way atypical of four decades of action films about Asia. The overwhelmingly present theme of the non-human-ness of the non-white prepares us to accept, without flinching, the extermination of our "enemies" (as John Wayne commented in *The Searchers*, 1956, there's "humans" and then there's "Comanches.") and just as surely it helped prepare the ideological way for the leveling and near-obliteration of three Asian areas in the course of three decades.

It is useful, in this light, to compare the cinematic treatment of the European front in World Wars I and II with that of the Pacific front. From *The Big Parade* (a silent film) on, a common and often moving convention of movies about the wars against Germany went something like this: The allied soldier finds himself caught in a fox-hole (trench, farmhouse, etc.) with a wounded German soldier. He is about to shoot when the young, begrimed soldier holds up his hand in what is now the peace symbol, but at the time meant "Do you have a cigarette?" Though speaking different languages, they exchange family pictures and common memories.[4]

The scene is meant to attest to man's sense of humanity and brotherhood over and above war and national hatred. Until very recently, such a scene simply did not appear in movies about the Japanese front. Between the American and his non-white enemy, a bond transcending enmity was hardly even considered. Instead, an analogous scene went something like this: A group of Japanese, shot down in a withering crossfire, lie on the ground either dead or severely wounded. The American soldiers approach, less from humanitarian motives than because they hope to get prisoners and information.[5] One of the Japanese, however, is just playing possum, As the American reaches down to give him water (first aid, a helping hand), he suddenly pulls out a hand grenade (pistol, knife) and, with the look of a fanatic, tries to blow them *all* to smithereens. He is quickly dispatched. (See, for instance, *In Love and War*, 1956)

The theme of alien intruders descending on embattled humans and being obliterated from an earth they clearly are not entitled to is most straightforwardly put in Science Fiction movies; for monsters turn out to be little more than the metaphysical wing of the third world. These movies represent historical events which have taken place only in the Western imagination. Thus, the themes of the cowboy (-third world) movie come through in a more primeval way. An overlay of fear replaces the suspense. Metaphorically, the world is the wagon train; the universe, the horizon. (Or, alternately, the earth space-ship is the wagon train; an alien planet, the horizon.) From that horizon, somewhere at the peripheries of human existence, from the Arctic icecap (*The Thing*, 1951), the desert (*Them*, 1954), the distant past (*The Beast from 20,000 Fathoms*, 1954), the sky (*War of the Worlds*, 1953), at dawn or dusk, hooting and beeping come the invaders. Enveloping whole armies, they smash through human defenses, forcing the white representatives of the human race to fall back on their inner defense line (perhaps New York or Los Angeles). Imperiling the very heartland of civilized life, they provide only one option—destroy THEM before THEM can destroy us.

In this sort of a movie, the technical problems involved in presenting the extinction of a race for the enjoyment of an audience are simplified.[6] Who would even think about saving the Pod People? (*Invasion of the Body Snatchers,* 1956) Ordinarily the question of alternatives to elimination barely comes to mind. If it does, as in that prototype "modern" Sci-Fi film *The Thing* (James Arness of Matt Dillon fame played the monster), usually the man who wants to save Them, "talk to Them," is the bad mad scientist as opposed to the good, absent-minded scientist (who probably has the pretty daughter being wooed by the cub reporter).[7]

Unfortunately for American movie-makers, Asians and others could not simply be photographed with three heads, tentacles, and gelatinaceous bodies. Consequently, other conventions had to be developed (or appropriated) that would clearly differentiate them from "humanity" at large. The first of these was invisibility. In most movies about the third world, the non-whites provide nothing more than a backdrop for all-white drama—an element of exotic and unifying dread against which to play out the tensions and problems of the white world. Sometimes, even the locales seem none-too-distinguishable, not to speak of their black, brown, or yellow inhabitants. It is not surprising, for instance, that the Gable-Harlow movie *Red Dust* (1932), set on an Indochinese rubber plantation (Gable is the foreman), could be transported to Africa without loss two decades later as the Gable-Kelly *Mogambo.* It could as well have been set in Brazil on a coffee plantation, or in Nevada with Gable a rancher.

As George Orwell commented of North Africa in 1939,

> All people who work with their hands are partly invisible, and the more important the work they do, the less visible they are. Still, a white skin is always fairly conspicuous. In northern Europe, when you see a labourer ploughing a field, you probably give him a second glance. In a hot country, anywhere south of Gibraltar or east of Suez, the chances are that you don't even see him. I have noticed this again and again. In a tropical landscape one's eye takes in everything except the human beings. It takes in the dried-up soil, the prickly pear, the palm tree and the distant mountain, but it always misses the peasant hoeing at his patch. He is the same colour as the earth, and a great deal less interesting to look at. It is only because of this that the starved countries of Asia and Africa are accepted as tourist resorts.[8]

Theoretically, it should have been somewhat more difficult since the Chinese and Vietnamese revolutions and other uprisings of the oppressed and non-white around the world, to ignore the people for the scenery. Yet we can't fault Hollywood for its valiant attempt. Generally, American films have hewed with unsurpassed tenacity to this framework—reproducing the white world whole in the Orient, with Asians skittering at the edges of sets as servants or scenic menace (as in the recent horrific extravaganza, *Krakatoa, East* [sic] *of Java,* 1969, where a volcano takes over the Lassie role and the Asian female pearl divers go under in the final explosions). This is even more true in films on Africa, where for generations whites have fought off natives and lions, not necessarily in that order.

A second convention of these films concerns the pecking order of white and non-white societies when they come into conflict. It is a "united front" among whites. Often the whites portrayed are the highly romanticized third-rate flotsam and jetsam of a mythologized American society—adventurers, prostitutes, opportunists, thieves (just as the films themselves, particularly when about Asia, tend to represent the brackish backwater of the American film industry). Yet no matter how low, no matter what their internal squabbles, no matter what their hostilities towards each other, in relation to the third world the whites stand as one: Missionary's daughter and drunken ferryboat captain ("I hate the Reds," he says to her, "because they closed a lot of Chinese ports where they have dames. Chinese, Eurasian, and White Russian. . . . Somebody pinned the bleeding heart of China on your sleeve but they never got around to me." / *Blood Alley,* 1955); soldier of fortune and adventurer-journalist, natural enemies over The-Woman-They-Both-Love (They escape Canton together, avoiding the clutches of the Reds in a stolen boat / *Soldier of Fortune,* 1955); sheriff, deputies and captured outlaws (They are surrounded by Mexican bandits / *Bandalero,* 196?); or on a national level, the British, Americans and Russians (They must deal with "the chief enemy of the Western World," Mao Tse-tung / *The Chairman,* 1970). This theme is, of course, simply a variation on a more home-grown variety—the Confederates and Yankees who bury their sectional hatreds to unite against the Indians; the convicts on their way to prison who help the wagon train fight off the Sioux, bringing the women and children to safety, etc. (See, for example, *Ambush at Cimarron Pass,* 1958, which combines everything in one laughable mess—a Yankee patrol and its prisoner team up with a Confederate rancher to fight off an Apache attack.)

The audience is expected to carry two racial lessons away from this sort of thing. The first is that the presence of the incomprehensible and non-human brings out what is "human" in every man. Individual dignity, equality, fraternity, all that on which the West theoretically places premium value, are brought sharply into focus at the expense of "alien" beings. The second is the implicit statement that, in a pinch, any white is a step up from the rest of the world. They may be murderers, rapists, and mother-snatchers, but they're ours.

When the inhabitants of these countries emerge from the ferns or mottled huts, and try to climb to the edges of the spotlight, they find the possibilities limited indeed. In this cinematic pick-up-sides, the whites already have two hands on the bat handle before the contest begins. The set hierarchy of roles is structured something like this: All roles of positive authority are reserved for white characters. Among the whites, the men stand triumphantly at the top; their women cringe, sigh and faint below; and the Asians are left to scramble for what's left, like beggars at a refuse heap.

There is only one category in which a non-white is likely to come out top dog—villain. With their stock of fanatical speeches and their propensity for odd tortures, third world villains provided the American film-maker with a handy receptacle for his audience's inchoate fears of the unknown and inhuman. Only as the repository for Evil could the non-white "triumph" in films. However, this is no small thing; for wherever there is a third world country, American scriptwriters have created villain slots to be filled by otherwise unemployable actors (though often even these roles are monopolized by whites in yellow-face). From area to area, like spirits, their forms change: the Mexican bandit chief with his toothy smile, hearty false laugh, sombrero and bushy eyebrows (see, f.i., the excellent *Treasure of the Sierra Madre* 1948, or the awful *Bandalero*); the Oriental warlord with his droopy mustache and shaven head (see *The Left Hand of God,* 1955, *The General Died at Dawn,* 1936, *Shanghai Express,* 1932, *Seven Women,* 1965, etc. ad nauseam); the Indian "Khan" or prince with his little goatee and urbane manner (*Khyber Pass,* 1954, *Charge of the Light Brigade,* 1936). Yet their essence remains the same.

Set against their shiny pates or silken voices, their hard eyes and twitching mouths, no white could look anything but good. In *Left Hand of God,* Humphrey Bogart, the pilot-turned-opportunist-warlord-advisor-turned-fraudulent-priest becomes a literal saint under the leer of Lee J. Cobb's General Yang. Gregory Peck, an "uninvolved" scientist-CIA spy, becomes a boy wonder and living representative of humanity when faced with a ping-pong playing Mao Tse-tung in *The Chairman.* How can you lose when the guy you want to double-deal represents a nation which has discovered an enzyme allowing pineapples to grow in Tibet and winter wheat in Mongolia, yet (as one of the Russian agents puts it) is holding it so that the rest of the "underdeveloped" world, "90% poor, 90% peasant . . . will crawl on their hands and knees to Peking to get it." All in all, these non-white representatives of evil provide a backboard off which white Western values can bounce in, registering one more cinematic Score for Civilization.

The other group of roles open to non-whites are roles of helplessness and dependence. At the dingy bottom of the scale of dependence crouch children. Non-white children have traditionally been a favorite for screenwriters and directors. Ingrid Bergman helped them across the mountains to safety (*The Inn of the Sixth Happiness,* 1958); Deborah Kerr taught them geography (*The King and I,* 1956); Humphrey Bogart helped them to memorize "My Old Kentucky Home" (*Left Hand of God*); Carrol Baker went with them on a great trek back to their homelands (*Cheyenne Autumn,* 1964); Richard Widmark took one (a little half-breed orphan girl—sort of the black, one-eyed Jew of the tiny tot's universe) back to the States with him (*55 Days at Peking*). And so on.

Essentially, non-white children fulfill the same function and have the same effect as non-white villains. They reflect to the white audience just another facet of their own humanity. Of course, if you ignore W. C. Fields, children have had a traditionally cloying place in American films; but in the third world movie they provide a particularly strong dose of knee-jerk sentiment, allowing the white leads to show the other side of Western civilization. It is their duty not just to exterminate the world's evil forces, but to give to those less capable (and more needy) than themselves. And who more closely fits such a description than the native child who may someday grow up to emulate us.

While it is children who demonstrate the natural impulses of the white authorities towards those who do not resist them, but are helpless before them or dependent upon them, it is women who prove the point. Even within the cinematic reflection of the white world, women have seldom held exalted positions. Normally they are daughters of missionaries, sweethearts of adventurers, daughters, nurses, daughters of missionaries, wives on safari, schoolmarms, daughters of missionaries, or prostitutes. (The exceptions usually being when women come under a "united front" ruling—that is, they confront Asian men, not white men. Then, as with Anna in *The King and I*, while their occupations may not change they face society on a somewhat different footing.) Several rungs down the social ladder, non-white women are left mainly with roles as bargirls, geishas, belly dancers, nurse's aids, missionary converts, harem girls, prostitutes. In such positions, their significance and status depend totally on the generosity (or lack of generosity) of those white men around whom the movies revolve.

However "well-intentioned" the moviemaker, the basic effect of this debased dependency is not changeable. Take that classic schmaltz of the 1950's, *The World of Suzie Wong*. William Holden, a dissatisfied architect-businessman, has taken a year's sabbatical in Hong Kong to find out if he can "make it" as an artist. (It could have been Los Angeles, but then the movie would have been a total zilch.) He meets ***Suzie Wong***, a bargirl who is cute as a Walt Disney button and speaks English with an endearing "Chinese" accent. ("Fo' goo'niss sakes" she says over and over at inappropriate moments.) He wants her to be his model. She wants to be his "permanent girlfriend." Many traumas later, the moviemakers trundle out their good intentions towards the world's ill-treated masses. They allow Holden to choose Suzie over Kay, the proper, American, upper class woman who is also chasing him. This attempt to put down the upper classes for their prejudices towards Chinese and bargirls, however, barely covers over the basic lesson of the movie: a helpless, charming Chinese bargirl *can* be saved by the right white man, purified by association with him, and elevated to dependency on him. (Her bastard child, conveniently brought out for his pity quotient, is also conveniently bumped off by a flash flood, avoiding further knotty problems for the already overtaxed sensibilities of the scriptwriters.) It all comes across as part act of God, part act of white America.

Moving upwards towards a peak of third world success and white condescension, we discover the role of "sidekick." Indispensible to the sidekick is his uncanny ability to sacrifice his life for his white com-

panion at just the right moment. In this, he must leave the audience
feeling that he has repaid the white man something intangible that
was owed to him. And, in this, we find the last major characteristic
of third world roles—expendability. Several classic scenes come to mind.
In this skill, the otherwise pitiful Gunga Din excelled (*Gunga Din,*
1939). Up there on a craggy ledge, already dying, yet blowing that bugle
like crazy to save the British troops from ambush by the fanatic Kali-
worshippers. Or, just to bring up another third world group, the death
of the black trainer in *Body and Soul* (1947), preventing his white
World Heavyweight Champion (John Garfield) from throwing the big
fight. Or even, if I remember rightly, Sidney Poitier, Mau Mau initiate,
falling on the Punji sticks to save the white child of his boyhood
friend Rock Hudson (*Something of Value*, 1957). The parts blend into
each other: the Filipino guide to the American guerillas, the Indian
pal of the white scout, that Mexican guy with the big gut and sly sense
of humor. In the end, third world characters are considered expendable
by both moviemakers and their audiences because they are no more a
source of "light" than the moon at night. All are there but to reflect in
differing mirrors aspects of white humanity.

While extermination, dependency and expendability have been
the steady diet of these movies over the decades, American moviemakers have not remained totally stagnant in their treatment of the
third world and its inhabitants. They have over the last forty years
emerged ponderously from a colonial world into a neo-colonial one.
In the 1930's, the only decade when anything other than second-rate
films were made about Asia, moviemakers had no hesitation about expressing an outright contempt for subjugated and/or powerless Asians;
nor did they feel self-conscious about proudly portraying the colonial
style in which most Westerners in Asia lived. The train in *Shanghai*
Express (1932) is shown in all its "colonial" glory: the Chinese pas-
sengers crammed into crude compartments; the Westerners eating dinner in their spacious and elegant dining room. Here was the striking
contrast between the rulers and the ruled and nobody saw any reason
to hide it.

During this period, with the European imperial structure in Asia
still unbroken, colonial paternalism abounded. No one blinked an eye
when Shirley Temple asked her grandfather, the British Colonel (*Wee*
Willie Winkie, 1937), why he was mad at "Khoda Khan," leader of
the warlike tribes on India's northeast border; and he replied, "We're
not mad at Khoda Khan. England wants to be friends with all her
peoples. But if we don't shoot him, he'll shoot us . . . (they've been
plundering for so many years) they don't realize they'd be better off
planting crops." [a few poppy seeds maybe?] Nor were audiences taken
aback when Cary Grant called his Indian sidekick a "beastie" (or alternately the "regimental beastie") in *Gunga Din;* nor when Clark
Gable kicked his Indochinese workers out of a ditch (to save them
from a storm, of course), calling them similar names (*Red Dust*).

A decade later such scenes and lines would have been gaffes.[9] In
the wake of the World War and its flock of anti-Japanese propaganda

flicks (whose progeny were still alive in the early 1960's), the destruction of the British, French and Dutch empires, the success of the Communist revolution in China, the birth and death of dreaded "neutralism," and the rise of the United States to a position of preeminence in the world, new cinematic surfaces were developed to fit over old frames. In their new suits, during the decade of the 50's, cowboy-third world movies flourished as never before. A vast quantity of these low-budget (and not-so-low-budget) films burst from Hollywood to flood the country's theatres. In the more "progressive" of them, an India in chains was replaced by a struggling, almost "independent" country; the "regimental beastie" by a Nehru (-Ghandi) type "rebel" leader; the Kali-worshipping, loinclothed fanatic by Darvee, the Maoist revolutionary ("You cannot make omelettes without breaking eggs."). Yet this sort of exercise was no more than sleight of hand. The Nehru character looked just as ridiculously pompous and imitative as did Gunga Din when he practised his bugle; nor did the whites any less monopolize center stage (holding, naturally, the key military and police positions); nor could the half-breed woman (Ava Gardner) any less choose light (the British officer) over darkness (Darvee and his minions). Soon, all this comes to seem about as basic a change in older forms as was the "independence" granted to many former colonies in the real world (*Bhowani Junction*, 1956).

If any new elements were to enter these movies in the 1950's (and early 60's), it was in the form of changes in relations within the white world, not between the white and non-white worlds. These changes, heralded by the "adult westerns" of the late fifties, have yet to be fully felt in films on Asia; yet a certain early (and somewhat aborted) move in this direction could be seen in some of the films that appeared about the Korean war (not a particularly popular subject, as might be imagined)—a certain tiredness ("Three world wars in one lifetime" / *Battle Circus*, 1953) and some doubts. The WWII flick's faith in the war against the "Japs", in a "civilian" army, and in "democracy" comes across tarnished and tired. The "professional" soldier (or flyer) takes center stage. ("We've gotta do a clean, professional job on those [North Korean] bridges." / *The Bridges at Toko-ri*, 1954). There is, for instance, no analogue in your WWII movies to the following conversation in *The Bridges at Toko-ri*. Mickey Rooney (a helicopter rescue pilot) and William Holden (a flyer) are trapped (shot down) behind the North Korean lines. Surrounded, they wait in a ditch for help to arrive. During a lull in the shooting, they begin to talk:

> Holden: "I'm a lawyer from Denver, Colorado, Mike. I probably couldn't hit a thing [with this gun] . . ."

> Rooney: "Judas, how'd you ever get out here in a smelly ditch in Korea?"

> Holden: "That's just what I've been asking myself . . . the wrong war in the wrong place and that's the one you're stuck with . . . You fight simply because you are here."

Within minutes, they are both killed by the advancing Korean soldiers.

Yet though the white world might seem tarnished, its heroes bitter, tired and ridden with doubts, its relationship to the non-white world had scarcely changed. If anything, the introduction of massive air power to Asian warfare had only further reduced the tangential humanity of Asian peoples. For in a movie like *Toko-ri* (as at Danang today), you never even needed to see the enemy, only charred bodies.

This attempt, particularly in westerns, to introduce new attitudes in the white world, increasingly muddied the divisions between stock characters, brought to the fore the hero-as-cynic, and called into question the "humanity" of the whites vis-a-vis each other. Such adjustments in a relatively constant cinematic structure represented an attempt to update a form which the world's reality put in increasing danger of unbelievability. By the early 1960's, the "adult western" had reached a new stage—that of elegy (see, for instance, *The Man Who Shot Liberty Valance*, 1962). Superficially, such movies seem to be in a state of sentimental mourning for the closing of the frontier and the end of a mythical white frontier life. However, westerns as a form were originally created amidst industrial America partially to mourn just such a loss. The elegiac western of the 60's was, in fact, mourning the passing of itself. Today, this form has come to what may be its terminal fruition in America, the "hip" western—*Butch Cassidy and the Sundance Kid* (1969), which is a parody not of the western, but of the elegiac western, since not even that can be taken totally straight any more.[10]

However, even in this extension of the western, one thing has not changed—attitudes towards the third world. When, for instance, Butch and Sundance cannot make a go of it in a hemmed-in West, they naturally move on, "invading" Bolivia. In Bolivia, of course, it's the same old local color scene again, with one variation: instead of the two of them killing off hundreds of Bolivians in that old wagon train scene, hundreds of unidentified Bolivians band together to kill them. It all boils down to the same thing.

Whatever *Butch Cassidy* may be the end of, I think we stand at the edge of a not totally new, but nonetheless yawning abyss—the "sympathetic" film. The first of what I expect will be an onslaught of these are appearing now. They have at least pretensions towards changing how we see relationships not only within the white world itself, but between the white and Indian worlds. And what is appearing in westerns today may be the transmuted meat of Asian or African films within the next decade.

The recent *A Man Named Horse* (1970?) is a good example. It seems to have been a sincere and painstaking attempt to make a large-scale, commercially successful movie about the Sioux (before they were overrun by the whites), to show from an Indian point of view their way of life, their rituals (recreated from Catlin's paintings) and benefits, their feelings and fears. Yet, at every turn, the film betrays the edges of older and more familiar frameworks.

It concerns an English lord hunting in the American West early in the 19th century. Captured by a Sioux raiding party, he is brought back to their village (where the rest of the film takes place). There he becomes a slave (horse) for an Indian woman (Dame Judith Anderson). Already a white "hero" has been slipped into this movie about Indians, betraying an assumption that American audiences could not sustain interest in a film without whites. Given the way we look at these films, he immediately becomes the center of our attention; thus, in the end, you are forced to relate to the Sioux village through his eyes, and to relate to the Sioux as they relate to him (aiding him or mistreating him). Second, by following the travails of this lord-turned-beast of burden as he assimilates to the tribe, the movie seems to prove that old adage, "put a white man among even the best of savages and you have a natural chief." (He kills enemy Indians, goes through the sun initiation ritual, marries the chief's daughter, teaches the tribe British infantry tactics, and, in the end, his wife and adopted mother being dead, he splits for the white world.)

His girlfriend has that Ali McGraw look which probably is supposed to allow the audience to "identify" better with the Indians, but looks about as fitting as it did among the Jews of New Jersey (*Goodby Columbus*). Even a stab at righting the wrongs westerns have done to language has a similarly dismal result. The movie's makers, reacting to the common use of pidgin-Hollywood by Indian characters in normal westerns, allow the Sioux in this movie to speak their own language. As all but two of the characters are Sioux, much of the movie is conducted in the Sioux language. If this were a French movie, there would naturally be subtitles; but as these are Sioux *au naturel*, and as there is already a conveniently English-speaking character, an alternate means is called upon. Another "prisoner" is created, an Indian who spent some time with the French and speaks broken English. At the behest of the English lord, he translates what is necessary to his and our understanding. In this way, the Indians, while retaining the dignity of their own language, are perhaps slightly less able to express themselves comprehensibly in this picture than in a normal western. More important, just as if it were the normal wagon train scenario, it forces us to see everything through white eyes.[11]

And as long as the eyes through which we see the world do not change, so long as the old frameworks for movies about the third world are not thrown away, "intentions" go for little indeed. It is hard even to think of examples of films where sympathetic intentions are matched by deeds. Certainly one would have to venture beyond the bounds of the U.S. to find them—perhaps *The Battle of Algiers* (which, in reverse, does for the French colonizers what we were never willing to do for the Indians). Its view begins at least to accord with the brutal history of the third world; to tell a little what it means, from the colonized point of view, to resist, to fight back, to rebel against your occupiers.

American moviemakers, however, are at heart still in love with an era when people could accept the six year old Shirley Temple telling Khoda Khan not to make war on the British because "the Queen wants to protect her people and make them rich." Their main substitution in later movies being to replace the Queen with (American) technology—machine guns to mow em down, and band-aids to patch em up. This mood is best captured by Gene Tierney in *The Left Hand of God* when Humphrey Bogart says, "China's becoming a nightmare, Anne . . . What are we really doing here? . . . We belong back in the States, marrying, raising a family." She replies, ". . . There's too much work to do here . . . the things we're doing here are what they need; whether medicine or grace. And we can give it to them . . ." Of course, the historical joke of this being uttered in China's Sinkiang province in 1947, a time when the unmentioned communist revolution is sweeping through the central provinces, passed the scriptwriters by. Yet, on the whole, just this distance between the film's "message" and Chinese reality about sums up the American approach to the third world. In the end, no matter where the moviemakers may think their sympathy lies, their films are usually no more than embroideries on a hagiography of "pacification."

Within such a context, there is no possibility for presenting resistance, rebellion, or revolution by the intruded upon in a way that could be even comprehensible, no less sympathetic. Quite the opposite, the moviemakers are usually hell-bent on glorifying those Asians (or other third worlders) who allied with the Western invaders, not those who at some point resisted either the invasion or its consequences. However, there is an insoluble contradiction here. The method for judging non-whites in these films is based on how dependent or independent they are of the white leads and the white world. To the degree to which they are dependent, they are seen as closer to humanity. To the degree to which they are independent (i.e. resist) they are seen as less liable to humanization or outrightly inhuman and thus open to extermination. ("Mitchell, we must stamp this out immediately." / *Gunga Din*). In other words, there is an inherent bias in these movies towards the glorification of those "natives" who have allied with us. Yet what makes the white hero so appealing is the audience's feeling that no matter how low he sinks, he retains some sense of human dignity. There is always that feeling (as Bogart and countless cowboy stars brought out so well) that despite appearances, *he is his own man*. Yet no movie Asians linked to the West can ever really be that. Though they can bask in the light of humanity, they can never be much more than imitation humans. In only one non-white role is this possibility open—that is the role of villain (he who refuses white help and actively opposes him). Only the villain, already placed outside the pale (sic) of humanity, can be his own man.

The result is a knotty problem. If those close to the whites are invariably dependent, they cannot but be viewed in some way with contempt, no matter how the movie makers go about trying to glorify them. On the other hand, if those most contemptible non-humans, the villains, are the only Asians capable of "independence" in these films, they are also the only Asians who are the cinematic equivalents of the white leads. Thus, we cannot help but have a sneaking respect for those who oppose us and a sneaking contempt for those who side with us. (How similar this is to the attitudes of many American soldiers in Vietnam towards ARVN and towards the NLF forces.) No doubt this is at least partly responsible for the extremes American movie-makers have gone to in glorifying one and despoiling the other.

What Lewis and Clark's Indian guide Sacajawea was to American history high school texts, Gunga Din was to third world movies. He makes the classic sacrifice for the white world, and in death theoreti-cally proves he is a "better man" than his British mentors. Yet how hollow this "triumph" is for the viewing audience. No one is fooled by the words. Doing his mimic marching shuffle, around the corner from the practicing British troops, what a pitiful imitation "human" he appears to be. And even his greatest hopes—to get one toe on the lowest rung of the white regimental ladder as company bugler—leave him second best to any white who comes along. On the other hand, the leader of the Kali worshippers (read: native resistance forces) is por-trayed in a paroxysm of caricature ("Rise brothers and kill . . . kill for the love of Kali, kill for the love of killing, KILL, KILL, KILL!"). He is a mad murderer, a torturer, a loinclothed savage, a megalomaniac with bulging eyes. Yet he is the only Indian in the film who has the real ability to "love his country" like a white man. "I can die as readily for my country and my fate as you for yours," he says and voluntarily jumps into the snakepit, yelling "India farewell!"

This inability, despite pulling all the stops, to deny the enemy a certain dignity is not extraordinary. Even Mao Tse-tung, in the other-wise rabid *The Chairman* proves in some grim sense, irrepressible. On the other hand, no matter how charmingly portrayed, our allies' de-pendency cannot be totally overcome. They are always, in a way, trained spies in the camp of their own people.

American movies about the third world should not be given more credit than is their due. Despite the impression you might get in the theatre, American moviemakers did not invent the world, nor even the version of world history they present in their films. However, they must be given full credit for developing a highly successful and satis-fying cinematic form to encapsulate an existing ideological message. With this form, they have been able to relegate the great horrors of Western expansion into the rest of the world, and present-day Ameri-can hegemony over great hunks of it, to another universe of pleasure and enjoyment. They have successfully tied extermination of non-white peoples to laughable relief, and white racial superiority to the natural order of things. They have destroyed any possibility for ex-plaining the various ways in which non-white (not to speak of white) people could resist invasion, colonization, exploitation, and even mass slaughter.

Cowboy (-third world) films are, in the end, a vast visual pacifica-tion program, ostensibly describing the rest of the world, but in fact aimed at the millions of people who for several generations have made up the American viewing audience. It's hardly a wonder that Viet-nam did not sear the American consciousness. Why should it have? For years, Americans had been watching the whole scene on their screens: REV DEV, WHAM, endless My Lai's, body counts, killing of wounded enemy soldiers, aerial obliteration, etc. We had grown used to seeing it, and thrilling with pleasure` while reaching for another handful of popcorn.

Such a "pacification" program is based on the inundation principle. It is not a matter of quality (probably there have been no good films on Asia since the 1930's), but quantity. So many cowboy-third world movies have rolled factory-style off the production line that the most minute change of plot is hailed as a great innovation. In the end, all the visual "choices" available to a viewer just emphasize the way in which America is strikingly a one-channel country. In fact, it might not be too far wrong to say that while pacification may have failed in Vietnam, its pilot project here in America has generally succeeded, that we are a pacified population, living unknowingly in an occupied country.

NOTES

1 The men who historically advocated or pursued such a policy in the American West openly and unashamedly referred to it at the time as an "extermination" policy.

2 One must at least credit John Ford, the director, with keeping the carnage down in several of his films (for example, *She Wore a Yellow Ribbon*, 1949) and with for allowing the Indians (*Fort Apache*, 1948) to emerge victorious, if no more comprehensible, from at least one movie in the history of the western film.

3 The land equivalent of the Kamikaze onslaught is the Banzai! charge (as in Fuller's *Merrill's Marauders*, 1962).

4 While somewhat harder to find in Nazi war flicks, see *The Enemy Below* (1957) for the World War II (and naval version) of the same scene. The last shot is of the opposing American and Nazi commanders who have disabled each other's ships and saved each other's lives, standing at the stern, sharing a cigarette and looking out together 'over the endless sea.

5 This is not to say that Americans are portrayed as lacking generosity. Quite the opposite, humanitarian gestures are second nature to them; however, those gestures tend to be directed towards humans. As in the scene where Merrill's Marauders, having smashed thru a mass of Japs, are confronted with a wounded comrade. "You wouldn't leave me?" he asks. "We never leave anybody," is the reply.

6 Extermination has, however, been spoken of quite bluntly in certain third world movies. This was particularly true of those movies made during the war against Japan. Take, for example, *The Purple Heart* (1944), about Japanese attempts to try the Doolittle flyers for "war crimes." At the trial, the leader of the American flyers tells the Japanese judge: "We'll come by night and we'll come by day. We'll blacken your skies and burn your cities to the ground until you get down on your knees and beg for mercy . . . This was your war. You asked for it. You started it . . . and now we won't stop until your crummy little empire is wiped off the face of the earth." The Japanese chief prosecutor immediately commits Hara-kiri because of loss of face in failing to break the American prisoners. Or again, *Objective Burma* (1945): the American journalist sees tortured and dead American prisoners. In anger, he says, "This was done in cold blood by a people who claim to be civilized . . . stinking little savages. Wipe em out. Wipe em off the face of the earth, I say. Wipe em off the face of the earth!"

7 Of all the forms discussed, only Science Fiction films exhibit certain themes which run against this grain. It seems to me there are two sources for this opening towards "deviation." First, in the particularly chilly years of the fifties, anti-nuclear, anti-military freaks flocked to this form whose very fantastical nature provided an allegorical legitimacy for their questionable messages. Thus, even the monster-eradication movies often hide a plea for "peace"/deliverance from incompetent military

defenders and their nuclear disasters, whose by-products are sci-fi's ubiquitous radio-active creatures. Second, a traditional tie-in with the sky, heaven, and God led to a semi-religious counter-theme of "divine intervention" and human (implicitly white) inferiority. This conception of wisdom descending from above to straighten out the stupid problems of blundering, incapable humanity is basic to *The Day the Earth Stood Still* (1951), in which "Klaatu" appears from space to tour Washington and plead for nuclear peace (and a fascist robot-police force to patrol the world); or *The Next Voice You Hear* (1950), in which God intervenes in person—via radio.

8 George Orwell, "Marrakech," in *Essays* (Doubleday, 1954), pp. 189–190.

9 There were, of course, some holdovers from the 30's. Particularly junk like *Khyber Pass* (1954), in which British lancer Richard Egan, getting ready to capture rebel leaders in a village, tells a fellow officer: "I don't want any of those devils to escape us."

10 Even John Wayne, the last of the cowboy superstars still in the saddle, is forced to mourn his own passing in *True Grit* (1968?).

11 For another recent example, see *Tell Them Willie Boy is Coming* (1970); and I feel certain (though I have yet to see it) that *Soldier Blue* (1970) will fall in the same category.

As for the newness of "sympathetic" films—at least a couple of historical ante-cedents come to mind: first, *The General Died at Dawn* (1936) with Gary Cooper, and Akim Tamiroff as the warlord Yang (seems to have been a pretty popular name among warlord's mothers). This Clifford Odets script hangs heavy with the hand of the 30's Left. ("You ask me why I'm for oppressed people, because I have a back-ground of oppression myself.") But despite its professed sympathy for the oppressed people of China, its protestations of Asian dignity and love for life, and its unbeliev-ably murky politics, it is loaded with all the normal stuff: white-centeredness ("Mr. O'Hara, from the time you leave this room until you deliver the money, the fate of China is in your hands."); a Chinese super-evil villain; and a mass suicide scene that only could have taken place among those for whom human life meant nothing at all (In the movie's climactic scene, General Yang—who is dying at dawn—has his troops line up in two facing lines several feet apart and shoot each other), to name just a few of the more salient points.

For an example from the earlier 60's, see John Ford's "bow" to the tribulations of the Indians, *Cheyenne Autumn* (1964). Exactly the same sort of process occurs and a good book by Marie Sandoz, written from the viewpoint of the Cheyenne, is de-stroyed in the bargain. Even its historical ending is twisted to imply that Secretary of the Interior Schultz (Edward G. Robinson) allowed the remnants of the Cheyenne to return to their homeland—which he most definitely did not.

Haves vs. Have-nots: The Economic Divide

3

Are the Rich Countries Getting Richer and the Poor Countries Poorer?

THEODORE CAPLOW

It is widely believed that the rich countries of the world are getting richer and the poor countries poorer. I propose to test that belief by examining empirical data about development trends in a large number of countries.

Development is the process by which a society improves its control of the environment through technology and organization. Development means an increased per capita supply of energy and commodities; higher productivity per worker and per acre; the sending and receiving of more messages per capita; an expanded transportation network; a movement of workers from extractive occupations to processing to service occupations; a drift of population from rural to urban places and from smaller to larger cities; a rising educational level; declining mortality; and an increased provision of food, protective services, information, and entertainment.

All the countries of the world can be placed on a rank-order list, showing how well or how little developed each nation is with respect to numbers of telephones, doctors, schools, steel factories, and other things for which statistics are available. If we examine these and many other indicators of development, the rank-order generated by any one indicator is very much like the rank-order generated by another. For example, taking recent (1965) figures available for 66 countries with populations over five million, the rank-order of these countries with respect to the per capita consumption of mechanical energy is very nearly the same [1] as their rank-order on such indices as the proportion of the population urbanized, the proportion of adults literate, the proportion of the school-age population in school, telephones per capita, newspapers and cinemas per capita, doctors per capita, and iron and steel production per capita. This same consistent pattern holds for about 30 other indicators, any of which could be used with fair accuracy to determine a country's position on the world development ladder.

Table 1 shows the 6 major countries ranked by 1965 per capita energy consumption, and divides them into three groups. In the upper third—from the United States to Japan—are what may be called *developed countries;* they are extensively industrialized and have the technological capacity to maintain continued progress without assistance. The middle third—from Argentina to Algeria—consists of *developing countries.* They are partially industrialized and modernized, but must import technology and capital on a large scale in order to continue their development. The lower third—from the Philippines to

Table 1
Per Capita Energy Consumption in
66 Major Countries, 1965

Country	Per Capita Energy Consumption*	Rank	Country	Per Capita Energy Consumption	Rank
Upper Third			Greece	784	29
(Developed Countries)			Taiwan	654	30
United States	9201	1	Peru	588	31
Canada	7653	2	Iraq	581	32
Czechoslovakia	5676	3	Colombia	532	33
East Germany	5460	4	Portugal	521	34
United Kingdom	5151	5	China	461	35
Australia	4795	6	South Korea	445	36
Belgium	4724	7	Rhodesia	399	37
Sweden	4506	8	Iran	391	38
West Germany	4234	9	Turkey	348	39
Union of Soviet Socialist			Brazil	347	40
Republics	3611	10	Malaysia	338	41
Poland	3504	11	Saudi Arabia	311	42
Netherlands	3271	12	Egypt	301	43
Venezuela	2974	13	Algeria	300	44
France	2951	14			
Hungary	2812	15	*Lower Third*		
South Africa	2716	16	*(Underdeveloped Countries)*		
Switzerland	2668	17	Philippines	209	45
Austria	2630	18	India	172	46
Bulgaria	2571	19	Morocco	153	47
Rumania	2035	20	Kenya	124	48
Italy	1787	21	Ceylon	114	49
Japan	1783	22	Indonesia	111	50
			Thailand	110	51
Middle Third			Mozambique	106	52
(Developing Countries)			Ghana	104	53
Argentina	1341	23	Pakistan	90	54
Yugoslavia	1192	24	Congo	83	55
Chile	1089	25	South Vietnam	73	56
Spain	1023	26	Sudan	69	57
Mexico	977	27	Tanzania	55	58
Cuba	950	28	Burma	47	59
			Nigeria	44	60
			Madagascar	42	61
			Uganda	42	62
			Afghanistan	25	63
			Ethiopia	10	64
			Yemen	10	65
			Nepal	8	66

*In equivalent kilograms of coal per capita.
Source: Based on the data files of the Profiles of Development Project, Bureau of Social Research Columbia University.

Nepal—consists of *underdeveloped countries* in which technology has not yet taken firm root. Their future progress is almost entirely dependent on outside help.

Table 1 also illustrates the magnitude of the distances between successive rungs of the development ladder. The per capita consumption of energy in Algeria, the lowest country in the middle third, is barely 3 percent of the per capita consumption of energy in the United States. The per capita consumption of energy in Nepal, the lowest country in the lower third, is less than 3 percent of Algeria's. These enormous disparities must be kept in mind to understand why differences in short-term rates of change do not have much effect on the rank-order.

The stability of the world development ladder is the fundamental background condition against which the question of whether the rich countries are getting richer and the poor countries poorer must be considered. When we compare the 1950 and 1965 rank-orders of major countries on each of a dozen diverse development indicators, none of the rank-order correlations is under .95; composite indices of development show even greater stability over time because the fluctuations of single indicators cancel out. In other words, hardly anyone moves up or down the world development ladder.

The stability of this ladder may be further illustrated by means of one of the best simple indicators of development, the number of telephones per capita. Because all telephone systems generate directories, the enumeration of telephones is simple and accurate. Telephone statistics are available for a longer period of time than almost any other modern economic index.

Table 2 compares the countries of the world which had the most telephones per capita on January 1, 1911 with those which had the most telephones per capita 56 years later, on January 1, 1967. The countries included in the list are the same. Not one has been added or subtracted, and their rank-order has changed remarkably little, considering the fortunes of war and politics over half a century.

How shall we visualize rich countries getting richer and poor countries getting poorer within a stable rank-order? One possibility is that countries ranking high on development indicators would show steady rises from year to year on those indicators, while countries ranking low would show steady declines. This condition would present a straightforward—and very serious—social problem, but fortunately it has not existed in this century. On the contrary, most countries have been improving on most development indicators most of the time.

In common-sense terms, the rich countries *are* getting richer, but the poor countries *are not* getting poorer. Nearly all countries get richer concurrently. Thus, for example, among the 39 countries for which the United Nations gathered information on iron production from 1953 to 1965, not a single country failed to increase its production substantially; the average increase for the 13-year period was 96 percent. Between 1950 and 1965 the per capita availability of physicians for the world as a whole increased from about 28 to about 42 per 100,000 of the population, while 55 of the 66 largest countries showed increases in the per

Table 2
The World's Leading Countries with Respect to
Telephones per Capita, 1911 and 1967

Country	Telephones per capita January 1, 1911	1911 Rank	Telephones per capita January 1, 1967	1967 Rank
United States	.087	1	.499	1
Canada	.037	2	.389	4
Sweden	.034	3	.479	2
Switzerland	.021	4	.392	3
Germany*	.016	5	.159	9
Gr. Britain	.014	6	.207	5
Netherlands	.011	7	.201	6
Belgium	.006	8.5	.174	7
France	.006	8.5	.132	11
Austria	.004	10	.149	10
Japan	.003	11	.161	8

*German Empire 1911, Federal Republic 1967.
Source: American Telephone and Telegraph Company, *Telephone Statistics of the World*, May 1912; and *The World's Telephones*, December 1967. Countries of less than five million population at either date are omitted.

capita availability of physicians and only 11 showed decreases. From 1963 to 1966 per capita consumption of mechanical energy increased in 151 countries and autonomous territories, and declined or remained unchanged in only 21. These achievements, all expressed in per capita terms, are even more remarkable when population growth is taken into account.

Suppose, however, that "rich" and "poor" have meaning only in a relative sense, the rich being considered rich only in relation to the poverty of the poor, and vice-versa. What might it then mean to say that rich countries are getting richer and poor countries poorer? There are two practical possibilities.

In the first—let us call it Model *X*—rates of improvement on development indicators would be greater for high-ranking than for low-ranking countries on the development ladder. This would not interfere with the stability of the rank-order, but the absolute difference between any two countries with respect to a development indicator would increase logarithmically.

The second possibility is Model *Y*, a situation where rates of improvement on development indicators would be the same for high-ranking and for low-ranking countries. Since such growth rates begin from a much higher base in the high-ranking countries, the absolute differences between high-ranking and low-ranking countries would increase at constant rates.

In general, Model *Y* fits the empirical data on national development better than Model *X*. There is no consistent tendency for high-ranking countries to show higher rates of improvement on development

Table 3

The Relative Progress of Rich and Poor Countries on Various Development Indicators, 1950 to 1965

Note: The rich country in each pair was that nearest the tenth percentile in 1950 in the world distribution of the given indicator; the poor country was that nearest the seventieth percentile.

Indicator	Rich Country	1950 Value	1965 Value	% Change	Poor Country	1950 Value	1965 Value	% Change
Energy kw consumed per capita	Czechoslovakia	3,006	5,676	+88	India	101	172	+70
Steel kg consumed per capita	United Kingdom	280	524	+51	Morocco	18	13	−28
Telephones per capita	Belgium	.0795	.1650	+108	Madagascar	.0013	.0030	+207
Printing Paper kg consumed per capita	United Kingdom	146	256	+75	Morocco	2.6	5.0	+92
Calories per capita daily	Switzerland	3,180	3,160	−1	Mexico	2,210	2,640	+19
Fertilizer tons consumed per hectare	East Germany	.1460	.2560	+75	Morocco	.0026	.0050	+92
Teachers per capita	Canada	.0065	.0108	+66	India	.0021	.0035	+67
School Enrollment proportion of population 5-14 in school	West Germany	.81	.75	−7	Madagascar	.22	.44	+100
Physicians per capita	Italy	.00122	.00177	+45	Malaysia	.00013	.00014	+8
Hospital Beds per capita	West Germany	.0106	.0101	−5	Peru	.0020	.0022	+10
Air Travel passengers-km per capita	Venezuela	47	64	+36	Ethiopia	2	9	+350

Source: Based on the data files of the Profiles of Development Project, Bureau of Social Research, Columbia University.

indicators than low-ranking countries. By way of illustration, Table 3 compares pairs of rich and poor countries on eleven development indicators from 1950 to 1965. For the rich countries the changes ranged from −7 percent to +108 percent, with a median of +51 percent. For the poor countries, the changes during the same period ranged from −28 percent to +350 percent, with a median of +70 percent. The poor countries show somewhat higher and much more variable rates of progress.

Insofar as rich and poor countries improve concurrently on development indicators at roughly similar rates, the absolute differences per capita will, of course, increase. But before we consider what this finding does to the "the rich get richer, the poor get poorer" hypothesis, two special situations should be noted.

1. Poor countries show *much* higher rates of improvement on certain development indicators than rich countries. For example, per capita air travel increased by 350 percent in Ethiopia from 1950 to 1965 and by only 36 percent in Venezuela. Air traffic is a comparatively volatile indicator of development, because it requires very little fixed investment in proportion to the cost of aircraft, and has a standardized technology that can be installed anywhere without much adaptation to local conditions. Differences of this order would be quite unlikely with respect to road or water transportation.

2. Daily per capita calorie consumption in Mexico increased from 2210 to 2640 calories—an improvement of 19 percent—between 1950 and 1965, while the comparable figures for Switzerland showed no appreciable change. Per capita calorie consumption is one of many development indicators that have built-in ceilings. Even the most affluent population is unable to consume much more than about 3200 calories per person per day. When a rich country approaches this level, its progress on the indicator effectively ceases (although the *quality* of its nutrition may continue to improve); and every poor country that is making normal progress begins to catch up. Other important development indicators that have built-in ceilings are literacy, infant mortality, and urbanization.

Apart from such special situations, the study of almost *any* development indicator discloses a distinctive pattern of growth that describes the past experience of developed countries and predicts—although not infallibly—the future experience of developing countries. Many of these patterns are nonlinear; as growth continues, rates of growth accelerate or decelerate. Consider, for example, the historic trend of telephones per capita.

In Table 4, I have ranked the 63 major countries reporting telephone systems in 1950 (column one), entered their telephones per capita in 1950 and 1965 (in columns two and three), and computed each country's percentage increase in telephones per capita between 1950 and 1965 (column four).

Despite population growth, civil wars, natural disasters, the shocks of decolonization, economic crises, and other convulsions, it is interesting to see that not one of these 63 countries registered a decline in telephones per capita during the 15-year period between 1950 and 1965. Indeed, the average increase per country exceeded 200 percent.

There were enormous variations in rates of progress among these countries during this period. For example, Mexico, which had .0110 telephones per capita in 1950, showed an increase of 81 percent by 1965. Algeria and Greece, starting at the same level as Mexico, showed increases of 9 percent and 445 percent respectively.

Column five of Table 4 presents a five-line moving average of the percentage increases in telephones per capita in these countries from 1950 to 1965. The first ten entries, representing the richest countries, are all lower than 150 percent, and eight of the last fifteen entries, representing the poorest countries, are higher than 300 percent. Elsewhere in the table, all but two of the entries fall in the middle range, between 150 percent and 300 percent. On this indicator, the richest countries seem to be getting richer rather slowly, and the poorest countries seem to be getting richer rather quickly.

This analysis suggests that with respect to telephones, the poor countries are slowly but surely closing the gap that separates them from the rich countries. But if we think of the rich country as a moving target whose velocity has varied in the past and will vary in the future, then we can see that further analysis is required.

Table 4

Increases of Telephones Per Capita in the World's Major Countries, 1950 to 1965

Country	Telephones Per Capita 1950	Telephones Per Capita 1965	Percentage Increases 1950 to 1965 By Country	Percentage Increases 1950 to 1965 5-line Moving Average	Country	Telephones Per Capita 1950	Telephones Per Capita 1965	Percentage Increases 1950 to 1965 By Country	Percentage Increases 1950 to 1965 5-line Moving Average
(1)	(2)	(3)	(4)	(5)	(1)	(2)	(3)	(4)	(5)
1. United States	.2823	.4780	70	—	32. USSR	.0076	.0340	348	199
2. Sweden	.2402	.4600	91	—	33. Morocco	.0076	.0090	47	185
3. Canada	.2123	.3770	78	81	34. Egypt	.0057	.0110	92	182
4. Switzerland	.1909	.3780	97	84	35. Peru	.0055	.0120	118	146
5. Australia	.1415	.2470	70	92	36. Yugoslavia	.0052	.0210	304	188
6. United Kingdom	.1073	.1950	82	106	37. Rhodesia	.0045	.0120	167	214
7. Belgium	.0795	.1650	134	114	38. Malaya	.0038	.0140	259	225
8. Netherlands	.0773	.1930	148	123	39. Taiwan	.0037	.0130	250	215
9. Austria	.0595	.1390	134	138	40. Iraq	.0037	.0090	143	223
10. France	.0576	.1240	115	121	41. Turkey	.0031	.0110	255	188
11. West Germany	.0479	.1480	157	107	42. Kenya	.0022	.0060	207	218
12. Argentina	.0464	.0670	49	128	43. Ceylon	.0022	.0040	83	278
13. South Africa	.0368	.0660	79	171	44. Iran	.0180	.0090	401	207
14. Czechoslovakia	.0311	.1050	237	194	45. Ghana	.0016	.0050	213	245
15. Italy	.0267	.1160	335	191	46. Madagascar	.0013	.0030	130	298
16. Spain	.0239	.0880	268	182	47. Philippines	.0010	.0050	400	448
17. Chile	.0222	.0300	35	246	48. Saudi Arabia	.0009	.0040	346	471
18. Cuba	.0219	.0300	37	265	49. South Korea	.0008	.0100	1,150	511
19. Japan	.0217	.1420	555	259	50. Mozambique	.0007	.0030	329	477
20. East Germany	.0181	.0970	435	279	51. Sudan	.0007	.0030	329	488
21. Portugal	.0181	.0600	232	342	52. Indonesia	.0006	.0020	232	312
22. Venezuela	.0135	.0320	137	247	53. Uganda	.0006	.0030	400	272
23. Hungary	.0124	.0560	351	162	54. Tanzania	.0005	.0020	300	226
24. Mexico	.0110	.0200	81	205	55. China	.0005	.0010	100	240
25. Algeria	.0110	.0120	9	187	56. Congo	.0005	.0010	100	190
26. Greece	.0108	.0590	445	185	57. India	.0005	.0020	300	160
27. Brazil	.0106	.0160	51	203	58. Nigeria	.0004	.0010	150	187
28. Poland	.0093	.0410	341	239	59. Afghanistan	.0004	.0010	150	213
29. Colombia	.0089	.0240	170	214	60. Burma	.0003	.0010	233	333
30. Rumania	.0083	.0250	189	274	61. Pakistan	.0003	.0010	233	383
31. Bulgaria	.0081	.0340	320	215	62. Thailand	.0003	.0030	900	—
					63. Ethiopia	.0002	.0010	400	—

Ideally, we might try to determine how many future years a poor country requires to reach the present level of a rich country. To estimate this by projecting development trends is an uncertain business, but something can be learned by retrospective measurement of time lags; that is, by calculating the years elapsed since the rich country passed the present level of the poor country.

In Table 5, I have taken advantage of the unusual longevity of statistics on telephones per capita in the United States (the records go back to 1896) to measure how much other major countries lagged behind the United States on this indicator in 1950 and in 1965. The table includes 34 countries. The remaining major countries of the world are omitted from this table because, as of 1950, they had not yet reached the 1896 U.S. level!

Column one of Table 5 arrays the 34 major countries by telephones per capita as of 1950. Column two of the table gives the year the United States was at the other country's 1950 level with respect to telephones per capita. For example, the entry for Sweden in this column is *1947,* meaning that Sweden's 1950 level (.240 telephones per capita) was approximately equal to the level reached by the U.S. in 1947 (.239 telephones per capita).

Column three of the table gives the year the United States was at the other country's 1965 level. The entry for Sweden in this column is *1964,* meaning that Sweden's 1965 level (.460 telephones per capita) was approximately equal to the United States' 1964 level (.458 telephones per capita). Column four of the table shows the lag as of 1950 expressed in the number of years another nation trailed the U.S. in providing telephones to its population. For Sweden, this was three years (1950 minus 1947). Column five shows the lag as of 1965. For Sweden, this was one year (1965 minus 1964). Column six of the table shows the change of lag between 1950 and 1965. There is a minus entry in this column if the lag was smaller than in 1950, as it was for Sweden (minus two years), and a plus entry if the lag was greater than in 1950, as it was for Canada (plus three years). Countries with minus entries in column six were catching up to the United States in telephones per capita; countries with plus entries were falling further behind.

The results of this comparison are dramatically different from those obtained by comparing percentage rates of growth. Of the ten countries closest to the United States in telephones per capita in 1950, only three (Canada, Switzerland, and France) failed to gain on the United States from 1950 to 1965; most of them gained substantially. Of the ten countries lowest in the table, none gained on the United States from 1950 to 1965. Indeed, all but one lost more than ten years. Looked at in this way, the rich counrties *were* growing richer and the poor countries poorer with respect to telephones during this period.

The secret of this unexpected outcome is as follows: the rich countries are those that progressed fastest in the past; they had much higher growth rates in the early stages of their development than they do now, but what is equally important, their growth rates 50 or 60 years ago were generally higher than the current growth rates of poor countries.

Table 5

Time-Lags Between the United States and Other Countries in the Increase of Telephones Per Capita, 1896-1965

Country in Rank Order of Telephones Per Capita, 1950	U.S. Equivalent Date for Telephones Per Capita in Other Countries		Time-Lag in Years		Change in Time-Lag 1950-1965
	1950	1965	1950	1965	
(1)	(2)	(3)	(4)	(5)	(6)
1. United States	1950	1965	0	0	—
2. Sweden	1947	1964	3	1	-2
3. Canada	1946	1958	4	7	+3
4. Switzerland	1943	1958	7	7	0
5. Australia	1936	1947	14	18	+4
6. United Kingdom	1916	1944	34	21	-13
7. Belgium	1910	1940	40	25	-15
8. Netherlands	1909	1944	41	21	-20
9. Austria	1906	1924	44	41	-3
10. France	1906	1920	44	45	+1
11. West Germany	1905	1937	45	28	-17
12. Argentina	1905	1907	45	58	+13
13. South Africa	1903	1907	47	58	+11
14. Czechoslovakia	1902	1915	48	50	+2
15. Italy	1902	1918	48	47	-1
16. Spain	1901	1911	49	54	+5
17. Chile	1901	1902	49	63	+14
18. Cuba	1901	1902	49	63	+14
19. Japan	1901	1936	49	29	-20
20. East Germany	1900	1913	50	52	+2
21. Portugal	1900	1906	50	59	+9
22. Venezuela	1899	1902	51	63	+12
23. Hungary	1899	1906	51	59	+8
24. Mexico	1898	1900	52	65	+13
25. Algeria	1898	1899	52	66	+14
26. Greece	1898	1906	52	59	+7
27. Brazil	1898	1900	52	65	+13
28. Poland	1898	1904	52	61	+9
29. Colombia	1898	1901	52	64	+12
30. Rumania	1898	1901	52	64	+12
31. Bulgaria	1897	1903	53	62	+9
32. USSR	1897	1903	53	62	+9
33. Morocco	1897	1898	53	67	+14
34. Egypt	1896	1898	54	67	+13

Source: American Telephone and Telegraph Company, Telephone Statistics of the World, May 1912; and The World's Telephones, December 1967. Countries of less than five million population at either date are omitted.

Countries that enter the arena of development late have opportunities to borrow technology and capital that the early comers may have lacked, but this advantage does not seem to offset whichever disadvantages retarded their development at an earlier stage.

As Table 5 suggests, these lags in development are greater than is commonly assumed. By 1965, only four countries surpassed the level of telephones per capita reached by the United States during World War II; only 11 surpassed its World War I level. Taking account of the countries omitted from the table, fewer than half the world's major countries enjoyed as ample a provision of telephones in 1965 as Switzerland in 1911. This "telephone gap" has broad implications. As noted earlier, there is consistency and very high correlation between the telephone data and almost every other statistical index of development we have.

Thus, rather unexpectedly, the grievance embodied in the inaccurate statement that the rich countries are getting richer and the poor countries poorer, turns out to be partly justified. If the time-lag between developed and developing countries lengthens from year to year, the relative progress of the developing countries is unsatisfactory, regardless of their high growth rates.

It is almost impossible to conceive of the low-ranking countries on the development ladder *overtaking* the high-ranking countries within the foreseeable future. Turkey had achieved the same level with respect to telephones in 1965 as the Netherlands in 1911. No matter how fast the Turkish telephone system expands, it must take a considerable number of years to reach the Dutch level of 1965. By that time the Netherlands, barring some catastrophic interruption of its progress, will have moved far ahead again. Even if it were possible for Turkey to close the "telephone gap," there would still be lags on scores of other indicators. To catch up with a rich country, a poor country must for many years produce energy, metals, trained manpower, and a long list of other things at a much higher rate than the rich country, although its capacity to do so is necessarily inferior.

Buckminster Fuller has shown that once a pound of refined metal enters the economy of a developed country, it circulates indefinitely, with negligible loss, and with a mean interval of less than 25 years between refabrications. The new mteal produced or imported in a given year is only a small fraction of the total supply of metal on hand. To rise on the ladder of development, a poor country must not only exceed the metal output of richer countries year after year, but must also overcome the accumulated disadvantages of the past. The same reasoning applies with nearly equal force to education, transportation, or any other development indicator.

Several conclusions, it seems to me, inescapably flow from this. Stated simply, they are as follows:

1. The rank order of wealth (or development) among the world's countries is relatively fixed, changes hardly at all in the short run, and is

surprisingly resistant to the effects of war, revolution, and economic planning.

2. Since the beginning of the Twentieth Century, availability of goods and services has been improving almost steadily nearly everywhere. In any given period, most development indicators register significant gains in most of the world's countries.

3. The rate of progress of a poor country, as measured by percentage changes in its development indicators, generally equals or exceeds the progress of a rich country; but the bases, the "starting places" for growth of rich and poor nations, differ so greatly that gaps between them tend to increase.

4. The time-lag in development among the richest countries is decreasing, but between them and all other countries it seems to be increasing.

5. The equalization of the world's countries with respect to development indicators is impossible to visualize in the immediate future, except perhaps by a catastrophic decline of all countries down to the level of the poorest countries.

6. The reduction of absolute gaps between unequally developed countries is mathematically incompatible with universal progress since, under normal conditions, poor countries have no means of outstripping the growth rate of rich countries by the wide margins necessary to reduce these gaps.

7. The reduction of time-lags between rich and poor countries seems to be a fair criterion for evaluating the development of the modern world as a whole. By this criterion, most countries did *not* make satisfactory progress between 1950 and 1965.

In this century there has been a relatively immutable hierarchy of development among nations. If present trends can be projected into the future, that hierarchy will remain. Nuclear war, world economic collapse, and other imaginable cataclysms and changes could alter the picture. But barring such unpredictable events, as long as the present structure of nation-states persists we can expect to live in a world whose nations are vastly unequal in wealth.

NOTE

[1] The statistical correlation is over .80 in each case.

4

The Developing World—
Should We Give a Damn?

ROBERT HUNTER

America's efforts to help the developing world are in trouble. Foreign aid is in disrepute. The Vietnam War has led to widespread disillusionment with any U.S. involvement in countries not central to our own security. And our problems here at home are competing for resources that might otherwise go overseas. In fact, saving the American environment has become more important than helping to feed the poor of the world.

Is something wrong with this argument? Why, indeed, should we give a damn about the developing world?

A few years ago, we thought we knew the right answer: we had to save the souls of people in the developing world. Even more important, we had to save them from communism—their fate if we didn't pitch in and help poor countries develop the bulwarks against internal subversion, either by political agents or by poverty, disease and lack of hope.

Today, these arguments are worth virtually nothing. Most people in poor nations don't want to be saved, either from perdition or politics; and they certainly don't want to be saved by rich Americans. Also, we no longer fear that we will gradually be surrounded by an international communist conspiracy. After all, look at Cuba—the one real success that the Russians have had in the developing world. It's now costing them dearly, for precious little return. In addition, Egypt, Syria, and Iraq have proved to be just as unruly under Soviet tutelage as under that of Britain and France. Even North Vietnam asserts its independence of China, despite years of debilitating war with us.

So we may as well forget the developing world. These countries can't really do very much to us, whatever happens. And we don't really get very much from them either, even when they aren't (as the saying goes) "kicking us in the teeth at the U.N."

But are we really so sure about all this?

Maybe not.

First, let's look at the condition of the world today—and how we fit into it. There is now some real hope that we can soon limit the arms race. At least we are talking seriously with the Russians about the problem. Things are also pretty quiet in Europe, a quarter of a century after the war. That's something we Americans helped to do: provide more peace than Europe has known in a long time.

As far as Asia is concerned, Vietnam has been one long tragedy; but now we're getting out. In the future, we may succeed in understanding better where our real security interests lie. In the Middle East, we're not in such a lather as we were a year ago, as the superpowers tell their local clients and friends not to cause trouble.

This looks like a good picture. Why, even the president now tells us that Vietnam may be our last war.

Maybe he's right. But maybe there are some other problems that we ought to be looking at—problems that we can spend more time on, now that some of the old issues are causing less trouble. In the Middle East, for example, there have been skyjackings by Palestinian guerrillas that have added new dangers to air travel. And there has been a spate of diplomatic kidnappings, creating another new cause of fear and uncertainty.

Many of these acts of violence are taking place in parts of the world where there are poor people, undeveloped economies, and high growth in population. Indeed, there is growing violence within countries from one end of the Third World to the other.

Nor is it clear that we are going to be able to insulate ourselves for very long. To make matters worse, we seem to be developing the notion that things happening in many parts of the world do not demand our attention. It would take a daring man, however, to say that we won't still be involved in Southeast Asia in a direct way several years from now. But it may make a difference *how* we are involved. So far, we've emphasized an approach based largely on military assistance. Perhaps we could do better with a different approach—by helping people in Asia to help themselves economically, and to try to provide for their own security. Primarily, this means local political, economic, and social development, with the U.S. offering resources and technical assistance, while at the same time recognizing the limitations of our free advice. If we can help people be more self-reliant, we should face fewer dilemmas of the sort that once led us into Vietnam.

These are matters to think about, even though we may believe now that we will no longer play a major role in other people's lives. But no matter what we do, we can't be sure that violence in the developing world will leave us alone. For example, nobody doubts that we are involved in the Middle East, and would have a hard time getting rid of our responsibilities there even if we wanted to. Here is one part of the developing world, prone to violence, where we are doubtful we could keep aloof from open conflict. But in other areas, violence doesn't seem like much of a problem for us—at least not now. And everyone knows that it is all but impossible to run a foreign policy that looks beyond next year, much less to the middle of the decade.

Yet despite that myopia we all have about foreign policy, there are two areas where we can see the trend of affairs. First, there is the fact of American trade with the developing world. What will happen to this trade if there are continued eruptions of violence? This isn't an idle question. For example, the civil war in Nigeria cost Britain its oil supplies from there, and a war in the Middle East could cause even wider disruptions in the world oil market. In fact, in those places where the West has trading relations with the developing world—especially where raw materials are involved—there are many possibilities of important sources being cut off.

Second, there is the question of American private investment abroad. This is a subject not talked about in some circles, for fear that one will be called "imperialist." Perhaps there is justification in the charge of imperialism against the U.S., and perhaps we need to listen more closely to what people in poor countries say about multinational corporations. But until we do that—and as long as we enjoy our affluence here in part because of our investments abroad—we should realize that they could be placed in jeopardy if there were a lot of violence in less-developed countries. And the consequences would affect us directly.

It may well be, therefore, that growing violence in the developing world will pose some problems for us. But how is development assistance going to help? To be honest, it's impossible to tell. In fact, some people think that a small amount of outside help may actually promote strife and conflict, by raising hopes and expectations faster than they can be satisfied. But that's no reason not to try. There will be development in these countries at some point anyway, with all the threat of violence and disruption that that process often entails. The only question is whether we will help, perhaps only with the faith that our helping will make the job easier than if we sit back and watch things take their natural course. Of course, developed countries also make war and have riots. But nothing is more certain than that poor countries just beginning to develop themselves will face a variety of violent upheavals.

Let's look more closely at the Middle East. The Arab conflict with Israel has gone on for so long in part because most Arab economies have barely begun to develop. Of course, there are very real conflicts of interest in the Middle East, and no one would argue that development efforts will quickly turn conflict into cooperation between Israel and her Arab neighbors.

But over time, it is possible that development in the Arab world could provide another focus of attention, and go hand-in-hand with a long-term resolution of the conflict. Moreover, constructive economic relations between the Arabs and the West might loosen the dependence of some Arab states on Moscow's support.

So far, this isn't an overwhelmingly convincing case for an American role in development assistance. But then, no great adventure to stave off what could become a problem in the future can be undertaken without hard thought about the distant future. In fact, just what kind of world is it in which we want to live?

For one thing, we want a world that can function. One clear requirement for this is a system of trade based on good faith and a fair exchange among all the parties. Indeed, if the trading system does not run on that basis, then we may not be able to have one that will work for anyone.

In the trade of raw materials, for example, the developing countries have been getting a bad deal for a very long time. We think that the prices we pay are right and proper, because that's what the prices are. We forget that we have the power to keep prices down, and the poor countries can't get together to push them up. But now some of them are trying to do just that. Oil producing countries in the Middle East have managed to get more money out of the consuming nations. And it may happen to copper next. What then should we do about it? Should we gang up on the developing countries so that they feel they need to nationalize our investments? Should we put on so much pressure that some countries will start searching for other markets?

There is a better way. It lies in taking seriously the problems that these countries have in developing themselves—not necessarily because we love them, but because if we don't realize that the relationship is a two-way business, we may lose by it. Again, it means taking a long view. Of course, we will have to pay more for some products. But that may happen in any event, under conditions we don't like. And a lot of foreign investment is going to be nationalized anyway in the next few years.

If we're smart, we can keep things from turning sour. After nationalization, somebody has to keep running the oil wells and marketing the products. Why shouldn't we do what we can to help poor countries develop economies that will both provide markets for us, and someday bring them to the point where nobody needs to help them at all? And why shouldn't we show enough good faith so that our relations with developing countries will benefit us even after investments are nationalized? Letting poor-country goods into the U.S. without paying duty, for example, wouldn't affect us very much. Naturally it will increase the pressures on the U.S. to adjust away from labor-intensive industries. But adjustment is a process that is taking place anyhow. Perhaps, therefore, we should give a try to preferential treatment for the products of poor countries, and see what they can do for themselves.

Trade isn't the only area where working together can help everybody. There is also the problem of pollution. Most of the problem centers in the big industrial countries, with land, water and air all being fouled. However, some of these problems can't be solved by the rich countries alone. What happens if developing countries increase their use of DDT just as we stop using it? What if they start polluting rivers as they discover industrialization, just as we start cleaning ours up? We can't expect them to help in the global search for ways of saving man from himself if we ignore their problems and expectations. We are all together on this planet, whether we like it or not.

We must also consider together what is happening to the world's resources. We use a good part of them right here in the United States—

over one-third with only one-sixteenth of the world's population. Some people say that that's unjust. But even if we want only to stay fat and happy and enjoy what we have, we will not be able to ignore what's going on elsewhere. The poor people of the world will inevitably be competing with us for scarce resources.

"Help 'em with birth control," some people say. That's one partial and needed approach, even though it is hard for rich, white North Americans to preach self-restraint to poor Indian villagers who want lots of children to take care of them in old age. Or maybe they just resent being told what to do. But even if poor countries do want to limit the size of their populations, it isn't so simple. Unless these countries are advancing economically, the people will have no incentive to cut down on family size. This means development; and it means that outsiders have to help, or populations will keep on expanding and placing ever more demand on limited resources.

These are some arguments for development assistance—but still not a compelling rationale, like having the Russians knock at the door of Europe. But if we once again ask ourselves what kind of world we want, we may recognize that it's more than just a planet free from war or having a good system of international trade.

Man is still a moral being—a fact that goes a long way toward explaining why he's different. Morality, however, does not stop at the water's edge. Men are still men, whether they live in Waco or Quagadougou. We can say that we have to "take care of our own" before we can take care of someone else's (not that we're doing a very good job even with our own). But that's misleading for two reasons.

First, there's a real question whether the rest of the world will wait for that. Right now, there is a momentum behind the development effort. If we retire from the effort now, that momentum may be lost. Also, many problems are likely to be much worse a few years from now, and our chances of helping solve them much less. Or we may find that we face new temptations to act militarily, as we did in Southeast Asia, simply because we didn't try the economic and human remedies first.

Second, the idea of "putting our own house in order first" implies that we have to choose one or the other. That might be true if Uncle Sam became the fount of charity, spilling treasure all over the world. But we need not do that; rather, we can say that the United States, as the richest country of all, can meet its challenges at home and still afford without hardship to help the rest of the globe make some development progress.

What does that mean in specific terms? Simply that our record of development assistance during the last few years, while it may reflect what some consider to be our short-term self-interest, certainly can't be called moral, or just, or any of the other words we like to use about ourselves when we think of the best human qualities. That's no reason for breast-beating; not many other people are particularly moral either in their day-to-day lives. But then Americans don't like to think of themselves as "other people."

In any case, we are certainly lagging behind others today in our material effort on behalf of poor countries, if we consider the percentage of gross national product used in this way. In economic aid in 1969, we ranked 12th among the members of the O.E.C.D.'s Development Assistance Committee, even with aid to Vietnam thrown in. And if we consider both economic aid and private investment, then we were last of the pack.

Maybe some of those Europeans, or the Japanese and Canadians, know something we don't. But at least they seem to have more faith that they can help do something in the Third World. Most of these countries, despite our popular belief to the contrary, tax themselves far more heavily than we do. Yet they are willing to see a greater percentage of their resources used to help people poorer than themselves.

Possibly it's self-interest; possibly people in these other developed countries simply want to feel better; or possibly they have some glimmering that it would be better to live in a world that has a bit more justice in it than to let things go on as they are.

In the end, each American must make his own decision on whether or not he believes his country should help the poor countries to develop. But he ought to remember that the United States looms large in the world; it's involved in places and in ways that bring us into constant contact with the developing countries; and it's going to have a loud voice in saying what kind of world people are going to live in during the coming years. . . .

Imperialism and Intervention: The Dynamism of the Strong

5

To Intervene or Not to Intervene

HANS J. MORGENTHAU

Intervention is as ancient and well-established an instrument of foreign policy as are diplomatic pressure, negotiations and war. From the time of the ancient Greeks to this day, some states have found it advantageous to intervene in the affairs of other states on behalf of their own interests and against the latters' will. Other states, in view of their interests, have opposed such interventions and have intervened on behalf of theirs.

It is only since the French Revolution of 1789 and the rise of the nation-state that the legitimacy of intervention has been questioned. Article 119 of the French Constitution of 1793 declared that the French people "do no interfere in the domestic affairs of other nations and will not tolerate interference by other nations in their affairs." This declaration ushered in a period of interventions by all concerned on the largest possible scale. For a century and a half afterwards, statesmen, lawyers and political writers tried in vain to formulate objective criteria by which to distinguish between legitimate and illegitimate intervention. The principle of nonintervention was incorporated into the textbooks of international law, and statesmen have never ceased to pay lip service to it. In December 1965, the United Nations General Assembly adopted a "Declaration on the Inadmissibility of Intervention in the Domestic Affairs of States and the Protection of their Independence and Sovereignty," according to which "no state has the right to intervene, directly or indirectly, for any reason whatever, in the internal or external affairs of any other state . . ." and "no state shall organize, assist, foment, finance, incite or tolerate subversive, terrorist or armed activities directed toward the violent overthrow of another state, or interfere in civil strife in another state." Yet again we are witnessing throughout the world activities violating all the rules laid down in this Declaration.

Both the legal commitments against intervention and the practice of intervention serve the political purposes of particular nations. The former serve to discredit the intervention of the other side and to justify one's own. Thus the principle of nonintervention, as formulated at the beginning of the nineteenth century, sought to protect the new nation-states from interference by the traditional monarchies of Europe. For the main instrument of the Holy Alliance, openly proclaimed in the treaty establishing it, was intervention. Thus, to give only two examples among many, Russia tried to intervene in Spain in 1820, and actually intervened in Hungary in 1848, in order to oppose liberal revolutions. Great Britain opposed these interventions because it was opposed to the expansion of Russian power. Yet it intervened on behalf of nationalism in Greece and on behalf of the conservative status quo in Portugal because its interests seemed to require it.

What we have witnessed since the end of the Second World War thus appears as a mere continuation of a tradition which was well established in the nineteenth century. There is nothing new either in the contemporary doctrine opposing intervention or in the pragmatic use of intervention on behalf of the interests of individual nations. What Great Britain and Russia were doing in the nineteenth century, the United States and the Soviet Union seem to be doing today. Thus, to cite again two spectacular examples among many, the Soviet Union intervened in Hungary in 1956 as Russia had done in 1848, and the United States intervened in Cuba at the beginning of the sixties as it had done in the first decades of the century. Yet there are fundamental differences between the interventions of the past and those of the present. Five such differences have significantly altered the techniques of contemporary intervention, have drastically reduced the traditional legal significance of the consent of the state intervened against, and have affected in a general way the peace and order of the world.

First, the process of decolonization, which started after the Second World War and is now almost completed, has more than doubled the number of sovereign nations. Many if not most of these new nations are not viable political, military and economic entities; they are lacking in some if not all of the prerequisites of nationhood. Their governments need regular outside support. Thus France subsidizes its former colonies in Africa; all the major industrial nations extend economic and financial aid to the new ones, and the United States, the Soviet Union and China do so on a competitive basis.

What makes this aid a lever for intervention is the fact that in most cases it is not just an advantage which the new nations can afford to take or leave, but a condition for their survival. The Indian economy, for example, would collapse without outside support, and in consequence the Indian state itself would probably disintegrate. Large masses of

Egyptians would starve without the outside supply of food. What is true of these two ancient and relatively well developed nations is of course true of most of the new nations which are nations within their present boundaries only by virtue of the accidents of colonial policy: the supplier of foreign aid holds the power of life and death over them. If a foreign nation supplies aid it intervenes; if it does not supply aid it also intervenes. In the measure that the government must depend on foreign aid for its own and its nation's survival it is inevitably exposed to political pressures from the supplying government. Many of the recipient governments have been able to minimize or even neutralize these political pressures by keeping open alternative sources of foreign aid and by playing one supplying government against the other. Some nations, such as Egypt, have developed this technique into a fine and highly successful art.

Second, our age resembles the period of history after the Napoleonic Wars, when the theory of nonintervention and the practice of intervention flourished, in that it is a revolutionary age. Many nations, new and old, are threatened by revolution, or are at one time or another in the throes of it. A successful revolution frequently portends a new orientation in the country's foreign policy, as it did in the Congo, Cuba and Indonesia. Thus the great powers, expecting gains or fearing disadvantages from the revolution, are tempted to intervene on the side of the faction favoring them. This is particularly so when the revolution is committed to a communist or anti-communist position. Thus China has almost indiscriminately intervened throughout the world on behalf of subversive movements, very much in the manner in which the Bolshevist government under Lenin and Trotsky tried to promote world revolution. In many nations, the United States and the Soviet Union oppose each other surreptitiously through the intermediary of governments and political movements. It is at this point that the third factor comes into play.

Of all the revolutionary changes that have occurred in world politics since the end of the Second World War, none has exerted a greater influence upon the conduct of foreign policy than the recognition on the part of the two superpowers, armed with a large arsenal of nuclear weapons, that a direct confrontation between them would entail unacceptable risks; for it could lead to their mutual destruction. Both have recognized that a nuclear war fought against each other would be a suicidal absurdity. Thus they have decided that they must avoid a direct confrontation. This is the real political and military meaning of the slogan of "peaceful coexistence."

Instead of confronting each other openly and directly, the United States and the Soviet Union have chosen to oppose and compete with each other surreptitiously through the intermediary of third parties. The internal weakness of most new and emerging nations requiring foreign support and the revolutionary situation in many of them give the great powers the opportunity of doing so. Thus, aside from competing for influence upon a particular government in the traditional ways, the United States and the Soviet Union have interjected their power into the domestic conflicts of weak nations, supporting the government or the opposition as the case may be. While one might think that on ideological grounds the United States would always intervene on the side of the government and the Soviet Union on the side of the opposition, it is characteristic of the interplay between ideology and power politics, to which we shall turn in a moment, that this has not always been so. Thus the Soviet Union intervened in Hungary in 1956 on the side of the government, and the United States has been intervening in Cuba on the side of the opposition. The Soviet slogan of support for "wars of national liberation" is in truth an ideological justification of Soviet support for that side in a civil conflict in which the Soviet Union happens to have an interest. In the Congo, the United States and the Soviet Union have switched their support from the government to the opposition and back again according to the fortunes of a succession of civil wars.

While contemporary interventions serving national power interests have sometimes been masked by the ideologies of communism and anticommunism, these ideologies have been an independent motivating force. This is the fourth factor which we must consider. The United States and the Soviet Union face each other not only as two great powers which in the traditional ways compete for advantage. They also face each other as the fountainheads of two hostile and incompatible ideologies, systems of government and ways of life, each trying to expand the reach of its respective political values and institutions and to prevent the expansion of the other. Thus the cold war has not only been a conflict between two world powers but also a contest between two secular religions. And like the religious wars of the seventeenth century, the war between communism and democracy does not respect national boundaries. It finds enemies and allies in all countries, opposing the one and supporting the other regardless of the niceties of international law. Here is the dynamic force which has led the two superpowers to intervene all over the globe, sometimes surreptitiously, sometimes openly, sometimes with the accepted methods of diplomatic pressure and propaganda, sometimes with the frowned-upon instruments of covert subversion and open force.

These four factors favoring intervention in our time are counteracted by a fifth one, which in a sense compensates for the weakness of the nations intervened in. Having just emerged from a colonial status or struggling to emerge from a semicolonial one, these nations react to their dependence on outside support with a fierce resistance to the threat of "neo-colonialism." While they cannot exist without support from stronger nations, they refuse to exchange their newly won independence for a new dependency. Hence their ambivalent reaction to outside intervention. They need it and they resent it. This ambivalence compels them to choose among several different courses of action. They can seek support from multiple outside sources, thereby canceling out dependence on one by dependence on the other. They can alternate among different sources of support, at one time relying on one, and at another time relying on another. Finally, they can choose between complete dependence and complete independence, either by becoming a client of one of the major powers or by forswearing outside support altogether.

This ambivalence of the weak nations imposes new techniques upon the intervening ones. Intervention must either be brutally direct in order to overcome resistance or it must be surreptitious in order to be acceptable, or the two extremes may be combined. Thus the United States intervened in Cuba in 1961 through the proxy of a refugee force, and the Soviet Union intervened in Hungary in 1956 by appointing a government which asked for its intervention.

II

What follows from this condition of intervention in our time for the foreign policies of the United States? Four basic conclusions can be drawn: the futility of the search for abstract principles, the error of anti-communist intervention per se, the self-defeating character of anti-revolutionary intervention per se, and the requirement of prudence.

First, it is futile to search for an abstract principle which would allow us to distinguish in a concrete case between legitimate and illegitimate intervention. This was so even in the nineteenth century when intervention for the purpose of colonial expansion was generally regarded to be legitimate and when the active players on the political stage were relatively self-sufficient nation-states, which not only were not in need of intervention but actually were opposed to it as a threat to their existence If this was so then, it stands to reason that in an age where large segments of whole continents must choose between anarchy and intervention, intervention cannot be limited by abstract principles, let alone effectively outlawed by a United Nations resolution.

Let us suppose that nation A intervenes on behalf of the government of nation B by giving it military, economic and technical aid on the latter's request, and that the government of B becomes so completely dependent upon A as to act as the latter's satellite. Let us further suppose that the local opposition calls upon country C for support against the agents of a foreign oppressor and that C heeds that call. Which one of these interventions is legitimate? Country A will of course say that its own is and C's is not, and vice versa, and the ideologues on both sides will be kept busy justifying the one and damning the other. This ideological shadowboxing cannot affect the incidence of interventions. All nations will continue to be guided in their decisions to intervene and their choice of the means of intervention by what they regard as their respective national interests. There is indeed an urgent need for the governments of the great powers to abide by certain rules according to which the game of intervention is to be played. But these rules must be deduced not from abstract principles which are incapable of controlling the actions of governments, but from the interests of the nations concerned and from their practice of foreign policy reflecting those interests.

The failure to understand this distinction between abstract principles and national interests as guidance for a policy of intervention was in good measure responsible for the fiasco of the Bay of Pigs in 1961. The United States was resolved to intervene on behalf of its interests, but it was also resolved to intervene in such a way as not openly to violate the principle of nonintervention. Both resolutions were legitimate in terms of American interests. The United States had an interest in eliminating the political and military power of the Soviet Union, which used Cuba as a base from which to threaten the security interests of the United States in the Western Hemisphere. The United States also had an interest in avoiding whatever would jeopardize its standing in the new and emerging nations. The United States failed to assign priorities to these two interests. In order to minimize the loss of prestige, the United States jeopardized the success of the intervention. Instead of using concern for prestige as a datum among others in the political equation—that is, as an interest among others —it submitted to it as though it were an abstract principle imposing absolute limits upon the actions necessary to achieve success. In consequence, the United States failed thrice. The intervention did not succeed; in the attempt we suffered the temporary impairment of our standing among the new and emerging nations; and we lost much prestige as a great nation able to use its power successfully on behalf of its interests.

Had the United States approached the problem of intervening in Cuba in a rational fashion, it would have asked itself which was more important: to succeed in the intervention or to prevent a temporary loss of prestige among the new and emerging nations. Had it settled upon the latter alternative, it would have refrained from intervening altogether; had it chosen the former alternative, it would have taken all the measures necessary to make the intervention a success, regardless of unfavorable reactions in the rest of the world. Instead, it sought the best of both worlds and got the worst.

The Soviet Union's intervention in Hungary in 1956 is instructive in this respect. The Soviet Union put the success of the intervention above all other considerations, and succeeded. Its prestige throughout the world suffered drastically in consequence. But Hungary is today a communist state within the orbit of the Soviet Union, and Soviet prestige recovered quickly from the damage it suffered in 1956.

The interventions of the United States in Cuba, the Dominican Republic and Viet Nam, as well as others less spectacular, have been justified as reactions to communist intervention. This argument derives from the assumption that communism everywhere in the world is not only morally unacceptable and philosophically hostile to the United States, but is also detrimental to the national interests of the United States and must therefore be opposed on political as well as moral and philosophic grounds. I shall assume for the purposes of this discussion that, as a matter of fact, communist intervention actually preceded ours in all these instances, and shall raise the question as to whether our national interest required our counter-intervention.

Ten or twenty years ago, this question could have been answered in the positive without further examination. For then communism anywhere in the world was a mere extension of Soviet power, controlled and used for the purposes of that power. Since we were committed to the containment of the Soviet Union, we were also committed to the containment of communism anywhere in the world. However, today we are faced not with one monolithic communist bloc controlled and used by the Soviet Union, but with a variety of communisms, whose relations with the Soviet Union and China change from country to country and from time to time and whose bearing upon the interests of the United States requires empirical examination in each concrete instance. Communism has become polycentric, that is to say, each communist government and movement, to a greater or lesser extent, pursues its own national interests within the common framework of communist ideology and institutions. The bearing which the pursuit of those interests has upon the interests of the United States must be determined in terms not of communist ideology but of the compatibility of those interests with the interests of the United States.

Subjecting our interventions in Cuba, the Dominican Republic and Viet Nam to this empirical test, one realizes the inadequacy of the simple slogan "stop communism" as the rationale of our interventions. While this slogan is popular at home and makes but minimal demands upon discriminating judgment, it inspires policies which do either too much or too little in opposing communism and can provide no yardstick for a policy which measures the degree of its opposition by the degree of the communist threat. Thus on the one hand, as part of the settlement of the missile crisis of 1962, we pledged ourselves not to intervene in Cuba, which is today a military and political outpost of the Soviet Union and the fountainhead of subversion and military intervention in the Western Hemisphere, and as such directly affects the interests of the United States. On the other hand, we have intervened massively in Viet Nam, even at the risk of a major war, although the communist threat to American interests from Viet Nam is at best remote and in any event is infinitely more remote than the communist threat emanating from Cuba.

As concerns the intervention in the Dominican Republic, even if one takes at face value the official assessment that the revolution of April 1965 was controlled by Cuban communists, it appears incongruous that we intervened massively in the Dominican Republic, whose revolution was, according to our government's assessment of the facts, a mere symptom of the disease, while the disease itself—that is, Cuban communism—is exempt from effective intervention altogether.

This type of intervention against communism per se naturally tends to blend into intervention against revolution per se. Thus we tend to intervene against all radical revolutionary movements because we are afraid lest they be taken over by communists, and conversely we tend to intervene on behalf of all governments and movements which are opposed to radical revolution, because they are also opposed to communism. Such a policy of intervention is unsound on intellectual grounds for the reasons mentioned in our discussion of contemporary communism; it is also bound to fail in practice.

Many nations of Asia, Africa and Latin America are today in a pre-revolutionary stage, and it is likely to be only a matter of time until actual revolution will break out in one or another of these nations. The revolutionary movements which will then come to the fore are bound to have, to a greater or lesser degree, a communist component; that is, they risk being taken over by communism. Nothing is simpler, both in terms of intellectual effort and, at least initially, practical execution, than to trace all these revolutions to a common conspiratorial source, to equate all revolutionary movements with world communism, and to oppose them with indiscriminate fervor as uniformly hostile to our interests. The United States would then be forced to intervene against revolutions throughout the world because of the ever-present threat of a communist take-over, and would transform itself, in spite of its better insight and intentions, into an anti-revolutionary power per se.

Such a policy of intervention might succeed if it had to deal with nothing more than isolated revolutionary movements which could be smothered by force of arms. But it cannot succeed, since it is faced with revolutionary situations all over the world; for even the militarily most powerful nation does not have sufficient usable resources to deal simultaneously with a number of acute revolutions. Such a policy of indiscriminate intervention against revolution is bound to fail not only with regard to the individual revolution to which it is applied but also in terms of its own indiscriminate anti-communism. For the very logic which would make us appear as the anti-revolutionary power per se would surrender to communism the sponsorship of revolution everywhere. Thus anti-communist intervention achieves what it aims to prevent: the exploitation of the revolutions of the age by communism.

In truth, the choice before us is not between the status quo and revolution or even between communist and non-communist revolution, but between a revolution hostile to the interests of the United States and a revolution which is not hostile to these interests. The United States, far from intervening against revolutions per se, has therefore to intervene in competition with the main instigators of revolution—the Soviet Union, Communist China and Cuba—on behalf of revolution. This intervention should serve two alternative aims: first, to protect the revolution from a communist take-over, and second, if we should fail in this, to prevent such a communist revolution from turning against the interests of the United States. Such a policy, substituting the yardstick of the American national interest for that of anti-communism, would obviously form a complete reversal of the positions which we have taken in recent years and of which our interventions in Viet Nam and the Dominican Republic are the recent prime examples.

If this analysis of our policy of intervention is correct, then we have intervened not wisely but too well. Our policy of intervention has been under the ideological spell of our opposition to communism and potentially communist-led revolutions. Yet while this ideological orientation has continued to determine our policy of intervention, the

Soviet Union has continued to pay lip service to support for "wars of national liberation" but has in practice relegated these wars to a secondary place in the struggle for the world. This softening of the Soviet ideological position has become one of the points of contention in the ideological dispute between the Soviet Union and China. In a statement of June 14, 1963, the Chinese Communist Party declared that "the whole cause of the international proletarian revolution hinges on the outcome of revolutionary struggles" in the "vast areas of Asia, Africa and Latin America" that are today the "storm centers of world revolution dealing direct blows at imperialism." In their reply of July 14 of the same year, the Soviet leaders opposed the " 'new theory' according to which the decisive force in the struggle against imperialism . . . is not the world system of socialism, not the struggle of the international working class, but . . . the national liberation movement." The Soviet Union's recent practice of restraint in fomenting and supporting revolution has matched this theoretical position. This ideological "revisionism" has of course not prevented the Soviet Union from intervening, as in Syria and Somalia, when its national interest appeared to require intervention.

One factor which cannot have failed to influence the Soviet Union in toning down its ideological commitment to intervention has been the relative failure of ideological intervention. The United States, China and Cuba have joined the Soviet Union in the experience of that failure. The new and emerging nations have been eager to reap the benefits of intervention, but have also been very anxious not to be tied with ideological strings to the intervening nation. After making great efforts, expending considerable resources and running serious risks, the participants in this worldwide ideological competition are still approximately at the point from which they started: measured against their ambitions and expectations, the uncommitted third of the world is still by and large an ideological no-man's-land.

This experience of failure is particularly painful, and ought to be particularly instructive, for the United States. For we have intervened in the political, military and economic affairs of other countries to the tune of far in excess of $100 billion, and we are at present involved in a costly and risky war in order to build a nation in South Viet Nam. Only the enemies of the United States will question the generosity of these efforts, which have no parallel in history. But have these efforts been wise? Have the commitments made and risks taken been commensurate with the results to be expected and actually achieved? The answer must be in the negative. Our economic aid has been successful in supporting economies which were already in the process of development; it has been by and large unsuccessful in creating economic development where none existed before, largely because the moral and rational preconditions for such development were lacking. Learning from this failure, we have established the theoretical principle of concentrating aid upon the few nations which can use it rather than giving it to the many who need it. While this principle of selectivity is sound in theory, its consistent practical application has been thwarted by the harsh political and military realities which may require economic aid which is economically not justified, as well as by political and military considerations derived from the ideological concerns discussed above.

This principle of selectivity must be extended to the political and military sphere as well. We have come to overrate enormously what a nation can do for another nation by intervening in its affairs —even with the latter's consent. This overestimation of our power to intervene is a corollary of our ideological commitment, which by its very nature has no limit. Committed to intervening against communist aggression and subversion anywhere, we have come to assume that we have the power to do so successfully. But in truth, both the need for intervention and the chances for successful intervention are much more limited than we have been led to believe. Intervene we must where our national interest requires it and where our power gives us a chance to succeed. The choice of these occasions will be determined not by sweeping ideological commitments nor by blind reliance upon American power but by a careful calculation of the interests involved and the power available. If the United States applies this standard, it will intervene less and succeed more.

6

Is America Imperialistic?

RONALD STEEL

Vietnam, as we have learned from the Pentagon papers, was no aberration. It resulted logically from the decisions made and the attitudes assumed throughout the cold war. It was Harry Truman who in 1950 provided aid to the French to put down Ho Chi Minh's independence movement. It was Dwight Eisenhower and John Foster Dulles who continued paying for France's colonial war and who threatened to intervene with American troops and atomic weapons. After that war was lost, they installed Ngo Dinh Diem and defied the Geneva accords calling for elections to unify Vietnam. Later it was John F. Kennedy, a true believer in the domino theory, who got rid of Diem when he ceased to be malleable and who dispatched American combat troops to ensure an anti-communist South Vietnam. The expansion of the war by Lyndon Johnson and the current efforts of Richard Nixon to achieve with air power and South Vietnamese mercenaries the victory denied American troops are all outgrowths of the same decisions about communism and America's role in the world.

To reject the war in Vietnam is to question the assumptions on which American foreign policy rests. It is to ask not only whether the prevalent conception of the cold war might now be wrong, but whether it was ever right. It means re-examining a set of attitudes, the decisions that flowed from them, and the perceptions on which they were based. This re-examination has been going on for some time in the work of younger historians, many of them disciples of William Appleman Williams and rediscoverers of Charles Beard. While their works are contentious and often heavily slanted toward Marxist economics, they have thrown new light on the cold war and its origins.

They differ from liberal historians in that they condemn not only American behavior, but the motives that lie behind it. For them there is no such thing as accident, inadvertence, or error. American policy is deliberate, single-minded, and determined by the larger economic forces that motivate the society. Whereas liberals and "political realists" criticize American postwar diplomacy for being too ideological or for displaying a faulty concept of the national interest, these radical revisionists see that diplomacy as the necessary instrument of the capitalist order.

Liberal critics such as Morgenthau, Lippmann, and Kennan see the nation swaying between the twin poles of isolationism and globalism, unable to balance its great power with an enlightened concept of its vital interests. They believe American statesmen are "unrealistic" in trying to impose moral judgments on the amoral behavior of nations. They believe like William Pfaff in his eloquently argued new book, *Condemned to Freedom,* that while Vietnam "has constituted the calamitous triumph of American hypocrisy and cant over American seriousness," nonetheless, "the regrettable truth is that the foreign policy of the United States in the postwar period has, for the most part, been a popular policy pursued out of Wilsonian motivations and for reformist, even utopian goals."

To be a liberal critic is not, of course, the same thing as being a liberal policy maker, and nobody is harsher on the politicians than these critics. As Pfaff, whose book[1] is a blistering account of the failure of liberal governments to preserve liberal values, has written,

> It took a visionary liberal administration fully to translate the globalism of American rhetoric, which the Republican party wholly shared, into a program of national action. Vietnam was consciously made into a test of liberal international reform by the Kennedy and Johnson administrations—of liberal "nation building," carried on behind a shield of Green Beret counterinsurgent warfare—against the Asian communist "model" of radical national transformation.

Damning though it is, this is essentially a liberal critique resting on assumptions that radicals do not share. It is not American "serious-

ness" that radicals question, for they believe that those who are responsible for American foreign policy are both serious and determined.
Rather it is that American diplomacy is based upon the demands
of the world capitalist system, of which the United States is the chief
beneficiary and defender. This, and not a condemnation of the Vietnam war or of militarism or of a national security bureaucracy, is what
separates them from the liberals. In fact, they deny that the military
exerts a heavy weight on foreign policy or that the bureaucracy has a
momentum of its own. To their minds American policy is not marked
by mistakes and shortsightedness; it has, for the most part, been remarkably successful in imposing an American order upon the world.

Radical historians see American policy as inherently, indeed in-
exorably, counterrevolutionary. They trace this policy at least as far
back as the era of imperial expansion at the turn of the century—
marked by the acquisition of the Philippines and Puerto Rico, and
the suzerainty over Cuba—and view the Open Door as the rationale
for imperial expansionism. Thus, following the analysis used by Williams in *The Tragedy of American Diplomacy,* N. Gordon Levin has
written that Wilsonianism "defined the American national interest in
liberal-internationalist terms in response to war and social revolution,
the two dominant political factors of our time." [2] Similarly, the struggle
over the League of Nations was not, as a conventional historiography
would have it, one pitting blind isolationism against enlightened involvement, but rather one over whether or not American economic
interests could be better protected by a free-hands policy, that is, by
unilateralism.

In their analysis of the more recent cold war period, radicals reject
the theory that the United States responded defensively to Soviet intransigence, or that, as Kennan and Lippmann would argue, a necessary aid program under the Marshall Plan became unduly militarized
in NATO and its sibling alliances. Rather they maintain that the
United States challenged Moscow directly by refusing to accept a
Soviet sphere of influence in Eastern Europe, by raising the specter
of a rearmed Germany, and by rattling the atomic bomb. Committed
to the triumph of capitalism and suppression of revolution, the United
States, in the words of Gabriel Kolko, one of the most impassioned of
the radicals, was committed to intervene "against the Soviet Union,
against the tide of the left, and against Britain as a coequal guardian
of world capitalism—in fact, against history as it had been and had yet
to become." [3]

According to this view, the Russians were not threatening Western
Europe and, initially at least, did not intend to dominate Eastern Europe by imposing a system of satellites. All the Russians wanted was
a sphere of influence along their borders, similar to the one that the
United States enjoyed in the Western Hemisphere, and a guarantee
against German militarism. However, when the United States refused
to accept this—and instead openly showed its hostility to the Soviet
Union by abruptly canceling lend-lease, ignoring Moscow's request for
a $6 billion loan, and refusing to honor the German reparations plan

tentatively agreed to at Yalta—the Russians had no choice but to exert full control over the satellites and build their defenses behind the Iron Curtain. (The brutality and terror used to exert this control have mostly been ignored by the revisionists, just as conventional historians have ignored the brutality of our own client states in Latin America and Asia.)

While the cold war began in Europe, it could not be confined there, since it involved far more than a struggle with Russia over access to Eastern Europe. Its true meaning, according to the radicals, has been the attempt by the United States to achieve a world order congenial to capitalist penetration and to consolidate a nonterritorial empire ("the free world") whose preservation is considered essential to American security. For a country like the United States, a diplomacy of counterrevolution is not a choice, but a matter of necessity. The empire stands or falls as a whole; it must always be defended at its weakest link. Thus the importance of Vietnam as a test case ("stand by our commitments") to preserve American hegemony and the capitalist order on which it feeds.

Radicals lean heavily on an economic interpretation of history to back up their analysis. But even liberals who reject this Marxist approach have nonetheless been influenced by elements of the radical argument and have had to revise some of their own theories. Thus Arthur Schlesinger, who in 1966 in a letter to *The New York Review* declared it was time to "blow the whistle" on revisionism, a year later wrote that "revisionism is an essential part of the process by which history, through the posing of new problems and the investigation of new possibilities, enlarges its perspectives and enriches its insights." [4]

Even the designation of the United States as an imperial power, which was once considered absurd, has been accepted by historians on the center and the right. Some, like George Liska, have extolled it,[5] while others, like Robert Osgood, have simply taken note of it by defining an imperial power as one whose "vital interests extend far beyond the protection of the homeland [to] embrace all the outlying areas of commitment . . . [these] become equivalent to the preservation of an international order and a distribution of power upon which order must depend." [6] By this liberal historian's definition the United States is clearly an imperial, if not necessarily an imperialist, power.

Robert Tucker, a colleague of Liska and Osgood at the Washington Center of Foreign Policy Research, takes the argument further by viewing American policy as maintaining a world imperial structure. For those determined to preserve that structure, he states, the war in Vietnam is an integral part of the containment policy that was originally applied to Europe in the late Forties, "and both are found to serve the same vital interests and to further the same over-all purpose of achieving and maintaining a desirable world order." [7] If the containment argument is accepted, then it is irrelevant to insist that the circumstances are different in Asia today from what they were in Europe—for obviously they are. The question is whether the reasons for following a containment policy remain valid.

Tucker comes close to the radicals' argument when he says that America became a counterrevolutionary power not because nationalistic revolutions dominated by the left would necessarily contribute to Russian or Chinese power, but because leftist regimes would resist American control. Thus Kennedy's well-known remark that he saw in "descending order of preference" three possibilities in the Dominican Republic following the assassination of Trujillo: "a decent democratic regime, a continuation of the Trujillo regime, or a Castro regime. We ought to aim at the first, but we really can't renounce the second until we are sure that we can avoid the third." Lyndon Johnson was simply following suit when he sent the Marines to suppress a popular insurrection in the Dominican Republic against a US-supported military regime in 1965.

Vietnam was part of the same pattern. The American intervention was based on the belief that the failure to contain communism in Southeast Asia would threaten the entire imperial system on which American economic and political hegemony rests. In official speeches this was usually described as the "preservation of world order," but its meaning was the same. W. W. Rostow, one of the most vocal advocates of the aggression in Vietnam, was particularly outspoken when he explained: "It is on this spot that we have to break the liberation war—Chinese type. If we don't break it here we shall have to face it again in Thailand, Venezuela, elsewhere. Vietnam is a clear testing ground for our policy in the world."

The question of interventionism, therefore, is not one of undifferentiated "globalism," but of ensuring political control wherever it is threatened. Interventions can, of course, be stimulated by domestic politics, as in the Cuban missile crisis, or by the effort to compensate for foreign policy setbacks in other areas. Thus, Kennedy's decision to send a man to the moon followed on the heels of the Bay of Pigs fiasco, and his expansion of the Vietnam war was stimulated by his disastrous encounter with Khrushchev at Vienna. As Chester Bowles has suggested in his recent autobiography, *Promises to Keep,* Kennedy, uncertain and eager to assert himself, "subconsciously at least, was searching for some issue on which he could prove at relatively low cost that he was, in fact, a tough President who could not be pushed around by the Soviets, the Chinese, or anyone else." Bowles vocally dissented from Kennedy's adventures in Vietnam and the militarized liberals who supported and encouraged it. This was one of the reasons he was eased out of the higher councils of the Administration.

Bowles, of course, is no radical, and like many other liberal critics of the war sees Vietnam as illustrating how a nation, "with the very best of intentions, once it loses touch with political realities, can delude itself and its people." Radical critics would deny both the good intentions and the self-delusion. But even if one does not accept all their premises, particularly the economic determinants, their argument is a powerful one which explains a good deal more about American foreign policy than the conventional liberal critique of "inadvertence" or excessive "moralism."

To be sure, ideology, idealism, and even domestic politics played a part in the decision to go into Vietnam. There were people who believed, or convinced themselves, that what we were doing in Southeast Asia was not only necessary for our own security, but good for the people who lived there. Moreover, no President has ever been willing to be responsible for the "loss" of any country anywhere to communism. According to Kenneth O'Donnell, John F. Kennedy said he would get us out of Vietnam—just as soon as the 1964 elections were safely over. As Daniel Ellsberg observed in these pages a few months ago,[8] "For twenty years,—since the 'fall of China' and the rise of McCarthy—Rule 1 of Indochina policy for an American President has been: Do not lose the rest of Vietnam to communism before the next election." Invoking the specters of Wallace or Reagan and a right-wing reaction to "bugging out" in Vietnam, Nixon, like Kennedy, has clearly shown that at least part of his policy of defending the "free world" is influenced by the next elections.

In addition to domestic political pressures, there is pressure, both public and private, from high-ranking generals and admirals who believe that wars of "containment," like other wars, are meant to be won—however reluctant they may be to get involved in them in the first place. While it is hardly fair to blame the military for getting us into Vietnam or for an imperial foreign policy that has been designed by civilian lawyers, academicians, and businessmen, the Pentagon nonetheless has a vested interest in an American empire that has to be defended with bases, fleets, and supply lines. In evolving less bellicose policies, any President has to reckon with the Joint Chiefs of Staff and with their powerful allies on Congressional committees.

Like a good many other liberal historians, Tucker has been persuaded by the radicals to see calculation rather than inadvertence in American interventionism, but has remained skeptical about the economic determinants of foreign policy. In his provocative new book, *The Radical Left and American Foreign Policy,* he gives the radicals their due on political grounds, but criticizes their "archaic" arguments of dependency on foreign markets and Third World raw materials. His refutation of the Marxist arguments used, for example, by Harry Magdoff in *The Age of Imperialism* seems convincing. In spite of his skepticism on these grounds, Tucker accepts the radicals' central thesis of the imperialist nature of America's counterrevolutionary diplomacy. "America's interventionist and counterrevolutionary policy," he writes, "is the expected response of an imperial power with a vital interest in maintaining an order that, apart from the material benefits this order confers, has become synonymous with the nation's vision of its role in history."

Adopting key elements of the radical critique, Tucker affirms that the postwar policy of universalism was simply a cover for a spheres of influence policy that the United States pursued for itself but sought to deny the Soviet Union, that the United Nations was manipulated to consolidate America's leadership, and that in the postwar period we have defined our interests in such a way that "the only policy the

Russians could have pursued which would not have incurred American hostility was one that placed Russian security—and not only security —largely at the mercy of the good intentions of others, above all, America." By this he means that the Russians could not realistically have been expected to accept such programs as the Baruch plan for the control of atomic energy, with its built-in American monopoly, or the restoration of anticommunist governments in Eastern Europe.

In arguing that American imperialism rests on the needs of capitalism for expanding markets and access to raw materials, radicals quote Dean Acheson's 1944 statement before a Congressional committee that the United States required foreign markets to absorb its "unlimited creative energy" if it were not to slide back into a depression, or Harry Truman's March, 1947, speech, in which he said, clearing the ground for the forthcoming aid program to Greece and Turkey, that "the American system could survive in America only if it became a world system." Although Tucker agrees that such statements are revealing of the attitude of American corporate leaders, he denies that they reveal the root of American policy, and suggests that "their purpose is largely to elicit support for a policy that is pursued primarily for quite different reasons."

Those reasons, he would argue, are rooted in the fear that the United States cannot be secure in a world hostile to its example. To American leaders "the prospect of the growing irrelevance of the American example must raise the issue of American security in the greater than physical sense." Thus he takes to task radicals who "cannot consistently accept the view that an interventionist and counterrevolutionary America has been motivated more by the prospect that the American example, and, in consequence, American influence, might otherwise become irrelevant than by the prospect that in a hostile world America would no longer enjoy the material benefits her hegemonial position has conferred."

For Tucker it is not the compulsions of capitalism, "it is power itself, more than a particular form of power, which prompts expansion." America behaves imperialistically because it has the power to do so. In this sense it is like any other imperial power of the past— regardless of its economic structure. Thus Tucker asks whether a socialist America would pursue a significantly different foreign policy, or whether it would also identify its security with a pro-American world equilibrium. This is a basic question which radicals have not satisfactorily answered, but which is central to any serious criticism of the use of American power. . . .

In re-examining the origins of the cold war, and the perceptions and motivations of American policy makers, radical historians have helped us to understand how the United States has become an imperial, self-aggrandizing power. Their research has shown that the form the Russo-American confrontation took was not inevitable, that the United States did not simply respond defensively to Soviet aggressive moves, and that there has been nothing inadvertent in our colonial wars and our acquisition of empire.

A weakness of the radicals is their characteristically American view of America's exceptionalism. Just as conservatives see this nation as the embodiment of goodness and justice, so radicals see it as the fount of evil. Similarly, there is something sentimental about the radicals' uncritical embrace of Third World movements, and their equation of imperialism with capitalist elites. For radicals, as for everyone else, Vietnam has been a traumatizing experience. But its lesson is not, as some radicals believe, that the United States will inevitably intervene anywhere and everywhere against popular reform movements. In overdrawing the lesson of Vietnam too many radicals, in Pfaff's words, "have unexpectedly discovered sin but not original sin."

In using its power crudely, immorally, and imperialistically, the United States has behaved like many great powers in the past. It has done so not for the noble motives claimed by every postwar administration, but for reasons of hegemony, control, and aggrandizement. The fact that the American empire is basically nonterritorial makes it no less imperialistic than its predecessors. Its major distinction is that it is considerably more hypocritical.

We now know that the professed ideals have been essentially a mask for expansionistic, and even immoral, behavior. This imperialist ambition is not fed exclusively, or even primarily, by economic need—although certainly there has been a determination to use American power to impose upon the world a democratic capitalistic pattern congenial to American economic interests. The imperialistic drive also rests on a missionary impulse to mold other societies in our own image ("We're going to turn the Mekong into the Tennessee Valley," Lyndon Johnson once proclaimed), to assure ourselves of the validity of our institutions by imposing them upon others, and from a sheer will to power that comes, almost irresistibly, from the possession of overwhelming power.

Vietnam has made us aware of the American empire, and the radical historians have helped us to understand how it came into being. The ordeal the society faces today is not simply how to disengage from a disastrous imperial war, but how to dismantle the empire—together with the imperial bureaucracy, the war machine, and the industrial superstructure of the warfare state—before it destroys the nation.

NOTES

1 Published October, 1971.

2 *Woodrow Wilson and World Politics* (Oxford, 1968).

3 *The Politics of War: The World and United States Foreign Policy 1943–1945* (Random House, 1970).

4 "The Origins of the Cold War," *Foreign Affairs*, October, 1967.

5 *Imperial America: The International Politics of Primacy* (Johns Hopkins, 1967).

6 Osgood, Tucker, et al., *America and the World: From the Truman Doctrine to Vietnam* (Johns Hopkins, 1970).

7 *Nation or Empire? The Debate over American Foreign Policy* (Johns Hopkins, 1969).

8 "Laos: What Nixon Is Up To." *NY Review of Books*, 1971.

Revolution: The Weak Respond

7

On Winning and Losing by Revolution

FRANCIS G. HUTCHINS

Americans have recently been forced to look at political problems in new ways. Outbreaks of violence, demonstrations, studied defiance of laws and courts, have revealed that many of our inherited assumptions about the nature of the political process are only assumptions, not the basic contours of reality. Abraham Lincoln, who understood many things Americans have since forgotten, once stated that "This country, with its institutions, belongs to the people who inhabit it. Whenever they shall grow weary of the existing government, they can exercise their constitutional right of amending it or their revolutionary right to dismember or overthrow it." [1] Americans have forgotten the "right of revolution"; they have forgotten that participation in politics can take many forms—violent, nonviolent, moderate, or defiant—forms whose legitimacy is contingent, not inherent. Americans have begun to realize, however, that it is necessary to think seriously about the nature of political activity extending beyond bargaining and agitation within a constitutional framework. Systems do break down, or are overthrown; those who ignore the potential of revolutionary politics may be condemned to become its victims.

Political systems, whether old-fashioned or newly established, are never entirely open or equitable. Whatever is, is in somebody's interest. But those who benefit from a system have no difficulty perceiving it in a liberal light. No elite imagines that it is repressive. There are always sufficient reasons for their existence and actions. They are the upholders of "law and order," and their self-justifications are usually variations on this theme. Constitutionalism, rights, legality—and their opposites—constitute an elite's realm of discourse. Those who espouse the inadmissible opposites are readily understood; they are selfish, sick, or immature. The system seems sufficiently open and flexible to permit legitimate ambitions to be fulfilled, legitimate grievances to be assuaged; an elite need only point to its own example.

It is thus not difficult to understand why so little effort has been devoted to attempting to understand the logic of revolution, or why variants of the assertion "We will not yield to threats or brute force" are always among an elite's last words. Yet it is impossible to cope intelligently with a revolutionary challenge without a sympathetic appreciation of its internal dynamism. Those who are satisfied with infinite variations on the theme of law and order are only talking to themselves. There are some signs that the emergence of a new radicalism in American politics has stimulated a new effort to think seriously about a more broadly defined political process, including an effort to transcend the interpretation of revolutions as diseases or accidents. The scope of potentially relevant comparative studies has been widened, as Americans come to realize that they can learn something about themselves by studying events and situations which once seemed remote. Americans have for some time assumed, for instance, that the world's "new nations" could learn much about the operation of stable democracy by studying current American practice. Both Americans and nationalists elsewhere can learn much about the *preconditions* of stable democracy by studying colonial nationalist revolutions. . . .

In a successful revolution a nation is born anew in a state of holy innocence. Legitimacy ends and begins; no subsequent act need or can be justified on anterior grounds. The fact of revolution is a self-sufficient act of creation. The revolution's agents are unanswerable to any law higher than revolutionary necessity. All extant rights, foreign and domestic, are subject to challenge. The manner in which America has followed its "Manifest Destiny" across America and more recently across the world is unparalleled except by the course taken by other postrevolutionary societies—for example republican France and Soviet Russia.

Purity begins at home; the revolutionary society cannot be a beacon for humanity if it harbors every variety of person, good and bad. Enemies of the revolution cannot be tolerated; they must be expelled, or at least neutralized, dispossessed and disenfranchised. The process, of course, is not as pure as its justification. Revolutionaries, reluctant to disown their own rhetoric, and equally reluctant to offer every specimen who calls himself a man the rights they have claimed as the due of all mankind, disqualify unacceptable groups by presuming them to be enemies of the revolution; by deciding that they ought to be, or probably secretly already are enemies of the revolution. Traitors have no rights merely as men, and are expected to demonstrate their own innocence if they wish to escape the wrath of the just. Thus, Americans helped to justify the exclusion of Negroes from postrevolutionary social rights by the argument that they had probably been pro-Tory. Indians have expressed parallel suspicions about the loyalty of Indian Muslims. Following every revolution there are some born traitors; some have treachery thrust upon them.

Whether groups who sit out the revolution become disadvantaged minorities within the new state, or elect or are forced into exile, or manage to salvage a state for themselves depends upon accidents of foreign intervention and geography. Many revolutions produce groups who suffer variously all of these fates. Those who are submerged or exiled may suffer greatly and remain problem minorities at home or in their country of exile, but their problems are largely their own, not initially those of the newly established revolutionary state. For the revolutionaries, such minorities are sources of profit and plunder. The formation of salvaged societies, in contrast, means the persistence for many years of serious military and political problems. A hostile adjacent state is created by the division of what may have been a natural geographic unit, making the defense of artificial boundaries necessary; moreover, the bitterness of displaced exiles, the intensity resulting from the division of friends and families puts the relations between two such states in a special category. The common memory of having participated in the larger political community of the past may encourage on both sides a yearning to set back the clock by incorporating the one state into the other. The result is often a series of wars which are ideologically unlimited, no matter how localized or stalemated they may prove to be. At least a generation is required before totalistic perspectives wane; divergent evolution, suspicion, and animosity may never disappear.

The main factors determining whether a salvaged society can be formed are the geographic concentration of loyalists and the role played by external powers. Canada contained a variety of groups hostile to the American Revolution for different reasons, and offered a commodious new home for exiles from the United States. Taiwan provided a convenient—if less commodious—place of exile for the Nationalist Chinese, having been under Japanese control until 1945 and therefore isolated from the revolution on the mainland. Protestant Northern Ireland was a logical nucleus for the division of Ireland on Protestant-Catholic lines. Contiguous areas of India with Muslim majorities proved a viable basis for the state of Pakistan. Many of South Vietnam's difficulties have stemmed from the lack of such a contiguous area of consolidated control; throughout South Vietnam areas exist which have long been under the control of Communist revolutionaries. Germany and Korea were divided following foreign conquests rather than as an outgrowth of the dynamic of indigenous revolution, although "revolutions from above" were subsequently sponsored in the Communist-controlled halves of these two formerly unified areas. Whether or not these divisions are irreversible is still an open question and depends upon the success of the officially-sponsored revolutions.

States salvaged from the path of revolution show a distinctive course of development traceable to the manner in which they were founded. This outcome has been well demonstrated in the case of

Canada.² Typically such societies have difficulty establishing unity because the diverse groups within the society have little in common except accidental proximity and antagonism to the dominant revolutionary force. Anomalies, bizarre social fossils, may also survive out of the mainstream in a postrevolutionary society, but in a salvaged society they are likely to be much more prominent. On Taiwan a full structure of government is maintained as if the Nationalist regime still controlled all of mainland China, with representatives in the legislature nominally representing the different regions of the Communist-controlled mainland. In Canada ethnic communities of all descriptions —including the dominant British—have remained much closer to their country of origin and less assimilated to a positive national identity than in the United States. Pakistan had an advantage in having Islam as an organizing principle, but even this bond has been a frail link between two areas so disparate and distant as East and West Pakistan. Antagonism toward India and more recently toward the Ayub government have done more than the common adherence to Islam to unify East and West. Significantly, princely states retained their autonomy much longer in Pakistan than in India, where they were almost instantly swept away.³ South Vietnam has also found it difficult to develop a positive national identity, given the division of the population amongst Buddhist, Catholic, and Confucian faiths and in other ways, ethnically, geographically, linguistically, politically, and given the fact that most of its leaders have been refugees from North Vietnam. The Southern regime with its largely Northern personnel sits on top of an assemblage of internally cohesive minority groups who have common enemies but few common goals.

America, Southern Asia, China, and Vietnam illustrate clearly the contrasting patterns of development in societies partitioned into revolutionary and salvaged segments. There are in addition several partly comparable international situations, for example the division of areas of the old Ottoman Empire into the modern states of Turkey and Greece; and the establishment of Israel as a postrevolutionary state and the consequent transformation of Jordan into a partially salvaged society. In these two cases, as to a lesser degree with India-Pakistan, the pure type of revolution-stimulated change verges on a situation of competing nationalisms; opposition to revolutionary nationalism is focused around a competing nationalism rather than a simple preference for the *ancien régime*. The relative intensity of the two nationalisms, however, has left Jordan and Greece with more characteristics of salvaged societies, Israel and Turkey with more characteristics of postrevolutionary societies.

Foreign sponsorship and assistance has usually been available to salvaged societies. This support may come from the defeated colonial power—Britain in the case of Canada, Northern Ireland, and Pakistan —or from other interested world powers. An accessibility to outside aid, whether or not it actually materializes, is a critical aspect of the strategic geography of a salvaged society. The American West was loyal, but boxed in. Some of India's princely states—notably Muslim-

ruled Hyderabad—flirted with ideas of independence or alliance with
Pakistan, but their geographic position, landlocked and surrounded by
Indian territory, doomed them to inclusion within India. Katanga and
Biafra, though comparable to salvaged societies in some respects, broke
away after the granting of independence to the Congo and Nigeria
because the brevity and superficiality of the nationalist revolutions had
not permitted the confrontation of divisive issues beforehand. In these
two cases, states were created without reference to geographic viability,
a further indication of the cost of a hasty and superficial revolution
which must be borne by the revolution's heirs. In Katanga, Belgian
assistance was critical. In Biafra, Britain held aloof, refusing to aid
the more Anglicized, Christian Ibos. Biafra broke away from Nigeria
some years after independence was granted by the British, and Britain
was no longer inclined to become deeply involved.

Newly established, badly integrated states may be unable to prevent
secessionist movements, especially if they are abetted by interested foreign powers. More commonly, groups who do not escape during the
course of the revolution itself have little luck in defying revolutionary
orthodoxy. The ultimate fate of plundered, exploited, submerged minorities in postrevolutionary societies is still an open question; as in
the United States with reference to the American Negro. . . .

. . . Every successful revolution, like every successful business venture, spawns a host of imitators who are loath to focus upon the handi-
caps or disabilities they possess which may prevent them from becoming
an equal success. For this reason successful and even partially successful
revolutions tend to become world-historical whether or not they set
themselves up consciously as examplars for the rest of humanity. The
American, French, Russian, Chinese, Indian, and Cuban Revolutions
have evoked imitative efforts, which have rarely succeeded, and which
have succeeded—as in Vietnam—only when adapted to local conditions,
and when the local conditions duplicate the main ingredients which
made for success in the first place. The chain of revolutions which
spread across Latin America in the years following the American and
French Revolutions proved abortive because they were superficial and
imitative; so have many of the nationalist revolutions in Africa and
Asia which arose in the wake of events in India and China. The plan-
fulfilling revolution of Che Guevara in Bolivia failed to find local
roots; the self-fulfilling revolutions of Ghana, Nigeria, Burma, and
Indonesia, among others, were too hasty and disorganized to produce
an adequately unified postrevolutionary society.

A great revolution can nonetheless be usefully analyzed in relation
to many nonrevolutionary situations if the lack of full comparability
is understood, because a revolution is an epitome of national experience, as a play can be of human experience. Revolutions usually do
not occur; individual lives are usually more inconclusive than tragic,
but the lessons are relevant even when the analogy is not complete.
When governmental rigidity is combined with national polarization
resulting from destabilizing developments in society and economy, and
exploited by creative leadership, a revolution may occur, if favored by

accidental circumstances. Revolutions may be accompanied by civil war. They may fail. If they succeed, they draw larger and sharper circles around the effective national community, expanding the active citizenry while decisively excluding some groups. Revolutions determine the course of national development for an indefinite period, establishing its myths, shaping its institutional prospects, and exhausting the national capacity for new initiatives. The heightened creativity of a revolutonary era builds, ill or well, for many years to come.

NOTES

1 Quoted in Harold Cruse, *The Crisis of the Negro Intellectual* (New York: William Morrow, 1967), p. 97.

2 See Louis Hartz, *The Founding of New Societies* (New York: Harcourt, Brace and World, 1964), and Lipset, *Revolution and Counterrevolution, op. cit.*

3 See Wayne Wilcox, *Pakistan: The Consolidation of a Nation* (New York: Columbia University Press, 1966), for an account of Pakistan's belated attack on the problem of the princely states.

8

Che in Bolivia: The "Revolution" That Failed

ROBERT F. LAMBERG

It is ironic—but not untypical of Fidel Castro's checkered course—that only a few months after he stage-managed a major demonstration of his influence on the Latin American continent (the conference of the "Latin American Solidarity Organization" convened in Havana in August 1967), the strategy of guerrilla warfare by which he and his followers hoped to achieve their revolutionary aims was emphatically and decisively repudiated—in the much celebrated misadventure of "Che" Guevara in Bolivia.

There are several reasons why it is important to examine the Bolivian guerrilla movement. First and foremost, it was the only insurgent force organized entirely on the basis of refinements in guerrilla theory that might be described as the third phase of the Castroite ideology.[1] Secondly, it was the only guerrilla action in Latin America that yielded a great deal of firsthand documentary material, so that it can be analyzed with a minimum of speculation. In the third place, it provided a graphic and striking illustration of the distance between the revolutionary idealism of the Castroites and the practical realities of Latin American life.

In the latter respect, we shall start out by considering what Che Guevara apparently did not—the specific political, social and economic conditions that characterize the Bolivian nation.

Bolivia has been called "a beggar on a throne of gold" [2]—a reference to the unhappy fact that despite enormously rich natural resources the Bolivian economy is greatly underdeveloped and the country is plagued by poverty. Eighteen years ago these conditions helped to bring about a revolution which, in terms of the changes it wrought in Bolivia's political and economic system, ranks among the three most important revolutions in Latin America in this century (the other two being the Mexican in 1910 and the Cuban in 1959). Carried out by the *Movimiento Nacionalista Revolucionario* (hereafter MNR) under the leadership of Victor Paz Estenssoro, the revolution of 1952 was decidedly "socialistic" insofar as its original goals and programs were concerned. Among the significant measures that it undertook were the nationalization of the country's most important natural resource, the tin mines; an extensive program of land reform; and the introduction of universal suffrage. If, in later years, there was reason to doubt the success of these programs in terms of their economic impact, they did at least succeed in converting a significant segment of the population to the socio-political outlook they represented.[3]

In November 1964 the Paz regime was overthrown by a military faction within the ranks of the MNR, and a new government was formed under the leadership of Generals René Barrientos Ortuño and Alfredo Ovando Candia.[4] The announced aim of the new regime was to depoliticize public life and to institute decision-making based on technological expertise. In terms of power relations, the three most important forces in the country now became the military, the farmers and the mine workers.

For both political and economic reasons which do not need to be elaborated here, Barrientos and Candia concentrated their efforts on curtailing the power of the mine workers while seeking support from the major peasants' organizations. By 1966 the regime felt strong enough to seek popular affirmation of its leadership, and Barrientos was duly endorsed as President of Bolivia in national elections. Barrientos' success in establishing a power base in the peasants' organizations later proved to be an important political asset, as we shall see.

The Barrientos regime could hardly be called democratic (for that matter, neither could its predecessor). At the same time, it certainly was not "counterrevolutionary"—on the contrary, it aimed, in its own way and according to its own notions, at spurring the slow pace of progress toward the goals of the revolution. It might also be pointed out that Barrientos and his colleagues acted with relative restraint in dealing with their political opponents (at least compared to the behavior of some Latin American militarists who have seized power by force). It is true that the mine workers were subjected to a number of repressive measures, including the outlawing of their union organization and the exile of their most active leaders. But otherwise the regime seemed to act with deliberate moderation. The ousted leaders of the Paz regime were spared brutal physical persecution, and though Paz himself was exiled, his supporters were soon able to regroup and return to the political arena without serious harassment from the regime. Various leftist groups, including Communist factions, emerged as legal political organizations, and the pro-Soviet Communist Party of Bolivia (PCB) even took part—unsuccessfully—in the elections of 1966 by organizing the collective front FLN (*Frente de Liberación Nacional*). While it is impossible to gauge the genuineness of the support extended to Barrientos, it is at least clear that he was offered relatively weak opposition in the presidential election and emerged from it with enhanced strength and status.

To all apearances, Ernesto "Che" Guevara's plan to establish a guerrilla force in Bolivia originated some time in 1963, preceding the *coup* that brought Barrientos to power.[5] It seems possible that he later considered other target areas (during the period of his much-publicized disappearance from the public scene in 1965–66) but in the end decided Bolivia offered the ripest ground for revolution. In any case, the observer cannot escape the impression that once "el Che" had embarked upon his course, he paid very little attention to the important shifts taking place on the Bolivian scene—an oversight that was to contribute significantly to his downfall.

To understand Guevara's course of action, it is necessary to know something about the revolutionary theory on which it was based. First formulated by Guevara in his book *Guerra de Guerrillas*—and elaborated over the years in the statements and writings of Castro, Guevara, and finally the Frenchman Jules Régis Debray—this theory departed from the traditional Marxist and Leninist views of the conditions necessary for revolution to propound the notion that a guerrilla force could serve as the "nucleus of armed insurrection"—or *foco insurreccional*—creating a revolutionary situation by its own momentum. According to Guevara, a small band of armed revolutionaries, by gaining popular support, could grow in numbers and strength to the point where it could defeat a national army. On the Latin American continent, the best locale for such an armed struggle was the countryside, where the guerrillas would have more mobility against enemy forces and would be less liable to exposure than in densely populated areas. More important, Guevara believed that the peasants—motivated by the desire to possess their own land and to crush the feudal agricultural structure—would join with the guerrillas in fighting the "oppressors"; thus he assigned the peasantry a key role in the revolutionary warfare that he envisioned would "liberate" the Latin American continent.

Guevara's theory was said to be based in part on lessons the Castroites had learned in the Cuban revolution of 1958–59. Both he and Castro, and later Debray, came to assert that the Cuban experience exemplified the successful creation of a revolutionary situation by a guerrilla force. Consequently, they preached that the Cuban revolution must be extended—or, to employ the usual term, exported—to other Latin American countries. They also became convinced that revolutionary action—that is, armed struggle—was the only possible way to achieve social change in Latin America. Finally—in defiance of the sacrosanct Leninist notion of party supremacy—they insisted that in the course of such armed struggle, the political element of the revolutionary forces (*i.e.*, the Communist Party) should be subordinated to the military element (*i.e.*, the guerrillas).

These, in brief, were the convictions that underlay Guevara's venture into Bolivia. His broad aim was to achieve an "internationalization" of the guerrilla force in a region reaching from the Peruvian and Bolivian highlands into his homeland, Argentina, and possibly including even southwestern Brazil and Paraguay. The Bolivian area was intended to serve as the center of the insurgency, providing both a training and a proving ground for the guerrilla troops. The whole guerrilla region was to become a "second Vietnam," as Guevara later described it in a manifesto to his followers issued in April 1967.[6]

Guevara seems to have been indifferent to certain early signs that his ambitions might be overreaching. For example, a small guerrilla force organized in Argentina in 1963 by Jorge Massetti, working in close collaboration with Guevara, initially played a part in the insurgents' plans, but it was annihilated by government troops in 1964. The previous year had witnessed the crushing of a peasants' uprising in upper Peru (Cuzco) led by the Trotskyite Hugo Blanco Galdos;[7] an effort was made in 1965 to supplant this rebel movement with a guerrilla band loyal to Castro, but it, too, was destroyed within a few months.

Seemingly undaunted by these developments, Guevara proceeded with his plans to establish the Bolivian base. As part of the advance preparations, Jose Maria Martinez Tamayo (referred to in rebel writings as "Ricardo"), a Cuban officer and later a member of the guerrilla force, reportedly made repeated trips to Bolivia between 1962 and 1966 to establish contacts, gather information, and make practical arrangements.[8] According to Cuban sources, Tamara Bunke ("Tania")—an East German woman who figured prominently in the later drama of the jungles—was sent to Bolivia in 1964 with the assignment of establishing an urban network to help the guerrillas.[9]

Early in 1966—probably while he was in Havana for the Tricontinental Conference—Mario Monje Molina, the Secretary-General of the Communist Party of Bolivia, was finally informed of Guevara's plans. Though Monje was later to refuse to support the guerrilla venture—a crucial factor in the events of 1967, as we shall see—a certain number of prominent Bolivian Communists at first collaborated with the Cubans on preparations for the rural guerrilla base and for the supportive urban network which Tania was working to set up. Two Bolivians who actually joined the guerrilla force were the brothers Peredo Leigue—Roberto ("Coco") and Guido ("Inti")—the latter a member of the PCB Central Committee. Following a period of training and planning in Cuba with Guevara, the Peredos were assigned the task of establishing a site for the guerrilla base. Somewhere around the middle of 1966 they chose a ranch north of Lagunillas on the Ñancahuazu River for the guerrillas' central training and supply camp. On November 7, Guevara arrived at the camp, masquerading as an Uruguayan businessman. At the end of that month the guerrilla force consisted of 13 men, mostly Cubans; according to plan, a number of other Cubans were to join the group, and at least 20 Bolivians were to be recruited in the intial phase of operations.[10]

Thus the guerrilla *"foco"* was formed which, according to the notions of Castro, Guevara and Debray, would provide the spark to set off the powder keg of revolution on the Latin American continent. Guevara's diary reveals that the guerrillas were at first in constant touch with Havana and had no trouble receiving the financial and political assistance they needed to pursue their "internationalization" activities. The urban network also seemed to be functioning as planned. An Uruguayan journalist in Fidel Castro's confidence, writing in the spring of 1967, stressed that Guevara's force was operating independently and without responsibility to any "specific party" (meaning the Communist Party)—thus constituting a genuinely new form of guerrilla movement along Debray's theoretical lines.[11]

Ironically, the revolutionaries' insistence that the guerrilla force be independent—which was intended, in part, to give flexibility to its political operations—had the opposite effect of contributing to its political isolation. On the last day of 1966, PCB Secretary General Monje arrived at the Ñancahuazu camp to confer with Guevara on the question of collaboration between the party and the *foco*. The talks got nowhere. According to reports by both men, Monje maintained that preparatory discussions should be held with representatives of the PCB and other Communist parties on the continent before the start of guerrilla activity; more important, he asserted his right—as head of the Bolivian party—to exercise authority over the political and military operations of the *foco*. This, of course, was totally unacceptable to Guevara.[12] In a later report to the party issued after the destruction of the guerrillas (and after he was no longer head of the PCB), Monje stated that "there was no commitment made to Guevara either before or after December 31 to assist him in the guerrilla warfare which he planned to conduct. . . ."[13]

In subsequent months, the attitude of the Bolivian party leadership revealed the dilemma it confronted. On the one hand, it had no wish to ruffle feelings in Havana or to open itself to charges that it was abdicating its "revolutionary avant-gardist" role. On the other hand, it wanted to demonstrate its fealty to the Moscow line—which prescribed a legal road to power for the Communist parties of Latin America—and it obviously resented the encroachment of the guerrilla force on its own political preserve; moreover, as a local force with pragmatic leanings, it sensed the suicidal character of Guevara's action. As a consequence, its course appeared ambivalent. In February 1967 Bolivian party leaders went to Havana to negotiate directly with Fidel

Castro, but the discussions came to nothing.[14] After Guevara's force
was discovered in March and came under attack by Bolivian govern-
ment troops, the PCB professed its "solidarity" with the guerrillas.[15]
Not long afterward Jorge Kolle Cueto, Monje's successor as Secretary-
General of the party, remarked ambiguously to newsmen that there
were "not only [sic] members of our community" in the guerrilla force.[16]
During the Latin American Solidarity Conference, which took place in
July-August 1967 in Havana, Castro was apparently furious with the
Bolivian Communist delegation because of the party's continued refusal
to collaborate with the guerrillas.[17]

The few Bolivian Communists who joined Guevara clearly did so
against the wishes of the party leadership, at least in the period after
December 1966. According to observers with seemingly reliable information, the guerrilleros recruited from the Bolivian Communist Party as
well as from other political groups were "marginal types, unconnected
with the core of their organizations." [18] Most of the guerrillas of
Bolivian nationality (numbering 29 in all [19]) were recruited from among
unemployed mine workers by a pro-Chinese Communist mine workers'
leader, Moisés Guevara Rodríguez; another group was made up of ac-
quaintances of "Coco" Peredos who, like him, had been taxi drivers;
and there were also some students among the recruits. The reliability
of the Bolivian combatants does not appear to have been high, since
one-third of them deserted and/or collaborated with the authorities
after being taken prisoner. In later interviews, Debray felt impelled
to refer to this element as Lumpen-proletarians.[20]

The alienation of the Bolivian CP was only one of the factors
leading to the isolation of the guerrilla force. Two other important
factors were the nature of the territory which the guerrillas chose as
their zone of operations and their inability to attract the support of
the local population.

To describe the area of operations briefly, Guevara and his lieutenants chose a zone in the southeast section of Bolivia comprising a
part of the two departamentos (or provinces) of Santa Cruz and Chu-
quisaca. On the eastern boundary of the area was a railroad line running
from Santa Cruz into Argentina, while to the south it bordered on the
rapidly developing oil production center of Camiri. Despite its proximity to the latter, most of the region was thinly populated and in-
accessible, containing both tropical jungles and arid mountain areas.
Once the fighting started, the terrain worked against the guerrillas,
since they were cut off from contact with the outside world and were
therefore unable to get supplies and maintain communications.

In terms of socio-political factors, the area was also a poor choice
for the foco. For a variety of reasons, the campesinos—or peasants—in
the area proved entirely unwilling to cooperate with the guerrilleros.
In part their attitude was a reflection of their way of life. The sparse
peasant population was clustered in a few settlements throughout the
area and lived mainly by extensive farming. Though the quality of the
land imposed a marginal existence, the peasants were not dissatisfied
with their lot. One important reason was that they owned their own

farms (under a regional land reform dating back to 1878). Moreover, the nearby oil industry at Camiri had been able to absorb those unable to make a living from the soil. Thus, in contrast to the mining districts in northwestern Bolivia, the Southeast had not experienced explosive social problems.[21]

Added to this, the Barrientos regime, as noted earlier, had gone out of its way to court peasant support, and Barrientos himself was well-liked by the farmers; thus, when the skirmishing began, the *campesinos* looked upon the government troops as their own and sided against the guerrillas.[22] A related factor in the peasants' outlook was their strong nationalistic sentiment and dislike of foreigners—and the farmers considered not only the Cubans and Peruvians but even the mine workers from northwest Bolivia as foreigners. Finally, a whole world of experience divided the *campesino* struggling with his workday cares from the ideologically-oriented *guerrillero* who, if he did not come from the middle or upper class himself, was at least led by men of middle or upper-class origins.

It may now be useful to review in detail the events that marked the ill-starred course of Guevara's venture. In retrospect it is possible to group the operations of the guerrillas into four phases.[23]

The first phase, from November 1966 to March 1967, witnessed the organization of the base at Ñancahuazu. During this phase the *foco* grew in number to about 50 men, including—at one point on record— 17 Cubans (of whom four were members of the Central Committee of the Cuban Communist Party), 29 Bolivians, and three Peruvians.[24] This phase ended abruptly on March 23, when—through a combination of carelessness and treachery—the location of the guerrilla force was revealed to Bolivian government troops and the first fighting took place. The initial skirmish actually took the government forces by surprise and cost them seven casualties; but the victory was a Pyrrhic one for the guerrillas, since the discovery of their whereabouts forced them to abandon their efforts to build up a guerrilla network and to concentrate all their energies on the immediate struggle. The outbreak of fighting was partly due to the bungling of the Cuban subcommander "Marcos" (Antonio Sánchez Diaz), whose lack of precautions precipitated the guerrillas' first contact with the enemy. But two other developments were also crucial: first, three Bolivian *guerrilleros* who deserted and were captured between March 11 and 19 furnished government troops with detailed information about the *foco,* its Cuban leaders, and the Ñancahuazu camp; secondly, the government forces uncovered a jeep in the jungle in which compromising documents had been left, through what appeared to be the gross negligence of Tamara Bunke.[25]

At the time of the first encounter, "Tania" was one of four key collaborators who were visiting the guerrilla camp; the others were Debray, the Argentinian artist Ciro Roberto Bustos, and a Peruvian named Juan Pablo Chang Navarro Levano ("Chino"). As a consequence of the premature hostilities, all four were forced to stay with the guerrillas—two until they were captured (Debray and Bustos) and two until they lost their lives (Tania and Chino).[26] Thus they were unable to complete contact work which they had been assigned or which Guevara had in mind for them. Debray, for example, was to have gone on important missions to Havana and France, Bustos to Argentina, and Chang Navarro to Peru; Tania was unable to return to La Paz, where she had been the main link with the urban guerrilla unit and where she had also held an important cover job in the Information Bureau of the government. The entrapment of these four thus contributed critically to the isolation of the guerrillas. Debray and Bustos later made an effort to escape past enemy lines, but they were taken prisoner on April 19.

The second phase of guerrilla activities lasted from March 23 until the beginning of July. In this period the guerrilla force—which now called itself the *Ejército de Liberación Nacional* (ELN)—was constantly on the move, and in fact split into two groups around the middle of April so as to gain greater mobility. The main contingent commanded by Guevara numbered 25 men; the second group led by the Cuban "Joaquín" (Juan Vitalio Acuña Nuñez) consisted of 17 men. Neither detachment included a single *campesino,* and by this time it must have been clear to Guevara that he would not be able to recruit any more followers. The split-up of the guerrillas was only supposed to last a few days, but the two groups were fated never to meet again. In subsequent weeks both groups undertook a forced march to the north; Guevara's party, after capturing the village of Samaipata, reached the northernmost point of its drive on July 6. In these several months the guerrillas engaged in many minor skirmishes with the enemy, but only one was of any significance—an action near Iripiti on April 10, in which the government lost 11 officers and men. The guerrillas' resistance was severely taxed, however, by the combined impact of miserable conditions, sickness, accidents, declining morale, internal dissensions, casualties, and—of course—isolation, described as "total" by Guevara as early as the end of April.

In the third phase of guerrilla operations, stretching from July to the third week in September, Guevara's group withdrew to the southwest as far as La Higuera, reaching there September 25. Meantime "Joaquín's" group had reached and continued to operate in the northern part of the Ñancahuazu district, but its strength was gradually reduced to 10 men. On August 31, this group was finally surrounded by government troops near Puerto Mauricio ("Vado del Yeso") and wiped out. Here, too, "Tania" was killed. Two weeks later the fragmentary urban network which she had established for Guevara was put out of commission by security detachments in La Paz.

By this time the army had been reinforced with newly-trained anti-guerrilla units (called "Rangers"), which stepped up efforts to surround and destroy the weary remainder of the guerrilla band. A fight near La Higuera of September 26 reduced Guevara's contingent to 16 men.

The fourth phase of developments marked the death gasps of the *"foco."* The final fighting took place between September 26 and October

8; on the latter date, in an action near Quebrada del Yuro, the guerrilla unit lost seven combatants—among them Guevara himself. According to widely published reports, Guevara was shot the day after he was taken prisoner. The rest of the now leaderless *guerrilleros* fled, with the "Rangers" in pursuit; over the next couple of months, some were captured and some surrendered voluntarily, while a few managed to make good their escape. Three Cubans eventually got back to their homeland via Chile. Two Bolivians, Guido Peredo ("Inti") and David Adriazola ("Dario") remained in Bolivia, working underground in a vain attempt to revive the guerrilla movement; "Inti" was finally killed in September 1969 in La Paz, where he was trying to organize a new urban revolutionary unit.[27] By that time the guerrilla episode was past history to most Bolivians.

Writing in 1968, a British observer seemed to state the obvious when he remarked that Guevara's small band of insurgents had attracted attention way out of proportion to its effective power, not only on the national level (as reflected in the reaction of the government, press, and people of Bolivia) but around the world.[28] In retrospect it seems amazing that so much exaggerated information pertaining to the strength and effectiveness of the guerrilla force managed to find its way into print. To cite a few examples from scattered sources, it was reported during the spring of 1967 that the *foco* consisted of at least 400 revolutionaries, that this force was being trained by guerrilla veterans from Venezuela, that it had a medical staff, and that it was broadcasting news over a powerful short-wave radio.[29] A French student of guerrilla warfare declared: "The new guerrilla focus seems to constitute the most serious revolutionary initiative in Latin America in the last ten years." [30]

Much of the "news" about the guerrillas issued from sympathetic sources—that is, from Havana and from Castroite supporters, who naturally wished to enhance the importance of Guevara's continental venture; in this effort they simply substituted imagination for information, since in the whole period of fighting Guevara only managed to smuggle out five communiqués.[31] But exaggerated stories were also circulated by other sources—for example, the Bolivian military and government authorities, who may have wished to spur more assistance from the United States. Obviously another reason for the enormous publicity that surrounded the venture was the fact that Guevara—already a legendary hero to revolutionaries around the globe—assumed personal leadership of the *foco*. By the same token, the role of Jules Debray—the ideologist of the so-called "third phase of Castroism"—as Castro's emissary to the guerrilla camp attracted international attention after his capture. The campaign for the release of the then 27-year-old revolutionary got press coverage on a scale that is not often equalled: everyone got into the act, from Debray's conservative and wealthy Parisian mother (who called him "one of France's most brilliant intellectuals" and a "spiritually deeply Christian apostle"), to *The New York Times'* C. L. Sulzberger (who called him "an egocentric hippie"), to Jean Paul Sartre,

Charles de Gaulle, the Vatican, and indirectly Lyndon B. Johnson.[32] All of this publicity cast a glow on the handful of *guerrilleros* in the jungles of Ñancahuazu.

While the attention focused on Bolivia may have had some influence on the Barrientos regime, the course it pursued during the period of the guerrilla challenge was dictated in the main by domestic political considerations. To all appearances, when Guevara's force was first discovered, the regime assumed that it had been organized by leftist opposition factions in Bolivia.[33] In terms of numerical strength, the most important of these opposition elements were the aforementioned MNR (*Movimiento Nacionalista Revolucionario*) and the PRIN (*Partido Revolucionario de Izquierda Nacionalista*), a party led by the exiled mine workers' leader, Juan Lechin Oquendo. These parties, *inter alia*, shared influence with Trotskyite groups and the pro-Soviet and pro-Chinese Communists in the mine workers' organizations.

After the first brush with the guerrillas in March, Barrientos took steps to curtail the activity of the MNR, the PRIN, and the Communists, as well as the Trotskyites in the divided *Partido Obrero Revolucionario* (POR). Following the fight at Iripiti in April, the regime declared a state of emergency which made southeast Bolivia a miiltary zone and outlawed all Communist and Trotskyite organizations.[34] Although the government subsequently relaxed its crackdown, continued restraints on political activity led to restiveness among the miners. In late June Barrientos apparently felt it necessary to order the military occupation of three mining districts (Huanuni, Siglo Veinte and Catavi), leading to an open clash between government soldiers and armed mine workers that reportedly took 21 lives and sparked unrest among university students in the capital.[35]

By this time, however, it had long since become clear to the authorities and to everyone else that no political forces in Bolivia were actively supporting the guerrilla movement. While propaganda friendly to the *foco* had been distributed in the mining areas, the regime made no charges of collaboration against the rebellious mine workers. Thus Barrientos was probably less concerned about the guerrillas than he was about reinforcing his political position when he made his next move: at the end of June he convened a congress of *campesinos*, who made it clear that the loyalties of the agricultural Southeast belonged to the President; they also adopted a declaration labeling the guerrillas an "anti-national" force and promising assistance to the army in its task of pacification.[36]

The convocation of the "National Congress of Peasant Workers of Bolivia" was the last extraordinary political measure taken by the regime in connection with the *guerrilleros*, even though they continued to be active for at least another three months. At no time did the guerrilla campaign seriously threaten the political power of the regime, again due to the fact that the guerrillas failed to establish links with any force of political significance in the country.

In the latter respect, there is a good deal in the public record to indicate either ignorance of, or indifference to, the guerrilla movement

on the part of precisely those groups who might have been expected
to be Guevara's natural collaborators. To the extent that verbal support
was expressed at all, it dwindled or was withdrawn as it became clear
that the guerrilla mission was doomed to failure. The reaction of the
pro-Soviet Communist Party of Bolivia—the one force which Guevara
seriously sought and failed to enlist as an ally—has already been described in detail. In the case of the MNR—a party long since weakened
by dissension and more tolerated than respected in Barrientos' Bolivia—
it seems clear from the statements of various leaders that none of them
had any information about the character of the guerrilla operation.
For example, after the existence of the *foco* became public knowledge,
the exiled MNR chief, Victor Paz Estenssoro, issued statements calling
it "an integral Bolivian phenomenon" and "the result of an internal
process" (sic!); initially he expressed "sympathy" for the guerrillas but
later prudently advised his followers against taking any part in the
movement.[37] Another MNR leader, René Zavaleta Mercado, spoke
vaguely of the need for "armed struggle" but did not encourage support for Guevara in specific terms.[38] By September 1967 Raúl Lema
Peláez, an MNR senator in La Paz, was ready to declare that the MNR
had "no connection with the guerrilla movement whatsoever." [39]

As for the PRIN group, Guevara's diary revealed that its aforementioned leader, Juan Lechin Oquendo, promised Castro in Havana early
in 1967 that he would publish a declaration of his party's support for
the guerrilla operation, and he fulfilled this promise in a manifesto
issued about the first of May.[40] That, however, was the last heard from
PRIN until October, when the party withdrew its "endorsement" of
the now-defeated forces whom it had hailed six months earlier as the
"liberators of the homeland." [41]

The Trotskyites of the POR (Guillermo Lora's group) expressed
"solidarity" with the guerrilla force in a Central Committee resolution
of April 1967, but that was all. Another Trotskyite group, the *POR—
Cuarta Internacional* was even more circumspect in its endorsement.[42]

According to all available evidence, none of these groups ever gave
active assistance to the guerrillas. The same was apparently true of the
pro-Chinese Bolivian Communist Party, though some confusion surrounded its role. For reasons that were not clear, Castro showed special
enmity toward the pro-Chinese Bolivians after the destruction of the
guerrilla force, accusing them of treason—even though one of their followers, Moisés Guevara Rodriguez, had been among the most dedicated
members of the *foco* and had indeed given his life for it.[43]

The remaining parties and factions in Bolivia, among them the
relatively important *Falange Socialista Boliviana,* were opposed to the
guerrillas from the start, as they made clear in their public statements
and commentaries.[44]

Insofar as active support from outside the country was concerned,
once the fighting began, the guerrillas were effectively cut off from all
but a trickle of help from Havana. By contrast, Barrientos was able
to count on assistance from the United States which, while modest in
absolute terms, was substantial in proportion to the small size and

strength of Guevara's force. The main U.S. contribution was to conduct an anti-guerrilla training course for several hundred Bolivian soldiers, providing the "Ranger" units which were instrumental in the final defeat of the guerrillas.[45] In the opinion of military observers, by the fall of 1967 the combat effectiveness of the Bolivian troops was sufficient for them to have put down a much stronger guerrilla force than that led by Guevara.

In the course of this paper, a number of the factors that contributed to the failure of Guevara's guerrillas have been suggested. To discuss these factors systematically, it may be useful to classify them in three categories, ranging from the least to the most significant.[46]

The first category covers errors, insufficiencies, or inadvertent developments of a technical or military nature. Certain factors—for example, losses due to illness—were of course beyond anyone's ability to control. But manifold errors were also made—among them, the poor political judgment used in the selection of some of the *guerrilleros,* accounting in part for later desertions and betrayals; their insufficient military training, which lessened the striking power of the *foco;* their mania to immortalize themselves in vast quantities of photographs, written documents, and even portrait sketches, which—once captured—were of great help to the government troops; and their initial casual methods of maintaining outside contacts (notably with Havana), stocking supplies, *etc.* All of these errors shed significant light on the military capacities of Guevara and his lieutenants, but they are of only marginal importance in explaining the failure of the guerrilla venture.

The second category consists of more serious inadequacies and errors that can be described as tactical in nature. Two crucial weaknesses of the guerrilla organization were the fragility of its urban network, operated by largely inexperienced personnel, and its virtual lack of security machinery. (In the latter connection, Debray expressed the suspicion that enemy agents had infiltrated the *foco*—without, however, naming names; for information pointing to "Tania" as a likely suspect, see footnote 25.) As for outright errors, first and foremost was the selection of the guerrilla zone—though this was also a matter of faulty strategic conception, as we shall see. Beyond the choice itself, the guerrillas showed negligence in failing to obtain sufficient information about the topography and other natural aspects of the zone of operations. A lack of proper precautions was responsible for a number of other tactical errors, including the premature discovery of the guerrilla base camp and the subsequent loss of supply depots. Taken together, these tactical weaknesses and mistakes would of themselves have been enough to doom the guerrilla adventure, and some observers—particularly those with Castroite sympathies—have tried to argue that they provide, along with the first category of problems, the most meaningful explanation of Guevara's failure.

However, there is another and by far more crucial category of reasons why the mission failed, and these have to do with the fact that the whole concept of the *foco* was based on fallacious strategic doctrines, principles and interpretations. The available evidence seems to indicate that not a single one of the Castroites responsible for launching the guerrilla movement made an objective study in advance of the Bolivian nation, the causes and consequences of its revolution of 1952, or the character of the regime elevated to power by the *coup d'état* of 1964. This alone could explain why the *guerrilleros* were so surprised by their isolation once they were encamped in the country. To the extent that they considered Bolivian factors at all, they misjudged the attitude of the *campesinos,* the strength of the Barrientos government, and the relative popularity of the Bolivian army, which had been overhauled after the 1952 revolution and which enjoyed respect, partly because it had participated for years in economic development projects.

The theorists of guerrilla warfare also ignored the existence of virulent nationalism in Bolivia; by insisting on the organization of an "international" guerrilla movement, they left the field free for Barrientos to appeal to patriotic sentiment and even opened themselves to the charge of neocolonialism *sui generis,* since all the key positions in the *foco* were held by Cubans.

The Castroites' stress on the priority of military over political struggle—and therefore on the need to subordinate political elements to the guerrilla force in any revolutionary situation—led them to forfeit the possibility of collaboration with the Bolivian Communists, whose assistance might not have been large in a concrete sense but would probably have been helpful for propaganda purposes. The same ideological rigidity led them to rule out from the start any possibility of compromise or cooperation with the other forces of the far Left which enjoyed some influence in Barrientos' Bolivia; it was assumed (probably correctly) that such "ideologically foreign" political groups would be non-compliant to the will of the *foco.*

Thus, both through ignorance of the realities of the Bolivian situation and through ideological preconceptions, Guevara's expedition was initiated according to a "grand plan" that relied exclusively on guerrilla warfare to achieve revolution. Ironically, "warfare" is what they got, and it soon revealed the *guerrilleros* for what they really were —a mere half-hundred armed foreigners and Bolivian *"marginados,"* gradually reduced to desperation by their isolated condition and waiting for a miracle that never came. In a sense "Castroism" in Bolivia was defeated by the Castroite strategy itself, meeting its end in a military mop-up action.

Going a step farther, in the final analysis the failure of the guerrilla movement in Bolivia—and in all Latin American countries—was the necessary consequence of a Cuban misreading of history. The ideologized reconstruction of Castro's victory, fashioned after the event in response to domestic political requirements and to Castroite aspirations in Latin America, opportunistically distorted the situation in Cuba during the years 1953-59.

In the first place, Castro's *"foco"* did *not* create a revolutionary situation where none had existed, as Castroite history would have it; the revolutionary situation existed in Cuba *before* the formation of the guerrilla movement. In the second place, Castroite ideologists have described Castro's guerrilla force as a "peasant army," implying that Fidel succeeded in mobilizing the Cuban peasantry in support of his cause; but in reality, the nucleus of Castro's force was drawn from a small group of middle-class revolutionaries. In the third place, the new history misrepresented the character of the Batista regime—at once dictatorial and weak—by equating it with those of Ydigoras Fuentes or Mendez Montenegro in Guatemala, of Romulo Betancourt or Raoul Leoni in Venezuela, of Lleras Restrepo in Colombia, of Belaunde Terry in Peru, and finally of René Barrientos in Bolivia. In so doing, it implied that all Latin American leaders were as vulnerable to revolutionary overthrow as Fulgencio Batista had been. In the fourth place, ridiculous parallels were drawn between the Cuban Sierra Maestra and the Bolivian Andes; between Cuban city youth on the one hand and upland *Indios* and Brazilian *cuboclos* on the other. In the fifth place, no mention was made of the assistance that had been extended to Castro by populist parties in Latin America and also by liberal groups in the United States of America, because such assistance did not fit the post-revolutionary image of the *Lider maximo*. Finally, no recognition was given to the fact that Castro owed a good deal of his success in the 1950's to his purposeful ambiguity concerning his ideological convictions, accounting for the support he won from all Cuban democrats (but *not* the Communists); hence, misleading comparisons were made between Castro's course and that pursued by his followers in the 1960's, who loudly proclaimed their adherence to a "Cuban" type of Marxism-Leninism (much as the validity of that ideological compound might be challenged by other leftists), and who as a result were opposed by all political groups of any consequence *except* the Communists (and even the support furnished by the latter was hesitant, ineffective, ambivalent and intermittent, as we have seen).

Given these fallacies built into Castroite historiography and *a fortiori* into the Castroite model of revolution, it is no wonder that Havana failed in its effort to export its revolution to the Latin American continent. Looking beyond Guevara's misadventure in Bolivia to guerrilla efforts in other Latin American countries, in no case has a guerrilla movement based on the Cuban model achieved enough strength to pose a serious threat to a ruling government regardless of whether the latter was a progressive regime or a dictatorship. In a few instances, other types of guerrilla forces have operated temporarily with somewhat more success, but none has escaped eventual extinction.

In Guatemala, for example, guerrilla forces have existed since the early 1960's. Those of Castroite persuasion have failed to shake the security of the government in any way; in fact, their acts of terrorism have been counterproductive in that they have contributed to public unrest and invited retaliation, giving aid and comfort to the extreme Right and impeding the economic and social modernization of the country. A Trotskyite guerrilla group which for years operated independently had some success in winning over the *campesinos* with its down-to-earth ideology; eventually, however, the Guatemalan army eliminated these revolutionaries as an effective force.

In Venezuela—which for a variety of economic, political and geographic reasons was long Castro's primary target on the continent—the guerrilla movement dwindled down to nothing after leadership conflicts led the Communist Party of Venezuela to sever relations with the guerrillas and government troops then decimated their ranks.

In Colombia, guerrilla activity has similarly died down. It is worth noting that armed insurgents were operating in Colombia long before Castro came to power—in fact, since the disastrous *violencia* that started in 1948. For several years, a guerrilla force led by the Colombian Communist Party managed to win the support of a portion of the peasantry in a few districts, but it disintegrated after the government succeeded in pacifying the countryside and the party changed its strategy to accord with the Moscow line of pursuing power by peaceful means. Several efforts were made to launch a Castroite guerrilla movement, the last in 1965; but the *foco* was unable to muster enough strength to become active, even though it attracted to its ranks a man of the stature of Father Camilo Torres.

In Peru, as noted earlier, armed peasant organizations operated with some success in the province of Cuzco in 1962–63, under the leadership of the Trotskyite Hugo Blanco. However, the Castroite guerrilla band organized in 1965 was destroyed within a few months. A number of small Castroite *"focos"* were formed in other countries (several times, in fact, in Argentina and Brazil), but they fell apart so quickly that the world press hardly had occasion to note their existence.[47]

The fiasco in Bolivia seems to have been the final straw that convinced Castro of the impracticality of his hopes for a "second Cuba." Today—some years since the orthodox Communists on the continent were assaulted by Havana for having abandoned guerrilla adventures—Castro himself is under attack by such adherents of the *"foco"* theory as Douglas Bravo in Venezuela and Fabio Vasquez Castaño in Colombia. Both have accused Castro of "betrayal of the guerrilla," indicating that Cuba—presumably because of Soviet pressure as well as domestic economic problems—has now made it clear she can no longer give them assistance.

Castro's belated realism cannot reverse the mistakes of the past. Let us hope, however, that it has helped to dampen the fervor of those who have glorified guerrilla warfare as the only means to achieve social and economic justice, not seeing that all it has really ever accomplished was to encourage political polarization and extremism on the Right as well as on the Left in the Latin American nations. If the futility of the guerrilla strategy has indeed become recognized, then a small step forward has been taken at least toward the understanding—if not toward the solution—of the complex social, economic and political tensions that characterize Latin American life.

NOTES

1 In the writer's view, it is possible to distinguish three distinct phases in the evolution of Castroite ideology. In the first, theoretical notions were formulated *ex post facto* to explain and glorify Castro's successful revolution in Cuba; the classic

expression of these theories was Guevara's famous volume, *Guerra de Guerrillas,* published in Havana in 1960. In the second phase, Castroism was elaborated and infused with doctrinal concepts that placed it unmistakably in the ideological orbit of communism (see, for example, the "Second Declaration of Havana," *Revolucion* (Havana) Feb. 5, 1962; Guevara's "Guerra de Guerrillas: Un Metodo," *Cuba Socialista,* September 1962; and other sources). The third phase witnessed the amendment of Guevara's theories of guerrilla warfare to emphasize the need for armed struggle by guerrillas operating independently from political control (reflecting Havana's impatience with the peaceful politics and tactics of the pro-Soviet Communist parties on the continent). The chief articulator of this last phase of ideology was the Frenchman Jules Régis Debray. See in particular his *Revolution in the Revolution,* New York, The Monthly Review Press, 1967.

2 Robert J. Alexander, *The Bolivian National Revolution,* New Brunswick, N.J., Rutgers University Press, 1958, p. 3.

3 On the 1952 revolution and its results, *cf.* Robert J. Alexander, *The Bolivian National Revolution,* New Brunswick, N.J., Rutgers University Press, 1958; and Mario Rolon Anaya, *Politica y partidos en Bolivia,* La Paz, Editorial Juventud, 1966.

4 On the Barrientos *coup* and its consequences, *cf.* William H. Brill, *Military Intervention in Bolivia: The Overthrow of Paz Estenssoro and the MNR,* Washington, D.C., Institute for the Comparative Study of Political Systems, 1967.

5 See Fidel Castro's introduction to *El Diaro del Che en Bolivia,* Mexico City, Siglo XXI Editores, 1968. See also the report of a special OAS commission entitled *Estudio del "Diario del Che Guevara en Bolivia,"* Washington, D.C., Pan American Union, Mimeographed document, Sed. L/X.II.23, Dec. 20, 1968.

6 Ernesto Che Guevara, "Mensaje a la Tricontinental," in *Obra revolucionaria,* Mexico City, Ediciones ERA, SA 1967, pp. 640 ff. See also Castro's introduction to Guevara's diary, *loc. cit.;* Ricardo Rojo, *Che Guevara—Leben und Tod eines Freundes,* Frankfurt, S. Fisher Verlag, 1968, pp. 137 f., 176; Ted Cordova Claure, "Un Vietnam en Bolivie?" *Marcha* (Montevideo), May 19, 1967; and Richard Gott, "La experiencia guerillera en Bolivia," *Estudios Internacionales* (Santiago), April-June 1968.

7 Blanco's peasant movement was crushed in May 1963; in any case, it is unlikely that Blanco and Guevara would have been able to collaborate, since both showed strong ideological and psychological tendencies to go it alone. According to Guevara's diary and other sources, Havana tried to establish a new guerrilla force in Peru in 1966–67, following the destruction of the first Castroite unit. See "Mensaje al Che No. 37," in *Punto Final* (Santiago), July 30, 1968; Agence France Presse (AFP), report from Camiri, Nov. 14, 1967; and the entries in Guevara's diary for March 20 and 21, 1967, *loc. cit.*

8 Jesus Lara, "Una renuncia remece al PC Boliviana," *Punto Final,* Feb. 25, 1969. See also *Verde Olivo* (Havana), Aug. 3, 1969.

9 *Bohemia* (Havana), Jan. 17, 1969.

10 See Guevara's entries in his diary for Nov. 27, 1966, and his monthly summary for November. See also Gott, *op. cit.;* and *International Herald Tribune* (Paris), July 2, 1968.

11 Carlos Maria Gutierrez, "Bolivia: otra forma de guerrilla," *Marcha,* May 12, 1967.

12 *Cf.* entry in Guevara's diary for Dec. 31, 1966; and Mario Monje, "Las divergencias del PC boliviano con Che Guevara," *Punto Final,* Feb. 27, 1968.

13 Monje, *ibid.*

14 Entry in Guevara's diary for Feb. 14, 1967; OAS report, *Estudio . . . ,* p. 17; Lara, *loc. cit.*

15 *Cf.,* for example, a PCB declaration published in the Uruguayan Communist paper, *El Popular* (Montevideo), dated April 29, 1967, signed by three high-ranking party officials, including Monje himself.

16 *El Popular,* May 19, 1967.

17 See Havana's message to Guevara of Aug. 26, 1967, published in *Punto Final,* July 30, 1968. In this message Castro used the scathing term *"mierda"* to refer to the PCB delegation to the Solidarity Conference.

18 *International Herald Tribune,* Oct. 16, 1967.

19 *Estudio . . . ,* pp. 49 ff.

20 The *Times* (London), Oct. 28, 1967; Debray estimated the number of deserters at 15 and 17, but this seems exaggerated. *Cf. Estudio . . .* , p. 51, f.

21 *Cf.* René Zavaleta Mercado, "Bolivia y America Latina," *Marcha,* May 30, 1969.

22 On the latter point all observers seem to agree; even Guevara's diary offers confirmation, at least indirectly.

23 The account that follows is based mainly on Guevara's diary entries and on information in *Estudio . . .* , *loc. cit. Cf.* also Gott, *op. cit.*

24 *Estudio . . .* , pp. 49 ff. The guerrillas' urban network consisted of 15 persons at the most.

25 Whether Tania was guilty of "negligence" or betrayal later became an issue. Months after Guevara's defeat, it was alleged that Tania had been an agent of the East German State Security Service (SSD) since 1961 and had been charged with shadowing Guevara and reporting on his activities: see the statement of Günther Männel, a former SSD officer, about Tamara Bunke in *Welt am Sonntag* (Hamburg), May 26, 1968. See also the *International Herald Tribune,* July 16, 1968; and *Bohemia,* Jan. 17, 1969.

26 See Guevara's diary entries for March 20 and 21, 1967, as well as his monthly summaries for March and April.

27 The only known activity of the new ELN commander "Inti" was to issue unrealistic manifestos and communiques that were distributed by Havana to Latin America's left radical press. *E.g.,* see *Punto Final,* Feb. 27, July 30, and Aug. 27, 1968. On "Inti's" death, see AFP and Reuter's reports from La Paz, Sept. 10, 1969; also *Granma* (Havana), Sept. 12, 1969.

28 Gott, *op. cit.* Gott himself estimated the number of guerrillas at 150—three times the actual strength later revealed by Guevara's diary.

29 See, *e.g., The New York Times* (Paris edition), April 4, 1967; Associated Press (AP) report from La Paz, April 4, 1967; and AFP and AP reports from La Paz, March 29, 1967.

30 Marcel Niedergang in *Le Monde* (Paris), May 18, 1967.

31 *E.g.,* see *Boletin Tricontinental* (Havana), July 1967; and Ojarikuj Runa, "Bolivia—analisis de una situacion," *Pensamiento Critico* (Havana), July 1967. Guevara's communiqués were later printed in *Granma,* No. 28, 1968, and *Punto Final,* July 30, 1968.

32 *E.g.,* see reports of AFP and the Italian news agency ANSA from La Paz, May 6, 1967; and the *International Herald Tribune* (Paris), Oct. 4, 1967.

33 *E.g.,* see United Press International (UPI) report from La Paz, March 31, 1967.

34 AFP report from La Paz, April 12, 1967.

35 *Cf.* Ruben Vasquez Diaz, *La Bolivie a l'heure du Che,* Paris, Francois Maspero, 1968, especially Chapter I.

36 Discussed, *inter alia,* in Edgar Millares Reyes, *Las Guerrillas: Teoria y Practica,* Sucre, Bolivia, Imprenta Universitaria, 1968, p. 40.

37 See *El Popular,* May 16, 1967; *El Diario* (La Paz), June 16, 1967; Interpress Service (Lima), Aug. 2, 1967; Vasquez, *op. cit.,* pp. 118 ff.; and finally an interview with Paz in *Ultimas Noticias* (Caracas), Aug. 5, 1967.

38 Vasquez, *ibid.,* pp. 111 ff.

39 Millares, *op. cit.,* p. 140.

40 See Guevara's diary entry for April 15, 1967, and AFP report from La Paz, May 2, 1967; see also *International Herald Tribune,* July 2, 1968.

41 *Presencia* (La Paz), Oct. 31, 1967, as cited in Millares, *op. cit.,* p. 126.

42 Millares, *ibid.,* pp. 115 f., 119 f.; Vasquez, *op. cit.,* p. 116.

43 *Cf.* Castro's introduction to Guevara's diary, *loc. cit.,* as well as the pro-Chinese Communists' pronouncement, *Oscar Zamora responde a Fidel Castro,* Montevideo, Ediciones del MIR, 1968.

44 Pertinent references may be found in Millares, *op. cit.*

45 Juan de Onis placed the number of Bolivian soldiers trained by U.S. Army personnel at 400: *Internationalist Herald Tribune,* July 2, 1968. Another observer, Jay Mallin, estimated the number at a few hundred more: "Che Guevara: Some Documentary Puzzles at the End of a Long Journey," *Journal of Inter-American Studies* (Coral Gables, Fla.), Vol. X, No. 1. See also UPI report from Washington, D.C., March 10, 1968.

46 The text that follows incorporates some conclusions drawn, *inter alia*, by Gott, *op. cit.;* Debray, the *Times* (London), Oct. 28, 1967; Jacques Arnault, *L'Humanité* (Paris), Nov. 17, 1967; Juan de Onis, *loc. cit.;* and Antonio Arguedas Mendieta, *El Siglo* (Santiago), July 25, 1968. However these sources generally limit themselves to the technical and tactical aspects of Guevara's failure—in other words, to the first two of the author's three categories.

47 A new type of "armed struggle" has sprung up in the last few years, particularly in Uruguay and Brazil, in the form of "urban" guerrilla units; however, they appear to be only indirectly tied to or motivated by Castroism. So far police efforts to curb their activity have had indifferent success; at the same time, it is impossible to imagine that they could achieve genuine revolutionary victories.

9

The Meaning of Revolution in Viet Nam

JOHN McALISTER, JR., and PAUL MUS

Is there a meaning to revolution in Viet Nam? Do the seemingly kaleidoscopic events of the past quarter of a century add up to something more than a situation of apparent anarchy? Can a pattern really be discerned in the struggle for power that has devastated Vietnamese society for more than a generation? Yes, there is a pattern, these events do have a larger significance, and there is an easily understood meaning to revolution in Viet Nam. This meaning is best explained by first referring to the contrasting bases of power between the two principal competitors in the struggle and then pointing out how these differing sources of strength have affected the pattern of conflict that has now persisted into the 1970s.

The revolutionary struggle in Viet Nam is a conflict between two modern cultures created by antagonists who still share an old culture in common. Both sides in the struggle want the same thing: a new Viet Nam that is united, independent of foreign involvement, and modern in its economy and society. The differences between them over how to achieve this new Viet Nam are not, however, merely political in the sense of being a disagreement over short-run strategies and priorities. These differences are much more profound. They are cultural, which is to say that they are based on sharply contrasting conceptions of the way a modern society ought to be organized. They clash over opposing ideas about social status and social cohesion, over what a man's place in society should be and what values should link him to other men.

Too frequently, the values of a society have been regarded by Westerners, especially Americans, as the same thing as ethics and morality. Values and morality are, of course, inseparably intertwined. But values are more than principles for personal conduct; they are also sources of social cohesion and guides for social action. Without common values men find it difficult to work together toward common goals. They either don't trust each other or they don't understand each other. Words don't have the same meaning to people who have different values. Moreover, without the discipline derived from shared values the efforts of men lack force and can easily be dissipated by quarrelsome divisions among them. In a society like the one in Viet Nam, where old values are no longer relevant to the new lives men must live, conflict over values is not merely an ethical and moral controversy—it is also, and most conspicuously, a struggle over political power.

It is because they are so critical in determining the capacity of people to work together that questions of values are also questions of power. In the most general sense, power is the ability to affect people's actions or, simply, the ability to get compliance with a demand. In politics, power implies sanctions for noncompliance, and these sanctions often depend on coercion and force. But power based solely on coercion is an extreme that is normally avoided, because it is more difficult to maintain and less dependable than power based on common values. When values are shared, people usually comply readily with demands made upon them, because they accept the legitimacy of these demands. This is why those whose power is primarily coercive always seem to try to get their values accepted by the people they wish to control. Voluntary compliance, their actions seem to confirm, will be a more certain and less arduous way of holding power within a society than coercion.

From the perspective of the role of cultural values in Vietnamese politics, the powerlessness over the past quarter-century of pro-Western, urban-oriented governments becomes easier to understand. These governments have, by and large, been limited to urban bases of power precisely because they have not had values relevant to the lives which village people have had to lead. The sharp dichotomy in culture between the cities, where about one-fourth of the Vietnamese live, and the countryside, where about three-fourths live, has been a barrier which these governments have not really been able to overcome.

They have, of course, tried to exercise authority in the rural areas, but primarily through administrative representatives and military force. These instruments, strong though they have been at times, have not been transformed into durable power because rural people have not respected them as legitimate institutions of authority or complied with their decisions. Even if there were no rural-based revolutionaries, these governments, it seems, would still have had difficulty in conducting such routine functions as collecting taxes and administering public programs.

Generalizations about the numerous pro-Western governments that have come and gone over the past twenty-five years are, admittedly risky. These governments have run the political gamut from a transparently colonial regime under the ex-emperor Bao Dai, to a self righteous dictatorship under Ngo Dinh Diem, to the rule of American-trained military officers under Nguyen Van Thieu. But despite their differences in style these governments have had a conspicuous common denominator: a dependence on foreign troops and foreign financing to keep them in existence.

This dependence can be brought into clearer focus by recounting the steady expansion of pro-Western military forces in Viet Nam during the past several decades. As late as 1938, seven years before revolution broke out, only 11,000 French troops aided by a 16,000-man Vietnamese militia were able to maintain France's colonial control throughout the whole of Indochina—an area nearly half again as large as France itself. But after the revolution was launched a force that dwarfed this colonial contingent of the thirties was able to control very little territory on any permanent basis. Up until 1954, an expeditionary force of 70,000 French regulars, 68,000 Legionnaires and Africans, and 300,000 Vietnamese—or a total of about 450,00 men—fought in vain to uphold the claim of Bao Dai's regime, the State of Viet Nam, to be the only government for the whole country from the China border in the north to the Gulf of Thailand in the south. Though these forces were potent enough to capture territory they could not get the compliance from rural people that less than 30,000 troops had gotten in 1938.

As the 1970's begin, military forces in Viet Nam have grown to a size dwarfing even those that existed in the early 1950's. Yet the political future of the Saigon government, which has tried to rule in only the southern portion of Viet Nam, remains in doubt. Its military support, however, consists of over a million men—more than twice as great as the force which fought to sustain the Bao Dai regime. Why has there been this greater and greater dependency on foreign forces in a vain attempt to hold on to a smaller and smaller amount of territory? Why is it that 538,000 Americans plus their air and naval firepower cannot quell the armed opposition to the Saigon government? What has happened in Viet Nam to make it impossible for truly massive Western military force to prevail in Viet Nam in the 1970's when only 11,000 French troops were able to control a vastly larger territory with hardly firing a shot just thirty years before?

Some American critics feel that Western military power in Viet Nam has been unduly shackled by political constraints. Without restrictions on heavy bombing and orders against "hot pursuit" of the enemy into privileged sanctuaries, the military results of the war, they believe, would have been quite different. In the French era of the fighting they would have advocated the massive bombing of Dien Bien Phu by American air power and the denial of a safe haven across the China border to the Viet Minh. In the American era they have called for the bombing of Haiphong and the end of sanctuaries in Cambodia, Laos, and northern Viet Nam itself. These criticisms and others like them are calculations about power, specifically about the military power balances in the war, and it is natural that they should be made. But these calculations don't go far enough. They don't explain the enormous change between 1938 and 1970 in the effects of military power and the quantity of it required to have an impact in Viet Nam. They don't get at the very essence of the power relationships in the struggle in Viet Nam.

The reason these criticisms have been able to explain so little about the military dilemmas in Viet Nam is not hard to understand. Expectations about the war—by both critics and supporters alike—have been based on the usually correct assumption that most armies are trained to fight for control over territory. Armies must have bases, sources of supply, avenues of retreat, and rear-area sanctuaries where they can regroup. All the requirements for keeping an army in the field clearly point to the need for a territorial base. And since adversaries normally expect each other to defend the territorial sources of their strength, they measure the prospects for victory by their capacity to capture the other's territory.

More important than these tactical considerations, armies must control territory because they are instruments of governments which are committed to protect the people they govern. Governments are usually thought to derive their legitimacy through the exercise of sovereign authority over a territory, and when they can no longer control such a territory their legitimacy is brought into question. But in Viet Nam, Communist-led revolutionaries have won widespread political legitimacy and secured military bases without having to rely on territorial sovereignty.

The Communist substitute for territorial control has been a political link tying together a steadily larger portion of the people in the countryside. So resilient has this tie been that it does not depend on military protection to be maintained. So formidable is the power derived from this popular link that it is hard to overestimate it. In military terms alone it has meant that the Communists have almost never had to defend territory or fixed positions. Since their adversaries, the pro-Western governments, have, by contrast, depended almost entirely on control over territory as their primary source of legitimacy, an asymmetrical pattern of warfare has developed. In fighting each other the two contenders have been pursuing quite different strategic goals— goals which are obvious indications of the sharply contrasting bases of power the antagonists have depended upon.

Although the scale of the war has escalated enormously during the quarter-century since revolution broke out, the asymmetry of the conflict has remained substantially the same. The Communists' goal in mobilizing the potential power of the rural people by organizing them politically has been to tie down larger and larger numbers of their opponent's troops in static defense of territory. This strategy has struck at the critical vulnerability in pro-Western governments: their dependence on military force to maintain political power. If they abandoned their static positions they would lose control over a segment of the rural population and possibly not be able to win it back again. Yet by re-

maining in static positions they become convenient targets for their
elusive enemy and they also lack the mobility to seize the initiative to
search out and pursue the quick-moving Communist units. Here is how
the quagmire has been made, here is why more and more troops have
been required: to maintain political power by occupation of territory.
Here is why Viet Nam has been a war not for land but for people.

The disadvantages to pro-Western governments from such a strategy
are so clear that their continuing need for extra military power should
not be surprising. Without a means of transforming control over territory into popular political loyalties, these governments have simply not
been able to compete on the same plane with their Communist adversaries. They have had no choice but to rely on military force; it has
been virtually the only instrument of power they have possessed. Its
effectiveness, however, has declined, and the amount of it required
to hold on to portions of the countryside has mounted as the Communists' village-based political organization has grown. Unlike 1938 or
1945 or even 1960, popular compliance caused by coercive sanctions is
in deep decline; coercive power now finds itself thwarted by the power
developed around a set of common values that have slowly been adopted
by ever-larger segments of village Viet Nam.

[We have] tried to analyze in cultural terms how and why the
Communists have been successful in mobilizing political power in Viet
Nam. Among the many reasons for Communist success the most essential one is the relevancy of their values to the lives villagers must lead.
This relevancy springs from a conception of society as a communal as
distinct from a secular organization—a conception which offers a comprehensive explanation for a new sense of community in which rural
people can participate.

The longing for a new sense of community has been no abstraction
among village people. Their spiritual traditions have left them with
the belief that men must be linked closely together in a bond of communal identity. But as a practical matter this spirituality has not offered
values explicit enough to make this bond a reality. The need has been
for values to replace the Confucian traditions which once linked the
villagers to a larger community and gave them a sense of being able
to acquire a status of recognized significance. The relevance of Communist values, therefore, has been in the possibility of using them to
establish a new communal spirit guided by the traditions and forms of
the past.

Relevant though they are, these values have not been adopted in
the Vietnamese countryside without great violence and extreme coercion. The struggle over who is to govern in the villages of Viet Nam
and how, has, certainly, been one of the most tragic examples of political
violence since the end of World War II. Moreover, even if the
Communist-led revolution had not been opposed by the French, the
Americans, and the anti-Communist Vietnamese, there still would
have been violence—the rural people are unlikely to have accepted a
new scheme of values through a peaceful mass conversion.

Rarely have the values by which people live been changed fundamentally without a fight. Even in their vestigial form the values which tenuously held Vietnamese villages together prior to 1945 conferred status on some villagers and denied it to others. A change in values meant, therefore, a loss of status to the privileged, and from the first days of the revolution village notables have, almost routinely, lost their lives. But a change in values has also meant an opportunity for an increase in status for villagers who otherwise would have led dreary lives of little consequence within a static village hierarchy.

Worse than the dreariness was the uncertainty—the lack of any really precise identity within a declining village community that also had lost its own identity. How did one establish his distinctiveness under such circumstances? There no longer were examinations in Confucian learning to set a standard for achievement. Also unlike earlier eras, there was no new land to be opened up in the south to which one could move from one's home village. There was only the limited horizon of the village—a village no more a part of a spiritually endowed kingdom but now the object of alien bureaucratic control. Then came the revolution. Along with the new ideas came a way to act upon them. There were a multitude of new organizations to be formed, all of them having a legitimacy as part of the revolution and conveying a new status for those who participated in their activities.

Although access to this new form of status has been open to everyone in the countryside—even landowners if they agreed to a redistribution of their lands—advancement to higher status positions of authority has been strictly based on performance. In much the same way that examinations testing a person's knowledge of Confucian traditions once determined who would be chosen as mandarins, a knowledge of the ideology of revolution has become the criterion for choosing the new, revolutionary cadre from the village people of Viet Nam. Written examinations, of course, are now archaic; the real test of a person's knowledge of the revolutionary program comes in action. If he is to be successful the beginning revolutionary will need not merely a spirit of daring but also a capacity to mobilize his fellow villagers and coordinate their actions within the larger scheme of revolutionary strategy.

Mastery of the ideas and values of revolution has, therefore, become a source of power and an opportunity for upward mobility in the Vietnamese countryside. By contrast with Confucian learning, this mastery has not required years of enforced inactivity for studying the Chinese language in order to learn the classics of Confucius in their original version. Mastery has come through action—action that teaches the need for acceptance of new values as a means of establishing discipline and motivation in even the smallest village guerrilla team. In other words, mastery over these values has come through using them and recognizing that the greater their acceptance the more successful the revolution—and the larger the opportunity for upward mobility.

This access to political power by Vietnamese villagers is the most essential characteristic in the meaning of revolution in Viet Nam. It represents a new way of mobilizing and sharing power that is not only a unique departure from the country's past experience in organizing political power but is also a prime example of the worldwide phenomenon of the entry of peasant people into modern "mass" politics. Through revolution instead of economic development and industrialization these villagers have had their first chance to abandon passive lives of unchanging routine and by action of their own initiative to acquire a totally new status. Officer rank in the army and leading cadreman in the revolutionary party have been the most sought after positions. But because of the enormous number of local organizations for mobilizing the countryside in tying down enemy troops and supporting revolutionary forces, there have been plenty of opportunities for participation.

The popular responsiveness to these opportunities for participation has resulted in a revolutionary movement powerful enough to dominate northern Viet Nam and to stalemate a massive American force in the south for over five years. A major explanation of the motivation for this response is the relevancy of revolutionary values to Vietnamese traditions. But probably as important has been the feeling that within the revolutionary movement there is a predictability and equity in the access to power. At the lowest levels there seems to be a tested conviction that mobility to positions of authority comes to those whose performance is most notable. And throughout the movement a firm belief appears to exist in a kind of simple justice: the sharing of power on the basis of a mastery of the values and strategy of revolution.

Yet if there is a relevancy of the values of the revolution to Vietnamese traditions and if there is a sense of equity in the sharing of power within the movement, then why hasn't the revolutionary cause been adopted by all Vietnamese? Why has the revolutionary struggle gone on for so long? Why does a substantial portion of Vietnamese society still oppose the revolution? All revolutions have, naturally, been opposed by those who benefit from an existing regime as well as those who are uncertain about what a future regime might bring. But as protracted as revolutions usually are, few have endured as long as has revolution in Viet Nam. Foreign intervention has, of course, made a major difference by prolonging and intensifying the conflict through the commitment of troops to fight on behalf of pro-Western governments.

From this intensity have come deeper cleavages in Vietnamese society and an emphasis by both sides in the struggle on coercion in winning political allegiance. Terror and brutality have mounted as techniques for obtaining popular bases of power as the war has escalated. It is impossible and undoubtedly useless to attempt to assess which side has been the most brutal. Neither side has clean hands. Their conflict has made pawns out of fellow Vietnamese; the score is now kept by the number of their countrymen each side can claim to "control." But despite the inhumaneness of this violence an assessment can be made about its consequences and, particularly, about its relevance to the meaning of revolution in Viet Nam.

The Communist revolutionaries have prided themselves on the selective use of terror. By carefully relating their terror tactics to specific political goals, they have sought to break down the resistance of vestigial village cohesion and to persuade the villagers to adopt their scheme of revolutionary values. Killing a rich landowner or an informer for the pro-Western governments has been their way of communicating both revolutionary goals and revolutionary power. Forcing young villagers to join local militia units and then indoctrinating them on the strategy of revolution has been their technique of winning new recruits by force. When terror is indiscriminate, they feel, people may be drawn together out of a common fear rather than being divided and won over through tactics which forcefully yet skillfully coerce them to a part of the revolutionary movement.

Pro-Western governments in Viet Nam have never relied on tactics of selective terror. Their political goals have instead called for force to be used in occupying and controlling territory. Somehow they have expected this control to lead to political allegiance. Perhaps they have thought that if rural people were given some protection they would be grateful. Yet, clearly, they have expected too much from such a concept of passive allegiance. But a more active form of popular allegiance has been out of the question. Pro-Western governments have simply been unwilling to share power with the people in the countryside. In part this has been motivated by a desire to have power concentrated in a few hands. Yet beyond such selfishness there has been the larger problem of being unable to devise a scheme of values to form the base of a community encompassing the modern world of the cities and the traditional world of the villages. Without any values to master as a means of gaining access to power and without local-level organizations for participation in national politics, allegiance from the countryside has been lacking.

In the discussion of the alienation of the Westernized elite from Vietnamese traditions, [we] tried to suggest some of the reasons why Viet Nam's upper class has not been able to offer leadership to the countryside. Divorced from their country's past, these new mandarins have nevertheless expected and demanded the compliance that previous Vienamese elites had gotten. Yet they have not realized that this earlier compliance was based on shared values. The old mandarins were respected because their intellectual achievement could be measured in terms that villagers understood and according to values by which villagers lived. These country people cannot now share the values on which this new Westernized upper class is founded because for them they are unattainable. These values were obtained primarily through education in an alien scientific culture. If, earlier, this upper class had tried to relate their modern values to the world of the village, they might have won the loyalty of the villagers for which they have been fighting. But they have been an exclusivist upper class, concerned more with the maintenance of their privileges than in forming a community with the countryside.

Increasingly larger military forces have been required to maintain anti-Communist, urban-oriented governments in Viet Nam. The political impact of these forces has, however, been disproportionately small in comparison with their massive size. The governments they have desperately tried to sustain have steadily been losing ground because they have been unable to consolidate the potential power which military force has given them in the Vietnamese countryside. Clearly the meaning of this tragic conflict is that force alone cannot cope with the mass mobilization of peasant people for involvement in revolutionary struggle. Without some competitive program for mobilizing and sharing power in the countryside Western military force can only fight a rear-guard action.

[We have] tried to bring a fresh perspective to the repetitious pattern of conflict in Viet Nam by emphasizing some time-tested insights about the nature of Vietnamese society. Despite the enormous scale of violence and the far-reaching changes in the country the most important aspects of the struggle remain the same. Pro-Western governments are still trying to wrest control over the countryside away from rural-based revolutionaries who have developed power by relating their strategy and values to Vietnamese traditions. The meaning of revolution in Viet Nam is that the opportunity for predictable access to political power by village people is a more potent form of power than a primarily military force arrayed against them. In Viet Nam, therefore, the technological power of the West has had its weaknesses exposed by the political power of a peasant people. The embarrassment this exposure has brought might well have been avoided, of course, if, sometime over the twenty years since the ideas [here] were first presented, the meaning of revolution in Viet Nam had been understood.

10

The Palestinians and Israel

SHLOMO AVINERI

Three years have now passed since the Six-Day War, and there seems to be no end in sight to the impasse into which it has led Israeli-Arab relations. In the summer of 1967 hope was in the air; most Israelis shared the belief, nurtured by a mixture of naiveté and arrogance, that the war had finally opened the door to peace. If before June 1967 most Arabs had believed that Israel could be easily defeated, the Six-Day War—so the reasoning went—proved that Israel was here to stay. Hence, the argument continued, the Arabs would now realize that they had no choice but to cut their losses and pursue an alternative, and to them less costly, policy. In return for peace, i.e., recognition on the part of the Arabs of the legitimacy of Israel, Israel had quite a formidable package to exchange: the territories she had captured from Egypt, Jordan, and Syria.

We all know better now. The net gain of the 1967 war was not a diminishing of the Arab-Israeli conflict, but rather an intensification of it. However the war may have affected the political consciousness of the Arabs, it certainly did not reconcile them to the existence of Israel, nor did the prowess of the Israeli armed forces cow them into submission. Those Israelis who in the past had been accustomed to assert that the only language the Arabs understand is the language of force, proved to be as wrong as ever. Humiliation breeds stubbornness, and the very fact of Israel's victory served only to widen the chasm between her and the Arabs. The dialectic of the self-fulfilling prophecy was at work again. Israel could beat her breast in genuine innocence, proclaim that she had no expansionist aims, that she had been pushed into a corner by the Arabs in May 1967, and that consequently she had to strike back in despair and self-defense. But do not the Israelis now control, as a result of the war, the whole area from Kuneitra to Kantara, from Mt. Hermon to the Suez, and do not Israeli leaders make it clear that a return to the frontiers of June 5, 1967, is quite unthinkable? As Cecil Hourani so pointedly tried to tell his fellow Arabs, their total rejection of Israel had consistently redounded to Israel's advantage. Had they accepted the UN partition plan in 1947, a much smaller Israel, and one with a sizable Arab minority at that, would have been established alongside a more populous Palestinian Arab state; similarly, had they not rocked the boat in 1967, Israel would still be encased in her precarious borders of 1949, with a narrow waistline around Natanya, with Jerusalem still half in Jordanian hands, and with Eilat rather than Sharm el-Sheikh as Israel's southernmost point. . . .

Finally, there are the Palestinians, who in the two decades between 1949 and 1967 were subsumed under the various Arab states, but who now, due to the inability of the Arab governments not only to regain for the Palestinians their lost home, but even to defend their *own* borders, have come to the fore as an almost independent element in the conflict. To be sure, Palestinian guerrillas had been operating for several years before 1967; but during that time they were totally subservient to the various Arab governments that subsidized them. Thus, the Palestine Liberation Organization was an adjunct of Egyptian foreign policy, while *Al Fatah* was organized by the Syrian intelligence services. Since 1967, however, the *fedayeen* have become an autonomous power, far more active against Israel than before the war. . . .

These guerrilla organizations have so far shown no signs of succeeding in their aim of dislodging Israel from the occupied territories and destroying her as a state, and there is no reason to believe that in the future they will be more successful than hitherto. Nevertheless, . . .

by continuing to wage a war of terrorism against Israel after the massive Arab defeat in 1967, the Palestinians have kept the conflict open and have prevented both the solidification of the ceasefire lines into mutually accepted, semi-permanent frontiers, and the emergence of an accommodation between Israel and at least some of the Arab regimes.

The ideology of the Palestinian organizations has hardened since 1967—a development not usually noticed in the West, where the Palestinian propaganda machine, having learned that the rhetoric of genocide does not pay, is now trying to convey quite the opposite image of the guerrillas. Before 1967, the Palestine Liberation Organization was ready, at least on paper, to allow those Jews who had entered Palestine before 1948 to remain in the country after the destruction of Israel was accomplished. Now, according to the Palestinian National Covenant, as amended by the Fourth Palestinian Council in Cairo in July 1968, similar rights will be accorded only to those Jews who were in Palestine in 1917. All others will not be considered "Palestinians" and will have no place in the country after the destruction of Israel. Anyone taken in by *Al Fatah* propaganda about a secular Palestine, in which "Moslems, Christians, and Jews" will live peacefully side by side, should be reminded that most of the 2,500,000 Jews of Israel would be excluded from such a state. To an even greater degree than other Arab communities, the Palestinians have become more, not less, extreme since 1967.

The conflict is thus very much with us. But what sometimes disappears under the newspaper headlines and the daily flux of events in the Middle East is the nature of the conflict itself, and it is to this topic that I wish to turn now. It is perhaps easiest to begin by trying to explain what the conflict is *not*. Despite appearances, it is not—and never was—a struggle between the two Great Powers, though the powers have always had a stake in it. This statement may at first glance seem fantastic, especially at a time when the Arab-Israeli conflict has taken on the classical visage of an overt arms race and when on the one hand Israel is portrayed by the Soviets and the Arabs as the spearhead of U.S. imperialism, and on the other hand some of Israel's friends in America try to present her as the best ally the U.S. and Western democracy have ever had in the Middle East. Yet despite all this, the Middle East conflict has never truly been susceptible to analysis in cold-war terms.

At the risk of restating the obvious, let us examine the positions adopted by the Great Powers in each of the three outbreaks of war between Israel and the Arab states (1948, 1956, 1967). The UN proposal of 1947, that the British-mandated territory of Palestine be partitioned into a Jewish and an Arab state, was supported *jointly* by the USSR and the U.S. When the State of Israel declared its independence on May 15, 1948, the only arms at its disposal (aside from those stolen from the British) came from Czechoslovakia, and were delivered in token of Soviet support for Israel—a fact now conveniently forgotten by both the Soviets and the Arabs, and, on occasion, even by some Zionists. Not only did Israel not receive any arms from the West, the

U.S. went so far as to declare an embargo on arms shipments to the Middle East, which, though intended to be nonpartisan, in effect worked against Israel alone.

Both the USSR and the U.S. granted immediate diplomatic recognition to Israel, but whereas the Soviet recognition was *de jure,* the Americans limited themselves for the first year of Israel's existence to mere *de facto* recognition. In the summer of 1948, when the Soviet and American envoys arrived in Tel Aviv, only one hotel (the Käte Dan) was considered fit to house foreign dignitaries of such stature; so the Hammer and Sickle and the Stars and Stripes were displayed side by side on the hotel front—an unusual sight in 1948, the year of the Czech *coup d'état* and the Berlin blockade. Soviet spokesmen, including the present Foreign Minister, Andrei Gromyko, waxed eloquent over the right of the Jews to their ancient homeland, condemned (with customary Soviet vehemence) the Arab attack on Israel, and called upon the Arabs to abide by UN decisions. It was Harry Truman who in the spring of 1948 appeared ambivalent over the partition question, and who for a time entertained the idea of some form of UN trusteeship and of scrapping the Jewish state altogether. At one stage during the war of 1948, Ben-Gurion decided to make public the names of the members of the Israeli General Staff (still kept secret in good conspiratorial fashion); his reason for doing so was to disprove rumors circulating in the Western press to the effect that Russian generals were directing the Israeli war effort: few people in 1948 were prepared to believe that the Jews could fight.

While Israel was thus supported—though in different forms—by *both* the Soviet Union and the United States, the Arab countries drew their support from the British and the French, who were still the paramount powers in the Middle East. Britain had military bases in Egypt and in Iraq, and trained these two countries' armies; Jordan's Arab Legion was even commanded by regular British army officers, headed by Brig-Gen. Sir John Glubb Pasha. Syria and Lebanon were still very much under French influence. Late in the 1948–49 war, when Israeli forces penetrated a few miles into Sinai, a British ultimatum was dispatched to Israel, and British aircraft were sent in to convey to the Israelis that Britain would not tolerate any closer approach to the Suez Canal and its installations. The Israelis shot down five British Spitfires, but then Ben-Gurion (always the first among Israeli leaders to give in to foreign pressure) ordered a hasty withdrawal.

The mixed pattern of Great Power support for the local belligerents in this early period can be easily explained; in the years immediately after 1945, the Jewish *Yishuv* in Palestine was the only force in the Middle East fighting British imperialism and actively engaged in the attempt to dislodge England from the area. In restricting Jewish immigration to Palestine, even in the face of the emergency created by the Holocaust, Britain was catering to the wishes of its Arab client-states, for the Arab regimes—King Farouk in Egypt, Nuri Said in Iraq, Emir Abdullah in what was then Transjordan—were the instruments of British policy and the mainstays of British support in the Middle

East. Obviously, then, the Soviet backed the only group, tiny and weak as it might then have seemed, which was trying to oust the British altogether. U.S. support for Israel was of a different order: in part it could be traced to bad conscience after the Holocaust, in part to the influence of the Jewish vote on a Democratic administration, and in still another part to a combination of idealistic enthusiasm for a new, vigorous, and democratic country and the shrewd calculation that the establishment of a Jewish state might lessen the pressures on the U.S. to admit Jewish refugees from Europe (the British were not altogether incorrect in their oblique references to the outright cynicism of some American demands for allowing Jewish immigration into Palestine). In no case was U.S. support motivated by any grand design of American foreign policy: the State Department was against the recognition of Israel,[1] and the American oil interests of course strongly supported the Arabs and opposed Israel (as they still do today).

By 1956, the picture had changed completely. Britain and France, anti-Israel in 1948, now supported Israel, and in the case of France even egged her on. The French at the time were engaged in a war in Algeria, where the FLN was heavily dependent upon Nasser's support. Both British and French interests had been substantially damaged by the Egyptian nationalization of the Suez Canal. With the emergence in the Arab world of nationalist anti-Western regimes like Nasser's, the Soviet Union had switched its support to the Arab cause, and the United States, though generally supporting Israel, opposed her and the French-English-Israeli alliance on the specific issue of Israel's war with Egypt in 1956. After the Sinai campaign, the U.S., together with the Soviet Union, put pressure on Israel to withdraw from Sinai without first having achieved peace terms. In 1956, then, as in 1948, the Soviet Union and the United States took the same line, the only difference being that in 1948 the line was pro-Israel, whereas in 1956 it was pro-Arab.

In 1967 the kaleidoscope pieces fell into yet another pattern: while the Soviet Union continued to support the Arabs, U.S. support for Israel (though hedged, especially on account of America's interest in Jordan) was stronger than ever before; France now abandoned its 1956 marriage of convenience (or, rather, concubinage) with Israel and reverted to its 1948 position of support for the Arabs; and Britain, though generally behind Israel, was much more lukewarm about it than in 1956. Britain clearly wished to emerge from the 1967 war as a possible honest broker in subsequent negotiations, although its eyes, of course, were also on the vestiges of British influence in the Arab countries.

Over the past twenty years, then, the great powers have repeatedly switched their basic positions and have played a complicated game of musical chairs with both sides in the Middle East conflict, yet the conflict is still there and still somehow involves none of the Great Powers directly.[2] Unlike all other post-1945 disputes, in which the roots of discord may always be seen to lie in the clash of Western vs. Soviet (or Chinese) policy, in the Arab-Israeli conflict Great Power rivalry is a secondary and derivative factor. The same can be said of ideological differences: there are probably more Marxists in Israel than in the whole Arab world, but the Soviet Union could not care less about that. Nor is it of any importance that in most Arab countries (including Egypt) Communist parties are outlawed and individual Communists rot in jail, whereas Israel is blessed with *two* Communist parties, both of them represented in the Knesset. Nothing along such lines could be envisaged in Korea, Berlin, Cuba, or Vietnam.

The real conflict in the Middle East is not between the Great Powers, nor is it a conflict between imperialism and anti-colonialism, or between "democracy" and "Communism." Basically and ultimately it is a conflict between two movements for national liberation. Both of these movements are relative newcomers to political consciousness; both are internally problematical; both movements have suffered from a series of historical traumas; both are terribly unsure of themselves and groping toward self-identity. On top of everything else, both the Jewish and the Arab national movements lay claim to the same piece of land, historic Palestine, *Eretz Israel*—though for the Arabs, of course, Palestine is just one part of the great Arab homeland, while the Jewish national movement claims only *Eretz Israel* as its patrimony.

Though Jews and Arabs have been around for millennia, it was only in the last decades of the 19th century that a secular national movement emerged among either of them. And among both Arabs and Jews, this movement arose in response to challenges from the external society and to the impact of these challenges on the society itself. Zionism, in the case of the Jews, was a response to the secularization of Jewish life and to the emergence of national movements and ethnically-conscious nation-states in Eastern and Central Europe. In the case of the Arabs, the contact betwen the Ottoman Empire and the West, as well as the emergence of a secular, ethnic nationalism among the Turkish ruling group—a development that threatened to transform the Ottoman Empire from the religious home of the Believers (*Dar al-Islam*) into a secular state based on the ethnic superiority of the Turks —served to make the Arabs aware of their own ethnic and linguistic heritage as against that of the Ottoman Turks. Though in its later stages Arab nationalism took for its main target the Western colonial powers, its initial impetus was directed in opposition to the ruling Turks, and both the British and the French were welcomed by Arab nationalists as disrupters of the old Ottoman Empire. It was as an ally of Arab nationalism that the West appeared among the Arabs—and "West" in this context includes also the American missionaries who founded the American University in Beirut, and whose efforts were directed toward making Christian Arabs conscious of their secular Arabism in order to weaken their connection with the Islamic Empire of the Turks and hence to win another battle in the Christian war against the infidels.

Arab spokesmen these days tend to emphasize the support given the Zionist movement by the British through the Balfour Declaration; they tend to forget, however, that at the same time that British diplomats were seeking the support of Jewish nationalism against the Turks and the Germans, British agents were aiding the Arab revolt against the

Turks in the Hedjaz; for every Balfour there was a T. E. Lawrence. In point of fact, both national movements, the Jewish and the Arab, made ample use of any support they could get. In 1917, both had a common enemy—the Turks—and both had a common ally—the British. That it was naive, if not cynical, of the British to believe that they could play both cards simultaneously, attests to nothing other than the narrow-mindedness of those British statesmen who liked to pooh-pooh the impact of nationalism generally—that is, until nationalism blew the British Empire out of existence. But in 1917, at least, the leaders of the two national movements still believed that they could arrive at a common platform, as the short-lived agreement between Chaim Weizmann and King Feisal shows. Inexplicable as it may now seem, none other than Haj Amin el-Husseini, the Mufti of Jerusalem and latter-day collaborator with the Nazis in the "Final Solution," was among the participants at the dedication ceremonies of the Hebrew University; his name appears among the signatories of a document buried in the university's cornerstone.

Both the Jewish and the Arab national movements were faced with a similar social problem, one that took the form of a lopsided social structure. But in their approach to this problem the two movements took separate paths, and it is in this divergence that one can locate the essential distinction between Jewish and Arab nationalism. For while it is possible to maintain that the Jewish national movement succeeded in combining a national revolution with a social one, the Arab movement remained almost exclusively political; an Arab social revolution, indeed, has yet to be undertaken. The successful synthesis of the social and political realms gave Zionism its peculiar dynamism and strength, whereas the purely political nature of Arab nationalism, in Palestine as well as elsewhere, is at the root of its present tragic dilemma.[3]

The Jewish problem, as it was defined by Zionism, was not merely territorial in nature, nor did Zionism aim only at a geographical concentration of Jewish people in Palestine. From the start Zionist theorists realized that the creation of a social infra-structure for a Jewish national home in Palestine would require a radical restructuring of Jewish social life as it had evolved in the Diaspora, where almost all Jews had been pushed into the ranks of the middle classes; there was in the Diaspora no Jewish peasantry, and hardly a Jewish proletariat. Nation-building, therefore, involved the creation of a Jewish working class and a Jewish peasantry in Palestine—in other words, the overall development of a differentiated social structure. Jewish immigration to Palestine was structurally different from Jewish immigration to the United States, England, or South America; those who left Eastern Europe to make a new home in the West did so in hopes of achieving a higher status in society, but Jewish immigration to Palestine represented *the only intentionally downwardly mobile social movement ever experienced in the history of immigration*. The typical *halutz* was a young middle-class Jew, usually quite well-educated for the circumstances of his age and society, who in going to Palestine turned his back both on the Diaspora and on bourgeois society, and set out to find personal and communal redemption by becoming a worker or a peasant.

In Zionism, then, social vision went hand in hand with nationalism; Zionism could succeed only insofar as it was combined with socialism. Hence the strongly socialist bias of Israel, hence the *kibbutzim, kvutzot,* and *moshavim,* hence the establishment of the Histadrut not as a mere trade-union organization, but as a Society of Laborers (*Hevrat Ovdim*), owning industries, paramount in the economic field, leaving its impact on all spheres of Israeli life; hence the hegemony of the labor movement in the political life of the *Yishuv,* hence the insistence on Jewish labor. The entire thrust of the Zionist movement was against the creation of a white, *colon*-like society. The facile analogy that is nowadays made between Israel and South Africa or Algeria is pure nonsense: Zionism called for self-reliance, doing one's own labor (*avoda atzmit*), the creation of a Jewish working class, absolute opposition to the exploitation of cheap Arab labor by Jewish settlers—in short, the exact opposite of the economic ideology of French Algeria or present-day South Africa.

In turning our attention to Arab society we find a dilemma similar to that faced by Zionism. One tends to forget that before the British and French established themselves in the Middle East, the Arabs were not a self-governing nation: ever since the 13th century, the Arabs in the Middle East had been ruled by a succession of foreign, albeit Moslem, invaders: Seljuks, Osmanli Turks, Mameluke slaves (in Egypt). Even Saladin, victor over the Crusaders at the Horns of Hittin, was a Kurd, not an Arab. When Arab nationalism emerged triumphant from its confrontation with the West, the Arabs, like the Jews, were essentially lacking in the experience of statehood. But because of the militaristic ethos of Islam—an ethos that harks back to the *Conquista* of the Mediterranean by Islamic Arab warriors in the 7th and 8th centuries—Arab society was also characterized by a strongly anti-commercial orientation; indeed, an urban, commercial middle class scarcely existed among Moslem Arabs. For centuries, the commercial middle classes in Arab society consisted of ethnic and religious minorities: Maronites, Greeks, Armenians, Jews, Copts. Arab society was as imbalanced as Jewish society in the Diaspora, though its tilt leaned precisely in the opposite direction.

Very little has been done within the Arab national movement to redress this imbalance, since very little social thought (as distinguished from political ideology) went into the making of Arab nationalism. The greatest trauma suffered by Arab nationalism was the regression of Arab Islamic society from the cultural grandeurs of the High Middle Ages to the dismal backwaters in which Arab society found itself on the threshold of the 20th century, when it came into contact with Europe and found its civilization profoundly inferior to Western culture and technology. In the same way that traditional Islamic thought had paid far less attention to social philosophy than had Christian medieval thought, so modern secular Arab nationalism has consistently stressed political reconstruction at the expense of social reconstruction: according to Arab nationalist ideologies, Arab society would be regenerated once the yoke of Western imperialism was broken. Moreover, the original leaders of the Arab national movement were themselves members of the traditional elites of Arab society, and were naturally disinclined to consider the need for social transformation. Hence the complete and rapid breakdown of the quasi-constitutional political structures left in Arab countries by the departing Western powers, and the frequent replacement of those structures by military regimes.

Western observers usually interpret the emergence of the military as a sign of modernization and a guarantee of rapid, if forced, progress. Within the Arab context, however, the emergence of military regimes in Egypt, Syria, Iraq, Libya, Sudan, and Yemen has not signified a breakthrough to modernization, but a reversion to the traditional, legitimate form of government accepted and revered by the Arabs and by Islam for the past fifteen hundred years. Islam, after all, is the Army of the Faithful, the Caliph the Commander of the Faithful. Within the political culture of Arab society, military power equals political legitimacy, and for this reason military leaders have had very little difficulty establishing their authority in Arab countries. That very few voices have ever been raised in the Arab world to question the place of the army in politics is easily understandable: in Arab society, it is as natural and as legitimate for the army to take over power as it is in a Latin American country, or as it was for the Praetorian Guard in the late Roman Empire to become the repository of political authority. In societies created by conquest (Rome, Latin America, and the Arab world), political power not only grows out of the barrel of a gun, it is identical with the gun.

Even in as highly mobile an Arab group as the present-day Palestinians, many of whom have been uprooted from their traditional mode of living and whose condition of exile makes them far less conservative than any other Arab group, the kinds of leadership and political integration that have emerged appeal to the traditional imagination of a people whose history is one of conquest, of continuous warfare, of military glory, and especially of subjugating the vanquished infidel. To a somewhat ignorant Westerner, Yassir Arafat may appear to be a new phenomenon; as a social type, however, he belongs in the same category as Fawzi Kaukji, Hassan Salameh, and Abd el-Kadr el-Husseini—the Palestinian military leaders who in 1948 led their fellow Arabs into tragedy and defeat in their first confrontation with Israel.

It is in this respect too that the Arab military regimes, however radical their ideology, differ in social *praxis* from the revolutionary armies of China, North Vietnam, or Cuba. For in each of these latter countries the traditional, conservative army was overthrown and destroyed, and replaced by the revolutionary people's army which became the new ruling force. In the Arab countries (with the exception of Algeria, whose history is altogether different due to the country's century-long occupation and administration by the French, who completely pulverized the traditional Arab society) it was the *traditional* army that took over political power: no people's army, no revolutionary war. In some cases, as in Egypt, the army then tried to create a social organ as an alternative integrative force, but the Arab Socialist Union of Egypt is hardly anything more than a front. In Syria, the Ba'ath party is an adjunct of the army: the different factions within the party reflect only the different formations of the Syrian army commands and the different ethnic-religious groups (Alawis, Druzes, Suni Moslems) within the army.

The lack of a cohesive social *praxis* in Arab nationalism is reflected in the fate of the Arab refugees. The claim, made by Israel, that the plight of the refugees from the 1948–49 war has been cynically exploited by the Arab governments is, of course, true, though it obviously also serves as a convenient alibi for the Israelis to do nothing about the refugees themselves. But there is something else at work here too, something which became evident to Israelis only after the Six-Day War, when they could visit the camps on the West Bank and in Gaza. A visitor to any of these camps might have expected to find a plethora of Arab voluntary relief organizations actively at work. Certainly a visitor from a Western society, or anyone familiar with similar situations in a Jewish context, might have realistically expected some form of philanthropy or do-goodism, some expression of bad conscience which, after all, does help to make the life of the wretched of the earth a little more bearable. Nothing of the sort. Insofar as voluntary work has been done in the camps (aside from the work of UNWRA), it has been done by various Christian, Western church-relief organizations. In a camp near Ramallah (the most sophisticated and affluent town on the West Bank), one looked in vain for evidence of local efforts to do something concrete for the refugees; the equivalents of Hadassah, ORT, or the JDC were conspicuous by their absence. Every Ramallah burgher, on the other hand, would upon questioning fervently assert his belief in the sacred right of the refugees to be reinstated in their former lands, and his willingness to provide the refugees with all the political support they needed, verbal or otherwise; when it came, however, to a feeling of solidarity, of social responsibility, of a shared fate, the response was total silence. Social relations between Ramallah—and other townships on the West Bank and in Gaza—and the camps were limited to the brutal fact that the camps supplied the town with cheap labor.

It is clearly possible in Arab society for political rhetoric about the rights of refugees to go hand in hand with their severe social exploitation without creating all the uneasy questions such a situation would create in any other society. Even among the refugees themselves, no socially radical movement directed against the socially-entrenched classes has ever emerged. The internalized norms of Arab society operate as strongly among the refugees as they do among the established classes. Thus, the question is not why Arab society has failed to absorb the refugees economically and socially; one can well understand that leaving the refugees in camps is a rational, if cruel, means of keeping the issue alive. The question is why Arab society has done nothing for the refugees on an interim level, and the answer is to be found not in considerations of politics or propaganda, but in the sheer absence of those societal orientations that make voluntary mutual aid in times of crisis almost an institutional necessity in, say, Jewish social life. The lack of a social dimension in Arab nationalism is as much the scourge of the refugees as it is of Arab society in general.

Yet whatever the social nature of Arab nationalism may be, the conflict is still a conflict between it as a movement and the Jewish national movement as embodied in the State of Israel. Indeed, a general recognition of the fact that the conflict is between two movements, rather than between states as such, may perhaps become the key to a possible solution of the Middle East problem. Ultimately, there is no conflict between Israel and Egypt, or between Israel and Syria; the conflict is between Israel and the Palestinians. It is true that this conflict has been in abeyance most of the time between 1949 and 1967, but the reason is that those parts of the British mandate of Palestine that were not incorporated into Israel in 1948 also did not emerge as an independent Arab Palestinian state; rather, they were either annexed by Jordan (as in the case of Judea and Samaria, the so-called "West Bank") or kept under Egyptian military occupation (as in the case of the Gaza Strip). But it is likewise true that scarcely anyone officially recognized Jordan's annexation of the West Bank and of East Jerusalem (most significantly, *no Arab country recognized the annexation*), and everyone who knew anything about the Middle East was well aware that the Palestinians were far from happy under the rule of King Hussein and his Bedouin army, whom they considered inferior to them in culture and learning (Hussein springs from a dynasty whose historical abode has been the Hedjaz, now in Saudi Arabia, and his grandfather had been installed in Transjordan after World War I by the British). Nevertheless, although all this was known, nobody really bothered about the Palestinians, since the uneasy stalemate between Israel and the Arab countries created the illusion that the basic problems would somehow be solved with the passage of time. Came the 1967 war, and all the old questions were ripped open again, and the Palestinian Arabs were now brought into the consciousness—and conscience—of the world.

It now seems clear that any settlement of the Arab-Israeli conflict that does not deal with the problem of Palestinian self-identity will fall short of the requirements of a truly peaceful solution. The Palestinian organizations have said time and again—and their statements should be taken seriously—that even if the Arab *states* make peace with Israel, they will go on fighting. Under such circumstances, the border situation between the Arab states and Israel will remain tenuous in the extreme. The same can be said of what would happen in the case of an "imposed solution" by the Great Powers—a settlement short of peace but guaranteeing cessation of hostilities. Those who desire such a solution—their number includes some Israelis—have in mind a model drawn from the situation in 1957, when Israel was forced to retreat from Sinai under Great Power pressure and in return was given some guarantee that the border with Egypt would be kept quiet, as it really was until May 1967.

But 1970 is not 1957. The powers may impose a settlement on Israel and the Arabs (I myself tend to doubt the possibility of this, but am ready to grant it for the sake of argument), but neither the United States nor the Soviet Union can impose a settlement on the Palestinian organizations. The options open after the Sinai War of 1956 are simply not open today, since one has now to deal not only with Egypt and Jordan, but with the Palestinians as well, and the latter will not abide by any settlement to which they are not a party. For it has been precisely the Palestinians who have by their activities succeeded in frustrating what little hope there was after 1967 of reaching an accommodation between Israel and Jordan.

The trouble, of course, is that the Palestinians today are committed to the same maximalist policies that spelled their doom in 1948, when they rejected the UN partition plan and thereby jeopardized their chance to establish an Arab state in a part of Palestine. As a "war of liberation," the guerrilla effort is hopeless; it can cause a great deal of damage to Israel's image, it can kill quite a number of Israelis, but it cannot win a war, "liberate" the occupied territories, or destroy Israel. The West Bank is less than half the size of New Jersey; it contains no swamps, jungles, or mountain ridges. Anyone who thinks in terms of Algeria or South Vietnam is deluding himself; the geography of the West Bank simply cannot become the territorial base any guerrilla movement needs in order to succeed. This is why the Arab guerrilla effort has characteristically fallen back on personal and indiscriminate terrorism. But while terrorism of this kind often *accompanies* a true guerrilla war (again, Algeria and South Vietnam may serve as examples), in the Palestinian case terrorism has become a *substitute* for guerrilla war. Exploding a bomb in a supermarket or university may kill a lot of people, but it will not win a war. Throwing hand grenades at Arab refugees in front of an Israeli labor exchange may deter them from cooperating with Israeli efforts at economic rehabilitation; it will not win a war. Ultimately, this kind of terrorism is a sign of failure. Indeed, it is reminiscent of the terrorism practiced during 1936–39 by followers of the Mufti; in each case, guerrilla warfare, having failed in its objectives, deteriorated into a dirty, indiscriminate orgy of murder, which in the end killed more fellow Arabs (suspected of collaboration or of selling land to the Jews) than Jews or British soldiers. In the 30's the ideology flowing out of the barrel of terrorist guns was fascist rather than quasi-Marxist, but the Israeli confronted with a bomb in a bus station has the uncanny feeling of *déjà vu.*

Nevertheless, in my opinion, it is the Palestinians, despite their failure to achieve their aims through military or terroristic means, to whom one may look for a way out of the present impasse. For the purposes of the ensuing discussion, I will rather mechanically divide the Palestinians into two categories: (a) those under Israeli rule in

Judea and Samaria (the "West Bank") and in the Gaza Strip; and (b) those on the East Bank of the Jordan (the old Transjordan), in the rump of Hussein's Hashemite Kingdom of Jordan. Let me begin with the latter group, those under Hussein's rule, both because with regard to them Israel can do very little to effect possible developments and because it seems to me that precisely with regard to them Israel should begin to rethink some of her conventional political wisdom.

Before 1967, Jordan was, next to Lebanon, the most accommodating of Israel's neighbors, and accordingly Israeli political thinking grew accustomed to the notion that Israel had a stake in the continuation of King Hussein's rule. Indeed, Israel had made it clear several times that she would have to react in the event of a radical, pro-Egyptian coup in Jordan. There is little doubt that because of this stance Israel has more than once prevented a Nasserite takeover in Jordan. In 1958, in the wake of the Iraqi *coup d'état*, Israel allowed British aircraft to overfly her territory en route to Jordan to bolster Hussein's regime against a possible revolt. And after the Six-Day War, Israeli hopes focused on Hussein as the Arab ruler most likely to be willing to negotiate with Israel; in the summer of 1967, government leaders as diverse in their political opinions as Moshe Dayan and Abba Eban adopted a policy of "waiting for the phone to ring" from Amman.

Today, it appears improbable that King Hussein, even if he were willing, would be able to move toward an accommodation with Israel. . . .

Out of inertia and a spirit of accommodation, Israel has continued to stake her chances on Hussein. But the truth is that Hussein is now an obstacle to peace. Were he to vanish from the scene—a prospect that is particularly painful for the U.S. to consider—a chain of events might be set in motion that could be more conducive to eventual peace than his continuing presence has proved itself to be.

The majority of the Jordanian population east of the river is Palestinian in origin; Transjordanian Bedouins are a minority. Historically speaking, Transjordan was always a part of what has been considered Palestine, and it was included in the territory given by mandate to Great Britain after World War I. However, in order to find a throne for Britain's protégé Abdullah, Winston Churchill in 1922 ruled that the provisions of the Balfour Declaration did not apply to the area east of the Jordan. Transjordan was thus turned into a semi-autonomous Emirate, but until the end of World War II the British High Commissioner for Palestine was also vested with ultimate power with regard to Transjordan.

Now, it is my view that if tomorrow the Palestinian guerrillas were to overthrow King Hussein . . . a Palestinian Arab state, populated by more than a million Palestinians, would come into existence, albeit in only a part of what the Arabs consider the whole of Palestine. The Palestinians would thus come back into their own. I entertain no illusions that this would satisfy the maximalist Palestinian claims, and I have no doubt that the Palestinians would in all probability continue to hope for the destruction of Israel. Nevertheless, the grievance at the root of the conflict—the frustration of the Palestinians—would be greatly alleviated. Palestinian Arabs would have a state of their own, their "homelessness" would be to some degree remedied, a place would be set for them in the councils of nations with an army, a flag, and all the trappings of sovereignty. They would, in other words, regain their consciousness of existing on a political level.

Some observers, especially in Israel, consider such a development highly dangerous, since they claim that it would mean a radicalization of Jordan and the replacement of the moderate Hussein by an extremist like, say, Yassir Arafat. But . . . one of the paradoxes of Arab society is that only radicals can afford to be moderate, while moderates tend to play to the radical gallery (compare the violent behavior of the moderate Hussein with the moderate behavior of the radical Syrians on June 5, 1967). It may well be that a new, radical Palestinian regime in Jordan would behave in reality very much like the present military regime in Syria, which has managed since the Six-Day War to combine the most radical ideological anti-Israel stance with a surprisingly moderate and pragmatic attitude in the field; . . . It is a historical truism that an underground movement, once come into formal, political power, tends to become responsible, and respectable, in the exercise of authority. In all, I think it eminently worthwhile for Israelis, who shudder at the thought of *Al Fatah* taking over Jordan, to have second thoughts on the matter.

But these developments, to repeat, are outside Israel's sphere of direct involvement, and Israel can do very little to bring them about. Israel can, however, initiate a number of steps with regard to the other category of Palestinians—those now under her rule on the West Bank and in the Gaza Strip.

The kind of military administration set up by Israel in these territories after the Six-Day War was a brilliant improvisation; as a temporary measure, it provided Israel with maximum security while allowing minimum interference in the life of the local population. The general idea was that the less the military administration meddled in the daily affairs of the population, the better, and the result is that today Arab municipal self-government on the West Bank and in Gaza remains intact, and Jordanian and Egyptian laws are still the law of the land. Yet, basically, this entire policy was conceived as a stopgap measure, intended to maintain law and order until negotiations between Israel and the Arab states got under way, as most Israelis were sure they would. Now, three years after the war, one must deal with the real possibility that the provisional will be transfigured into the semi-permanent. Liberal and minimalist as this sort of administration may be, furthermore, it still is a military form of government, and Israel is considered an occupying power by the local inhabitants. All the benevolent care taken by the military administration in matters of agriculture and medical and social services is, ultimately, offset by the need to protect Israel from the guerrillas, which means arrests, interrogations, and the imposition of curfews when a grenade is thrown at a tourist bus or at a group of Jewish worshipers in Hebron or at Israeli housewives in Gaza. Israel has refrained from passing death sentences on perpetrators of such acts, but the long prison terms meted out do not endear the Israelis to the local population.

In my opinion, what Israel has to do now is to make clear its readiness to discuss peace terms not only with the Arab states, but also with the representatives of the Palestinians. What I have in mind specifically is a discussion with the Palestinians now under Israeli rule concerning the possibility of establishing a Palestinian Arab state on the West Bank and in Gaza.

Such a proposal, of course, comes up against a host of difficulties: the envisioned state will need access to the sea, as well as facilities for secure communication between the West Bank and Gaza; Jerusalem will undoubtedly be a thorny problem, and Israel will have to insist on some guarantees for her security along the Jordan river. But, once negotiations were undertaken, the fundamental issue would have been breached, for the Palestinians would then be the first Arab group ever to acknowledge the legitimacy of Israel. Premier Golda Meir once said, in rejecting a proposal that Israel negotiate with the Palestinians: "Is what the Arabs need a fourteenth or fifteenth state?" The Arabs may not need such a state; the *Palestinians* do. Israel too may not need a fourteenth Arab state—but she is in dire need of the *first* Arab state to accept her existence and to be willing to enter into negotiations.

But why, it may be asked, should the Palestinians under Israeli rule wish to do what no other Arab state has ever been ready to do—accept Israel's legitimacy? Some, like Aziz Shehade, himself a refugee from Jaffa and now a lawyer in Ramallah, and perhaps the most courageous Palestinian leader on the West Bank, say openly that this may be the chance the Palestinians missed in 1948 to establish their own state. Others, like the Mayor of Hebron, Sheikh Ali al-Ja'abri, may be more cautious, believing that some arrangement will eventually be made, either directly between Israel and Jordan or diplomatically through the Powers, that will bring Jordanian rule back to the West Bank. But on various occasions Ja'abri has indicated that if this does not happen in the near future, then it will be up to the Palestinians to negotiate with Israel on their own, psychologically difficult as that may be. To all the Arab *states* Israel has very little to offer in return for negotiations; to the Palestinians it can offer independence, sovereignty, and honor.

Ja'abri and his colleagues are aware that once they entered into negotiations with Israel they would be branded as traitors by their fellow Arabs. But, as the present stalemate continues, more and more Palestinians in the areas under Israeli rule may come to realize that the choice before them, though brutal, is also simple: either do nothing and continue to be ruled by Israel, or negotiate in order to achieve independence. Given Arab pride, and the utter unwillingness of Arab states to recognize Israel even at immense cost to their own societies, this may be a long and agonizing process; but more and more Arab intellectuals on the West Bank are beginning to think along the lines of possible negotiation, though few have as yet mustered the courage of Shehade to say in public what they are ready to concede in private.

Israel, in all events, must be prepared for such an eventuality. It would be foolhardy for Israel to come out with an actual plan for a Palestinian state or even to state publicly that she "recognizes" such vague concepts as a "Palestinian entity," as some rather naive do-gooders have suggested she do. At the outset Israel should limit herself to stating clearly and unequivocally that she considers the Palestinians as partners for future negotiations in the same way that she is ready to negotiate with any Arab government. This would give an immense push to those Palestinians who are at present toying with the idea, but who would never come out into the open unless assured in advance that Israel will not turn them down flat.

The question, of course, arises as to who are the proper representatives of the Palestinians. Roughly speaking, one should name first the indigenous leadership on the West Bank, people like Ja'abri, the Mayor of Hebron; Hamdi Canaan, the ex-Mayor of Nablus; Hikmet al-Masri of Nablus, the former Speaker of the Jordanian Parliament; and many others. I myself, however, would be ready to go further. In Israel, any suggestion that Israel negotiate with the Palestinians is immediately challenged by the question: "Suppose Yassir Arafat wishes to negotiate; are you ready to sit down and talk with him?" I would answer in the affirmative, although, to be frank, I do not think there is any chance whatsoever that Arafat, given his maximalist program, would wish to negotiate with Israel. Of course, should a serious shift occur in Arafat's political posture, and should he then indicate a willingness to negotiate, I believe strongly that Israel—taking all the necessary precautions—should respond positively; an Arafat willing to negotiate with Israel would represent a very different political animal from the present Arafat, who is committed to her destruction.

It is naturally difficult, if not downright impossible, to spell out in detail what kind of relationship one would like to see emerging between Israel and the proposed Palestinian Arab state. In a way, the proposal itself goes back to the substance, though not to the details, of the principle at the root of the UN plan of 1947: since two national movements claim a relationship to the land, the most equitable solution would be partition. Seen from this angle, the question as posed today has very little to do with the traditional claims of traditional Zionism; whatever views one may entertain about the historical claims of Zionism, the issue today is existential, not historio-philosophic: there *are* two and a half million Jews in Israel who view it as their home, as the expression of their national self-consciousness. Just as it is impossible to overlook the legitimacy of Palestinian Arab nationalism, it is impossible to deny the same right to the Israelis.

Since the establishment of a Palestinian Arab state could today become possible only if the Palestinians on the West Bank accepted the legitimacy of Israel, one might hope that the relationship between these two states, if not cordial or friendly, could still be based on something approaching minimal decency. Ultimately one would probably like to see a federation established, but that is a long-term hope;

federation is based on mutual trust, a commodity conspicuously absent today but one which may be encouraged to develop through a less formal structure of cooperation between the two states. There is no doubt, for example, that part of Israel's burden in any accommodation with the Palestinians would be generous financial aid toward the rehabilitation of the refugees on the West Bank and in Gaza.

The inclusion of Gaza in the proposed Palestinian Arab state would, it is true, impose on the new state a territorial discontinuity, but I believe that preferable to the retention of Gaza by Israel. In human and political terms the Gaza Strip represents the most stubborn refugee problem of all, and Israel would lose any genuine chance of solving the problem if it tried to hold on to Gaza and its 250,000 refugees. In general, tempting as it may be for academics (myself included) to argue the fine points of an eventual settlement, it is at this stage a futile exercise. The first priority, for Israel and the Palestinians alike, is mutual recognition of the legitimacy of one another's national movement. Once mutual recognition is achieved, the territorial details, formidable as they may now appear, will lose much of their intractability.

There is, however, a more potent objection to the idea of establishing a Palestinian Arab state on the West Bank. This objection does not stem from considerations of ideology, but is based on the simple argument that so long as the Palestinians in other countries, mainly in Jordan east of the river, do not accept such a solution, it will, after all, solve nothing. The Palestinians on the West Bank and in Gaza may make their peace with Israel, but *Al Fatah,* or a section of it, will go on fighting Israel. What, then, will have been achieved? There is no doubt a very strong element of truth in this contention. But in putting forth a proposal for the establishment of a Palestinian state on the West Bank and in Gaza I have tried to be as pragmatic—and as minimalist—as possible, and have attempted to eschew more grandiose, and hence utopiàn, solutions. It would of course be ideal if Israel could make peace with *all* of the Palestinians; but if this is at the moment impossible, should she not at least try to achieve some kind of understanding with *some* of them? Nobody, after all, argues against a detente between the U.S. and the Soviet Union on the grounds that it will not solve the American dispute with China.

But to be more concrete: a situation in which about half the Palestinians will make peace with Israel is, after all, very different from a situation in which *all* of them reject Israel's legitimacy, lock, stock, and barrel. And a partial solution, in which some significant proportion of Palestinians can achieve self-determination, self-esteem, and dignity, and live peacefully with Israel, might point the way toward the acceptance of Israel by other Palestinians as well. There is no doubt that even moderate Palestinians—I have met many on the West Bank since the Six-Day War—are in a way forced into a posture of extremism by the total refusal of official Israel policy to accept their legitimate claims. It is a safe assumption that many Palestinian moderates in Jordan east of the river may similarly gravitate toward a less brutal solution than the one advocated by *Al Fatah* if they were given a chance by Israel to realize, even in a small Arab Palestine, their aspiration for self-assertion. . . .

It may be that mutual recognition between the two movements for national liberation, and the establishment of a Palestine Arab state on the West Bank, are a distant prospect. But as a possible solution, perhaps the only solution, to the clash between the two national movements, it is manifestly superior to, as well as more realistic than, the vague proposal, put forward in some quarters, for a "non-denominational," "bi-national" Palestine, in which Arabs and Jews would live peacefully side by side. In such a state, one community is bound to emerge as a majority, the other as a minority. As an Israeli, I certainly would not like to live as a member of a minority Jewish community in a country with an Arab majority; neither would I like to be a member of the Jewish majority in a country that had an Arab minority of about two million people. "Bi-nationalism," noble as it may sound, overlooks the dynamism of modern nationalism and in a way fails to take seriously both the Jewish and the Arab claim for nationhood and sovereignty. Cyprus and Nigeria provide two rather poor examples of bi- or multi-nationalism in a situation of tension; even Belgium and Canada show serious internal strains precisely because of the fact that "bi-nationalism" tends to institutionalize rather than to resolve tensions, suspicions, and national traumas. Arab nationalism, it should be noted, has been particularly nasty in its treatment of ethnic or religious minorities—as the examples of the Kurds in Iraq or of the blacks in Southern Sudan suffice to demonstrate.

Over the last century the Jews and the Palestinian Arabs have emerged into national movements, each craving a home, a place in the sun, a corner of the earth it can call its own. Throwing both of them into a state which would be neither Jewish nor Arab would make it impossible for either movement to overcome mutual tension and start cooperating with the other. A "bi-national" state, moreover, would run immediately into problems such as the relations between the Jewish sector and world Jewry, immigration, and links with the Arab world; how on earth could questions like these, which are at the root of the present conflict, ever be peacefully resolved within a single body politic? Instead of giving each national movement its due, a "bi-national" state would castrate and frustrate both national movements. Advocates of such a solution even overlook the fact that their program founders on the seemingly trivial but very fundamental question of name. Following *Al Fatah* propaganda, they take it for granted that their proposed state ("democratic," and "secular") would be called Palestine. But why should two-and--a-half million Israeli Jews consent to live in a state called Palestine, any more than two million Palestinian Arabs should consent to live in a state called Israel? When it comes to national movements, it is the grossest folly to ignore questions of consciousness—of symbols, dates, historic events, heroes, and national imagery. Both the Palestinians and the Israelis have rich national cultures, and both wish to develop those cultures and maintain their specific links to groups all over the world to which they feel allied: the Israelis to world Jewry, the Palestinians to the Arab world and Islam. In this connection, the example of Lebanon, which is often cited as a paradigm, is seriously misleading. For in Lebanon, the various groups—Muslims, Christians, Druzes—all consider themselves Arabs, use Arabic as their language, and relate directly to Arab culture and Arab history; their differences lie in the religious sphere. The Israelis, however, are emphatically *not* Arabs of the Jewish religion.

The conflict between Israel and the Arabs that arose in historic Palestine can come to an end if both protagonists will accept each other's legitimacy. Israel has to accept the legitimate claim of the Palestinian Arabs to a state of their own on the West Bank, ultimately also perhaps integrating Transjordan; the Palestinians have to accept the legitimacy of Israel. It is the tragedy of the Palestinians that at present every one of their organizations (PLO, *Al Fatah*, PFLP, PDFLP, *et al.*) denies the legitimacy of Israel and thus helps to frustrate any possible Israeli attempt to accommodate to the facts of Palestinian Arab nationalism. On the Israeli side, the great hope is the younger generation, which bears the brunt of the battle, and which is far more open-minded about the Palestinians than its elders; were the Israeli government to give some concrete expression to the mood of younger Israelis, an important step forward will have been taken. At that point it will be the turn of the Palestinian Arabs on the West Bank to take up the challenge, and by accepting the legitimacy of Israel pave the way for taking their place in that historic land which, for better or worse, they have to share with the Israelis.

One of the leading scholars of Arab nationalism, George Antonius, ended his *The Arab Awakening* in 1938 with the warning: "The logic of facts is inexorable. It shows that no room can be made in Palestine for a second nation except by dislodging or exterminating the nation in possession." Because the Arabs have behaved according to his formula, events have tended to prove Antonius right. But his words were nothing more than a self-fulfilling prophecy, and hence he shares, with many other Arab intellectuals who think like him, some of the moral responsibility for the tragedy of the Palestinians. Israelis and Palestinians *can* coexist in the area of historic Palestine, each in its own sovereign state. But the path to coexistence leads neither through the force of arms alone nor through the somewhat impotent channels of diplomacy. Since it is a conflict between two national movements, it is a conflict also over consciousness, and as Hegel rightly pointed out, such conflicts can be solved only through mutual recognition. This is the challenge which now confronts both Israelis and Palestinians.

NOTES

1 George Kennan's remarks on this subject in his *Memoirs, 1925–1950* are typical of the anti-Israeli attitude then prevalent in many circles of the government, and especially in the State Department. Quite a lot of this tradition is still alive and kicking in Foggy Bottom.

2 The above was written prior to the recent disclosure of Soviet air activity in Egypt. Disquieting as this development may be, it does not substantially affect the thrust of my argument here.

3 The tragic nature of the Arab-Israeli conflict is recognized by most Israeli writers on the subject, a recognition that gives their own nationalism a peculiarly introspective and liberal edge: they are able to perceive the point of view of the other side, even if they do not accept it. Among Arab intellectuals, on the other hand, very few perceive the conflict as tragic or see it as a conflict between *two* claims. One of the most sophisticated Arab writers on the subject, who otherwise brings to it a sensitivity rare among his compatriots, goes so far as to reject altogether the applicability of the tragic dimension, basing his rejection on the claim that tragedy is not "a Semitic idea." See Edward E. Said, "A Palestinian Voice," *Columbia Forum* (Winter 1969).

11

Violence in Ireland: Another Algeria?

CONOR CRUISE O'BRIEN

"The people have risen," according to Miss Bernadette Devlin.

"Polarization between Catholics and Protestants is complete," according to Mr. Tom Connaty, Chairman of the (Catholic) Central Citizens' Defense Committee in Belfast.

"The people" of whom Miss Devlin speaks are in fact the half-million Catholics of Northern Ireland. The Protestants, one million people, are not part of "the people" in the sense in which the various leaders, spokesmen, and pamphlets of the present insurrectionary movement are now actually using the term "the people."

There has been a change here. Two or three years ago, the leaders of the Civil Rights movement in Northern Ireland were actively—not just formally—discouraging the trend toward sectarian conflict between Protestant and Catholic. So was the Irish Republican Army—a left-oriented organization at that time. Then in vogue were various forms of a general theory that the civil rights conflicts and parallel militant activity on nonsectarian social issues would raise the level of consciousness of the working class (thought of as including Protestants and Catholics) and would eventually precipitate a genuine class war.

Vestiges of this concept remain in the language of the best known spokesmen—no longer really the leaders—of the Civil Rights successor movements when they address international audiences. But in reality no one any longer thinks in terms of revolutionary unity, of the solidarity of Protestant and Catholic workers. More and more openly, the real revolutionary leaders based in the Catholic ghettos acknowledge that the Protestant working class is a part of the enemy: they are not seen as Irish; they are settlers, *colons*.

Those who hold their view most plainly are the Provisional IRA: those who broke with the official leadership of the IRA in January, 1970, on the ground that that leadership was too Marxist, too theoretical, incompetent, insufficiently military, and insufficiently grounded in traditional Irish Republicanism. One of the ways in which the official leadership had been too theoretical was in its scrupulous care to avoid sectarian conflict, in conditions where sectarian conflict formed such a conspicuous part of the environment. The Provisionals accepted this fact of life from the beginning, and prospered accordingly in the Catholic ghettos. And the IRA "Officials," where they survived, did so by imitating the Provisionals.

The reality of a war of Catholics (natives) against Protestants (settlers) continues to be formally denied, but with less and less conviction. The socialist convictions or professions of so many of the revolutionary or militant intellectuals (including some of the more intellectual of the Provisionals) make a formally anti-sectarian position obligatory. More important, because affecting a deeper emotional level, is the Irish Republican tradition.

The founders of the Irish Republican tradition were Protestants, many of its earliest martyrs were Ulster Protestants. The IRA of today—both sections—were brought up on the writings and lives of these eighteenth-century men and women. But the militant Republicans now pursue an Irish national concept which—so far as any mass identification is concerned—has become a Catholic affair. And it is to these militant Republicans—the IRA—that the Catholics of the Northern ghettos look, as their defenders and, as they hope, their liberators. Defenders against or liberators from the Protestants, as far as the ordinary Belfast Catholic—not traditionally a Republican—is concerned.

The Republican defenders have increasingly accepted this role. But they have done so uneasily. They would much rather think of the struggle as one against England, against British imperialism, and they have had considerable success in making it look like that, especially in the present phase. To many people following events in Northern Ireland at a distance, through press and television, it must seem that the British army is waging a kind of war on the people of Northern Ireland, using tactics similar to those of the Black-and-Tans in the Twenties. This impression is partly correct. So far as the tactics used against Catholics are concerned the parallel has been, in some cases, shockingly close. Yet when the British troops were first deployed, in August, 1969, it was mainly for the protection of the Catholics—both in Belfast and Derry—against the sectarian police force of the Stormont regime and against armed Protestant mobs. At that time anyone could see—I saw it myself—

the Catholics welcoming the troops, fraternizing with them, offering them cups of tea.

Later, within the ghettos, the IRA in its new, more militantly aggressive form built itself up, with some help from Dublin and elsewhere, into a considerably more aggressive and somewhat better armed force than it had been in 1969. Ironically, this happened behind the screen which the British provided as a protection from the Stormont police apparatus. For the Catholic population generally the British troops were welcome in that capacity. But, from the viewpoint of the IRA they could not be welcome in any capacity. Harassment of the British troops and occasional skirmishes against them, fomented by the IRA, led to the inevitable results: retaliations often involving innocent people and arms searches in the ghetto, roughly conducted by troops determined to stand no nonsense from people who had shown themselves ungrateful for the protection they had received. As early as midsummer of last year relations between the Catholic population and the British troops were definitely bad: almost no trace remained of the friendliness of a year before.

This process was then speeded up by three factors, each of which reinforced the others. One was the change of government in England, bringing in the Tories, traditionally more sympathetic to the Northern Unionist oligarchy, and given to toughness in the repression of "lawlessness." The second was the anger of the Protestant population at the relative immunity which the IRA had seemed to enjoy behind the British army screen, the so-called "no-go" areas. The third was the increasing tempo of the IRA attacks on the British forces, and the killings of several soldiers, on and off duty.

The troops, originally restrained under provocation, were authorized to ease this restraint. Where CS gas had been the response to stone throwing, now a stone thrower might be shot dead on suspicion of being about to throw a bomb. After two such killings in Derry, the killing in Belfast of a completely innocent man, and the beating up by the soldiers of his equally innocent companion, the atmosphere in the Catholic areas of Northern Ireland by the second week of August this year [1971] was electric.

It was in these conditions that the Stormont government, with the concurrence of Westminster, started interning citizens without trial. Those who were interned were well-known activists—often not military activists—from the Catholic area exclusively (although Protestant terrorists had also been active against Catholics). Their arrests provoked an eruption of whole Catholic communities and a shoot-out between the British and the IRA, which soon ran out of ammunition. The greatly embittered resistance of the Catholic population then began to take the form of civil disobedience—mainly refusal to pay rents and taxes. This is announced as a nonviolent movement, but it seems improbable that the IRA will not try to make use of it, and regroup under cover of it. Whatever happens, and however tactics may change, the IRA is likely to remain for some time to come the main force in the ghettos of the North.

What can happen now? The IRA—especially the Provisional IRA
—is almost alone in having a fairly clear picture of what it thinks will
happen. The picture is like this:

The Catholics of Northern Ireland have become ungovernable.
This condition, and the inability of the army to deal with it, will
provoke such serious trouble among the Protestant community that
only a government of the far right (Paisley, Craig) will any longer be
acceptable to that community (the majority in Northern Ireland, on
which every government in Northern Ireland has always exclusively
rested). A government of the Protestant far right will not, however, be
acceptable to Britain, because damaging to Britain's international image.
Britain will therefore resort to direct rule, suspending or abolishing
the Stormont parliament. But direct rule also can be made unworkable.
The Catholics will be encouraged to resist it: their hopes for a united
Ireland will be all the higher after the abolition of the hated Stormont
system.

But the Protestants also will be disaffected and will resist the operation of direct rule. In these conditions, the pressure on Britain to disengage—a pressure already perceptible—will become irresistible. British
troops will be pulled out and then—possibly after an interval in which
a United Nations peace-keeping force will hold the lines in Northern
Ireland—Ireland will be united. The Protestants of Northern Ireland
are—in the belief of the IRA—hardheaded realists who will understand
that the game is up once the British pull out.

It is true that the Protestants are in a majority of almost two to
one in Northern Ireland but—as Mr. Rory O'Brady, the head of the
Provisionals, has stressed—they are in a minority of one to three and a
half in Ireland. So they will negotiate, find they can get satisfactory
guarantees, come to terms, accept their role in a United Ireland. A
small number of extremists who cannot accept this will emigrate to
Britain or elsewhere.

This scenario is quite credible, up to a point: that point is the
departure of the British troops. Even after that, it still seems credible to
some outside observers, relying on apparently close analogies: in Algeria,
for example, the *colons,* for all their bluster, made no attempt to stand
their ground once the French army was withdrawn. The Europeans of
Kenya and Zambia capitulated in the same way.

I believe that this analogy contains very serious flaws: so serious
that people thinking in these terms may inadvertently lead the Catholics
of Belfast to their doom. These flaws might be listed as follows:

Even if all Ireland is taken as the unit, the Protestants constitute a
much larger minority—more than twice as large—than did the Europeans of Algeria. They are also much more compact. They constitute a
clear majority in the densely populated eastern part of Northern Ireland, whereas Europeans did not form a majority in any city of Algeria.
(The Kenya and Zambia analogies being much less close may be ignored
here.)

The majorities and minorities in question are also qualitatively
different. The majority that Mr. Rory O'Brady is thinking of is made

up of both Southern and Northern Catholics. But most Southern Catholics, having had a very different historical experience from Northern Catholics, especially in the present century, are in only a rather vague sympathy with their Northern co-religionists. For centuries there have been important differences between the two groups. Fifty years of partition have widened these.

In the South, some politicians, some journalists are speaking and writing as if engaged in a kind of crusade: the *Irish Press* (controlled by President de Valera's son Vivian) has written of an impending "final solution." But so far there is little sign of a mass response proportionate to such appeals. There is not, in fact, anything like the same emotional solidarity among Irish Catholics generally (embracing both North and South) as there was among Algerian Moslems generally, preceding the independence of Algeria and the capitulation of the *colons*.

Moreover, the Protestants of Northern Ireland are not really very like the *colons*. As a community they are very much older. Their deepest roots go three times as deep: the colonization of Ulster began at the beginning of the seventeenth century, that of Algeria only toward the middle of the nineteenth century. In this regard, and many others, the Ulster Protestants are much more like Afrikaaners than they are like the former Algerian *colons*. They have an archaic but serviceable ideology, many generations of conditioning to a siege mentality, a blazingly simplified conception of history and of the history of their enemies. They also have a military tradition and are well armed.

In these conditions it seems to me extremely unlikely that these Protestants will simply cave in if the British troops pull out. It seems much more likely that if that happened, the Protestants, resisting incorporation into an Irish state, would try to fend off such an outcome by crushing the Northern Catholics. Specifically, they would go into the Catholic areas of Belfast—where Catholics are heavily outnumbered—looking for the IRA and its weapons. As they would be resisted, and would be uninhibited in their response to resistance, the outcome could only be the liquidation of the Catholics of Belfast, sectarian mass murder throughout the province generally, and the intervention of the small army of the Irish Republic in the South.

This army would be capable of restoring order to the Catholic-majority border areas of the present Northern Ireland, but not capable of subduing the hard-core Protestant industrial area including Greater Belfast. A cease-fire line would become a new border. The new Northern Ireland would be smaller, but it would have no Catholic minority. In both parts of Ireland such a struggle would bring right-wing extremists to the top, Green and Orange forms of fascism.

It is easier to see that this is where the combined escalation of violence must lead than it is to see how it can be averted. Far-reaching reform to assure the Northern Catholics of their political rights, at the insistence of London, seemed probable—and did begin—after August, 1969.[1] The IRA revival and its inevitable repercussions set it back. It may be that it is now too late for reform, that Northern Ireland—and Ireland generally—is now on a collision course. Yet this is not necessarily so: there are many people, in both communities, who see the full extent of the danger—and actual experience of the results of limited violence may well increase their numbers.

I have argued elsewhere (*The Times,* London, August 14) that any settlement that could hope to bring peace to the area would have to include granting power to Catholics in Northern Ireland in proportion to their numbers. It would also have to include a clear recognition by the Dublin parliament of the legitimacy of a Northern Ireland in which the Catholic minority received such a degree of recognition and power. This would mean that Belfast would have to drop the idea of "a Protestant parliament for a Protestant people," and Dublin would have to drop the quest for imposed political unification.

At the moment the Lynch government combines nominal support for the minority's civil disobedience campaign with a reiteration of the claim for unification and tolerance for IRA activities inside the Republic directed against Northern Ireland. It would be hard to think of a better formula for uniting Ulster Protestants against any concessions to the minority, but these Lynch positions constitute a reflex to the Heath government's get-tough-with-Catholics policy. Genuine reforms in Northern Ireland on a scale sufficient to impress the elected representatives of the Northern minority would certainly elicit a positive response in Dublin.

Moreover the majority of the population in the Republic are appalled by the news from the North and clearly more interested in seeing peace return there than in the unification claim. But if any progress is to be made in the desired direction the initiative must come from London, which should recast the political structure of Northern Ireland so as to include the Catholics and request Dublin to acknowledge the legitimacy of this reconstituted entity and to cooperate in deterring attempts to subvert it. These things are within the bounds of possibility and the London government should seek to secure them.

Those who can influence the Tory government should seek to influence it in that direction, not just in the direction of pulling out the troops. Everyone would like to see the troops out, but what is important is to create political conditions such that the troops can leave without precipitating massacres. It will be very hard to create such conditions, but as long as a serious possibility of doing so remains—and I believe it still does—to call for absolute and unconditional withdrawal of the troops, as a section of the British left, among others, is now doing, is cruelly irresponsible.

In all such discussions, the Algerian parallel plays little specific or overt part. But the general idea of decolonization plays a very important part. Both the Irish press and an important sector of the British press regularly evoke in connection with Northern Ireland the image of the imperial flag being pulled down in so many places, the departure or capitulation of so many one-time loyalists. Most of these stories bear little or no relation to Northern Ireland: the comparison of Britain's role in Northern Ireland to that of the United States in Vietnam, for example, is merely a street orator's weapon.

Among decolonization situations, the closest parallel is Algeria. I have tried to show that that apparent parallel is dangerously misleading. Northern Ireland is unique: a long, grim history has made it so. The measures to be taken for it and in it should be specific to its problems, not just the application of routines applied elsewhere. To places like the Kingdom of Ashanti the British came for the first time, and went forever, during the lifetime of one man. But Ulster Protestants have been in Ulster as long as white men have been in what is now the United States. And Irish Catholics have been there, coping with the English Question, much longer still.

NOTE

1 Northern Ireland is the poorest part of the United Kingdom, and Catholics make up a larger proportion of the poor than of the total population. It is not, however, true to say that the roots of the problem are economic. There are more poor Protestants than there are poor Catholics and appeals for class solidarity across religious lines have been a total failure. Well-off Catholics are as disaffected as poor ones and poor Protestants are as loyal as rich ones. See Richard Rose's recent illuminating study *Governing Without Consensus* (Faber & Faber, 1971).

PART
II
The Burden of the Strong

We turn now from the tensions between great and weak powers and between groups of differing ethnic and ideological identification to a discussion of relations between the great powers. In the Nixon–Kissinger era, American policy has been redirected toward increased interest in the great powers: the Soviet Union in particular, but also China, Japan, and Europe. This perspective contrasts with a greater interest during the 1960s in the patterns and developments within the Third World. The Nixon Administration seems to have believed that the creation of a balance of power among the major states would produce a more stable international system, at least on the higher levels where America's interests are most directly affected. In Part II we first examine bilateral relations among specific great powers and then move on to assess the vision of a balance among great powers and to consider whether or not such a balance can be achieved without weaker state support; finally, we analyze the effect of great-power armaments policies in the international milieu.

The first section opens with a consideration of Soviet–American relations in Hans Morgenthau's profile of the options which both major powers face in their relations with each other. This article was written before the improvement in Sino–American relations, a development which has placed greater pressure on the Soviet Union. It was also written before the Moscow summit conference between President Nixon and Communist Party Chief Brezhnev in May 1972. At that conference the United States and the Soviet Union reached major agreements concerning nuclear arms control (which will be discussed shortly) and agreed to a declaration of principles governing their relations with weaker countries as a means of limiting the likelihood of direct confrontation around the globe. The two leaders also ratified a large number of agreements relating to matters of health, the environment, science, technology, and space, including the announcement of a joint docking between Soviet and American spacemen in 1975. Finally, they laid the groundwork for later trade agreements between the two countries, agreements which have since progressed apace. One of the unique aspects of this summit was that the Soviets allowed it to occur even though the United States had mined the harbor of Haiphong barely two weeks before. Though Morgenthau's article does not deal with these later developments, he demonstrates the basic dynamics of Soviet–American relations and the pressures which have since led to agreements. The United States and the Soviet Union have certainly not achieved a condominium over world events, but for domestic as well as international reasons they have both found it in their interests to limit the scope of their competition, a competition which nevertheless persists.

Though China is far from equal in power to either the United States or the Soviet Union, its relations with both affect the nature of the global balance of power. China's improving relations with the United States and the continuing intensity of the Sino–Soviet conflict have meant greater flexibility for the United States and increased pressure upon the USSR. Richard Lowenthal appraises the state of the Sino–Soviet dispute, the geographical, historical, ideological, doctrinal, and power elements of the conflict. Though his article, like Morgenthau's, was written before the Nixon trips to Peking and Moscow and the normalization of Sino–Japanese relations during 1972, the basic issues in the Sino–Soviet controversy remain unchanged. His analysis of the alternative directions which the conflict may take is therefore still applicable. He also considers the balancing role of the United States in the conflict, a role which has become more central to world politics since the visit which Allen Whiting describes in the article that follows. Whiting reviews the major developments of President Nixon's trip to Peking in February 1972, a trip which symbolized not only a turning point in Asia but a dramatic alteration of great-power politics throughout the world.

Finally, George Ball takes a look at Japanese–American relations, which have become more fluid as a result of American initiatives toward China and the Soviet Union. He argues that "we are playing a dangerous game with Japan" and proceeds to illuminate the delicate nature of Japanese–American relations, especially considering Japanese economic strength, U.S. pressures for Japanese assistance with its balance of payments problems, and American inattention to Japanese concerns. The fluidity of Japanese–American relations is further symbolized by the establishment of diplomatic relations between China and Japan by the new Japanese government under Prime Minister Tanaka in September 1972.

Having reviewed the state of relations among individual great powers, we move to the next section of Part II, which comprises two examinations of the state of the great-power balance and its relation to the rest of the world. Richard Barnet, an American critic of the Nixon Administration's foreign policy, examines the Nixon dream of a "generation of peace," demonstrates the ways in which it differs from previous administration policies, and analyzes the issues on which present tactics and aims are consistent with earlier patterns. He considers "big power deals" and technology as essential ingredients of the Nixon Doctrine. Next a European, Alastair Buchan, explores both the adequacies and deficiencies of the Nixon concept, which views the United States, the Soviet Union, Japan, China, and Europe in a state of potential balance. Buchan concentrates particularly on the two evolving multiple balances in Europe and East Asia. Both Barnet and Buchan conclude their examinations with warnings about the reaction of weaker states to a constellation of great-power arrangements. Barnet condemns the "politics of indifference," while Buchan stresses the United Nations and local groupings as means of giving weaker states a stronger voice in world affairs.

In the third and final section of Part II we turn to the most significant single element in great-power relations: the existence of nuclear weapons. Both Soviet and American policies have been moderated by fear of the nuclear holocaust that could be precipitated by a direct confrontation. The United States and the Soviet Union both possess invulnerable second strike capabilities; each is currently capable of wreaking unacceptable retaliation by killing millions of citizens resident on its adversary's territory if attacked. Neither side at present maintains a first strike capability sufficient to prevent such a frightening retaliatory blow. The SALT talks, the first phase of which reached a culmination at the 1972 Moscow summit, represented a recognition by both sides of these conditions and a parallel desire to limit the nuclear arms race so that they could avoid some of the considerable expenditures that technology demanded—e.g., for anti-ballistic missiles (ABM's) and multiple independently targetable reentry vehicles (MIRV's)—expenditures that would only result in bringing the two powers back to a condition of parity that they had already achieved. The first phase of the SALT talks limited ABM's but not MIRV's. Benjamin Lambeth reviews the accomplishments of SALT I and the possibilities of the future as he assesses the state of Soviet–American nuclear relations.

George Quester discusses the effects of possible nuclear proliferation upon international affairs, especially given the fact that two of the five nuclear powers (China and France) have not signed the nonproliferation treaty. He also pays special attention to South Africa, which not only did not sign the treaty but is also one of the world's three major suppliers of uranium. Quester has important things to say about the effect of nuclear proliferation on both great-power relations and local disputes. Nuclear proliferation could radically alter the course of world politics, reversing the present trend toward concentration by the great powers on one another by forcing the great powers to return to a preoccupation with small states.

Competitors and Allies: Pas de Deux

12

Changes and Chances in American-Soviet Relations

HANS J. MORGENTHAU

Our reactions to Soviet foreign policy have a way of jumping from one extreme to another, both in the long and short run, with more regard for changing superficial appearances than permanent objective factors. During the last year of the Second World War, we tended to idealize the Russians, Stalin became "Uncle Joe" to be charmed by Roosevelt into cooperation, and the United Nations, having done away with "power politics," was supposed to be the vehicle of that coöperation. From 1947 onwards, the Kremlin was perceived as the headquarters of the devil on earth, causing all that was wrong with the world and, more particularly, scheming the destruction of the United States. These extreme swings of the pendulum can also be observed in much shorter time spans.

On August 27, 1970, *The New York Times* reported from San Clemente that "authoritative White House sources have declared that the United States is prepared to join the Soviet Union in a two-nation peacekeeping force to maintain a settlement of the Middle East conflict. . . ." The reader was left with the clear inference that both the President and Mr. Henry Kissinger, his adviser on national security, had something to do with this statement. If Mr. Nixon had made such a statement ten years ago, it would have been judged at best to be utterly eccentric and at worst might have jeopardized the then Vice President's political career, and if Professor Kissinger had made such a statement 20 years ago, the House Un-American Activities Committee might have investigated him as a likely subversive.

Yet less than a month passed, and the atmosphere was drastically transformed. For the Soviet Union had not only violated the ceasefire agreement in the Middle East on a massive scale but seemed to have intended doing so from the outset. Furthermore, the Soviet Union was suspected to be building a submarine base in Cuba. Thus, Secretary of State Rogers, at his news conference of December 23, 1970, discounted as "totally impractical" the idea of such a peacekeeping force as had been adumbrated in August and denied that the United States had ever given any thought to such a possibility.

Yet beneath these fluctuations of mood and tactics the perennial question about the future of American-Soviet relations persists in demanding an answer: Is it possible to move from sterile confrontation to meaningful negotiations? While 20 years ago such a question was purely rhetorical since the negative answer was a foregone conclusion, it can now be asked seriously, and it deserves a serious answer, derived not from the changing mood of the day but from the objective factors which in the long run determine the relations among nations. What has happened during the last 20 years to account for the possibility of posing that crucial question seriously?

II

Five factors have transformed the relations between the United States and the Soviet Union: the rejection of nuclear war as an instrument of national policy; the ideological decontamination of foreign policy at least with respect to each other; the failure of the competition for the allegiance of the third world; the implicit recognition by the United States of the status quo in Eastern Europe; and the Chinese threat to the Soviet Union.

The fear of mutual destruction through nuclear war has imposed effective restraints upon the foreign policies of the superpowers in two respects: the avoidance of direct military confrontation and, when it inadvertently occurs, its speedy liquidation. The United States has fought in Korea and Vietnam wars for limited objectives, falling short of military victory, because of the fear of such a confrontation. It has kept its hands off a series of East European revolts against Soviet domination. For the same reason, the Soviet Union has not followed up with action its repeated demands—twice in the form of ultimatums with a precise time limit—for a change in the status quo of West Berlin. In the Middle East, Russia has come close to a military confrontation with America, but the latter has not responded in kind, and both powers have joined in an initiative to restore peace. When there was military confrontation during the Cuban missile crisis of 1962, both sides went as far as they dared without compelling the other side to take steps that might lead to nuclear war, and retraced their steps in partial retreat.

Sharing the conviction of the suicidal irrationality of nuclear war, the United States and the Soviet Union have thus in a sense helped each other to avoid it; they appear to have concluded that the sole legitimate purpose of nuclear arms is not to win a nuclear war but to deter it. Nevertheless, they have continued an unlimited nuclear arms race as though there did not exist an optimum of nuclear preparedness sufficient for deterrence, beyond which to go is utterly irrational. They have thus pursued the rational goal of nuclear deterrence with the irrational means of an unlimited nuclear arms race. Recognizing this irrationality, they have joined in the Strategic Arms Limitation Talks (SALT), searching for an agreement which could bring the nuclear arms race under control.

While the United States and the Soviet Union have begun to deal with each other as one great power with another, having certain interests in common and being at loggerheads with regard to others, there was a time, not much more than a decade ago, when we took the communist dogma much more seriously as a guide to policy than did, for instance, Stalin, who with utter cynicism and brutality used communism and communists as a means to further the traditional ends of the Russian state. Yet we saw in Stalin the heir of Trotsky who was out to accomplish the communization of the world, begun in Eastern Europe at the end of the Second World War, while in truth Stalin was the heir of the Tsars, seeking the traditional goals of Imperial Russia with the new instruments communism put at his disposal. The Russians, in turn, interpreted our insistence upon democratic governments in Eastern Europe and our verbal commitment to "rollback" and "liberation" as evidence of the undying hostility of capitalism which since 1917 had used every opportunity to try to destroy the Soviet Union.

The emancipation of American and Soviet foreign policies from these dogmatic ideological stereotypes—again I must emphasize, limited to their mutual relations—has been the result of the impact the facts of life have made upon the thoughts and actions of the governments concerned. Foremost among these facts has been their failure to win the ideological allegiance of the nations of the third world in Africa, Asia and Latin America. The third world was supposed to be the decisive battleground in the struggle for men's minds, a struggle which would decide the fate of the world. Khrushchev, for instance, used to assure us that the third world would follow the lead of the Soviet Union and thereby seal the doom of the West. Nothing of the kind happened. The new nations of the third world have apparently preferred to be miserable in their own way to being made happy by the United States or the U.S.S.R.

This failure of ideological competition has led both superpowers to the conclusion that it is not worth the expense and the risk of a direct military confrontation, and they have given it up. The absence of any ideological reference and the explicit disavowal of ideological commitment in President Nixon's message to Congress on the state of the world of March of last year [1970] at least provides verbal evidence of this fundamental change in our approach to certain aspects of foreign policy. On the other hand, the Soviet Union has banished, a few exceptions to the contrary notwithstanding, ideological considerations from its policies in the third world. It has [had] very close relations with the United Arab Republic whose communists are in jail, and it supports Latin American dictators against their communist parties, which are in turn supported by Cuba, the ally of the Soviet Union. That is to say, it practices old-fashioned power politics, unencumbered by ideological considerations.

It is part and parcel of this victory of the facts of life over ideological blinders that the United States has for all practical purposes recognized the Soviet predominance in Eastern Europe. True enough, we have contained the Soviet Union at the line of military demarcation of 1945; but now we and the Soviet Union realize that the United States, too, has been contained at that very same line. This realization has removed from the cold war its main issue: the territorial status quo, especially with regard to the two Germanys. The recent treaty between the Soviet Union and West Germany makes explicit what had been implicit in the policies of the two superpowers: the recognition by all concerned of the territorial boundaries established at the end of the Second World War. This normalization of East-West relations in Europe has also deprived the status of West Berlin of much of the leverage which Stalin and Khrushchev used against the West. They threatened the status quo of West Berlin in order to compel the West to recognize the territorial status quo in Eastern Europe. Since that recognition has now been forthcoming, the status of West Berlin as a pawn in the hands of the Soviet Union has markedly decreased, although it still retains its usefulness as an instrument of annoyance.

Finally, even if these two developments had not greatly contributed to stability in Europe, the Soviet Union would have a vital interest in such stability. For the Soviet Union must cope at its Chinese frontier with endemic instability which might well escalate into war, and in such a contingency it must be reasonably certain that its western frontiers are secure. It needs that certainty in particular because its élite is obsessed with the fear the Americans will gang up with the Chinese. The Russian leaders suffer from the same "cauchemar des coalitions" which disturbed Bismarck's sleep (only he had better reasons than they). Thus they are not likely to provoke the United States in Europe as long as the insecurity at their eastern frontiers persists.

Considering the beneficial impact these factors have had on the relations between the United States and the Soviet Union, it is tempting to conclude that, undisturbed by contrary tendencies, these factors will continue to exert their pacifying and normalizing effect. This conclusion is particularly tempting for those who have conceived of our relations with the Soviet Union primarily, if not exclusively, in ideological, that is, anti-communist terms. Since we do not need to worry any more about the Soviet Union as the spearhead of communism bent upon destroying us, so the argument runs, there is really nothing at all to worry about. This position, simple if not simplistic and superficially attractive since it caters to our wishes, is, however, vulnerable to three arguments: the elimination of ideological considerations from our foreign policy is partial, and tenuous where it exists; the power politics of the Soviet Union contains residues of ideological commitment; the U.S.S.R. is a great power whose interests and the policies serving it, regardless of ideology, may run counter to the interests of the United States and the policies serving it.

Nor does the ideological decontamination of our relations with the Soviet Union signify that our foreign policy has been altogether freed of its ideological ingredients. We still think about foreign policy in demonological terms and allow our actions to be influenced by them. Why are we fighting in Indochina? In order to prevent the communist takeover of South Vietnam is the official answer. Why did we send our troops to the Dominican Republic? Because we cannot have another communist government in the Western Hemisphere, said President Johnson. Thus it appears that the struggle against communism still influences our actions. Only the devil's place of residence has changed. He could at a moment's notice move back to the Kremlin, and his reappearance in his old haunts would rekindle the ideological animosity between the United States and the Soviet Union. As William Graham Sumner put it: "The amount of superstition is not much changed, but it now attaches to politics, not religion," and, one can add, it attaches to one locale rather than another as circumstances seem to require.

This propensity for political demonology finds support in the nature of the Soviet state and the foreign policies it pursues. It is true that since Stalin the Soviet Union has used ideological factors as means to the end for the Soviet state and in consequence has been able to switch with great alacrity its ideological preferences and stigmatizations from one country to the other. Thus the German "fascist beasts" became comrades-in-arms against Western imperialism after the Molotov-Ribbentrop past of August 1939, and the "neo-fascists" and "revanchists" of West Germany transformed themselves into respectable partners, once they were willing to recognize the territorial status quo. China was embraced as a junior partner in the world communist movement as long as it was satisfied with that junior position. It was read out of the Marxist-Leninist camp altogether when it struck out on its own in competition with the Soviet Union.

But it is also true that the Soviet Union regards itself not only as one nation among others but also as the "Fatherland of Socialism," the leader of all "progressive" forces throughout the world. It is this position, now to be maintained against China's competitive claims, that imposes upon Soviet foreign policy certain ideological burdens which the Soviet Union would not need to bear if it conceived of its national interests in strictly traditional terms. What happens in Cuba has no bearing upon the interests of the Russian state traditionally conceived, but it bears heavily upon the position of the Soviet Union as leader of the "progressive" forces of the world. For that reason, the Soviet Union subsidizes Cuba to the tune of approximately $1,000,000 a day even though Castro supports subversion and civil war against the very Latin American governments with which the Soviet Union deals on a pragmatic basis. It is for the same reason that the Soviet Union supports

North Vietnam with military aid, carefully limited so as not to provoke
the United States to escalate the war, but sufficient to prevent an American victory.

Thus the ideological conflict between the United States and the
Soviet Union is not dead but only dormant. As long as the interests of
the two superpowers do not openly clash, the ideological conflict may
remain in its present state of suspended animation. But if and when
one superpower shall again openly encroach upon the interests of the
other, the ideological demons are also likely to be awakened from their
slumber. Here is indeed the crux of the future relations between the
United States and the Soviet Union. Can they pursue their respective
interests without encroaching upon each other's?

III

Since the downfall of Khrushchev, the Soviet Union has unobtrusively
and effectively expanded its political and military influence in the eastern Mediterranean, the Middle East, South Asia and the Indian Ocean
in the best tradition of great-power politics and has enhanced its economic influence throughout the world in the best tradition of a capitalist
trading nation. The pattern of that expansion has been constant: Russia
has moved into the spaces left by the liquidation of the British and
French Empires, thereby bringing close to consummation the Tsarist
aspirations which during the better part of the nineteenth century had
pitted Russia against Great Britain over the "Eastern Question."

Yet there are less spectacular and potentially as important achievements as well. The following story from the London *Financial Times*
of February 14, 1968, points out that Moscow has seen considerable
commercial advantage to gain from the blockage of the Suez Canal.
Across the Soviet Union lie "straight-line" routes from Western Europe
to most of Asia, and the Russians are beginning to exploit this fact.

> Already [the Russians] have developed two alternative water routes of
> their own to the East—the waterway system linking the Baltic Sea with
> the Caspian, and the Northern Sea route from Europe through the Arctic
> Ocean to the Pacific. Distances by these routes are shorter than via Suez
> (unlike the corresponding Cape journeys) and in the event of a long
> closure could well capture some of the traffic permanently. Iran's use of
> the Baltic-Caspian waterway has reached an advanced stage already. This
> route . . . is cutting 2,700 miles off the Suez route between Germany
> and Iran.

The *Financial Times* goes on to report that Russia had also announced that she would be "opening her previously tightly guarded
Arctic shipping lane across the top of Siberia to foreign ships." Such
a new sea route would put Yokohama only 8,500 miles from London
whereas the Suez passage totals 12,500 miles.

Instead of remembering how in the sixteenth century the center
of power shifted from the Mediterranean to the nations bordering on
the Atlantic in consequence of the opening of new trade routes, we
have been hypnotized by the ideological aspects of the Indochina war.

While we put our minds to beating the Russian communists to the moon and keeping the Vietnamese communists out of Saigon, the Soviet Union has occupied much of the middle ground between these cosmic and parochial goals. Thus the absence of open conflict between the United States and the Soviet Union or, to put it in positive terms, the improvement in U.S.-Soviet relations is in good measure the result not of the settlement of outstanding issues or of the absence of points of conflict, but of American failure to compete with and oppose a Soviet Union steadily expanding its power throughout the world. What looks to the naïve and the wishful thinkers as a new harmonious phase in American-Soviet relations is in truth a by-product of our military involvement in Indochina. We have been too busy with trying to save Indochina from communism to pay much attention to what the U.S.S.R. was doing in the rest of the world and to compete with it or oppose it as our interests require.

As long as our main national energies and human and natural resources remain absorbed by Indochina, we will continue to enjoy "good" relations with the Soviet Union. The "good" quality of these relations will be the result not of the identity or the parallelism of interests derived from the settlement of outstanding issues, but of letting the defense and promotion of our interests go by default. After all, it takes two to quarrel. If one side does not object to what the other is doing, there will be harmony, but it can be harmony at the former's expense. Thus, paradoxically enough, the lack of controversy in American-Soviet relations results in good measure from the pathological inversion of our national priorities caused by our involvement in the Indochina war. Once we terminate that involvement and conduct our foreign policies again on the basis of the rational assessment and ordering of our national interests, we are likely to find ourselves again in competition and conflict with the Soviet Union.

IV

Four issues, if they are not settled, are likely to revive the competition and opposition between America and Russia: the nuclear arms race, the status of Germany, the balance of power in the Middle East, and the ferment in the third world.

The restraints which the fear of mutual destruction has imposed upon the foreign policies of the United States and the Soviet Union are predicated upon the certainty of that destruction. That is to say, they depend upon what Churchill called a "balance of terror," in which B, after having suffered unacceptable damage from nuclear attack by A, would still be able with what remained of its retaliatory nuclear force to inflict unacceptable damage upon A, and vice versa. It is this psychological conviction that a nuclear war is a genocidal and suicidal absurdity which has preserved the peace and at least a modicum of order in the relations of the superpowers.

However, the indefinite persistence of this conviction cannot be taken for granted. It is threatened by two assumptions: that one or the

other side has acquired a first-strike capability which would destroy
the enemy's retalitory capability or at worst reduce it to tolerable proportions, and that one or the other side or both sides have developed
a defensive system which at worst would reduce nuclear damage to
tolerable proportions. It is irrelevant for the purpose of this discussion
whether or not these assumptions are correct; it is sufficient that they
might be held. If they were held, they would be bound to exacerbate
drastically the nuclear competition between the United States and the
Soviet Union; for them the question before us would no longer be the
relatively simple one of maintaining mutual deterrence, but how to
assure for oneself, and deny to the enemy, the ability to wage a successful nuclear war. The restraints which, as we have seen, have characterized the foreign policies of the superpowers would then follow mutual
deterrence into oblivion; for the avoidance of nuclear war appears
no longer as a precondition for physical survival if a nation is convinced that it can win a nuclear war either through irresistible attack
or impenetrable defense.

It is this dire possibility that makes the success of the SALT talks,
seeking a way to control the nuclear arms race, so crucially important
for the future of American-Soviet relations. If they fail, a drastic deterioration of these very relations is likely to result. If they succeed,
they will not only have stabilized the nuclear arms race on a level sufficient for mutual deterrence, though not for a first strike or effective
defense, but they will also have demonstrated the ability of the two
superpowers to translate their common interest in survival into opera-
tive policies.

While this issue, overshadowing all others, is still in the balance,
the normalization of the relations between West Germany and the
Soviet Union through the former's recognition of the territorial status
quo has brought to the fore a conventional issue which touches the
vital interests of both the United States and the Soviet Union: the
future orientation of West Germany. Almost 20 years ago, West Germany joined the Western alliance in order to contain the Soviet Union
and to assure powerful backing for its claim to be the sole legitimate
representative of the whole German people, East and West. It succeeded
in the first, and failed in the second, objective. That failure was due to
the East German government's staying power and the Soviet determination to contain the West at the 1945 demarcation line.

For West Germany, however, the relations with East Germany
and West Berlin have remained crucial. Bonn has come to recognize
that the only power which can improve and secure these relations is
the Soviet Union. By the same token, the Soviet Union knows that the
security of its European empire depends upon West Germany's position. A West Germany which is the dissatisfied spearhead of a hostile
alliance is a constant threat; a neutralized and friendly West Germany
is an invaluable asset. For a Russo-German combination would become the master of the Eurasian land mass, reducing what remains of
Western Europe to an insignificant promontory. This has been the
long-range aim of Soviet foreign policy at least since Khrushchev.

Khrushchev expressed time and again in private conversation his conviction that there would be another Rapallo, that is, another understanding between Germany and the Soviet Union after the model of the Rapallo Treaty of 1922; that it would come not under him and not under his successor but under his successor's successor; that it was inevitable; and that the Soviet Union could wait. The Soviet Union, in the treaty with West Germany recently concluded, has taken the first step in the direction sketched by Khrushchev.

This treaty, on the face of it, performs the function of a peace treaty—a quarter of a century overdue—in which West Germany recognizes explicitly the territorial status quo of 1945. This recognition has been implicit in the policies which West Germany and the United States have pursued for two decades vis-à-vis the Soviet Union and the nations of Eastern Europe, but the revisionary rhetoric accompanying it, especially in the 1950s, could not help but create doubts as to whether that implicit recognition could be relied upon if opportunities for a change in the territorial status quo should arise. These doubts have now been laid to rest.

However, it is hardly necessary to point out that the development so confidently predicted by Khrushchev would run counter to the interests of the United States and would nullify the policies Washington has pursued in Europe since the end of the Second World War; for it was the major aim of these policies to prevent all of Germany from being drawn into the Russian orbit. In the course of such a development, the Soviet Union, by replacing the United States as the predominant power in Western Europe, would achieve another of its long-term aims: the expulsion of the United States from Europe.

Here is indeed a potential source of serious conflict between the United States and the Soviet Union. Whether or not that conflict will materialize depends upon two factors: what other steps may follow after the initial step taken by the Soviet Union and West Germany, and whether the United States, remaining aware of those interests in Europe over which it fought the cold war, is still willing to support those interests with appropriate policies. As concerns the last point, domestic support for the proposal to reduce drastically our military presence in West Germany must give us pause.

At present it is the Middle East which appears the most obvious point at which the interests and policies of the United States and the Soviet Union appear to collide. The Soviet Union seeks to maintain and expand its predominant presence in the region, while the United States tries to contain it. In order to realize its aim the Soviet Union must support the Arab aspirations up to the point where the survival of Israel is in jeopardy; for much of the Soviet leverage in the Arab world depends upon the continuation of the enmity between the Arabs and Israel. Paradoxically enough, the Soviet Union has an interest in the survival of Israel, however precariously placed in the midst of continuing Arab hostility. On the other hand, the United States, too, is interested in the survival of Israel, secured through the acceptance of the Arab states; for such acceptance would reduce the Soviet leverage to a minimum and improve the chances for American influence re-asserting itself. Thus American and Soviet interests with regard to Israel are both contradictory and run for quite different reasons along parallel lines. They make for conflict as well as coöperation.

The third possible point of friction between the United States and the Soviet Union, the revolutionary ferment in the third world, differs from the others in that it is highly speculative. In theory, both super-powers are committed to incompatible positions on this issue. The Soviet Union has repeatedly come out in favor of "wars of national liberation," while the United States favors stability, which means in concrete terms the defense of the status quo against revolution from the Left. In consequence of these incompatible positions, the United States and the Soviet Union have found themselves on opposite sides of the fence in the Congo, the Middle East, Cuba, Vietnam. But, as pointed out before with regard to Latin America, the Soviet Union has not hesitated to abandon this position in favor of a pragmatic pursuit of its national interests as a great power. And the United States, after the Indochinese experience, is not likely to intervene openly in Africa or Latin America in order to defend the established order against rev-olutionary change. In view of the abatement of ideological commitment on both sides, this source of friction may appear remote at present, but it might become acute overnight if an unforeseen event, domestic or international, should suddenly awaken the slumbering ideological pas-sions.

The amicable or at least peaceful settlement of the substantive issues outstanding between the United States and the Soviet Union is greatly complicated and under certain conditions may well be jeopard-ized by a peculiarity of the Soviet approach to negotiated settlements. The Soviet Union has been painstaking in keeping the agreements—both political and commercial—that were in its interests to keep, and this is about all one can expect from any nation; for all nations will disregard—either openly or surreptitiously—those agreements which no longer serve their interests. It is peculiar to the Soviet approach to negotiated settlements to enter sometimes into such settlements with the intention not to honor them. It is one thing to disregard agreements when they no longer serve one's purposes; it is quite another to pledge one's word to an agreement with the intention not to honor it. The former is accepted diplomatic practice, however morally repugnant. The latter is treachery—Gromyko assuring Kennedy of the absence of Russian missiles in Cuba while the President had photographic evi-denc to the contrary; the Soviet Union agreeing to a ceasefire for the Middle East and violating the agreement at the very moment of its coming into operation. The experience and the resulting expectation of such treachery may well make the difference between accord and con-flict and, when the chips are down, between peace and war.

Thus the future of American-Soviet relations is shrouded in un-certainty. Neither amity nor enmity is foreordained. Those who pro-claim the inevitability of conflict on ideological grounds are as wrong as are those who assert the inevitability of peace, or even friendship, because the United States and the Soviet Union have become more restrained in words and deeds in dealing with each other. The future depends first of all upon how the two governments conceive of their respective interests and how they will go about defending and protecting them. If they conceive of them in compatible terms and pursue them with appropriate concern for each other's sensibilities, the future might well witness the realization of Roosevelt's dream, Stalin's grand design, and Mao's nightmare: the coöperation of the United States and the Soviet Union in establishing and maintaining a modicum of order in the world. Otherwise, the world will continue to hover on the brink of self-destruction.

The outcome, however, will no longer depend exclusively upon the actions of the superpowers vis-à-vis each other, but to an increasing extent upon the actions of secondary power centers—China, Japan, West Germany, either alone or in concert with a politically and militarily united Europe—and the reactions of the two superpowers to them. Thus the issues dividing the two superpowers will remain susceptible to peaceful settlements only in the measure that the superpowers are able to prevent their relations with the secondary power centers from exacerbating their relations with each other. When they deal with each other, they must also, as it were, look over their shoulders to see what other nations are doing and to anticipate what they are likely to do. While the freedom of manoeuvre which the secondary power centers are likely to enjoy will introduce a new element of uncertainty and risk into the relations between the superpowers, concern with the interests and policies of the secondary powers may well strengthen the self-restraint with which America and Russia have been dealing with each other because of the fear of nuclear war.

13

Russia and China:
Controlled Conflict

RICHARD LOWENTHAL

It is now eleven years since an ideological dispute between the Chinese and Soviet communist parties burst into the open on the occasion of the 90th anniversary of Lenin's birth, and almost eight years since the pattern of world affairs became definitely "triangular" with the open break between the two leading communist powers. Since then, the view of some Western dogmatists that personal rivalry between Khrushchev and Mao Tse-tung for the control of "world communism" was the only cause of the rift was plainly refuted as it continued after Khrushchev's fall; but at the opposite extreme, forecasts about tension between the two communist giants building up steadily toward nuclear war appear hardly more plausible at the present time. What events have tended to show so far is rather the persistence of controlled conflict between Moscow and Peking, with the ups and downs of crisis and relative détente familiar from other great-power conflicts of the nuclear age.

It is useful to recall at the start that history and geography oppose China and Russia far more to each other than they oppose either to the United States. They are neighbors with the longest common frontier in the world; and among the European powers which took advantage of China's weakness in the nineteenth century, Tsarist Russia was the closest and territorially the most rapacious. It was revolutionary ideology alone that tended to bridge this "natural" conflict of interest after 1917, and the bridge remained imperfect and fragile at best. Soviet Russia's Mongolian and Manchurian policies ensured that Chiang Kai-shek never ceased to distrust the powerful ally—even in his early days as a national revolutionary leader. Mao Tse-tung rose to leadership of the Chinese Communists after experiencing, in 1927 and 1934, the disastrous consequences of the party's obedience to Soviet advice; he rose to national power by repeatedly defying that advice; and he had to pay for Soviet support not only by "leaning to one side" in world affairs, but by signing—in February 1950—the last of the unequal treaties in modern

China's history. So conscious was Mao of Stalin's tendency to use the Chinese Communists as expendable pawns, and of the potential conflict underneath the ideological solidarity, that from his Yenan days he deliberately trained his cadres to follow their own model of revolutionary strategy, and only his own ultimate authority. Outwardly, he had to tolerate Soviet bases in Manchuria and to fight Russia's war in Korea while Stalin lived; but once the Vozhd was dead, Mao hastened to depose and arrest Kao Kang, long Russia's trusted man in the Chinese leadership, and to negotiate a revision of the unequal treaty. The different ideological emphasis, developed in following an increasingly independent road to power, now became a compass for an increasingly independent national policy.

The death of Stalin had given China equality of status within the alliance; the crisis of de-Stalinization seems to have been viewed by Mao as a chance to win major influence on Soviet policy without conflict. In the fall of 1957, he offered to Khrushchev the support of his intact authority for overcoming the crisis in the bloc and at home—at a price. His demands included substantial new capital aid, delivery of the latest weapons including in due course atomic bombs, and a more forward joint policy in Asia—and at least the first two were apparently promised to him. But the state of Soviet resources and the East European situation prevented major capital aid to China, while the Soviet view of the world relation of forces combined with the vulnerability of the advanced Soviet economy to limit Moscow's willingness to take major risks on Peking's behalf. Furthering atomic proliferation to build up an independent great power bordering Russia must have appeared to the Kremlin as the most foolhardy risk of all. From the end of 1957, the differences in the situations and interests of the two powers thus led to a whole series of Chinese disappointments—over capital aid, over atomic proliferation, over Middle Eastern diplomacy, over military aid in the Quemoy crisis, over Soviet-American and over Chinese-Indian relations. To those disappointments, the Chinese reacted in the course of 1958 and 1959 first with implied, then with increasingly explicit, attacks on Soviet ideological positions, in the hope of exerting effective pressure on the Soviet leaders by hitting their vulnerable spot—the weakness of their ideological authority. It was the public appearance of such symptoms of an "ideological dispute" that first indicated the existence of the underlying power conflict to the non-communist world.

II

But once the common ideology is no longer sufficient to bridge the conflicting policies of communist states, conflicting ideological arguments will be advanced to justify those policies—and will make compromise more difficult. As each side seeks to present its own practice as orthodox and its opponent's as heretical, it attacks by implication the legtimacy of the rival leader, and is perceived by him as threatening the stability of his rule. The very first disappointment—Russia's inability to supply the capital needed for China's industrialization—led Mao not only to launch the "People's Communes," but to proclaim them as a shortcut to the "higher stage" of communism—a challenge to the Soviets' birthright as pioneers on that road which they were bound to reject. True, the economic setbacks of the "Commune" experiment led the Chinese to withdraw that challenge in early 1959, and the first muted ideological dispute was thus patched up; but the same setback led one of Mao's domestic critics, Marshal P'eng Teh-huai, to seek Khrushchev's support—an approach which the Soviet leader failed to discourage. When Mao learned of this, he must have felt that both his own control and China's independence were threatened by Soviet subversion. His second, less muted ideological attack, which culminated in the Lenin anniversary speeches and articles of April 1960, was thus prompted not only by the growing conflict over foreign policy, military support and international revolutionary strategy, but by a sense that he was fighting for his survival as leader of an independent great power.

On the other hand, the fact that both V. M. Molotov, then Soviet Ambassador to Mongolia, and the Albanian Communists began to argue on Chinese lines soon convinced Khrushchev and his associates that they had to defend the cohesion of their empire against a subversive attack from Peking. The brutality of the total withdrawal of Soviet technicians from China in the summer of 1960 and the persistence of the Chinese challenge in the face of that blow, disproportionate and irrational in relation to the original policy conflicts, become comprehensible only in the light of the ideological broadening of those conflicts to encompass the domestic and imperial control of both leaders.

By the time of the last joint world conference of communist parties, held in Moscow in November and December 1960, the Chinese leaders were thus convinced that they would have to go their own way without Soviet help, unless and until there were radical changes in Soviet leadership and policy. In the circumstances, the compromise hammered out at this conference could be tactical only, and it proved short-lived because it had a different tactical meaning for each of the two sides. The Soviets had formally renounced their "leading role" in the world movement because they wanted to be rid of ideological debates: relying on their superior material strength to impose their course in foreign affairs, they were willing to stop criticizing what Mao did at home if Mao would stop criticizing what they did in Russia and East Europe. The Chinese, on the contrary, were interested in maintaining formal unity only as a basis for carrying on a long-term ideological struggle throughout the world movement—including Russia and East Europe.

When the difference became obvious in the Chinese support of Albania against Soviet pressure, a third and open phase of the dispute started, in October 1961, with the clashes at the 22nd Congress of the CPSU. But now, because of the adoption of a new party program at that congress as well as the increasingly apparent internal struggles in China over methods of industrialization, the basic divergence of the domestic development of the two became involved in the dispute. The need of an advanced industrial (and nuclear) power for continuity of production, hence for domestic stability and internal peace, and its reliance on a highly graded scale of material incentives and privileges seemed directly opposed to the need of an overpopulated, agrarian country with immense problems of modernization for a harsh régime of sacrifice. China needed to keep the masses fired by revolutionary enthusiasm and by the spirit of a besieged fortress. As Mao Tse-tung engaged in a bitter struggle for the distinctively Chinese form of revolution within his own party, he had to hold up the post-revolutionary materialism of Soviet society in the sixties as a warning example of the revisionist degeneracy to which any alternative road would lead. The consequences of different national conditions and stages of development were thus raised to the rank of incompatible principles; the objective divergence of the Russian and Chinese roads was magnified by ideology; and the earlier doctrinaire differences about the international struggle against imperialism were absorbed into two complete, mutually exclusive versions of what had once appeared as a common, Marxist-Leninist doctrine.

With the sense of a basic community of goals thus destroyed, the earlier conflicts about the proper contents of a common strategy on the world scene were soon replaced by outright power rivalry between the two nominally still allied states. Even before the rival doctrinaire structures had been fully worked out by their creators, the dual international crisis of the fall of 1962, in the Caribbean and on the Sino-Indian frontier, showed that all sense of solidarity between Moscow and Peking had disappeared: the Chinese delight in embarrassing the Soviets during their retreat from Cuba was matched by the Soviet willingness to aid Indian rearmament. As the Caribbean defeat led to a Soviet decision to seek a détente in relations with the West, regardless of Chinese denunciations, the last official meeting between delegates of the Soviet and Chinese communist parties, held in Moscow in the summer of 1963, was conceived by each side solely as an occasion to "unmask" the other, and its breakdown marked the effective end of the Sino-Soviet alliance: during the year that followed, the public exposition of the two competing ideological systems and the splitting of a number of communist parties along those lines was paralleled by a series of official disclosures about the earlier conflicts in foreign and military policies, and by a growing number of frontier incidents.

Yet compared with the fundamental power rivalry and the divergence of roads of development, the friction at the borders constituted a subsidiary phenomenon. Its first high point was reached when Mao, in an interview granted to Japanese visitors in the summer of 1964, complained about the massing of Soviet forces on the borders of Kazakhstan and Sinkiang, and Moscow failed to deny the charge. But what Mao feared was clearly not a Soviet attempt at territorial conquests, but a preventive strike at China's fledgling nuclear installations. A few months later, the fall of Khrushchev and the first Chinese atomic explosion ended that particular fear.

III

Khrushchev's successors do not seem to have been under any illusions that the former ideological unity of the communist powers could be restored—not, at any rate, while Mao was in power. But they have made

repeated if not consistent efforts to achieve the more modest goal of a
"normalization" of Sino-Soviet relations. They aim at a state of affairs
in which the two communist great powers would pursue their respective
interests independently, now in coöperation, now in conflict with each
other, but without fanatical and systematic hostility. Given that the
Soviet Union was necessarily opposed to Chinese pressure on India and
Chinese influence in Pakistan, could it not at the same time coöperate
with China against the Americans in Vietnam? While taking their precautions along the border, seeking to deter Pakistan from relying on
China in her conflict with India, and working to forestall a growth of
Chinese influence in Japan, the Soviets have therefore not only repeatedly offered a cessation of hostile ideological polemics, and invited the
Chinese Communists to join another international conference of communist parties, but have made specific offers for a "united front" in
support of North Vietnam, both on the government and party levels.

The Chinese have consistently refused those offers, to the dismay
of the independent communist parties of Asia. As many of their earlier
sympathizers turned into ideological neutrals while their most promising
allies, the Indonesian Communists, suffered disaster in the fall of 1965,
the prospect of a powerful bloc of pro-Chinese communist parties vanished. Yet Mao was willing to pay the price of growing international
isolation because by then the domestic power struggle had absolute priority in his eyes; and for that he needed the bogey of Soviet revisionism
leading to a restoration of capitalism. If Liu Shao-chi had to be branded,
in the course of the cultural revolution, as the "Chinese Khrushchev"
walking the capitalist road, evidently no united front was conceivable
with Soviet leaders whose policy had been unmasked as "Khrushchev-
ism without Khrushchev."

In the course of the cultural revolution, Soviet-Chinese relations
thus fell to their lowest point yet; as insults to each other's diplomatic
personnel led to the withdrawal of both ambassadors, Chinese propaganda called for the overthrow of the revisionist traitors by the Russian people and Soviet propaganda for the overthrow of Mao Tse-tung,
the destroyer of the Chinese communist party. The Soviets, at least, may
for a time have believed that such an outcome was possible. However,
as Mao's domestic victory became evident with the approaching end of
the upheaval, the Soviets returned once more to their earlier efforts to
work for a pragmatic normalization.

In fact, the end of the cultural revolution has brought a growth of
pragmatic influence in the Chinese leadership and a return to a more
"normal" conduct in foreign affairs—but at first, Sino-Soviet relations
remained an exception. Though evidence on the responsibility for the
Ussuri River incident of March 1969 remains conflicting, an analysis of
possible political motives strongly suggests a Chinese initiative. The
disputed islands themselves are worthless. The prospect of a multiplica-
tion of similar incidents along the endless frontier offered to the Soviets
no possible gain, but the nightmare of having to tie down large forces
for recurring, indecisive battles against an enemy specializing in hit-and-

run warfare and disposing of inexhaustible manpower. The Chinese, on the other hand, whose propagandist exploitation of the incidents was far better prepared—with detailed maps—could make excellent use of them for maintaining the "besieged fortress" spirit in general and popular hostility to the "new Tsars" in particular beyond the end of the cultural revolution.

Conversely, it seems plausible that the Soviets were responsible for the subsequent renewal of clashes on the border of Sinkiang, as they were certainly responsible for spreading the rumor, in the summer of 1969, that they might still decide on the preventive strike against China's nuclear installations which Mao had feared five years earlier. However unconvincing the rumor was in view of the probable cost of such an attempt at this stage, it may have helped to bring the Chinese to the negotiating table after Kosygin's meeting with Chou En-lai in September of that year, and to end the frontier fighting for the time being.

The course of the negotiations has so far been inconclusive—apparently not because of any substantial difficulty in agreeing on the demarcation of the existing frontier, but because of the Chinese insistence that the Soviets should formally and publicly admit that this frontier was the result of unjust and unequal treaties imposed on China by the Tsars. In demanding this admission, the Chinese assert that they claim it merely as a matter of undeniable historical truth, without any thought of actually changing the frontier to reverse the Tsarist annexations. But the Russians clearly feel that they cannot make such a formal admission without laying themselves open to later substantive Chinese demands. Hence the Chinese appear to have hit on a means for keeping the frontier question open, and thus maintaining popular hostility, without dangerously provoking the Russians by actual fighting. In a similar spirit, Peking finally agreed to resume the exchange of ambassadors with Moscow, and on the occasion of last year's November celebrations for the first time publicly reciprocated the wish for the normalization of state relations which the Soviet government had repeatedly expressed. At the same time the Chinese continue to emphasize their uncompromising ideological struggle against Soviet "revisionism" and "social imperialism."

Yet while that distinction is in principle acceptable to the Soviets and indeed corresponds to the kind of modus vivendi they have long proposed, in practice the Chinese persist in drawing the line between state relations and ideological struggle in a manner which endangers vital interests of the Soviets and cannot be tolerated by them: for the Chinese concept of ideological criticism includes the right to conduct propagandist attacks on the Soviet domination of Eastern Europe, and even on the unity of the nationalities of the Soviet Union. True, the Chinese attacks on the Soviet invasion of Czechoslovakia took place while the cultural revolution was still in progress and before any talk about normalization of state relations. But in December 1970, Chinese propaganda interpreted the crisis of the Polish régime, in which the Soviets were not visibly involved, in exactly the same spirit as a revolt

of the Polish working class against the "revisionist" régime in which
the Soviets had allegedly threatened to intervene, and forecast the ultimate victory of the Polish people over "Soviet social imperialism."

To the Soviets, such propaganda naturally appears as incompatible
with "normal state relations"; and this applies even more to the continuing Chinese efforts to encourage separatist national movements
among the Ukrainians and other constituent nationalities of the Soviet
Union. More than a year after the start of negotiations between the
governments, Russia and China thus seem back at the point at which
the last compromise between the parties broke up a decade ago: at the
Chinese refusal to accept the Soviets' control over their own power
sphere as the minimum basis for a modus vivendi.

IV

In trying to evaluate the prospects of the conflict, it may be useful to
start by separating its components. The first striking fact is that the
basic power rivalry between the two communist giants has survived the
disappearance of many of the original policy issues of the late 1950s—
issues that were linked to the situation of China's material dependence
on a richer and more powerful ally. As a nuclear power with an independent role in world affairs, China is clearly determined never again
to rely on Soviet economic or military aid for achieving its policy aims;
nor has the Soviet Union any more grounds to fear that it might be
drawn against its will into risky adventures by the now defunct alliance.
What has remained, however, is the power rivalry itself—the interest
of Russia in slowing down the growth of the industrial and military
might of its eastern neighbor, and the determination of China to overcome the obstacle.

At present, the rivalry manifests itself above all as a struggle for
influence in Asia. That struggle takes the form of political competition
in North Korea, which has become independent of both, and in North
Vietnam, which both have supported without ever coöperating directly.
It takes the form of primarily economic competition with Japan. It
appears as a direct clash in the Mongolian Peoples' Republic, where
China is trying to undermine Soviet control, and in South Asia, where
the Soviets are objectively aligned with the United States for the protection of India and have profited from the collapse of Chinese influence
in Indonesia.

The importance of the frontier issue in the wider power conflict
remains highly controversial among outside observers. The nature of
China's overpopulation is not such as to constitute an urgent compulsion to expand her territory: China remains short of capital rather than
land. Nor is there the slightest evidence of a Chinese inclination to engage in dangerous military adventures at the present stage—rather it is
the contrast between wild language and cautious behavior that continues to impress the student. Even for the longer run, assuming an
absolute and relative growth of China's military power and an eventual
exhaustion of the reserves of arable land with a further increase of her

population, it is by no means "fatalistically inevitable" that she must seek to expand at Russia's expense, at the risk of nuclear war, rather than move south against weaker neighbors or seek peaceful economic solutions. But neither can the possibility of such a development be excluded from the Soviet point of view in the light of the growth of Chinese armaments, of her present hostility, and of her insistence on the illegitimate origin of the present frontier. Seen from Moscow, the rise of China to the full status of a modern world power, which may be slowed down but is unlikely to be prevented, remains a potential long-term threat to Soviet territorial security—by now presumably the only serious threat of that kind.

If we now turn to the ideological aspects of the conflict, the struggle for control of the nonruling communist parties has lost much of its earlier importance because of the comparative failure of Chinese efforts in this field. The dominant fact here has been the collapse of the hopes for a bloc of major Asian communist parties under Chinese leadership since 1965, with the turn of the Korean and Japanese Communists and even the Indian left-Communists toward "neutral" independence and the catastrophe of the Indonesian party. But in Latin America, too, the Chinese have been unable to establish a solid influence among the more or less "Castroist" groups opposing Moscow's "peaceful road" to power, or to prevent the Cuban party itself from attending the Moscow world conference of 1969.

In Europe, the Chinese-oriented splinter groups have nowhere become more than a nuisance for the established communist parties, able at best to delay the evolution of the latter into potential participants in government coalitions useful to Soviet diplomacy. Nor has the Maoist influence among the student "New Left" become more than one unstable element in a general ideological ferment, as it met in the course of time increasing competition from the old-line communists in Western Europe and from the Trotskyites in the United States. The Chinese themselves seem to have come to realize their failure as an international doctrinaire center: there is evidence that for the propagandist struggle against the West and the Soviets, they are relying more and more on supporting militant movements of an outright nationalist character, like the Palestinian guerrillas, rather than left-wing ideological sects.

By contrast, the ideological legitimation of divergent roads of domestic development has remained a far more vital element in the conflict; but it is also far more liable to be affected by changes in the leadership and domestic policy of either country. Among the latter, changes in China are likely to have a more far-reaching impact on Sino-Soviet relations. A Soviet turn toward a new effort at modernizing reform could now only produce an intensification of Chinese ideological invectives, while a turn toward a wholesale rehabilitation of Stalin's memory and methods, from which its more primitive advocates are said to expect an ideological reconciliation with the Chinese, would leave the basic differences unaffected and only deprive the Maoists of the tactical pretext that they are defending the Stalinist tradition. In fact, the basic features of Soviet society which form the counterfoil to Mao's vision, such as its reliance on highly differentiated material incentives and its rigid bureaucratic stratification, go back to Stalin's own decisions, as Mao knows perfectly well; and they are unlikely to disappear through any change in the Soviet leadership conceivable at this stage.

On the other hand, a turn on China's part in a more "materialist" and therefore more Soviet-like direction, with more stress on material incentives and continuity of production and less reliance on revolutionary enthusiasm, is conceivable after the disappearance of Mao. Indeed the signs are not lacking that forces favoring such a "pragmatic" turn have increased their influence in the Chinese leadership since the end of the cultural revolution, and that they are the same who have pressed for a normalization of state relations with the Soviet Union (so far, as we have seen, with limited success). In that sense, a decline in bitterness of China's ideological hostility toward the Soviet Union and a move toward a climate of peaceful coexistence between independent communist powers building different types of "socialism" would be a possible development after Mao's demise. But it would not, of course, end the power rivalry between them; it might even, by speeding the success of China's modernization, make her a more formidable rival for Russia at a quicker pace. The power rivalry, then, will continue to be decisive for the substance of the conflict, while ideological factors may influence its more or less acute and intensive forms at particular times. That substance excludes a true "reconciliation" between the two leading communist powers in the sense of a return to a stable alliance based on the primacy of common ideological convictions and goals. But given a measure of rationality of the leadership on both sides, the fact of a serious conflict of power interests makes nuclear war between them no more inevitable than between either of them and the United States.

The continuation of limited and controlled conflict between Russia and China thus remains a far more plausible prospect than its end by either reunion or catastrophe. But in an increasingly triangular world, that leaves unanswered a question of decisive practical importance for the West: the question of priorities. In a triangular constellation, different combinations of coöperation and conflict are possible at different periods, with two of the major powers combining on different issues against the third. Yet it is in the nature of such a constellation that the combination that will become effective at any particular time is not predetermined, and therefore not predictable. It will be decided by the choice of the most urgent issues at any given moment, and that depends on the political skill of the leaders of each of the new Big Three—including the United States.

14

Turning Point in Asia

ALLEN S. WHITING

President Nixon's trip to Peking can best be characterized in Mao Tse-tung's favorite terms: it was a diplomatic "great leap forward" and a "turning-point in history." The visit began with Mao's historic hand-shake with Nixon in the intimacy of the Chairman's home, communicated throughout China by newspaper and television. This closed the book of fear and hatred against the "US-Chiang" gang on which all Chinese children have been raised over the past two decades. The visit ended with the President's pledge of "the withdrawal of all US forces and military installations from Taiwan" and his acknowledgment that "there is but one China and Taiwan is a part of China." Thus began our necessary extrication from the Chinese civil war, an involvement which has locked us into confrontation with one-fourth of mankind since June 27, 1950.

Both sides wish to blur their positions and concessions. Mao's ideological and national interests dictate a continuing struggle against "US imperialism." Specifically this means support for Communist insurgencies throughout the world and opposition to US bases and security treaties encircling China's periphery in East and Southeast Asia. President Nixon likewise hopes, for political as well as national interests, to cover his disengagement from Nationalist China. Conservative critics could cost him votes in the forthcoming election. Moreover, delaying the final US withdrawal from Taiwan permits allies in Asia to be reassured that this step does not affect their security relations with either Peking or Washington. In the meantime the Nationalists and Communists can grope for a formula that ends the civil war and returns Taiwan to mainland rule.

But the essence of the Mao-Nixon exchange should not be obscured. More than political rhetoric underlay the President's frequent allusion to "a generation of peace" and his repeated references to the future interaction of today's youth on both sides of the Pacific. For 20 years millions of Chinese children in state supervised schools have prepared themselves mentally for war with a demonic Uncle Sam. They are not like the Hitler *Jugend* who were nurtured on the bile of frustration and aggression to prove themselves through forceful conquest. But defensive anxieties over external threats were heightened by the symbolic US octopus whose tentacles reached from Taiwan into China through reconnaissance aircraft, sabotage teams, and support to Tibetan guerrillas.

Projecting ahead, this indoctrination could increase the risks of misperception, triggering escalation amidst confrontation, as this new generation of Chinese matures into political responsibility. To be sure, the image of an American threat was already on the wane as fear of attack by "Soviet revisionism" prompted millions to dig air-raid shelters and tunnels throughout China's major cities during the past three years. However, the decisive change came with the publicity Peking gave to the Nixons' various activities. Experts can disagree on who actually makes policy behind the scenes. But there is no mistaking the public impact of China's top three—Mao, Chou and Madame Mao—all of whom promoted America's "top two" as they eagerly experienced ballet, gymnastics, communes, factory and venerated shrines of antiquity.

American newsmen mistakenly lamented the absence of Peking's masses dutifully marshaled to hail such distant rulers as Emperor Haile Selassie in the ritualistic motorcade through Tien An Men Square. Far more important for Chinese audiences, however, was the unprecedentedly personal interaction between Mrs. Nixon and cooks, schoolchildren, peasants and workers. The word was out: these are honored guests who appreciate what New China has done.

Just as these meetings and their message qualitatively changed mass Chinese perceptions of the US as a potential threat, so did the joint communique decisively redefine the the US position on Taiwan to meet Peking's basic concerns. Until recently, notions of "real estate" dictated the security rationale for maintaining the status quo. Pentagon access to air and naval facilities on Taiwan controlled our basic relationship with China and thereby with all of East Asia. Ever since 1957 when construction began on the strategic bomber base of Ching Chuan Kang, the air force has coveted Taiwan as an unsinkable carrier, secure against local turmoil thanks to the police-state repression of the Chinese Nationalists. More than 6000 US servicemen make this base operational for the Vietnam War. As Okinawa became increasingly unreliable as a storehouse for nuclear weapons as well as strategic bombers, the Joint Chiefs pushed harder for Taiwan's inclusion in the permanent line of US defense arrangements in Asia. That prospect is now ended, once and for all.

Equally important from the Chinese view was suspicion that Washington might suddenly discover self-determination on behalf of the Taiwanese. That nightmare was also laid to rest by the joint communique, although unlike American forces and bases there was no serious prospect of this becoming reality. In 1947 Nationalist troops massacred some 10,000 Taiwanese including the bulk of professional, politically oriented individuals. Since then no evidence of a strong independence movement has emerged on the island, despite protestations to the contrary by Taiwanese exiles abroad. A combination of dramatic economic growth and subtle political suppression far outweighed the numerical imbalance between 12 million islanders and two million mainlanders. Nonetheless, over the past two years Chinese Communist insinuations and accusations linked Washington and Tokyo in alleged collusion to prevent Taiwan's return to mainland rule. That too has ended, provided both sides in the civil war can peacefully unite.

Beyond these major changes, the communique showed agreement to disagree, which had been anticipated by the participants and amply reflected in their respective advance warnings to various audiences. Thus Washington refused to withdraw recognition from Taipei and to terminate its defense commitment. Peking refused to compromise on its insistence that only this final step could permit the full normalization of relations. Contrary to another favorite maxim of the Chairman, neither East Wind nor West Wind prevailed, leaving the dignity if not the diplomacy of both sides intact.

However, it is precisely in diplomacy with third countries, most notably Japan, where partisan criticism from such leading Democrats as Averell Harriman and George Ball seems most justified. Whatever the reasons for secrecy prior to the surprise announcement last July of the Peking visit, subsequent months revealed a steady deterioration of Japanese comprehension of and confidence in US-China policy. Nor did symbolic summitry at Anchorage and San Clemente alleviate the apprehension of Premier Sato and Ambassador Ushiba. Seeing *is* believing, and while the Tokyo commentators differed on "who won" in Peking, they agreed that Japan had been wholly closed out of this Asian game. It was too late for the diverse talents of Assistant Secretary Marshall Green from the eclipsed State Department and John Holdridge from "Dr. Kissinger's staff." Their post-Peking mission to Tokyo could not overcome suspicion that "two's company, three's a crowd" with Washington and Peking aspiring for a duumvirate at Tokyo's expense.

Objectively, nothing should concern Japanese politicians other than pique over being left behind, although such sensitivities can be inflamed in the tumultuous interaction of opposition parties and public opinion. The United States has no way to compete with Sino-Japanese trade, already approaching one billion dollars. No change in the Taiwan Strait can conceivably jeopardize Japan's security in the foreseeable future. But it is often subjective fears, not objective facts, that increase international tensions. White House protestations notwithstanding, the handling of Japan has unnecessarily damaged our most important alliance in Asia, the full effect of which may not be apparent for some time.

Less serious though no less irresponsible has been the administration's refusal to explain the rationale behind its China policy to the American people. Last fall, according to a Gallup poll, more than half the respondents saw China as "the greatest threat to world peace in the next few years." Trading on that fear to justify a "journey for peace" is a deceitful as well as a dangerous game. The White House knows better, as was revealed by the President himself at Guam in July 1969. Although only *The New York Times* "leaked" its full-page version of that backgrounder, reports from follow-on briefings by top US officials in Indonesia, Thailand and India confirmed the foundation of the administration's self-proclaimed "Nixon Doctrine" in Asia.

Three critical assumptions underlay the new approach to China. First, China poses no serious subversive threat because its revolutionary and developmental models no longer seem attractive to others. Second, China is not an expansionist threat because the regime is preoccupied with problems at home. And third, China is not a potential nuclear threat because the United States offers its nuclear deterrence to any US ally or neutral in Asia that is the target of Chinese nuclear bluff or blackmail.

This simple summary of the basic rationale that climaxed with the historic handshakes and the communique in Peking has never been publicly stated by President Nixon or Secretary Rogers. To do so would not only risk conservative wrath, it would make the annual allocation of more than $15 billion in US military expenditures in Asia, excluding Vietnam, subject to heavy congressional cuts.

But the sudden and seemingly superficial alteration of our image of "Red China" was too much for the media, as reflected in the anachronistic Cold War commentaries from Peking. By forbidding any contact between knowledgeable government specialists and the press, the White House guaranteed no leaks or distortion of its policy. However it also guaranteed that a frustrated news corps would be wholly unprepared for the culture shock of Mao's China.

Regardless of grumblings in Moscow or Orange County, the credibility of our policy and its acceptance by domestic opinion cannot but be improved by complete candor on the crucial question of the so-called Chinese threat. Reeducation of audiences at home and abroad is essential to prepare for the international rearrangements that may eventually follow from the exchanges in Peking. For the indefinite future, token trade and travel will limit bilateral Sino-American developments until the US military is withdrawn from Taiwan and the Nationalists have dissolved their government in favor of mainland rule. Presumably Chiang Kai-shek's role must end before his colleagues can make this final move.

In the meantime, multilateral relations pivot on the Sino-American detente, particularly in Northeast Asia. Whether the two Koreas confront one another with a perpetually interacting arms race or formally end their 22-year conflict and move toward normal relations depends as much on the Peking-Moscow-Washington triangle as it does on the Seoul-Pyongyang line. This in turn affects Japanese perceptions of security needs. The 1950 Sino-Soviet alliance, defensively aimed at Japan and any state allied therewith, has long since passed into obscurity. It is time for a fundamental reexamination of Japan's defense policy, in the context of alternative prospects for the interaction of China, the Soviet Union and the United States in Northeast Asia.

These new security situations are matched by new economic possibilities, illustrating the futility of isolating bilateral Sino-American relations from the larger scene. To the simpleminded question, who won in Peking, must come the answer: except for Taipei, nobody lost, including the anxious absentee onlookers from Moscow to Hanoi and from Tokyo to Saigon. Chiang Kai-shek may merit sympathy as an injured party but the loser's fate in a civil war is foreordained. Never has it been so delayed as for the supporters of Nationalist China, and even that "ultimate" moment lies in the distant future. If President Nixon's courage was not matched by his candor on this question, Mao's patience has proven the possibility of sidestepping the Taiwan issue for the mutual interest in changing images on both sides of the Pacific.

Summitry rarely lives up to expectations or is worth the risk of failure at the highest level. On balance, however, the view from the top made it well worth the climb this time.

15

We Are Playing a Dangerous Game with Japan

GEORGE W. BALL

Although a year ago Americans would have thought the idea preposterous, some strangely prescient Japanese have long been haunted by the fear that the United States might sometimes arrange a *rapprochement* with China without their intermediation or even their knowledge, leaving them isolated. Last July 15 [1971] they saw that nightmare beginning to come true.

The surprise announcement that President Nixon would visit China was particularly awkward for Prime Minister Eisaku Sato's Government, for in response to Washington's heavy hand, he and his predecessors had been holding back mounting pressure from Japanese intellectuals, from the left-wing parties and even from significant elements of the ruling Liberal Democratic party to move independently toward the "normalization" of Japanese relations with Peking.

Thus it was only natural that the announcement should stir bitter resentment. Those who had sturdily supported America's leadership felt betrayed; other less friendly hailed the President's action as a "liberation"—an excuse for the Japanese to pursue autonomous lines of policy, to break free at long last from Washington's guiding hand.

But whether betrayal or liberation, the effect was the same. The pressures for an independent course of action toward China have now become irresistible because the insensitive handling of the President's China visit has impaired, if not destroyed, that mutual trust which holds alliances together.

If anything, Japanese suspicions have been intensified by further actions taken since Mr. Nixon's surprise announcement of his China trip. One month later, by an abrupt ukase, the Japanese were informed of the President's new economic policy, which was overtly designed to reduce Japan's trade advantage. Then Tokyo was enlisted in a kamikaze effort to block China's entry into the United Nations, which our Government foredoomed to defeat by its own activities.

In less obvious ways, the Nixon Administration has also signaled to the Japanese that their friendship is low on our list of priorities. Disregarding their expressed desire that we send as Ambassador to Tokyo an experienced diplomat with whom they could carry on a dialogue in depth, the President instead appointed Robert S. Ingersoll, a businessman with no prior diplomatic experience. To reassure the Japanese, Henry Kissinger traveled to Tokyo . . . and consulted with Premier Sato. But the belated completion of the twice-postponed trip seemed a grudging afterthought.

Even more important, some of President Nixon's [1972] statements have flatly negated the alliance relationship that Tokyo has long assumed under the Mutual Security Treaty with the United States. Those comments, which disclose a basic obscurity in the Administration's policy formulations, deserve the most careful scrutiny, since the Japanese may well be more alert than Americans in detecting the drastic change that has occurred in our basic position.

For many years the United States has rested the security of Europe primarily on the Western Alliance (NATO); equally central to the defense of the Far East have been our alliances with Japan, Taiwan and Korea. So long as China remained introverted and discussions with the Soviet Union were concentrated on other parts of the world, there seemed little reason to involve Japan in the diplomacy of the giants in the same way that the United States has closely involved its Western allies in policy decisions affecting security of the Atlantic area.

Nonetheless, most Japanese took it for granted that we would fully consult their Government in advance of any superpower talks that affected Asian power relationships—in other words, that we would treat Japan as a full-fledged ally.

Yet faith in that assumption, already severely shaken by the announcement of the China trip, was further undermined when President Nixon, in an interview reported in *Time* last Jan 3, disclosed his ideas of grand strategy. His point of departure was a concept of "five superpowers" which he had first mentioned six months before in a media conference in Kansas City. "We must remember," the President told the *Time* correspondent, that "the only time in the history of the world that we have had any extended periods of peace is when there has been a balance of power. It is when one nation becomes infinitely more powerful in relation to its potential competitor that the danger of war arises. So I believe in a world in which the United States is powerful. I think it would be a safer world and a better world if we have a strong, healthy United States, Europe, Soviet Union, China and Japan, *each balancing the other, not playing one against the other, an even balance."* [italics added]

It was these last words that the Japanese read with astonishment and anxiety, for the idea of five powers "each balancing the other" seemed clearly to confirm that American policy had fundamentally shifted. In announcing his trip to China without consulting Tokyo, the President had clearly not treated Japan as an ally; now, in his conception of the five balancing powers, he had made explicit—or so it seemed to the Japanese—that he had no intention of doing so.

It is therefore easy to understand why many Japanese are now convinced that, during the 15 hours of formal talks the President held with Chou En-lai and the much longer periods Henry Kissinger spent with Chou on his two earlier trips, the Americans almost certainly reached understandings with the Chinese that could threaten Japanese interests. They find it absurd to think that the President would fly 5,000 miles to China and stay eight days merely to move the ambassadorial talks from Warsaw to Paris, make arrangements for tourists to visit the Great Wall, and trade musk oxen for pandas.

The deep suspicions—amounting to mistrust—resulting from all this have created corrosive doubts about the durability of the American security commitment to Japan at the same time as they have pushed the Japanese toward "normalizing" relations with Peking. That Japan feels toward China deep cultural affinity—almost an obligation—seems clear enough. Though the old comparison of Japan as the Rome to China's Greece is far from the mark, the Japanese still feel a sober respect for the depth and richness of China's civilization. Today one even detects a certain pride in the achievements of the People's Republic in turning vast, sprawling China into an orderly, if regimented, nation-state. Added to this is a feeling of guilt. Beginning toward the end of the last century, Japan participated in the sordid rape of China by the great powers; from the invasion of Manchuria in 1931 through the Second World War, Japan was responsible for perhaps as many as 15 million Chinese deaths.

Yet pride and guilt do not tell the whole story. In addition, it is becoming fashionable in sophisticated Japanese circles to express regret that Japan betrayed her Asian heritage when she opted 100 years ago to follow Western patterns in her economic and political development. As a result some thoughtful Japanese now suggest that if their nation's modern industrial society seems empty and insipid, it is because Japan turned her back on the cultural riches of her spiritual fatherland without receiving enough of value from the West. Even at this late date should not the Japanese again try to tap the abundant wellsprings of Chinese culture and wisdom?

Little wonder that this strange chemistry of history and nostalgia has loosed an explosive political force that seems destined to drive any post-Sato Government toward Peking. Nor should one expect resistance from the more materialistic elements in Japanese society, since—though reality may give the lie to hope—most Japanese business-men see China as a source of needed raw materials and a potential market of almost unlimited dimensions as the mass of the Chinese people gradually achieve incomes above the subsistence level. . . .

. . . We must ask ourselves what the forces now in motion may ultimately mean for the higher geometry of Far Eastern *Realpolitik*.

To answer that question one must take account of the striking fact that Japanese history has never been charted by the same kind of wavering curve that has marked the progress of other countries; in-stead it resembles more a succession of straight lines, broken periodically by sharp angles as the whole nation, moving full speed ahead, has suddenly wheeled like a well drilled army corps to follow a new course.

There is nothing in all human experience to match it. From the seventh to the ninth centuries, Japan borrowed and assimilated the culture and administrative apparatus of China, creating an eclectic but distinctive civilization of her own; then in 1638, fearing the infection of Western ideas, she abruptly seceded from the world, sealing herself off in almost total isolation for more than two centuries. Not until a hundred years ago did the Japanese once again sharply alter direction as a new generation perceived that, to cope with the Western barbarians at the gates, they must borrow not only their technology—which they mastered—but political institutions alien to their traditions—which they only partially understood. In retrospect it was a fateful decision. To acquire Western weapons while retaining a warrior tradition sent Japan down a dark imperialist road—a road that led to Korea, Port Arthur, Manchuria, Pearl Harbor and Hiroshima until final and total surrender on the battleship *Missouri*.

Once humiliating defeat had been followed by occupation, there came still another turn of the rudder, revealing a resilience that de-ceived the experts. Bereft of faith in her prewar institutions and blocked off from China by Mao Tse-tung's takeover, Japan turned for guidance to the America that had defeated her, sublimating her power drive in spectacular industrial achievement. Nor has Japan wavered during the past two decades. As a rising industrial nation, she has fixed her eyes steadily on the West, stubbornly repressing the atavistic pull of the mainland.

Yet it has been a strangely unsatisfying time. Though the Japa-nese have more than proved their superb competence in the com-mercial and industrial arena of Western business, they have never felt a full member of the club. For once, to use an obnoxious cliché where it has real meaning, Japan has become a nation in search of an identity.

Where that search will lead—what sharp new turns of the rudder it may produce—cannot be foretold with certainty. Obviously a move toward China rules out anything resembling an alliance with the

Soviet Union. But that was never a serious possibility, since dislike of the Russians has strong roots in Japanese history. The Russo-Japanese War at the turn of the century left a bitter memory of diplomatic frustration, while 40 years later, as the Japanese saw it, the Russians stabbed them in the back at Yalta, tearing up their treaty of neutrality in a sordid rush to grab a share of the spoils. Undoubtedly, economic interest provides some countervailing attraction, but though Japan would no doubt like to take the lead in exploiting the natural resources of Siberia—including both oil and gas—it is hardly likely to give economic hostages to the one country that might pose a serious military threat.

None of these problems exists with regard to China, and the time seems ripe for a reconciliation. President Nixon's decision to go to Peking was, in Japanese eyes, a clear indication that the United States no longer considers China an expansionist power. At long last the Pentagon's frantic insistence that China must be "contained"—which reached peak intensity in 1965 following the publication of Lin Piao's famous dissertation on "Wars Of National Liberation"—has yielded to the reassuring belief that China's primary interest is in buffer areas and the integrity of her borders. It is hardly surprising that the Japanese have welcomed this analysis as giving legitimacy to their own views, for though wary of the Soviet Union's expanding naval ambitions, they feel no imminent threat from a China with vast internal problems, an unusable nuclear arsenal, little air capability and no navy beyond that needed for coastal defense.

How then are Sino-Japanese relations likely to develop? Once haggling over the conditions of "normalization" has been completed —and it will take a long time—a kind of honeymoon period might ensue: Japan would pay for "normal" relations with what amounts to neutralism, while China would seek to exploit Japan's potential as a source of technology and capital. But it is hard to envisage much survival value in such a marriage; the inherent contradictions in the relations of a backward China and an industrially striving Japan are almost certain to lead to rivalry for hegemonic primacy in the Far East—a rivalry that will pit the magnetic pull of China's vast population against Japan's increasing economic leverage over the whole of Asia.

Two such proud and regionally dominant nations cannot avoid competition. China is far too determined to control her own economic development to accept more than minimum dependence on a Japan she basically mistrusts, and already there is the foreshadowing of a bitter struggle for raw materials—oil under the China Sea, for example—that will inevitably lead to serious dissension.

Not that such dissension is likely to involve military force; yet as the interests of Japan and China clash in more and more sectors, as Tokyo's faith in America's security commitments grows gradually dimmer and as the Soviet Union seeks to fill more and more of the vacuums created by a diminishing United States presence, it would be quite unrealistic to expect Japan forever to refrain from translating her extraordinary industrial competence into the traditional muscle of military strength.

Without doubt, a Japanese decision to build a full-scale military force would encounter formidable domestic resistance, but one institutional obstacle to re-militarization has already lost much of its potency. Only seven years after Gen. Douglas MacArthur insisted on writing into Article IX of the Japanese Constitution the flat promise never to maintain "land, sea, and air forces," this self-denying ordinance was interpreted to permit the maintenance of a modest defense capability.

Today, as Japan's prosperity coincides with our new isolationism, American resentment at Japan's "free ride" on our security commitment has become increasingly vocal—to the point where we now seem to be urging the Japanese to do what we had once demanded they should never do. Particularly since the enunciation of the Nixon Doctrine our *sotto voce* suggestions that they should shoulder a larger share of the defense burden have given way to more strident exhortations, with the result that Japan is not at all sure what America expects of her.

Nor does she any longer take at face value formal statements by the Nixon Administration suggesting that Japan increase her military establishment only enough to protect the Japanese islands from external aggression. Secretary of Defense Laird, presumably expressing the Pentagon view—and speaking almost as a separate sovereign— recently indicated that Japan might need to send a fleet as far afield as the Indian Ocean in order to defend her long sea lanes from the Persian Gulf, while mutterings from the Secretary's staff suggested that a nuclearized Japan might even be necessary.

Though this latter idea was subsequently denied it gained a kind of tentative credence in Japan because our Government has recently appeared to change its position—or at least its tactics—with respect to the Nuclear Nonproliferation Treaty. We no longer urge Japan to ratify the treaty but insist instead that it is an issue Tokyo must decide for itself. Correct as this position may be in traditional diplomatic terms, it contrasts so sharply with the Administration's blunt manners in bilateral economic discussions that many Japanese believe the United States no longer cares about limiting the number of nuclear powers.

All this deepens Japan's nuclear quandary. Sentiment against becoming a nuclear power is still a powerful force in public opinion and one should not underestimate the internal political agony Japan would face in revising her Constitution so as to go down the nuclear road. Yet pressure is mounting in that direction, especially as China moves to develop operational ICBM's capable of reaching North American targets. "Who is foolish enough to believe that America would jeopardize her homeland by firing nuclear weapons in Japan's defense?" the skeptics will ask. It is de Gaulle's old question, but it may find a special echo in Japan.

Still, the greatest pressure on Japan to become a nuclear power is less likely to stem from anxieties over security than from a desire for political status. Alert Japanese are impressed by the fact that with the admission of Peking to the United Nations the five permanent members of the Security Council are precisely those powers that have nuclear weapons, and they have noted the implications of President Nixon's statement that his China trip was necessary because of the "great danger of the most populous nation in the world becoming a major nuclear power" 15 or 20 years from now.

Clearly there is no problem of capability. Apart from the social and political upheaval that might be involved in opting to be a nuclear power, Japan unquestionably has the scientific competence and industrial might to build a modest nuclear arsenal within a remarkably short time. The working principle is generally recognized as the goal of "N-2," which means that she will keep her technology constantly up to date so as to be able to produce operational nuclear weapons within two years after a decision to proceed.

Such a principle is, of course, welcomed by Japanese businessmen who believe that nuclear weapons technology would offer valuable spin-offs to private industry. As one might expect in the highly involuted algebra that shapes Japanese policy, the managers of heavy industry provide a key element of pressure for re-militarization—and to an extent we strengthen their hand when we continue to push Japan to increase expenditures for her military establishment. From experience in our own country we should know enough not to expect that a highly industrialized nation such as Japan will long continue to buy from us the military hardware her own enterprises can produce quite as well. And we should never lose sight of the fact that the uniquely intimate structure of Japanese business and government relationships is tailor-made for the emergence of a "military-industrial complex."

If the Japanese do decide to become a nuclear power, what of it? To the abstract question, the answer may be that it would not much matter—which is a view that may well prevail in the top reaches of the Administration. Why should we worry if there is one more nation with a nuclear arsenal? After all, there are five already, and the nuclear stalemate still seems to work.

Like all issues in international politics, however, the question will not arise as a sterile academic problem but in a context providing special color and meaning. Thus it seems clear from the circumstances I have described that the Japanese will go down the nuclear road only if they feel alienated from the West and strongly nationalistic—and these are the very conditions that might render Japan's nuclear power disruptive and dangerous.

It is this that makes our recent conduct particularly reckless. It is one thing to envisage a nuclearized Japan tied closely to the West and quite another to have to cope with an alienated nationalistic Japan armed with nuclear weapons. A great nation such as Japan, rootless and turned in on itself, could be an unpredictable force in world politics, threatening the stability of the Far East like a loose cannon on a ship in high seas. If that is so, why have we let the genie out of the bottle?

One reason we have failed to recognize the future importance of Japan in international politics is that the Japanese most Americans now encounter appear as narrowly focused economic men. It is their misfortune that they often seem to caricature the notorious American qualities of thinking in short time spans and carrying pragmatism altogether too far.

Yet in regarding the Japanese too narrowly in economic terms we Americans disclose an ideological bias that has frequently led us astray—our tendency to swallow the Marxist myth that all nations (except, of course, the United States) shape their foreign policy in slavish conformity to their presumed economic advantage, despite the fact that history is filled with situations where the opposite occurred. Thus we are tempted to take it for granted that because the United States is currently the most important single outlet for Japanese goods, we can behave pretty much as we wish toward Tokyo "because the Japanese have nowhere else to go."

But pride, nationalism and often downright irrationality are more likely to shape Japan's political relations than any informed calculation of economic interest. In spite of the current vogue for "linkage," we will never persuade Japan to adopt a political course at odds with her popular consensus, whether by threats of protectionism or commercial policy concessions. Let us not forget that when we sought to discourage Japan's expansionism in 1940 by cutting off her petroleum supplies, we did not stop her from going to war; we merely speeded her timing.

Nor should we draw false conclusions from a mistaken conception of her economy. Japan is not a Hong Kong that lives by importing raw materials, transforming them and selling them on the markets of the world: She is first and foremost a vast and burgeoning internal market. In contrast to a nation such as West Germany, whose exports total almost a fourth of her gross national product, Japan's exports and imports each constitute not much more than 10 per cent—or considerably less than one year's annual growth. Certainly Japan is dependent on imported raw materials, but most of these are obtainable from the so-called Third World, including China, and if Japan should find herself increasingly excluded from Western markets—or if she should find her major political interests jeopardized or disregarded by the West—she is far more likely to seek a privileged position with such developing countries than to bend her political policies to appease or mollify the United States or Western Europe.

This by no means suggests that the problem posed by aggressive Japanese competition is unimportant or that it does not demand intense and careful attention. Within the past few years, as our own external trade balance has deteriorated, many Americans in both business and government have felt angered and frustrated by Japan's behavior in international trade, and though they sometimes overstate the problem, they unquestionably have a legitimate complaint.

Unhappily our reaction has been uninformed by a coherent policy.

Under pressure of the individual complaints of particular industries, we have resorted to restrictionist improvisations worked out through bilateral discussions. We have ignored the point that Japanese industry has its own special history, structure, institutions and relationships; to bring it into a trading system constructed largely in response to Western institutions and habits of thought is an intricate task that cannot be accomplished by America alone, but only by a common effort of all the industrial trading nations.

But if preoccupation with Japan as an industrial competitor has led us to overlook her political significance, that only partially explains our aberrant actions during the past year. Fully as important as our preoccupation with Japan as an industrial competitor has been the lack of professionalism that has increasingly marred the execution of policy ever since the White House opted to become its own foreign office—or, more accurately, sought to get along without one.

Troublesome as this problem has been for our relations with other parts of the world, in regard to Japan it has got completely out of hand. It is significant that there is no Japanese expert among the 165 members of Mr. Kissinger's White House staff; and, since the State Department's own experts are no longer consulted, it is easy to understand why we have disastrously underestimated Japan's capacities for good or evil.

Still, it would be oversimplifying the problem to attribute Japan's threatened estrangement merely to the obtuseness of a White House too egocentric to delegate, for it has also reflected a self-conscious decision by the Administration to regard the reactions of Japan as of only secondary interest.

And this brings us back to the President's image of five balancing powers, which deserves a closer second look. In terms of present-day realities it would be fanciful to speak of "an even balance" among entities of such disparate size and weight as the United States, Western Europe, Russia, China and Japan. Two have massive nuclear arsenals, two have relatively puny nuclear capabilities, and one has no nuclear weapons at all; two have world-circling political interests and activities while the political interests and activities of the other three are merely regional in scope; four are major industrial powers while one is a vast underdeveloped country.

Even if Europe someday achieves real political unity and Japan becomes a world political force, the conditions would not exist for a static equipoise of five equidistant powers. Something of that kind was possible among the Italian city-states of the 15th century and later among the sovereigns of Europe; in those cases the political units shared a common intellectual and social heritage. But historical, social, ideological and economic differences could not be more profound than among the five powers the President says he would like to see in even balance. Thus the conditions clearly do not exist for a static equipoise, nor can one envisage a balance of power in the 19th-century pattern, with alliances reversing and coalitions shifting to prevent any one nation from gaining a position of hegemony over the others.

For one thing, there is no pivotal power to "hold" the balance

—a role that Great Britain played by throwing its weight with whichever seemed the weaker side. And given the fundamental ideological
cleavages both between the Communist powers and in the rest of the
world, it is bizarre to think of the United States combining with China
against Japan or Western Europe, just as it is difficult to believe that
Japan might combine either with the Soviet Union or China against
Western Europe or the United States. Thus the Japanese and informed
Europeans interpret the President's concept of five balancing powers to
mean only that the United States has abandoned a strategy based on
alliances in favor of a strategy of maneuver and independent action.

Certainly that is the game the White House seems to be playing
today, dealing bilaterally with Moscow and Peking, trying to play
one off against the other, while we let our allies—particularly Japan
—shift for themselves. In the case of Europe this may do little harm,
provided it does not inspire a flurry of bilateral diplomacy with each
small European state trying to make its own separate deal with the
Russians and thus producing a weak and fragmented West. An opti-
mist might even hope, on the contrary, that a lone-wolf American
policy could speed Europe toward unity—which would clearly be a
good thing. With a shared heritage of institutions and ideas and a
settled habit of talking easily with one another, the Atlantic nations
are quite unlikely to work at cross-purposes, whether or not our alliance relations are institutionalized.

But Japan is a different matter. Ties across the Pacific are of
brief duration and dangerously fragile, and we face enormous problems in trying to understand one another. Nor could a Japan alienated
from America and left to her own devices avail herself of anything
resembling the kind of constructive alternative that the Europeans
can find by unifying; her only realistic alternative would be nationalism.

That is why many of us have contended for many years that America
should take the lead in building a coalition of major non-Communist
industrialized nations by first turning the United States-Japanese Mutual
Security Treaty into a mature coalition, then progressively integrating
that relationship into an expanded Atlantic partnership that would
include in its purview the Far East as well as the West.

The assumption underlying this proposal was that over the years
ahead Europe would slowly expand its political horizons to resume an
interest in Far Eastern affairs, while Japan would, along with its
global industrial role, extend its political interests on a worldwide
basis. Thus by bringing Japan into existing Atlantic economic institutions and developing political institutions to include the Far East,
we might in the long run be able to build a broad and solid base
from which a reconciliation could gradually be worked out with the
Soviet Union and China.

It was a bright vision but it is rapidly fading, and if we persist
in our present course of action, it will fade irrevocably. Perhaps it has
already during this past traumatic year [1971–1972].

The Global Balance of Power:
Can the Great Powers
Rule the World?

16

Nixon's Plan to
Save the World

RICHARD J. BARNET

Richard Nixon once remarked that the nation did not really need
a president to conduct its domestic business. And indeed, it is not as
the man who cleaned the air, made the streets safe, balanced the
budget, found enough jobs, or made Americans feel better about their
country that Nixon has sought re-election and a place in history, but
as the architect of a new "structure of peace" designed to last a generation. This promised generation of peace is to come from a radically
revised vision of the world, a modernized military strategy, and an
updated political rhetoric. All reflect the official lessons of the Vietnam
war.

    There is a new map of the world in the White House which
bears little resemblance to the one that McGeorge Bundy and Walt
Rostow once used. In the official US world view the Soviet Union
and China are no longer centers of an international conspiracy. They
have become nation states. The Soviet Union, according to the Nixon-
Kissinger analysis, is not primarily interested in promoting the world
communist conspiracy or committing "indirect aggression" by sub-
verting free world nations, but is absorbed with problems of securing
its borders, building its economy, controlling its own population.
China is far more interested in what is happening in China than in
the politics of any other place. Nixon's gamble that the Soviet Union
and China would put up with the humiliation of the Haiphong

blockade to protect possible profitable trade relations with the United States was based on a nonideological reading of Soviet and Chinese motives unknown in the Kennedy-Johnson era.

Nixon is now prepared to accept the overwhelming historical evidence that the Soviet Union has consistently sold out revolutionary movements. Soviet leaders, contrary to the official view in the Dean Rusk era, are not primarily in business to humiliate the United States. With a judicious mixture of tough talk, ostentatious display of military power, and attractive economic concessions, one can make them offers they can't refuse.

Nixon has become the first President since Franklin Roosevelt to recognize the Russian revolution of 1917 and to accept the Soviet Union as a fixture of international politics that will neither "mellow" (in George Kennan's sense) nor collapse, and he is the first President ever to recognize the Chinese revolution of 1949. His generation of peace, as he has said, calls for "a strong healthy United States, Europe, Soviet Union, China, Japan, each balancing the other. . . ." In effect the President has offered the Soviet Union something like the junior partnership in world management that Stalin sought after World War II. He is offering an agreement among great nations not to push each other too far and to conduct their continuing rivalry within mutually advantageous rules of combat, such as the SALT agreements, which forbid exactly those weapons both sides would prefer not to build.

In arranging the new relationship with the Soviet Union Nixon has adopted several notions promoted in the early 1960s by critics of the cold war. He has appeared on Soviet television, and as part of an election-year pitch he has tried to evoke sympathy from American viewers for the "little Tanyas" of Russia. He has made an agreement regulating the access rights to Berlin—no one talks any more about who will die for whom over Berlin. The world's most expensive ritual, the preparations for the great ground war with the Soviets in Europe, continues, but the deployments in the center of Europe are being brought more into line with the actual expectations of the two sides. Indeed, agreements for "thinning out" or "balancing" military forces in Europe can be expected within the next two years. Although the Soviet Union is growing more powerful in staking out interests far from its own territory, the principal problems among the NATO nations during the 1970s increasingly concern the Russians less and the Americans more.

The United States is abandoning the familiar ground rules of the cold war because it can no longer afford them. The new issues in Europe, as indeed almost everywhere else, will be economic rather than military, and the competition will involve former allies more than erstwhile ideological enemies. Conflicts over such crucial matters as monetary policy, scarce resources, and new markets make the largely irrational military confrontation of the past too expensive a luxury. John Connally has already served notice upon the "free world partners" that the US does not intend to share most of the big decisions of world economic management and that it will use shock, surprise, maneuver,

and threats to get its own way. The competitive struggles between the
United States and its fully recovered European protégés are growing
much more intense, and the new look in US foreign policy is in large
part based on this reality.

On the new White House map the "Third World" looks even
newer. During the Kennedy days the number one official fear was of
the "war of national liberation," identified as the Kremlin's secret
weapon. This preoccupation with counterinsurgency reflected the anxiety of the Kennedy Administration that Cuba and Vietnam were
models for the revolutionary transformation of the former colonial
world. Guerrilla leaders, incredibly, were seen as Kremlin or Maoist
agents, as Mao himself was once seen as Stalin's agent.

Under Nixon the worry about insurgency is by no means di-
minished. But the Sino-Soviet dispute, the willingness of both communist powers, in spite of dozens of sharply worded notes, to "stand idly by"
while their ally is subjected to the heaviest bombardment in history,
the hunting down of Che Guevara and the crushing of guerrilla movements in Brazil and elsewhere in Latin America have made possible
a new, more relaxed view of how to handle the Third World. Vietnam and Cuba, it now seems, were historical exceptions. The two
billion people who live in Asia, Africa, and Latin America are not,
Che Guevara and Lyndon Johnson notwithstanding, about to rise
up and take our wealth from us. They are hungry, divided, and
vulnerable, and all the more so because the US-Soviet detente makes
it much harder for small countries to play one giant off against another.

Small nations, even those as dependent upon the Soviet Union
for material aid as Egypt was, have demonstrated, nevertheless, a
strong impulse to resist Soviet domination. The split in the communist world, with Russia and China each accusing the other of
having formed a cabal with the United States, has helped to convince
Nixon that the ideological attraction of communism for the poorer
nations is waning. Most Asian, African, and Latin American governments are in the hands of military dictatorships, rightist regimes, or
technocratic modernizers, all eager for US military aid, loans, and
private capital. Many of the "unstable," "romantic" revolutionary
leaders who used to upset Walt Rostow so much—Sukarno, Nasser,
Nkrumah—are gone, replaced by men prepared to serve as pillars for
Nixon's "structure of peace."

It is a totally different picture of the world from the one Nixon
presented to the American people during his nine previous electoral
campaigns. Accordingly, it calls for a different military strategy. The
Nixon Doctrine contains some important new elements, but as Virginia
Brodine and Mark Selden point out in their revealing commentary,
Open Secret: The Kissinger-Nixon Doctrine in Asia, it is mainly an
attempt to update traditional US counterinsurgency thinking. The
authors find the basic elements of Nixon's new policy as it applies to
Southeast Asia scattered throughout his speeches and articles written
during the Eisenhower and Pepsi-Cola years: The United States is
a Pacific power and cannot accept a defeat anywhere in the Orient

—since the Pacific, as he warned the Executives Club of New York in 1965, would then become a "Red Sea" and the dominoes would fall. In 1967, in an article in *Foreign Affairs,* he outlined the premises of his thinking on Asia:

> I am not arguing that the day is past when the United States would respond militarily to communist threats in the less stable parts of the world, or that a unilateral response to a unilateral request for help is out of the question. But other nations must recognize that the role of the United States as world policeman is likely to be limited in the future.

The reliance on what the Pentagon calls "indigenous troops" is of course the cornerstone of the new "low profile" policy. Asian soldiers, according to Pentagon statistics, cost only one-fifteenth of what is spent for their American counterparts, and neither they nor their parents vote in US elections. As John Dower, a contributor to *Open Secret,* points out, Vietnamization is a very old dream. A National Security Council policy statement of early 1952, released as part of the *Pentagon Papers,* calls for the development of "indigenous armed forces [in Indochina] which will eventually be capable of maintaining internal security without assistance from French units." It has been conventional wisdom in the Pentagon since 1951 that the United States should not fight a major land war in Asia. The most prominent military critics of the Vietnam war, General James Gavin and Matthew Ridgway, were members of the "never again club" who remembered that Korea was the wrong war in the wrong place.

The Nixon Doctrine explicitly expresses the view that other nations, rather than a US expeditionary force, should do the fighting to protect US "vital interests" on their territory. That, of course, has always been our preference. In the same way, the United States has always indicated its readiness to send such a force if the indigenous troops are incapable of fighting on their own. Melvin Laird told the House Armed Services Committee in March, 1971, that "when required and appropriate," US help "could include ground combat support." Following the first Nixon State of the World message on February 18, 1970, Max Frankel reported in *The New York Times* that "Mr. Nixon's aides concede . . . that there is nothing in his new doctrine that excludes a Dominican-style intervention in defense of vital interests."

There is nothing either in Nixon's rhetoric or in his practice to suggest that the United States has adopted a less imperial definition of its "vital interests." The principal threat in Asia, according to Laird, is still "internal insurgecy supported by external assistance." The United States will keep all its treaty commitments to some forty-two governments to protect them where necessary from their own people. Even "political agitation" has been identified in Department of Defense documents as a military threat requiring a counterinsurgency response. Although certain minor bases have been phased out and forces in such forward battle stations as Korea have been thinned out, the Administration has abandoned no major outposts of American power, and indeed has even staked out new "vital interests" in two critical areas: the Indian Ocean and southern Africa.

Although the Nixon Administration no longer believes that all insurgencies are masterminded in the Kremlin, and no longer conjures up LBJ's picture of successful Asian revolutionaries sweeping under the Golden Gate Bridge in sampans and junks, it obviously does believe that "stability," which is the prize of statecraft, is jeopardized by guerrilla movements throughout the world. The situation in the Philippines is serious enough for the Marcos government to impose martial law, shut down the press, and arrest liberals. Insurgents in Thailand, Cambodia, and Laos have controlled important territory for years, and the Cambodian rebels continue to gain ground. There are almost 3,000 highly organized guerrillas in the Dhofar area of Oman. In the Portuguese territories in Africa, according to the private estimate of a UN expert, about one-fourth of Angola is administered by the rebels and about two-thirds of the rural area of Guiné Bissau is in the hands of the liberation movement.[1] In view of America's continuing counterrevolutionary commitment and the possibility that guerrilla activity around the world may continue to grow, how can the United States hope to avoid future Vietnams?

War Without End, Michael Klare's well-documented study of US military planning, gives the best available account of the tactics behind the strategy for maintaining a Pax Americana without casualties, inflation, dissent, or guilt. The contours of the new strategy are visible in Vietnamization. Nixon's first domestic task was to disengage the country from the war without losing it. He did this by reducing American casualties and promising to end them entirely, by curbing inflation through wage-price controls, and above all by making use of technology. Nixon gambled that the very Americans who were outraged by an indecisive land war in Asia, with it 1,000 American battle deaths per week, would passively support an air war in which the equivalent of twelve Hiroshima bombs are dropped each month. According to the latest polls he is winning that gamble. What makes the strategy of military engagement and psychological disengagement possible is technology, and Klare gives a useful account of it in his book.

Perhaps his best chapter is on the "electronic battlefield." "We are making unusual efforts to avoid having the American young man stand toe to toe, eyeball to eyeball, or even rifle to rifle against the enemy that may outnumber him on the battlefield," Major General Ellis W. Williamson told a Senate subcommittee in 1970. "We are trying to fight the enemy with our bullets instead of the bodies of our young men—'firepower, not manpower.' " Some of these unusual efforts include olfatronic detectors such as the XM-2 Concealed Personnel Detector Aircraft Mounted, a General Electric product universally known in Vietnam, Klare tells us, as the "people-sniffer," which detects ammonia emitted from the human body. There are also many varieties of infrared detectors which locate human bodies from the heat they emit. Operation Bedbug, the army's experiment with the use of bedbugs wired with amplifiers as a warning system, was a failure because while bedbugs let out a "yowl of excitement" when they come in contact with human flesh, they turn out to be excited most of the time.

There is an extensive network of research laboratories in major universities, corporations, and military installations inventing equally ingenious devices for carrying on long-distance war. In his book, Klare traces a number of these weapons systems from the laboratory to the battlefield magnetic detectors, surveillance radars, seismic detectors, acoustic detectors, and other advances in lethal technology.

Eventually, the Pentagon tells us, they will be able to tell when the enemy shoots, what he is shooting at, and where he is shooting from. On the battlefield of the future, says General Westmoreland, "we can destroy anything we locate through instant communications and almost instantaneous application of highly lethal firepower." The technology of fighting wars by remote control is an essential component of the Nixon Doctrine. It is also, as Haynes Johnson and George C. Wilson demonstrate in their important survey *Army in Anguish,* a requirement of the military itself.

Johnson and Wilson, both *Washington Post* reporters, conducted extensive interviews with military people, from generals to privates, and they concluded that the army is beset with extraordinary problems most of which directly derive from the Vietnam war—drugs, fragging, desertion, a crisis of leadership and morale. (The army's desertion rate in 1971, according to DOD, was seventy-three men per 1,000.) Since "the army's problems are America's problems," as several senior officers told them, the answer is to "professionalize" the army, which means, among other things, to detach the services as much as possible from American life. Thus the Nixon Doctrine not only requires new equipment, such as the C5A airplane, which can carry six Greyhound buses, to get soldiers to "trouble spots" around the globe in a hurry. It also demands a new kind of soldier—professional, technologically trained, and unobtrusive.

Klare's account of the science-fiction weapons our taxes buy is frightening, but he takes the claims of the military too much at face value. Revolting as the new technology of death is, one has more doubts than are raised in his book about its effectiveness for the political purposes it is designed to accomplish. Boatloads of "people-sniffers" sent to Vietnam have not prevented the successive defeats of the ARVN. No one has yet devised a weapon, including the "smart bomb," that can keep South Vietnamese soldiers from selling gasoline to the NLF. It appears that even war cannot be dehumanized to the extent desired by the Pentagon.

The Nixon Administration is aware that even a modernized American elite corps cannot police the world by itself. Nixon's "structure of peace" is to be maintained by the sharing of "responsibilities," with "stable" nations acting as deputy peacekeepers. Klare describes what he calls the "science of mercenarization," i.e., how the military aid and counterinsurgency programs work, particularly the counterinsurgency research program called Project Agile and the stepped-up support for local police forces in Asia, Africa, and Latin America. In Thailand, for example, Stanford Research Institute designed elaborate technology for internal spying, a multi-million-dollar "Village Information System" for retrieving and storing "information about conditions and events in the villages and towns" for the benefit of the Thai army. Many of the police techniques used by the Brazilian police for extracting information from suspected insurgents have been developed with American advice and equipment. American military personnel have charged that there are torture chambers in the Brazilian Navy Ministry in Rio right next to the offices occupied by the US naval mission.[2]

America's deputy peacekeepers, as Kissinger suggested fifteen years ago in *Nuclear Weapons and Foreign Policy,* are to play a crucial role in "local defense" and "regional cooperation." The US role is to be limited to whatever will "make the difference between success and failure." Outside the region the US "must be free to act alone or with a different grouping of powers if our interest so dictates."

Nixon has openly assigned a deputy peacekeeper role to Japan. For many years he has urged Japanese rearmament. In 1967 he called for "a greater role both diplomatically and militarily in maintaining the balance in Asia" for Tokyo, and in the Okinawa accords he made his ideas about Japan's new role explicit.

However Japan is not only a deputized peacekeeper but an increasingly formidable economic rival of the United States. Some US multinational corporations are beginning to demand that the federal government play the same active role in direct support of their activities as the Japanese government plays in support of Japanese firms overseas. As competition with Japan increases such pressures will be hard to withstand, particularly for an administration already so protective of the interests of the multinational corporations. There is an obvious contradiction between Japan's role as a stabilizing military and economic presence in the Orient and her emerging role as the world production center and marketer of high technology, particularly as the United States becomes more and more of a service economy and net importer with rising unemployment.

In Latin America Brazil has already given active support to the Bolivian junta and is engaged in making Uruguay an economic dependency, thus imitating the traditional US role elsewhere in the hemisphere. But like Japan, Brazil, harboring a century of resentment about its treatment at US hands, may not always be willing to play its assigned part in the Nixon scheme for "peace."

The most ominous use of the "deputy peacekeeper" concept is in Africa. Over two years ago the National Security Council adopted NSSM 39, which, according to *The New York Times,* calls for "deliberately expanded contacts and communication with the white governments of southern Africa." In pursuit of the new policy, the US has authorized the sale of previously forbidden jet aircraft to Portugal and South Africa. It has authorized the sale to South Africa of helicopters and civil aircraft which are easily convertible to military use.

It has violated UN sanctions against Rhodesia and has facilitated the granting of substantial new credits to South Africa.

Even more significant was the renewal of the Azores base agreements with Portugal under which the United States promised an aid package of $436 million. This is roughly the equivalent of Portugal's annual military expenditure, most of which goes to the support of the three colonial wars in Mozambique, Angola, and Guiné. According to a recent report in the London *Sunday Times* (July 9, 1972), South African mercenaries in cooperation with the Portuguese Air Force have been waging chemical warfare against nationalist guerrillas in the jungles of northern Mozambique in order to wipe out rebel food supplies.

Chemicals produced in South Africa, including Convolvotox, which kills broad-leafed plants and inhibits fertilization, have been sprayed by South African pilots who, according to the *Times,* receive more than $72 an hour for their services. The State Department, when questioned, has refused to say whether US defoliants are being used in Portugal's colonial wars. But in a paper delivered at the annual meeting of the Africa Studies Association, Jennifer Davis reports that in the first eleven months of 1970, the year the Portuguese began using defoliants in Africa, the export of herbicides by US firms to Portugal was four times greater than the total exported in 1969.

Rhodesia and South Africa have stepped up their "peacekeeping" activities in the Portuguese territories because the Portuguese, even with increased US aid, are unable to prevent the guerrillas from occupying large parts of the countryside. For as in Vietnam, the foreign power can hold on to the towns while losing control of the surrounding rural areas. South Africa has rushed planeloads of arms to help Hastings Banda's government of Malawi fight a rapidly growing guerrilla movement. The white governments believe in the domino theory in its purest form. As the Rhodesian Secretary for External Affairs put it in 1969, "If we go, Mozambique can't hold out for six months; the others would fall in order."

The white regimes of southern Africa are important to Nixon's new policy not only because the navy thinks that the Cape route is a vital substitute for the Suez Canal and there is a "power vacuum" in the Indian Ocean but because those regimes symbolize "stability." In Nixon's neo-Metternichean politics, the liberal disdain for African fascism that marked the Kennedy-Johnson era is a dangerous luxury. The white regimes are a bulwark against communism and fanatical nationalism, and they offer the most hospitable climate anywhere for American business. The average rate of profit in 1972 on the one billion dollar US investment in South Africa was higher than 17 percent. A sharply rising proportion of the total NATO requirements of several vital minerals, including asbestos, iron, and tungsten, is now derived from southern Africa. For these reasons the United States (under the rhetoric of containing violence and preventing war) now appears ready to step up its assistance to the minority racist and colonial governments in beating back challenges to their rule.

The new rhetoric is as important to Nixon's "generation of peace" as the new strategy. Gone is the tone of cold war hysteria and in its place is a tone of complacency, even euphoria, designed to make Americans feel more comfortable, safer about the world. It is a law-and-order world, managed by limited agreements among the powerful. Nixon's definition of "peace" is flexible enough to accommodate genocide, as in Burundi, mass starvation, as in Nigeria, crippling malnutrition, as in much of Latin America, and obscure fratricidal wars among what the British used to call the minor races.

After the disastrous efforts of the Kennedy-Johnson years to export the Great Society, Nixon has discovered the politics of indifference. Since the poor of the world cannot hurt us, they can be ignored or quietly repressed. The United States, with 6 percent of the world's population, can continue to burn, melt, or gobble up over 52 percent of the consumable resources, as Barry Goldwater happily reported to the Republican Convention, and perpetuate the poverty of the undeveloping nations.

The sense of concern about the mounting human misery in the world that John F. Kennedy projected ten years ago is gone. The American efforts in the Kennedy era to direct peaceful revolutions in the Third World from above were tragically naïve and had grotesque consequences, but at least they reflected an understanding that no stable world order can be built without far-reaching reforms in desperate societies. The need for radical changes in the decolonizing world is now much more obvious. But the essence of Nixon's strategy is that peace can be bought by suppressing such changes through a combination of big power deals and modern technology.

NOTES

1 The rise of international terrorism—hijackings, kidnappings, bombings by mail—poses a new and quite different threat to the "generation of peace." The new terrorism, unlike the traditional assassinations of people in power in guerrilla wars, holds no promise of overturning governments or enlisting popular support. It stems not from revolutionary politics but from a politics of desperation. It is designed solely to dramatize political grievances for which there are no apparent solutions, not even revolutionary ones. The new terrorism is a poor instrument for toppling authority, for the killing of the innocent has the opposite effect. Its purpose, one must surmise, is to serve notice on the powerful nations that they will not be allowed to enjoy their control over events.

2 See AP dispatch, *Miami Herald*, February 25, 1971.

17

A World Restored?

ALASTAIR BUCHAN

In the issue of *Time* of January 3, 1972, President Nixon is quoted as follows: "We must remember the only time in the history of the world that we have had any extended period of peace is when there has been balance of power. It is when one nation becomes infinitely more powerful in relation to its potential competitor that the danger of war arises. So I believe in a world in which the United States is powerful. I think it will be a safer world and a better world if we have a strong, healthy United States, Europe, Soviet Union, China, Japan, each balancing the other, not playing one against the other, an even balance."

It is a curious statement if taken at its face value. In the first place, it is historically untrue—a pentagonal balance of power produced two periods each of about 40 years of peace between the battles of Waterloo and the Marne and hardly existed afterward; in "the history of the world" the periods of deepest peace have been those of partial or universal empire. In addition, it negates a long-standing American declaratory position against a multiple power balance, symbolized by President Wilson's famous description of it at the Guildhall in 1918 as "a thing in which the balance was determined by the sword which was thrown in on one side or the other . . . the unstable equilibrium of competitive interests . . . maintained by jealous watchfulness and an antagonism of interests."

It abrogates at least a decade or more in which it was the conventional wisdom in Washington that the United States should be "infinitely more powerful in relation to its potential competitor." And finally, it assumes that, as in the eighteenth century, the five powers concerned have broadly the same range of resources at their disposal. This simply is not true today. The Soviet Union and the United States possess a degree of strategic, military and economic resources which the other three partners do not. Western Europe, the United States and Japan are advanced technological powers of a kind which the Soviet Union and China would like to be but are not. Western Europe has still only the characteristics of a supermarket and it will take many years to acquire those of a single actor in world politics. Japan is not a military power in the ordinary sense and if she were to become one it might destroy the very system of balance of which the President speaks.

Before discussing whether the President is talking in archaic terms or not, one has to make one's own assessment of what are likely to be the most significant forms of power in the 1970s. The United States has lost its old strategic dominance over the Soviet Union. But is strategic power, that is to say nuclear weapons and long-range means of delivery, going to be the crucial means of exerting influence, the dominant expression of national power, in the years ahead? I am inclined to think that "the balance of prudence" has become the norm here, and last year's Soviet American agreements on the handling of a nuclear crisis or accident would seem to confirm this.

Moreover, one can, I think, detect a diminishing confidence on the part of the smaller nuclear powers that their own armories give them either real influence in the world or real security, which is not to say that they will dispense with them, especially as China perceives the Soviet Union as an active menace to her territorial integrity. But one factor which is common to all the nuclear powers, great and not so great, is concern with the cost of accepting the dictates of technological innovation and a growing readiness to distinguish between the possible and the desirable. These considerations are also present in the councils of advanced non-nuclear powers even though they may wish to keep their options open. The nonproliferation treaty is still a fragile instrument; but I detect less concern with the old Nth-power problem than, say, five years ago.

To say this is not to challenge the conventional wisdom that nuclear weapons would still probably provide the most potent source of influence in a situation of deteriorating or uncertain security for the major powers and in the crisis points of the world. All I would argue is that they now provide a relatively static form of influence, which seems not only less likely to be challenged or diffused than, say, a decade ago, but also one that will play a less central part in a somewhat more fluid calculation of interests and affiliations than was the case in the postwar decades.

Whether we are still in a bipolar situation or a multiple relationship of major powers, conventional forces also remain important. Force in being, the potential use of force, can be as important a form of political influence as force in battle. One of the factors which one cannot discount is that for over 25 years Soviet military power has been potential rather than employed, except for brief and decisive interventions in Budapest and Prague, whereas American military power, to say nothing of British and French, has been frequently deployed in action with all the shortcomings that the conduct of real conflict shows up.

But how politically significant this distinction is I am not sure because the readiness of the big powers to intervene with military force seems to me to be declining. I do not see any American administration being ready to repeat the Lebanon intervention of 1958 or that in the Dominican Republic in 1965 unless it had the direct mandate of a large number of other states as well. And despite the growing Soviet Navy, does not the active voice of China make Russian intervention in the third world—a landing in support of some African régime, for instance—less probable? Within Eastern Europe itself the difference in the Soviet handling of the Czech crisis, the Polish uprising and the sustained Rumanian defiance of the Kremlin's leadership is instructive even if it is not decisive. It is military aid rather than deployed force which has become the accepted form of intervention in the third world.

It is now becoming a Western interest—and in this I include the Japanese—to minimize the military aspect of power in a sense that was not true in the 1960s. And I find it difficult to see that it is in China's interest to maximize it. One can argue that this is not the Soviet view. But may they not be making a serious misjudgment about the temper of our times? May not the cumbrous decision-making machinery in Moscow have deduced from Cuba and Vietnam that they were entering a period when military power was the decisive aspect, only to find that by the time the ships and the missiles are built, the rules of the game are changing?

II

If strategic weapons appear to have become a rather less dynamic form of power and the exercise of conventional military force is to be hedged about with important limitations, does this make the exercise of political influence, both within the industrial world and in the developing world, relatively more significant? Obviously in the world as we know it, political influence cannot be wholly divorced from strategic and military potential. But the possession of force and influence have never been synonymous, even though the latter may be difficult to quantify and define. Considering a great power which is also a great civilization, one important aspect of influence is clearly the internal dynamism of its society. Does it provide the magnet for those that are trying to modernize or humanize their own societies? Britain had this effect from the day in the early nineteenth century when Pitt asserted that "Britain has saved herself by her exertions and will, as I trust, save Europe by her example," until 50 years later when Taine vividly exposed the cruel and seamy side of her Industrial Revolution. Germany in the latter part of the last century with its industrial vigor, Bismarck's social legislation and the strength of its great universities (which provided the model for their American counterparts) played a similar role. For a while in the interwar years before the Stalin purges, it looked as if the Soviet Union might play it; but, as Isaiah Berlin pointed ont many years ago, it was the success of the liberal pragmatism of the New Deal which weaned my own generation away from Marxism. Without question the United States was the magnetic power from the immediate postwar years until problems like race riots, student trouble, crime, the overloading of the legal system and the evident problems of the cities destroyed—temporarily, one hopes—the unique quality of the United States as the world's great experimental society. Perhaps China, if she would let more people look at her achievements more openly and more closely, could use this form of influence effectively, especially with the leaders of the developing world who face problems not dissimilar from those with which Peking found itself faced a generation ago.

A second element of political influence is national will—on which so many Teutonic and Anglo-Teutonic theses have been written—not necessarily the will to fight, but national will as an aspect of determination to change or maintain the nation's external environment. What proportion of its resources is a country prepared to devote to the achievement of its external goals, not necessarily in terms of armed forces but of involvement in the destinies of other states? What risks is a government prepared to take? To what extent is it prepared to assume the political consequences of external economic involvement? To what extent are its primary concerns domestic and its élites inward rather than outward-looking? How much authority does a government command among the young and the energetic?

Third, how good is its diplomacy? How sensitive to external susceptibilities is its decision-making apparatus? How consistent is its pursuit of its objectives? And lest anyone should think that I have in mind the well-documented vagaries of American policy over the past ten years, important though these have been in the loss of American influence in the world, it is worth remembering that in 1966 Prime Minister Harold Wilson told a Labour Party meeting that Britain's frontier was on the Himalayas and 15 months later took the final decision to withdraw all British military power from East of Suez. Moreover, diplomacy now has an altogether wider meaning, for it implies an ability to control the activities of one's own nationals, whose independent operations, as for instance in the multinational company, may conflict with broader national objectives.

No one can draw up an accurate balance sheet of the relative political power or influence of the major actors on the world stage today. In terms of political and social magnetism, what writers like Lord Acton have called the "moral factor" in diplomacy, the situation has become, and may well remain, that of a zero-sum game in the sense that no one power, society or capital city is now regarded as the central magnet; for what the United States has lost in terms of influence neither the Soviet Union nor China has gained as yet, nor Europe either, despite the many close ties of its component countries with different parts of the developing world. Nevertheless, it is a bleak fact that in terms of the will to extend control of its external environment and consistency in its pursuit of this goal, the Soviet Union is in some places gaining ground which the United States and Europe have lost: in the Middle East, in the subcontinent, in parts of Southeast Asia. Three new treaties of mutual assistance with Egypt, India and now Iraq—the first such treaties negotiated by the Soviet Union with noncommunist powers since the war—represent the ratification of a major extension of Soviet political commitment.

There remains the fourth level of power, economic power, whose external influence is related, though only partially, to the other three. Here there is a real danger that we may be entering a period of "power politics," something quite different from the acceptance of a balance of power, a preoccupation with the welfare of my side rather than the general health and stability of the international landscape. If democratic governments in particular are unable to find the answer to the unfamiliar phenomenon of growing inflation coupled with growing unemployment, then some of the dangerous features of the 1930s are likely to recur. If the United States, Western Europe and Japan cannot find limits of accommodation in both the trade and monetary fields quite soon, then the prospects of a stable balance of power, not only between themselves but with the communist powers as well, are poor indeed.

If one combines the four planes of power, then I suppose we have achieved a sort of pentagonal relationship, uneven though their interaction may be.

But in terms of the interface of the four levels of power, it seems to me more realistic to think in terms of two different foci of international politics, Europe and East Asia, with only the two superpowers actively engaged in each, even if certain kinds of developments in one area may have an indirect bearing on developments in the other. In both areas the key concept to the maintenance of a stable balance is what Marshall Shulman has recently described as "access," or the right of interpenetration, the resistance of any claim to an exclusive sphere of influence.[1] I note with encouragement a recent statement by Secretary Rogers that in effect repeals the Monroe Doctrine and accepts the principle of mutual accessibility in Latin America.

III

In Europe, we are groping our way toward a new relationship on two and eventually three fronts: among ourselves, toward the Soviet Union, and eventually toward the United States. The first process has started very late in the day because the 1960s were dominated by an argument about the balance of power in Western Europe itself, whether it would be a French-run system or a genuine coalition of equals. What is involved is not merely the enlargement of the Community, which itself is a difficult process, but the evolution of political institutions which can enable the European governments to speak with similar if not identical voices in their dealings with the rest of the world.

At the level of strategic power there is no serious question of Europe playing the role of equilibrist. Not only is there no requirement to counterbalance American strategic predominance as President de Gaulle mistakenly assumed, but it is acknowledged, in Paris nowadays as well as elsewhere, that the security of Western Europe still depends crucially upon the continuing commitment of American strategic power —on the maintenance of the Atlantic Alliance—and that the development of autonomy on the strategic plane is not on Europe's agenda in the foreseeable future.

But the problem of maintaining adequate deployed military manpower in Europe to make a European crisis manageable is going to present us with a difficult set of choices. Should we by some means or other bribe the Americans to stay in Europe at the level of five divisions, 26 air squadrons and a two-carrier fleet? I am not sure that it would be possible even if we decided to, given the domestic constraints on American military manpower and expenditure. Moreover, a mercenary relationship is rarely an enduring one. Should the active European members of NATO consolidate their relatively successful coöperation in their Euro-Group or should they invite France to join with them in creating a new European defense community or system as a counterpart of the Economic Community, even though nuclear weapons are excluded for the time being? Somewhere in the next few years—not more—the road forks toward the evolution of a less powerful European grouping within an integrated NATO framework and a more powerful, more autonomous European system under the umbrella only of the collective alliance. It is difficult to believe that the 1970s can pass without a radical reorganization of the structure and probably the strategy of NATO.

These questions are important, for conventional military force continues to be an aspect of balance in Europe, even though the center of the stage may be held in the next year or so by the preparation and staging of a European Conference on Security and Coöperation. It is at the third level, of political influence, that the tripolar or triangular relationship is beginning to assert itself. Valuable as such events as President Nixon's visit to Rumania may have been in establishing the principle of access, indispensable as was the unity of the Allied negotiating position on Berlin, the fact remains that it is the countries of Western Europe themselves which are playing the leading role in creating a new relationship between the two halves of Europe. Herr Brandt's *Ostpolitik* may suffer some temporary political setbacks in Bonn, but he remains one of the central figures in developing the conception of a Western Europe with interests of its own "interwoven," to use his own phrase, "with the rights and duties of the two superpowers." And the support of conservative figures like Heath and Pompidou for what we may call the Brandt conception is significant. What we are witnessing in Europe is a continuation of bipolarity at the level of strategic power; and the slow beginnings of a triangular situation at the level of political, economic and perhaps military power. But there is no question of the balance becoming fully triangular as the Soviet-Chinese-American has been for some years.

IV

If the development of a sort of tripolar balance of power in Europe, a small continent scarred with centuries of conflict, with very high levels of mobilized force on either side, is going to be a gradual and tentative affair, the evolution of a major power balance in Asia is already occurring more rapidly. In my own view this is primarily a quadrilateral relationship. If you consult the text books they will tell you that a quadrilateral balance is inherently unstable because it must either polarize into two against two or three against one. But it can also become two against one against one. Moreover, if you have only four actors you cannot invent a fifth simply for the sake of symmetry or intellectual orthodoxy.

I think that Europe, however rapidly it coheres, will play much the same interested spectator's role in relation to Asia that Japan will play in relation to Europe, with the difference that, in certain circumstances, individual European powers can continue to play a useful but quite limited role in the process of nation-building in Southeast Asia. By the same token I think it unlikely that India will play a decisive part in the Asian balance. Now that she is a Soviet ally her freedom of maneuver may well be restricted. But in any case her ability to project power of any kind at any distance from her borders is limited. She will be much more concerned with the new power balance in the subcontinent, and even if she were to develop operational nuclear weapons, these could be for purposes of local deterrence only. Indonesia, the other potential partner in the Asian balance, has her hands full with domestic reconstruction for years to come.

It may well be asked whether the United States is going to remain a central actor in East Asia. I believe that it will; that David Hume's remark about the Athenians who, "finding their error in thrusting themselves into every quarrel, abandoned all attention to foreign affairs," is not applicable to the American position in the Pacific, or elsewhere. Though indeed President Nixon has narrowed and refined the definition of American interests, more particularly in Asia than in any other part of the world, a European observer cannot fail to be struck by the long history of American concern with Asia. After all, her own metropolitan territory stretches halfway across the Pacific, and an irredentist Japan or an implacably hostile China could threaten not only her interests but her own security. What clearly is disappearing is an American sense of responsibility for order in the whole of non-communist Asia—the policy that prevailed from about 1952 to 1968—in favor of concentration on certain key countries. But it must, for instance, remain a high American interest to prevent Japan from quitting the Western military and economic system, even though her presence in it presents difficulties; clearly there is still a continuing sense of obligation to the Philippines and to Australasia. The difference between the past and the future is that there is little public and even less congressional willingness to consider the actual use of American force to maintain an Asian balance, though its latent use may still be an important factor. For the most part, American influence must be exercised more at the level of political influence and economic power.

The Soviet Union, as implied earlier, is a much more confident power than in the past but in East Asia its motives seem to be dictated as much by fear as by ambition. It is doing what it can to prevent the expansion of Chinese political influence in southern Asia and around the shores of the Indian Ocean. In an era of increasing Sino-American dialogue it cannot be certain that it could use nuclear weapons against China with impunity; this is one virtue of a multiple balance. True, it now has larger forces deployed along the Chinese border and in Mongolia than in Central Europe, but probably the very last contingency it could face is the prolonged exercise of the second level of power, conventional military force, against China at the end of very long lines of communication. This could weaken its position in Eastern and Central Europe disastrously. By the same token, it needs Western assistance in the development of Siberia though it has not as yet shown itself ready to pay a political price for it. In sum, though it has reason to fear Japanese or Chinese dominance in East Asia, the Soviet Union will be forced to tread rather more delicately there than in other parts of the world. A false step might either convince Japan that she had no alternative to an indefinite security relationship with the United States or that she must rapidly become a full-scale nuclear power—an autonomous actor at every level of power (a role which very few Japanese that I know wish to play). It might also make Peking see a new congruence of interests with both the United States and Japan, a new form of Triple Entente.

But China enters the international system with considerable skepticism about the credentials of the three other partners. Even though a mixture of fear, sense of historic wrong, ideological contempt and anxiety about superpower collusion has made her identify Moscow as the prime adversary for the time being, this implies no necessary confidence in Washington or Tokyo. Even if the Taiwan and Vietnam issues are gradually settled, as long as there are American military installations in Thailand, near her vulnerable southern border, the United States still has the qualities of an adversary state. China's distrust of Japan is based not only on jealousy of the economic dynamism of a country which was once a cultural province of China, but also on memories of recent aggression. China is not an expansionist state in the territorial sense. Yet she is proud, unused to participation in modern multilateral diplomacy, and on certain issues revisionist. She has, however, a clear sense of her own strategic vulnerability and will also play her hand with caution. If she has an external form of power to exert it is through the example she can set to the countries of the developing world and it must therefore be in her interest to widen the compass of the Asian balance.

Japan is a very uncertain actor at every level except that of economic power, and even here she may well have as much concern in the next 20 years with the social consolidation of her economy as with its growth. That she will acquire political interests as her dominance of the markets in Asia extends and as her preoccupation with the problem of access to sources of raw materials continues, there can be no doubt whatever. But I see no reason to assume that she must feel an instinctive urge to translate her economic strength into military and strategic power, unless she is deliberately encouraged to, or is frightened into it by some débâcle in the relations of the other three partners.

Here, then, we have a much more fluid balance-of-power situation than in Europe, operated by four partners of uneven strength, interests and perspectives. If we look some years ahead it is possible to conceive a number of variations in the combinations of the players: (1) A revival of the Sino-Soviet alliance to contain Japanese economic influence in Asia and oust Western influence for good—possible after Mao's death but improbable if one considers the deep and bitter national and ideological rivalries between the two countries. (2) A Soviet-American understanding emerging out of the SALT dialogue, to conduct parallel policies in different parts of Asia in order to neutralize the effect of Chinese nuclear weapons and to channel Japanese activity down paths that suit their interests; this would be certain to incur first Chinese then later Japanese hostility. (3) An American-Japanese-Soviet understanding to contain Chinese influence; possibly an attractive option for Japan, for it would ensure a continuing American strategic guarantee while giving her access to Soviet raw materials and possibly the Soviet consumer market. However, such a pattern would not only embitter China for generations but, being a rich man's club, would arouse the hostility of the rest of developing Asia. (4) A Sino-Japanese economic entente in a situation where the United States played a muted role in Asian politics; this prospect has certain cultural and economic attractions for Japan: the reuniting of the twin cultures, closer access to certain raw materials, the prospect of jointly exploiting the China Sea for oil. But it would be very difficult for China to embrace in ideological terms, despite the prospect of keeping Japanese military power at a low level as well as giving China access to her technology. If given concrete form it might well jeopardize the future of the Japanese-American political relationship and, of course, for the Russians it would represent the resurrection of the Yellow Peril in its starkest form. (5) A bilateral Russo-Japanese entente; this has some degree of probability if the Asian balance becomes governed largely by economic considerations. On the one hand, Japan could accelerate the exploitation of Siberia; on the other, the consumer market of European Russia may be ripe for the kind of products which the Japanese produce so well and so cheaply. But it would probably be a consequence rather than a cause of the change in relationships in Asia. If the United States and Western Europe were to turn increasingly hostile to Japanese commercial penetration it is a possibility that would have to be taken seriously, though, if Japan tried to play the role of balancing agent and gave a political context to such an understanding, it would forebode such a decisive shift in the balance of power in favor of the Soviet Union as probably to lead to a modification of European and American tariff and economic policies.

A number of other combinations can be envisaged, but while combination-making may be a useful intellectual exercise Asian politics will not consist of a continuous series of choices. The facts about modern international politics as we know them indicate that swift alignments and realignments are not possible as they were in earlier multiple balances; choices once made cannot be readily unmade.

What one can foresee, however, is a more elastic system of great-power interaction in Asia, in which the relationships of the major actors are not necessarily identical at the four different levels of power; in which, for instance, the Soviet Union and the United States maintain their current concern for the stability and safety of the overall strategic balance; in which China and the United States have a certain level of political relationship, one of reasonable diplomatic intercourse and adjustment without attempting to hedge in the Soviet Union by the appearance of a more intimate or more collusive bond; in which Japan is neither frightened nor encouraged into an active military let alone strategic role in Asia.

But, though I have argued earlier that the politics of the 1970s are not as likely to be dominated by the fear of nuclear diffusion as we feared, the one development which would impose a dangerous rigidity on the politics of East Asia would be the development of Japanese nuclear weapons. The United States would become dubious about the risks involved in its Asian commitments, China would freeze again into her shell, the Soviet Union would feel menaced by three nuclear powers and would behave either with truculence or with uncertainty, Japan herself would lose much of the influence and respect she is slowly regaining in the small Asian states.

The desirable balance in Asia, therefore, seems to me one in which the status quo is maintained at the strategic and military levels, namely a continuing Japanese-American security relationship, while the relationship between the four major actors at the political and economic levels has greater fluidity.

But such an outcome has two very important concomitants. First, there must be a reasonable degree of communication between all four major actors. The line between Peking and Washington is gradually getting cleared, that between Tokyo and Peking must now be built. For a stable relationship to exist, it is also a Western interest that communications and as high a level of confidence as possible be restored between Peking and Moscow. The other condition may take even longer to establish: it is nothing less than the acceptance by all four capitals of a common principle, that of mutual access in third areas—on the one hand, acceptance of the fact that in the rest of Asia and indeed the developing world in general, the various powers have acquired certain areas of primary interest, dictated by strategic, economic or historical affiliations, but that this endows none of them with the right to a hegemonial sphere of influence. The United States may legitimately argue that it has a primary interest in, say, the Philippines and Australia, the Soviet Union in India, China in the Asian states to her immediate south, Japan in Indonesia, the European countries in Malaysia and Singapore. But the difference between primary and exclusive interests must be accepted; all must be open to the political, ideological, or economic penetration of the others; he who claims an exclusive relationship with another country destroys the balance.

What the President is feeling his way toward, it seems to me, is not a resurrection of a classic pentagonal balance in the crude sense of countervailing power (though his Prince Metternich in the West Wing may use the language of an earlier age), so much as a philosophy of multiple coexistence. If this were the 1960s with its preoccupation with military power, as a consequence of Berlin, Cuba and Vietnam I would look with great suspicion on the whole concept and feel that the maintenance of the American-Japanese-European triangle was of far greater importance than any discussion of a pentagonal balance. But in an era when military power may play a less dominating role, there is one objective of the old multiple system which is worth emphasizing, namely the preservation of the autonomy of its members.

The world is still divided into different political and cultural civilizations, and the main rationale and function of a multiple balance in the past have been to preserve the freedom of its members, while in the process minimizing the risks and scale of war, for the reason that the destruction or crippling of one of them destroys the system. The importance of this question of autonomy can hardly be overstressed in looking at Asia, where what are, in fact, four different civilizations meet in the area of the China Sea; but it also has relevance to the European balance as well: Europeans are not Americans, and their civilizations are distinct though the two are closely linked. The autonomous state or civilization has a great deal of vitality and we are more likely to live in relative tranquility if we respect this differentiation while opposing the temptations of universality for our own values or the claims of other polities.

V

But what about the position of the smaller powers in a world dominated by such a pentagonal relationship? Not only do some of them, notably those at the interface of the focuses of primary interest, like Korea or Jugoslavia or the newly truncated Pakistan, fear that they will be the victim of some great-power agreement over their heads, that they will be the Polands or Taiwans of the future, but some of them are or will be tempted also to exploit the multiple balance.

Both aspects seem to me to give a new importance to the United Nations and its agencies. It has proved of limited value as an instrument of collective security, largely because it borrowed from the League of Nations, which in turn had unconsciously adapted from the Congress of Vienna the assumption that a concert of the great powers was feasible in an age when the meaning of power, the strength and objectives of those who wielded it, and the whole structure of the international system were about to change drastically. And even the ad hoc improvisation of U.N. peacekeeping is largely in abeyance because the concept has not yet been adjusted to the existence of a world of more than two great powers. Very possibly the next decade or so may see a regeneration of the United Nations, with China a member of the Security Council and with two Germanys in the Assembly. I, for one, wholeheartedly favor a permanent seat on the Security Council for

Japan opened up by the reduction of the Western European seats from two to one as the Community acquires political validity.

But even if the Security Council were to acquire a new effectiveness, I share Castlereagh's doubts about the legitimacy or durability of the idea of a concert of great powers as a means of keeping order in the world. I see the contemporary value of the United Nations in rather different terms. First, as a permanent seat of contact between the new partners in the two great multiple balances of the world. Second, as an arena where the smaller powers can hoist danger signals if they feel themselves the victims of the kind of great-power pressure which I have suggested is no longer legitimate in a multiple balance. Third, as a means by which they can drag as many resources as possible out of the developed world to accelerate their own development and mitigate the appalling problems which they face. In addition, of course, the smaller powers are, as in an ecological balance, acquiring new forms of coherence, new means of underpinning their own national identities by local combinations—ASEAN, LAFTA, OAU and, more valuable, some of the local groupings within the U.N. Economic Commission for Africa.

VI

In the last two generations we have forgotten, and by *we* I mean Moscow and Peking as much as Washington or Brussels or Tokyo, the means or the conditions for maintaining a multiple balance. One is the importance of diplomacy, which is both more onerous and more significant than in the simple world of the cold war; it involves a sensitive concern for the interests not only of adversaries but of friends, a skilled knowledge of the sensibilities of other governments and other cultures; a skill which is as important in embassies abroad as in the national capital and which in my view cannot be sustained by ad hoc teams of political advisers, however brilliant, but only by a permanent corps of experienced professionals. Occasional summit meetings, bilateral or multilateral, are no substitute for Bacon's maxim that "princes do keep due sentinel."

A second condition is consistency in policy, so that over a very long period of time governments have a clear sense of each others' central interests, which is by no means the same thing as saying that foreign policy must be excluded from domestic and electoral controversy.

Finally, there is the necessity for restraint or moderation in our demands upon the international system, economic as well as political; we know that a trade war among the democracies would undermine the prospect of balance at all other levels.

Lest it should be thought that these remarks are directed particularly at the United States, let me say that they present an equal challenge to all the major power centers. The Soviet Union seems at this moment to have some of the ambitions of an old-fashioned imperial European power and by its emphasis on exclusive spheres of influence to undermine the principle of accessibility or interpenetration which I believe is central to the notion of balance. It, therefore, may have the most to learn about the new rules of the great game. Japan has yet to learn the lesson of economic magnanimity as an essential constitutent of her autonomy. Western Europe has still to create the very decision-making machinery which is necessary to identify its essential interests.

We live by our own choice, and to a significant extent an American choice, in a plural world in which the important sources of power have become neither abolished, institutionalized nor diffused, but have tended to aggregate in uneven ways around a small number of great states. The intellectual challenge for the next generation is both to use and to modify our tradition, which is flawed but also enriched by sporadic failure, to find a temporary accommodation for other civilizations and ideologies in an intractable social order which limits our ambitions but must not suspend our efforts. Yet it would be a sorry world that risked alienating not only the small powers but our own younger generation as well, if they came to believe that a balance of power was the highest political achievement of which the new great powers were capable.

NOTE

1 "What does Security Mean Today?" *Foreign Affairs,* July 1971.

Arms: The Crisis Imposed by Technology

18

The Soviet Strategic Challenge Under SALT I

BENJAMIN S. LAMBETH

On the evening of May 26, 1972, the United States and the Soviet Union signed a major agreement on strategic arms limitation which Presidential Adviser Henry Kissinger later described as being "without precedent in the nuclear age, indeed in all relevant modern history." [1] The specific accord which Kissinger applauded so warmly (and also played a central role in bringing about) consists of a two-part interim conclusion to nearly three years of intensive strategic arms limitation talks (SALT) between the two superpowers, aimed at arresting and eventually reversing the strategic nuclear arms race. [2]

The first half of this agreement, a formal treaty requiring approval and ratification by the United States Senate, provides for an open-ended ban against the deployment of anti-ballistic missiles (ABM's) by both countries beyond two token sites for each. The second half of the package, an informal executive agreement between President Richard Nixon and Party Secretary Leonid Brezhnev, comprises a five-year quantitative freeze on the deployment of strategic offensive missiles by each country at the level of those presently in place or already under active construction. The two accords, which have collectively come to be called SALT I in the United States, provide both a significant curtailment of the arms competition which has dominated Soviet-American relations in recent years and a promising point of departure for the follow-on SALT II negotiations. [3] While it remains to be seen whether Kissinger was entirely justified in the fullness of his enthusiasm for the accords, there is no question that the conclusion of SALT I constitutes a major watershed in the evolution of the East-West strategic confrontation. Aside from representing the first instance in which either superpower has shown a willingness to observe significant self-restraint in the deployment of front-line strategic weaponry, it symbolizes the formal acceptance by both countries of the desirability of a stable mutual deterrence relationship and the apparent contentment of each, at least for the moment, to live with rough (if not precise) strategic equivalency to one another rather than to continue a costly and profitless arms race.

As one might well expect of such a trail-blazing agreement, however, SALT I has succeeded not only in winning the widespread acceptance and approval of the centrist majority but also in arousing considerable dissatisfaction on both ends of the American political spectrum. On the one hand, there is the liberal objection that because SALT I fails to prevent such qualitative weapons innovations as the supersonic B-1 bomber, the new Trident missile-launching submarine, the underwater long-range missile system (ULMS), and multiple independently-targetable reentry vehicles (MIRV's), the agreement not only fails to go far enough but indeed does so little as to be scarcely more than cosmetic in ultimate effect.[4] On the other hand, there is the conservative argument that because SALT I formally concedes to the Soviet Union a significant measure of ascendancy over the United States both in overall numbers of offensive missiles and in the combined throw-weight, or payload capacity, of its land-based ICBM launchers, the agreement consigns the United States to a distinct "second-rate" position in the superpower relationship. The conservatives fear that this might eventually oblige Washington to back down under the weight of nuclear blackmail in any future crisis with the Soviet Union.[5]

The liberal objection, while fair enough as a statement of general principle, is of relatively marginal consequence to the immediate success of SALT I both because its adherents do not oppose the accord *per se* and because, in any event, there is no absolute certainty that the new weapons which they do oppose will in fact be produced and deployed by the United States. Three of them, indeed (B-1, Trident, and ULMS), are being pushed explicitly by the Nixon administration as much for bargaining chips in SALT II as for actual follow-on strategic forces. Even if SALT II fails to provide an agreement which obviates the need for their deployment, moreover, it is far from clear at this point that Congress will abide by the administration's request for their full funding.[6] The conservative argument, on the other hand, deserves somewhat more considered attention and analysis because its proponents (largely within Congress and in the Department of Defense) are in a position and frame of mind to exert great efforts toward torpedoing the prospects for SALT I's success if the inequities and dangers which they perceive in the agreement are not satisfactorily explained away or accommodated.

In the discussion that follows, therefore, we shall examine the Soviet-American strategic weapons lineup which the SALT I accords envisage with a view toward clarifying and placing in perspective the following issues raised by the conservative argument: (a) the nature of the asymmetries which the treaty allows between the United States and the Soviet Union; (b) the extent to which the Soviet numerical edge in offensive missile strength and in ICBM throw-weight undercuts American deterrent and political bargaining capabilities; and (c) the propriety and advisability of American acceptance of SALT I given the quantitative and qualitative imbalances which the accord promises to ratify in favor of the Soviet Union.

By far the most significant accomplishment of SALT I is its formal treaty provision which sharply circumscribes each superpower's latitude to deploy ABM defenses. Under the terms of the agreement, the United States and the Soviet Union are both limited to two ABM sites consisting of no more than 100 interceptors each, with one allocated to the defense of each country's National Command Authority (NCA) in the respective capital cities of Washington and Moscow, and the other co-located with an ICBM complex no closer to the capital city than 1,300 kilometers (the distance provision being to assure that neither side might surreptitiously seek eventually to link the two ABM sites into a limited "area defense" system protecting a larger part of the country than that permitted by the treaty). The ABM agreement also places stringent limitations on supporting radar capabilities and on various sorts of hardware development and testing procedures to assure that neither the United States nor the Soviet Union may upgrade its extensive air defense missile force to ballistic missile intercept potential.

In effect, the ABM portion of SALT I essentially provides for a formal ratification of the prevailing *status quo*. The United States is allowed to keep its ABM site now under construction at Grand Forks, North Dakota; the Soviet Union is similarly allowed to retain its Moscow ABM network which has been operational since 1967; and, to redress the asymmetry, each country is allowed one additional ABM complex of the type which it lacks and the other side has. (In the Soviet case, this means one ICBM hard-point defense complex east of the Urals, and in the American case, an ABM defense of the Washington NCA.)

It would, of course, be simple for a skeptic to protest that in submitting to the ABM limitation agreement, the United States and the Soviet Union may well have done little more than reveal that they could be equally sanctimonious in formally pledging themselves not to do something they probably would have preferred not to do in any event. Certainly the Soviet Union has never expressed any serious public interest in deploying extensive ABM defenses around its landbased ICBM force, and there is considerable presumptive evidence that during the course of SALT I (if not indeed prior to it), the Soviet leadership also gradually lost whatever fascination it may once have had with city defenses of the Moscow ABM variety.[7]

In the United States, likewise, it has never been altogether clear how committed toward a massive ABM system the Nixon administration would be in the absence of a SALT treaty, if not because of lingering doubts about the technical efficacy of such a system against a determined offense, then certainly because of the serious question, whether Congress could be persuaded to authorize the vast financial resources its deployment would require. It would hardly follow from such an argument, however, that the ABM portion of SALT I is mere diplomatic window-dressing. The specter of an effective defense against ballistic missile attack has long been one of the most acute sources of instability in the East-West strategic relationship, because of the finite possibility that the eventual possessor of such a defense could come to find a first-strike posture feasible and thereby nullify the deterrent capacity of his adversary's nuclear retaliatory forces.

As a result, the ABM specter has been one of the principal forces energizing the quantitative race for strategic offensive force supremacy between the two superpowers. It was in part the perceived threat of an eventual Soviet ABM capability, for example, which inspired the initial development of MIRV by the United States in the early 1960's as a means of providing individual American ICBM's with enough separate warheads to assure that at least one of them could penetrate a concerted ABM barrage.[8] With the SALT I prohibition against significant ABM deployment by either superpower, this vicious circle of offense-defense interaction has been deprived of much of its former perniciousness. With the first-strike threat thereby substantially defused, both sides can accordingly feel far less concerned about the need to maximize the size of their offensive forces. For this reason alone, the ABM accord represents a signal advance in the effort to bring the nuclear arms race under control.[9]

It is not so much the formal ABM treaty as it is the offensive weapons bargain consummated in the informal SALT I executive agreement, however, that primarily raises the hackles of President Nixon's conservative opposition on the arms control issue. According to the terms of the agreement, each country is obliged to refrain for a five-year period from fielding any strategic offensive forces other than those already deployed or under construction. Furthermore, each country is allowed—if it so chooses—to replace its more obsolescent land-based ICBM's (in the Soviet case, 200 SS-7's and SS-8's, and in the American case, 54 Titan II's) with an equivalent number of advanced submarine-launched ballistic missiles (SLBM's). The problem with this formula in the eyes of the critics is that it formally concedes to the Soviets both a sizable quantitative lead in overall numbers of offensive missiles and a marked advantage in the throw-weight of its land-based ICBM force.[10] In the ICBM category, the agreement allows the Soviet Union approximately 1,600 launch vehicles (of which around 280 are of the heavy-payload SS-9 variety) to 1,054 for the United States. In the SLBM category it allows the Soviets a proportionally similar numerical advantage of up to 950 launchers, as compared with 710 for the United States.[11] In terms of ICBM throw-weight, finally, it allows the Soviets an edge by a factor of from 2.5 to 4 depending on which subjective calculation criteria one prefers to employ. Reduced to practical language, this suggests that if the Soviets were to MIRV their ICBM force (a move not proscribed by the executive agreement), they could potentially attain as much as a 4 to 1 superiority over the United States in numbers of deliverable nuclear warheads of equivalent size and yield.

Granted that the interim agreement confers these quantitative advantages on the Soviets, however, the relevant question is not simply whether Moscow can be said to have attained a measure of "superiority" out of the deal, but whether that superiority is meaningful in any practical sense. And on this latter score, for a variety of strategic and technical reasons, there is a strong answer to be made in the negative.

To begin with, the numerical ratio of offensive missiles in the Soviet-American strategic equation is only part of the overall picture and can be quite misleading if interpreted *in vacuo*. While the provisions of SALT I allow the Soviets theoretically a substantial quantitative lead over the United States in offensive launch vehicle strength, that putative advantage is offset by a more than two-to-one American counter-preponderance over the Soviet Union in the more significant category of individual nuclear warheads and bombs deliverable to independent targets. Including SLBM and manned bomber delivery vehicles as well as ICBM's, the figures top out at approximately 5,700 warheads for the United States as opposed to 2,500 for the Soviet Union, the difference being a product of the United States' monopoly on operational MIRV's and its substantial numerical superiority over the Soviets in manned strategic bombers. If one also includes the more than 400 nuclear-capable American forward-based tactical fighter aircraft in Europe and aboard carriers in the Mediterranean, the imbalance becomes weighted even more in favor of the United States.

Second, the quantitative missile supremacy granted to the Soviets by SALT I is far more potential than real at the moment. The Soviet SS-9 heavy-booster deployment program, for example, ground to a halt at around the 280-mark in 1970, leaving a force posture considerably short of the level which would be needed to threaten a disarming attack against the American Minuteman arsenal. To be sure, the interim agreement does permit each country to increase the linear dimensions of its ICBM silos by as much as 15 per cent, and there has been some concern expressed in various conservative circles that the Soviets may be in the process of taking advantage of that provision by procuring an entirely new ICBM even larger than the SS-9 and then deploying it extensively in upgraded versions of existing launch silos.

As best as one can gather from the publicly available evidence, however, that supposedly "new" missile has yet to be seen, let alone identified, by the United States intelligence community. Moreover, the notion that the Soviets would go to the inordinate trouble and expense of tearing down and then rebuilding all their SS-9 silos to accommodate a costly new missile offering scarcely more than a marginal increase in payload reflects, at the very least, a vast underestimation of the Soviet military-bureaucratic commitment to the retention of the SS-9 force which took such painstaking efforts to develop and deploy.[12]

The same can be said of the related concern about the ostensible Soviet advantage over the United States in ICBM throw-weight. By itself, missile throw-weight capacity is a meaningless asset. In order for it to be translated into an instrument for hurting an adversary like the United States who possesses a large and well-hardened nuclear retaliatory force, it must be coupled with enough accurate MIRV's to provide both a highly favorable warhead-to-target exchange ratio and a uniformly reliable hard-target kill capability for the attacker. Yet the

Soviet Union to date has not even flight-tested, let alone begun to deploy, MIRV's, and it is thus highly improbable that it could take significant advantage of its ICBM throw-weight superiority during the five-year course of the SALT I executive agreement even if it wanted to.[13]

In the SLBM category, the imbalance granted to Moscow by the executive agreement is entirely problematical because the Soviet Union at present has substantially fewer missile-launching submarines than the United States and will indeed only outnumber us by two (43 to 41) when its on-going Y-class submarine construction program is completed. As noted above, of course, the SALT I accord also allows the Soviet Union (as well as the United States) to replace its early-generation ICBM's with up-to-date SLBM's, a provision which, if implemented by Moscow, would succeed in bringing the Soviet missile-launching submarine force up to a ceiling of 62, or around 20 more than the number available to the United States. Even that numerical edge, however, would be largely illusory because it would have to be accompanied by an offsetting reduction of the Soviet ICBM force from 1,600 to 1,400 boosters. Furthermore, apart from the ICBM tradeoff it would involve, a Soviet decision to go for the full 62-submarine complement allowed by the agreement would still provide Moscow with only a functional equivalency in SLBM strength with the United States, because of the fact that geographical differences and the Soviet lack of overseas submarine bases require that the Soviet Union have at least three submarines for every two possessed by the United States in order to keep an equal number on station and ready to fire in the event of war.[14]

Nothing in the preceding discussion has been intended in any way to suggest that the SALT I accord (or at least that portion of it concerning offensive forces) is the best that the United States could have hoped for. One can legitimately share the liberal objection, for example, against waxing overly enthusiastic about a purported "arms control" agreement which not only fails to block such qualitative weapons innovations as MIRV, ULMS, and B-1, but which indeed does its very best to assure that the American defense budget will become even more astronomical in size than ever before. More important, one can also reasonably lament the fact that the executive agreement did not hold out for something more closely approximating Soviet-American numerical equality in offensive missile strength. A strategic arms control accord, ideally, ought to be structured in such a way as to have a dampening effect on the nuclear arms race by providing for a mutually satisfactory and equitable balance in which neither side need have any reason to consider itself penalized by the embarrassing and psychologically burdensome onus of perceived "inferiority" to its adversary. To the extent that the SALT I executive agreement has led many Americans to believe that the United States came out of the negotiations on the short end of the bargain and to insist, accordingly, on compensation in the form of unilateral American weapons improvements on the qualitative front, it has failed to live up fully to that ideal objective.[15]

Notwithstanding these technical reservations, however, the SALT I accord comes across on balance as a clearly remarkable and unassailable diplomatic breakthrough which deserves all the support it can get. If it does not offer both sides the best of all possible worlds (as no agreement could be expected to do anyway), it certainly advances the Soviet-American strategic relationship significantly closer to a mature and productive dialogue. For one thing, it has had the unprecedented effect of forcing military leaders in both countries finally to recognize and accept the notion that arms control negotiation is a legitimate and proper business for nation-states to be involved in. For another, it has been a clear testament to the Soviet Union's willingness to be a tractable negotiating partner as long as the United States gives it the respect due an equal and offers reciprocal concessions as well. Finally, and most significantly, it has provided both a notable partial limitation of the arms race by effectively freezing Soviet and American ABM and offensive missile deployments at approximately their current levels and a sound point of departure for the achievement of additional arms curbs in SALT II, such as offensive force-level reductions and selected bans on qualitative weapons innovations.[16]

The belief will persist in many conservative circles, however, that the United States "lost" SALT I because of the offensive force superiority which the accord in effect granted to the Soviet Union. Those of this persuasion will assert that the Soviet elite has long been committed to attaining strategic superiority over the United States, that SALT I virtually delivered it to them free of charge on a silver platter, and that in any future international crisis, the Soviets will be able to capitalize on their supremacy by forcing the Americans to back away just as we capitalized when the odds were reversed during the Cuban missile crisis in 1962. Already, such observers argue, the Soviets have shown a marked proclivity toward diplomatic muscle-flexing as a result of their steady strategic force improvements over the past half-decade, and it should only stand to reason, therefore, that they will continue to do so even more assertively in a SALT I environment which freezes the strategic balance to the distinct numerical advantage of the Soviet Union.[17]

To deal with this argument properly would require another essay altogether, but the present analysis would not be complete without a few brief remarks in response. First of all, given the multiplicity of criteria which can be used for measuring relative strategic power today, the concept of strategic superiority itself is highly subjective and is very much a matter of idiosyncratic definition. Just as an American observer can conveniently view as evidence of "superiority" the Soviet lead in offensive missile numbers and throw-weight capacity, so a Soviet analyst can equally see in the American preponderance in manned bombers and MIRV's an indication that the United States still holds most of the strategic cards.[18] So it is not at all clear precisely to what extent the Soviet Union really enjoys strategic superiority. For that matter, it is not clear whether the concept of strategic superiority even possesses any practical meaning at all.

Second, it is far from self-evident that the Soviet Union harbors any official doctrinal imperative aimed at the achievement of "strategic superiority" over the United States, however it may be defined. Of course, one can easily find any number of exhortations in the Soviet military literature urging strategic superiority as a policy goal, but such statements are inextricably bound up in internal Soviet bureaucratic in-fighting over resource allocations and hardly constitute authoritative expressions of official government policy.[19] A much closer approximation of the formal Soviet position on the issue may be found in Secretary Brezhnev's insistence that the Soviet Union share "equal security" with the United States, a declaratory perspective which seems far more analogous to President Nixon's own policy criterion of "strategic sufficiency" than to any sort of doctrine aimed at clear-cut "strategic superiority." [20]

Finally, the argument that American reticence in the face of Moscow's recent global military demonstrations and intrusions stems from the United States's loss of its former strategic nuclear ascendancy seems strangely oblivious to the corrosive effect which the war in Indochina, domestic dissent, and the resultant decline in the credibility of the United States government both at home and abroad have had cumulatively on the American capacity and willingness to maintain an interventionist foreign policy.[21] Given the pervasiveness of the domestic and international tribulations the war has imposed on the American leadership and populace, it is hard to imagine how the United States would have responded differently even if the Soviets had remained markedly inferior in the strategic balance.[22]

As for the future, one can scarcely venture a confident prediction, but it seems likely enough that the outcome of international crises will continue to be governed by considerations of relative commitment and resolve rather than by simple arithmetic calculations of which side possesses the larger or weightier array of strategic nuclear forces.[23] As long as American defense planners persist in wringing their hands over the supposed "superiority" SALT I has conferred on the Soviets and in lamenting the diplomatic disadvantage it allegedly imposes on the United States, they will assure the continued growth of a self-fulfilling prophecy ill-designed to shore up that American resolve which, in other contexts, they themselves deem so important to the diplomatic stature of the United States. All the same, however, the world will remain a dangerous place for both superpowers to live, and we may thus continue to rely, if not on the self-assurance of American critics of SALT I, then on the ever-present risk of nuclear escalation and inadvertent war to keep the Soviet Union safely delivered from the temptation to push its luck too far in the crisis arena.

NOTES

[1] Remarks at a congressional briefing, June 15, 1972, in *Documentation on the Strategic Arms Limitations Agreements* (Department of State, Bureau of Public Affairs, News Release, June 20, 1972).

[2] A brief historical overview of the SALT negotiations may be found in Bernard Gwertzman, "Strategic Arms Talks: Long Road to Success." *The New York Times*, June 18, 1972. On Soviet motivations and objectives in the talks, see Benjamin S. Lambeth, "Moscow and the Missile Race," *Current History*, Vol. 61 (October, 1971), pp. 215–221, and Thomas W. Wolfe, *Soviet Interests in SALT: Political, Economic,*

Bureaucratic, and Strategic Contributions and Impediments to Arms Control (The RAND Corporation, P-4702, September, 1971).

3 For the full range of specifics, see "Text of Treaty to Limit ABM's and the Interim Agreement on Offensive Missiles," *The New York Times* (May 27, 1972).

4 See, for example, Bernard T. Feld, "Looking to SALT II," *Bulletin of the Atomic Scientists,* Vol. 28, No. 6 (June, 1972), pp. 2–3.

5 The leading public proponent of this viewpoint is Senator Henry Jackson, closely followed by Defense Secretary Melvin Laird. For general background, see "Second Thoughts on SALT I," *Time,* July 10, 1972. For a detailed and sophisticated articulation of the conservative argument by a highly knowledgeable civilian defense intellectual, see also Donald G. Brennan, "When the SALT Hit the Fan," *National Review,* June 23, 1972.

6 A Princeton University study group has suggested that the proposed fleet of 241 B-1 strategic bombers, for example, when coupled with SRAM (Short-Range Attack Missile) armament and a supporting fleet of new tanker aircraft, could run as high as $75 billion, as contrasted with the $11.1 billion price tag put on it by the administration. See Peter J. Ognibene, "The B-1 Ballyhoo," *The New Republic,* June 17, 1972.

7 The Moscow ABM complex is estimated to consist of relatively primitive exoatmospheric interceptors and low-performance radars as compared with the technically more elegant American Safeguard system. Deployment of the Moscow system terminated in the late 1960's at 64 launchers, at about the same time that commentary began appearing in the Soviet military press deprecating the reliability of ABM's against a sophisticated attack. It may well be, therefore, that the Soviets simply found themselves stuck with a losing proposition and happily chose to cut their losses in SALT rather than press ahead with further deployments that would merely have wasted a lot of money.

8 There was also a counterforce target-coverage rationale underlying the initial MIRV concept. Whether that rationale or the ABM-penetration argument was the one primarily responsible for getting the MIRV program under way is not altogether clear from the available evidence. See James R. Kurth, "A Widening Gyre: The Logic of American Weapons Procurement," *Public Policy,* Vol. 19, No. 3 (Summer, 1971), pp. 383–385.

9 It does not, however, totally eliminate the offense-defense interaction dynamic. Research and development in high-energy lasers and in other ballistic missile defense schemes not based on missile interceptors are in no way affected by the ABM treaty.

10 Throw-weight, usually measured in kilopounds or fractions thereof, is a term used to denote the effective payload of an offensive missile. Its importance in strategic force calculations stems from the fact that it is more or less directly correlated with a missile's overall megatonnage capacity or number of deliverable independent warheads of equivalent size. As a general rule, the more throw-weight increases, the more versatile a missile becomes.

11 These and other figures cited in this article are taken from a Defense Department release published in *The Washington Post,* May 27, 1972. For a comprehensive run-down of Soviet and American strategic capabilities, see *The Military Balance, 1971–1972* (London: International Institute for Strategic Studies, 1972). See also the excellent analysis presented in Johan Jorgen Holst, *Comparative U.S. and Soviet Deployments, Doctrines, and Arms Limitation* (Chicago: Center for Policy Study, University of Chicago, 1971).

12 For a careful analysis which suggests that Soviet weapons deployment policies, like our own, are governed by considerable bureaucratic inertia and are less than readily susceptible to hairpin turns of this sort, see Matthew P. Gallagher and Karl F. Spielmann, *The Politics of Power: Soviet Decisionmaking for Defense* (Institute for Defense Analyses, P-774, October, 1971).

13 This is not to suggest that there will be no Soviet MIRVing at all throughout the span of the agreement. It is, however, to argue clearly that any such effort will not be able to offer the Soviets anything even approaching a credible counterforce capability against the United States. There is a rather hysterical view currently in circulation, perhaps best exemplified in Joseph Alsop's latest strategic disquisition, "The Arms Agreement," *The Washington* Post, May 31, 1972, which seems to believe that all the Soviets need to do to achieve a combat-ready MIRV for their SS-9 force is

simply to snap their fingers. In fact, there is plenty of evidence suggesting that the Soviets have had a great deal of difficulty with their MIRV development program and may even have been forced to go back to the drawing board. For the most recent official disclaimer of any rampant Soviet MIRV threat, see "Soviet Test of MIRV is Denied," *The Washington Post*, June 10, 1972.

14 It is probable, though not publicly confirmed, that the Soviets attempted in 1970 to establish a missile-submarine support facility in Cienfuegos, Cuba, and were compelled to scuttle their plan in the face of a quiet but firm American reminder that the understanding worked out during the 1962 Cuban missile crisis prohibited such a base. Whether or not the Soviets will make a similar effort elsewhere in the future remains an open question. For discussion, see George Quester, "Missiles in Cuba, 1970," *Foreign Affairs*, Vol. 49, No. 3 (April, 1971), pp. 493–506.

15 One is tempted to suggest that President Nixon, in his overweening desire to conclude a SALT agreement during his visit to Moscow for domestic political purposes, settled for a bill of sale that he clearly would not have accepted under less demanding circumstances, and that he could have perhaps easily induced the Soviets to back down from their ceiling of 62 SLBM submarines had he ignored his parochial political interests and allowed the negotiations to continue for several more months. This view, however, must be offset against the equally persuasive comment by a senior government official to the effect that "the President is still a hawk, and anyone who thinks he'd make a deal not in the country's interest for a short-term gain is just damned silly and superficial." Quoted in Michael Getler, "Defense Convinced U.S. Won't Be Hurt," *The Washington Post*, May 27, 1972.

16 For a useful discussion of the key issues which the next round of SALT will have to face, see Herbert Scoville, Jr., "Beyond SALT One," *Foreign Affairs*, Vol. 50, No. 3 (April, 1972), pp. 488–500.

17 This argument tends to be made more often by assertion than by analysis. For a representative example, see the article by Walter Darnell Jacobs, "Soviet Strategic Effectiveness," *Journal of International Affairs*, Vol. 26, No. 1 (1972), pp. 60–72, which bemoans the Soviet Union's incipient attainment of strategic superiority over the U.S., yet which fails to offer even a pretense of explaining how Moscow might be able to use that superiority to its advantage. For a vastly more sophisticated (though only slightly more substantiated) variant of the same point of view, see Uri Ratanan, *The Changing American-Soviet Strategic Balance: Some Political Implications* (Committee on Government Operations, Senate, 92d Congress, 2d Session, 1972).

18 Indeed, one can speculate that the Soviet Union held out for its offensive force advantage in SALT I precisely to counterbalance the American monopoly on operational MIRV's.

19 An excellent general discussion on this point may be found in David Holloway, "Strategic Concepts and Soviet Policy," *Survival*, Vol. 13, No. 11 (November, 1971), pp. 364–369.

20 See the relevant excerpt from Brezhnev's initial statement to this effect (made before a Moscow election meeting on June 11, 1971) reprinted in *Current History*, Vol. 61 (October, 1971), p. 240. For a discussion of President Nixon's concept of "sufficiency," see also Morton H. Halperin, *Defense Strategies for the Seventies* (Boston: Little, Brown and Company, 1971), pp. 72–86.

21 For further discussion, see the balanced analysis in Andrew J. Pierre, "America Down, Russia Up: The Changing Political Role of Military Power," *Foreign Policy*, No. 4 (Fall, 1971), pp. 163–187.

22 For that matter, it is not altogether clear just how much Soviet policy has been affected by the changed strategic balance. If the Soviet leaders have indeed become so impressed with their alleged superiority and so contemptuous of American diplomatic power and resolve, then one may fairly ask why they took both the renewed American bombing of North Vietnam and the mining of Haiphong harbor without so much as lifting a finger.

23 This point is developed at greater length in Benjamin S. Lambeth, "Deterrence in the MIRV Era," *World Politics*, Vol. 24, No. 2 (January, 1972), pp. 221–242. See also Alexander L. George and others, *The Limits of Coercive Diplomacy* (Boston: Little, Brown and Company, 1971).

19

Paris, Pretoria, Peking...
Proliferation?

GEORGE H. QUESTER

On a superficial first impression, there is a glaring weakness in the efforts of the United States and Soviet Union to stop the spread of nuclear weapons. The Nuclear Non-Proliferation Treaty limits possession of nuclear weapons to the five nations already in the "club," the U.S., USSR, U.K., France and China. Yet only three of these five nations intend to sign and ratify the treaty. These three will indeed refuse to give away nuclear weapons, and will assist peaceful nuclear projects only where IAEA (International Atomic Energy Agency) safeguards ensure that no weapons are produced. But won't the Treaty be meaningless if France and China are free to offer bombs to anyone that asks for them? Supporters of NPT can respond that the gap will be filled if most potential recipients of nuclear weapons sign the Treaty, i.e., promise not to accept such gifts. Yet abstentions by nuclear weapons nations may still make a great difference.

Some "near-nuclear" nations are already capable of making bombs without any assistance. Most however can do it much more easily with material or technical help from the outside. Indeed, if one were prepared to give complete bombs away, any potential receiving nation thereby becomes a "near-nuclear" power. France and China can give bombs away if they want; they have not legally promised not to. They can also give away technical information on how to produce bombs. Some other states are similarly significant in that they can sell or give away uranium, the material of which bombs are made. What if they also refuse to sign NPT?

For the moment, the attitude of Paris seems reasonably clear. France, its foreign minister has said, will not sign NPT, but will behave just as a signatory would. We will, of course, never receive an exact accounting of the assistance France rendered to Israel, or a denial that France left any bombs with its one-time partner. Also left unsettled are the rumors that Israeli scientists contributed to French progress on the H-bomb. Presumably, any such cooperation has now been terminated by political developments other than NPT.

We can also not be certain that nonsignatory France will interpret NPT quite as strictly as will signatory states. France will not give away bombs; but would she sell India or someone else crucial components, enabling that country to escape IAEA safeguards and then to make its own weapons? Even the signatories will argue about which sales are allowed and which are forbidden to a state rejecting safeguards. Whenever France and India negotiate any agreement on heavy water, etc., some part of the world public will again fear an undermining of NPT.

Bombs can be disseminated by nuclear-weapon nations and/or by nations controlling sources of uranium. In descending order, the three most significant sources of uranium are the United States, Canada and South Africa. As one of the nuclear-weapon nations that wrote NPT, the position of the United States is clear. Canada's position is also reasonably clear, a combination of moral objection to the spread of weapons and general aversion to the vagaries of the uranium market. Having suffered economically when the United States curtailed its own production of warheads abruptly in the early 1960s, Canada is not likely to become enthusiastic about potential uranium markets to be found in other countries. In any event, Canada has signed and ratified the Non-Proliferation Treaty.

I

The Republic of South Africa may be more of a problem. South Africa has not indicated as yet any intention of signing NPT. As a semi-outcast in the international community, Pretoria has a difficult path to tread. There might be gains to bypassing the international system with uranium sales in special circumstances, but there will also be strong arguments for cooperating with the system, tacitly or explicitly.

Of those states which are imminently interested in nuclear weapons, there are a number which would seem to be disqualified from partnership with South Africa. India, Pakistan and the United Arab Republic all have explicitly denounced the white regime. In extremis, one of these states might quietly accept uranium even from the devil, but it is hard to see what South Africa could be offered in return. Cash payments might more easily ease South African qualms on sales to Germany, Japan, Brazil, Australia or Argentina, if these states remain outside the NPT system. As will be seen, however, cash considerations can also make South Africa support NPT and the IAEA.

There has been speculation on cooperation between Israel and South Africa, some of it maliciously originating from Eastern European sources which like to lump together the regimes they oppose. Israeli involvement in Black Africa may superficially stand in the way of cooperation, as might the occasional anti-Semitism that emerges in South Africa, but both countries could indeed overlook this if grander projects were involved. One could obviously speculate on a deal whereby both states got nuclear weapons, combining South African uranium and Israeli expertise. Cooperation in the sharing of other military hardware might bring the two countries together also, as each is under a slightly different kind of arms embargo. Yet there will still be important arguments against South Africa so brazenly defying the world's consensus on proliferation.

II

First, because of the revenue they earn in selling uranium to the legitimate peaceful power reactor markets, South Africans will have to be concerned. This market promises to expand rapidly through the 1970s; but the appearance of a sixth nuclear power could substantially hamper this, as the United States and other technologically advanced states become reluctant to license or sell reactors, or to process fuel. The Republic has thus several times stated that it will not allow its uranium sales to be used to increase the number of nuclear-weapons nations.

There is also something dignifying and stabilizing for South Africa in being a supplier of uranium, just as in being a source of gold. But for this, the style might be more parochial, xenophobic or radical. If NPT induces the world to tolerate a great expansion of nuclear power production, it would be short-sighted and foolish for South Africa to rock the boat. Of course, NPT might hurt the uranium market by fracturing it into signatory and nonsignatory blocs, with conflicting incompatible control systems. If it wins widespread acceptance, however, it can ease barriers to fuel transfers and sales, as the IAEA safeguards become standardized and replace bilateral or Euratom arrangements. The Republic's reluctance to sign the Treaty thus may simply have reflected an uncertainty on how the Treaty will be accepted elsewhere, that is, whether it will stabilize or upset peaceful nuclear development.

For the moment, most of South Africa's uranium sales depends on the enrichment services of some other nation. The market for uranium is essentially divided into two clusters: installed power reactors which require enriched uranium as a fuel, and reactors which can utilize natural uranium. Countries with natural fuel reactors can come to terms directly with the Republic, and could presumably produce plutonium for atomic bombs directly from South African uranium. A nation requiring enriched uranium, however, will have to find some means to preprocess the South African product. For the moment, there are few such enrichment facilities available outside the current nuclear-weapon nations, indeed outside the United States. The USSR, France and China have facilities for enriching uranium; Britain has a facility which was shut down for a time, but may now be reopened if the commercial demand for enriched uranium makes it profitable. Proposals for gas centrifuge processes are under study by an Anglo-Dutch-German consortium, and in Japan. If these nations sign the Treaty, however, their facilities and any materials passed through them will also be under IAEA safeguards, whether or not South Africa signs NPT.

Pretoria may thus be dissuaded from delivering uranium to the "sixth" nuclear-weapon nation. Yet one must also consider the Republic's option of itself becoming the sixth. Under present circumstances, South Africa stands to gain less than it would lose in making nuclear weapons itself. The conventional superiority over any political opponents in Africa is so clear that it would hardly seem advisable to change the rules of the game. The Republic generally seeks to avoid publicity, and a nuclear-weapons program surely would focus the world's attention all the more on South Africa. If some other state, for example India, breaks the ice by becoming the sixth nuclear power, the Republic could then more easily contemplate conspiring with someone to become the seventh and eighth. At the moment, a move toward nuclear weapons would rouse great opposition and emotion, in Africa and out.

III

Several kinds of circumstances might thus be required to make South Africa willing to dispense uranium without safeguards. If NPT fails to pull in most of the significant near-nuclear nations, e.g., if Germany and Japan and Italy try to go it alone in refusing to ratify, South Africa could be guided in this direction simply by economic considerations. Even without safeguards, such markets would be difficult to pass up. Alternatively, if political and military events lead the Republic to feel a need for nuclear weapons, or for some other special kind of weaponry, it might be ready to offer its uranium in exchange. Finally, there might be some other special favor which another nation might be able to grant in exchange for assistance on nuclear weapons. If the analysis above is correct, however, it would have to be an extremely big and necessary favor to make such a defiance of NPT worthwhile.

None of this necessarily requires that the Republic sign NPT. South Africa can certainly observe the Treaty without signing it. As an important supplier rather than receiver of critical materials, it can afford to mold a policy of its own, demanding safeguards over most or all of its sales. There are some clear bargaining arguments for such a noncommittal position, whereby South Africa would cooperate with the NPT system, but not bind itself to do so forever. On a year-by-year basis, the threat of unsafeguarded uranium sales can be held in reserve to deter overly-stringent boycotts and embargoes, to force the United States and Britain to accommodate South African interests where such accommodation is crucial. In this light, it will be optimal for South Africa neither to surrender nor to exercise the option of spreading nuclear weapons.

Aside from this residual threat of selling uranium to weapons producers, the Republic might withhold an NPT signature simply to avoid unnecessary IAEA inspection of South Africa. Reactors purchased from abroad will, of course, have to come under IAEA safeguards on a project-by-project basis, but at least the uranium mines can escape inspection. At the moment, IAEA safeguards procedures do not extend to mining, but NPT seemingly calls for an extension of such inspection to mines as well as reactors. South African failure to sign the Treaty may thus reduce potentially troublesome access by outsiders to the

Republic. It could maintain a secrecy on exact amounts of gold and uranium production; the two are somewhat conjoined. Such secrecy is certainly important for merchandizing gold; it might someday also facilitate the clandestine sale of uranium.

IV

Peking, a third possible threat to NPT, normally draws the most speculation and attention. Chinese communist statements in the past have suggested that it would be desirable if all socialist nations possessed nuclear weapons. Other pronouncements have declared that no nation can deny another nation the right to such weapons. Denunciations of the Non-Proliferation Treaty have been forthcoming ever since it became clear that the U.S. and USSR might agree on such a pact.

Given Chinese interests in various parts of the globe, it has thus been quite plausible that Peking might deliver weapons to nations requesting them. Leaving aside various national liberation movements, which are not likely recipients of nuclear weapons from anyone, two specific possibilities have drawn some comment—Pakistan and U.A.R. There [have been] many similarities between the two. Each has a hostile neighbor known to be capable of early manufacture of atomic bombs. Each has despatched delegations of physicists to China; whatever the intention, this has encouraged speculation on nuclear weapons assistance from Peking.

At first glance, outsiders might wonder what will prevent such transfers from occurring. Pakistan will not sign NPT until India does, which probably means never. Egypt signed the Treaty under obvious Russian pressure, but will not ratify it unless Israel signs and ratifies. Peking is at least nominally committed to great sympathy for proliferation to such nations.

V

If India definitely acquires nuclear weapons, Pakistan might very much want to do the same. In the worst of situations, nothing else might suffice to deter the use of Indian bombs. Long before this calamity, the psychological inferiority suggested by Pakistan's non-nuclear status might seem undesirable. As long as India has not yet manufactured any nuclear explosives, a Pakistani request for such weapons may seem less likely, for Rawalpindi clearly prefers a non-nuclear confrontation with its only adversary. Unfortunately, however, New Delhi senses two adversaries, one of which, China, has already gone nuclear.

If Israel definitely acquires nuclear weapons, the U.A.R. may very much want to do the same. There have been rumors that Egypt sought a promise from the USSR that it would be provided A-bombs if Israel manufactured its own, a request which the Soviets rejected. The wording of NPT in any event makes it illegal for the Russians to give nuclear weapons to the U.A.R., even if Israel has acquired its own. Again the U.A.R. might be expected to turn to Peking for the same declaration, since Peking will not be bound by the Treaty. Indeed, Egypt might want to acquire nuclear weapons from China even before Israel had acquired them, for its hopes for peace are hardly higher than those of Pakistan with India.

VI

Yet there have been contrary considerations for both Pakistan and the U.A.R. which made any immediate transfer of nuclear weapons from China much less likely than the pessimistic picture would have it. The U.A.R. has been heavily dependent on Russian military assistance; Pakistan has been seeking to acquire such assistance. The Russians are opposed to proliferation and are at odds with China. For either Pakistan or Egypt to become so visibly involved with Peking might have alienated much more immediately necessary assistance in the conventional weapons field—the atomic bomb is not a panacea which quickly replaces all this. Moreover, neither Pakistan nor Egypt has totally burned its bridges with the United States, and would likely have done so if either one were to announce an agreement for nuclear weapons from Peking.

The reactions of the United States and USSR might go beyond cut-offs in aid. The United States, for example, might have tried to blockade all Chinese shipments to Egypt if it had been made clear that nuclear weapons were being handed over. World public opinion could well be marshaled behind strong sanctions against any nation which thus brazenly attempted to become number six in the nuclear club. Much would depend, of course, on whether Israel or India had already reached for the bomb and public opinion had been mobilized against them.

If the Chinese were willing to give bombs away, Pakistan and Egypt might be reluctant to accept them. Yet there is also good reason to assume that Peking has not been at all anxious to give them away. Since the first detonation of a Chinese bomb in 1964, there have been some significant hedges on Chinese statements on nuclear proliferation. There are pronouncements that the assistance of one nation to another is entirely appropriate in regard to the peaceful uses of nuclear energy, but that it is best for a nation seeking weapons to develop them itself. (Perhaps thus a nation may retain its independence and self-respect?)

Within the last three years, there have been more specific statements accusing the Japanese government of aspiring to manufacture nuclear weapons, and declaring that Japan under no circumstances should consider doing so. The Pro-Peking Communist Party in India has similarly opposed any Indian move toward nuclear weapons.

VII

Ever since detonating its first bomb, the Chinese Communist regime has declared its commitment to a "no-first-use" policy, whereby it would only use nuclear weapons if some other nation had done so first. No other nuclear-weapon nation has so clearly circumscribed the cases in which it would use its arsenal. The Chinese statements at times have suggested that nuclear weapons would not be used even if an American or Russian army were to invade China, as long as the invaders had not used them first. Releasing control over such weapons to other nations would appear to conflict with this apparent desire to keep all wars non-nuclear.

The statements to date thus do not firmly require Peking to refuse requests for nuclear weapons, but they certainly allow for such a refusal. The diplomatic reluctance of Cairo and Rawalpindi to become tied clearly to Peking will also make the Chinese reluctant to make firm offers of nuclear weapons aid. It would be humiliating, at the least, for Peking to be on record—publicly or even privately—with a firm offer as long as the recipients will not publicly commit themselves even to being interested. There is no evidence that private Pakistani and Egyptian talks with the Chinese have even gotten down to cases on possible proliferation; there are indications that they have not, that the Chinese have not been inviting discussion of this possibility at all.

The argument has been stated persuasively that donations of nuclear weapons might fit in well with the general Chinese approach to world political unrest, a low-cost donation with a high return of political confusion. Yet the opposite case can be persuasive as well. China has not professed to attach great significance to its own bombs; as mentioned above, they are to be used only if others use them first. Peking has attached more significance in its propaganda to well-founded guerrilla movements. To pass bombs around reverses all this in the eyes of the world. In the Middle East, it diverts attention from Al Fatah toward the U.A.R.'s government in Cairo. In general, it invites comparison with the strategic weapons Moscow could have offered; in techniques of guerrilla warfare, Peking might claim a special advantage, but in bombs it can not.

If one releases five or ten atomic bombs into the hands of the Arab governments, the follow-up influence one has earned may not be extensive. A long and gradual guerrilla campaign with Chinese instructors and Chinese machine guns promises much greater leverage, as well as being more consistent with the "man over weapons" ideological theme from which Peking has not yet deviated.

Despite earlier American charges against China, moreover, Peking has not been adventurist. The guerrilla movements it has supported by and large . . . had a modicum of mass following and a chance of winning. To give nuclear weapons to small guerrilla movements would be adventurism, perhaps diverting them from the tried and true paths to victory, perhaps making no difference at all. To give nuclear weapons to regimes already established, regimes which might topple overnight—as in Ghana—would similarly be adventurism. A war in which nuclear weapons were used by one or two regimes over which Peking had lost its control can hardly be viewed with equanimity in China. If nuclear weapons are used anywhere, their use anywhere else will be more likely, and Peking has shown every sign of hoping to reduce this risk to herself.

If there is one bona fide satellite or ally of China in the world, it is Albania. But Peking has said nothing about the appropriateness of Albania getting its own nuclear weapons. Rumors were spread in

1968 that China intended to deploy its own MRBMs (medium range ballistic missiles) to Albania, presumably thereby to be able to reach targets in Russia outside the striking range from Sinkiang. Yet even these would presumably have been under Chinese control, thus not constituting "proliferation," and no confirmation for such rumors is at hand. If one feared a Yugoslav-, Western- or Moscow-oriented take-over of Albania, nuclear weapons might indeed be a valuable deterrent; Chinese border conflicts with the USSR similarly might justify deployments allowing missile strikes along different azimuths. Yet the extent of Chinese caution is shown by Peking's unwillingness to comment openly on or confirm any such deployments; unadvertised, such deployments would lack much of their deterrent effect. Peking after all described Khrushchev's missile deployment to Cuba as "adventurism" (while labelling the withdrawal as "capitulationism").

VIII

The absence of French, South African and Communist Chinese signatures from the Nuclear Non-Proliferation Treaty does not immediately upset the Treaty. In our imaginations we are prone to exaggerate the indifference of such nations to a further spread of nuclear weapons. Yet to demonstrate that fears are groundless does not terminate their political significance.

As long as Peking does not definitively commit itself to resisting proliferation, it will still be possible for weapons to spread from this source. None of the barriers cited above are necessarily permanent. Changes of government can occur which might reduce the Soviet connection as a factor.

For the moment, the proliferation scenarios remain linked to other potential nuclear-weapon programs. Israel and India are close to the development of nuclear bombs themselves, and other decisions must adjust to this. For Peking and for a potential nuclear bomb recipient, several contingency strategies must thus be considered. Nuclear weapons could be supplied quietly before any rival weapons programs reach fruition, to facilitate some grand preemptive sneak attack. Alternatively, such weapons already in place could be announced directly after India or Israel announced theirs, thus to establish an immediate counter-deterrent. There are drawbacks to any such transfer prior to the explicit provocation; supplying weapons to a "seventh" will be diplomatically much easier than having supplied them to the sixth.

A second approach would be to announce mutual agreement that Chinese weapons will be transferred as soon as, and not before, India or Israel acquires them. Unless accompanied by a clandestine prior deployment, however, this risks an attempt by someone to interfere with or preempt the transfer. Everyone today assumes that Peking, Cairo and Rawalpindi will be more amenable to a transfer if India or Israel receive nuclear weapons. Proclaiming this in advance has the advantage of putting it down clearly as a commitment, but it also inspires talk of China having acquired satellites, or fears that nuclear bombs have already been transferred.

But the reasoning here does not stabilize at any primary level. Even if China had no intention of introducing nuclear weapons into the Middle East, it encourages such a development by the failure to commit itself to resisting proliferation. One linkage is as follows: Some Israelis will wish to avoid renouncing nuclear weapons and submitting to IAEA inspection; domestically they will note that such inspection can not ensure that Egypt has not quietly received such weapons from China, even if the USSR can be trusted. If the U.A.R. were to gain control over such weapons when Israel had none, the weapons could easily come into use, either because the Arabs expected to win a war thereby, or because revenge for past defeats was now possible even without victory, through bombs on Tel Aviv and Haifa. The Israeli government responds to this domestic sentiment by failing to submit to guarantees which could assure the Arabs that no bombs were being assembled in Dimona or elsewhere; the Egyptians then turn to China with a stronger argument for a U.A.R. bomb.

IX

In discussions of arms control, one must be careful to consider thoughts about physical realities, as well as the realities themselves. Even if the physical problem poses no real problems, fears around them can take on life of their own. It may thus only require a plausible name on either side to stimulate precautionary arguments that snowball both sides of a conflict toward nuclear weapons. China suffices on the left, South Africa or France a little more remotely on the right.

The disincentives to these sources upsetting the Treaty are serious, but will not certainly always remain so. Worse, we can not guarantee that the images thus aroused will not stampede some part of the world into making the proliferation threat real. It is worth trying to get Treaty signatures from France, China and South Africa. If we can not, our problem is not at all hopeless, but it is a little more difficult.

PART III
The Crises of Institutions

In Part III we deal with a variety of institutions: international and domestic, political and economic. We also examine the role of individuals in these organizations, as bureaucrats and as leaders.

The first section deals with the future of international institutions. What will the new world order be like? We have already discussed the concept of a balance of power. Those who are guided by this philosophy view the future as constituting a world very much like our own today, in which order evolves from a stalemate of forces between the greatest of powers, with the nation-state as the central institution. Many who believe in international integration argue that greater political or economic interdependence would discourage states from going to war. Economic integration, following the model of the European Economic Community, would mean that states of a particular region would become so dependent on each other that they could not conceive of preparing for war against each other. That increased interdependence will restrict conflict has also been argued by those who favor a balance of power among the great powers. Such a notion was at the heart of the agreements reached in the 1972 Moscow summit.

Many authorities believe that political union is a more effective means of restricting the ability of states to wage war than either increased economic interdependence or the balance of power. The successful federations within the United States, Canada, and Australia are often cited as examples of effective political integration despite the internal problems which have been present in each case. One of the original goals of the European unity movement was to restrict conflict among West European states, an objective which seemed particularly pressing after World War II. Today, many Europeans have other objectives for participating in the Common Market; these include economic strength, technological development, and political influence with respect to the rest of the world. It is still not clear whether the new European Economic Community consisting of nine states (the six original members, France, West Germany, Italy, Belgium, the Netherlands, and Luxembourg; and the three new members, Great Britain, Ireland, and Denmark) will remain an economic union or will advance to some form of political federation. Miriam Camps, in "European Unification in the Seventies," discusses this question and relates the future of Europe to the range of developments which are occurring in present-day international politics.

Many of those who have been concerned with ways of bringing order to the tension-ridden sphere of world politics have been intrigued with the possibility of world government—a global union in which a United States of the World would provide the supervision and restraint which have hitherto been lacking. Presumably through an international parliament with binding powers on its members, international conflict would be restricted. Others have viewed this solution as either unachievable or undesirable and have pursued instead the concept of collective security, which has been embodied in both the League of Nations and the United Nations. Although the organizational differences between the latter two institutions are many, both held out the hope that international politics could be partially ordered by agreement between states to deter and control conflicts between individual sovereignties. The League of Nations ended in dismal failure; and by 1970, its twenty-fifth anniversary, the United Nations seemed to have grown moribund through its failure to deal effectively, or often to deal at all, with the major crises of our times. Harlan Cleveland asks, "Can we revive the U.N.?" and suggests several avenues by which the U.N. might be made more effective in ameliorating international conflicts. Though many in this generation have become disillusioned with the United Nations and will question Cleveland's optimism, the ideas he presents—ideas which were once central to American foreign policy and have now become peripheral—are well worth our consideration. The article was written before the People's Republic of China was admitted to the United Nations, but Cleveland's observations seem as applicable today, since China's admission into the U.N. has not had the apocalyptic effect which many had predicted.

The notions of world order discussed thus far all rely on the continued existence of the nation-state in some form. The multinational corportion, however, presents the possibility of an alternate direction for world politics. The growth and increasing role of multinational corporations has made it possible to conceive of a world in which the major units would no longer be nation-states but economic conglomerates composed of directors from a variety of countries. Conceivably, these multinational corporations could overcome cultural differences between peoples since individuals from a variety of backgrounds would work together in a common global operation. In the resulting world order, economic institutions rather than political institutions would prevail, and dollars, francs, or pounds might replace missiles and tanks as "weapons," with a concomitant diminution of violence. Yet, as Robert Heilbroner suggests in his article, "The Multinational Corporations and the Nation-State," it is still not clear precisely what role this comparatively novel institution will play in the international politics of the future. Most multinational corporations are still run by individuals who are based in, and citizens of, a particular nation, and it is not entirely evident whether these corporations are simply extensions of the most powerful nation-states which now exist or whether they represent a new kind of institution entirely.

Although the articles in the second section of Part III focus explicitly upon the United States, they deal with problems of bureaucracy and authority that affect the actions of all governments and hence the level of tranquility and stability in international relations.

In "The Ten Commandments of the Foreign Affairs Bureaucracy," Leslie Gelb and Morton Halperin demonstrate the importance of the role that bureaucratic interests play in the conduct of American foreign policy, and they refer to a variety of historical examples to substantiate their position. Showing that the interests of lower echelon personnel may be quite different from the goals of the national leadership, Gelb and Halperin caution against the patterns which emerged in the Johnson and Nixon Administrations. In the former, the bureaucracy succeeded in hiding the diversity of views in a makeshift consensus which they called "option B"; in the latter, the Kissinger apparatus was used to bypass the bureaucracy entirely. Gelb and Halperin suggest a third alternative in which the conflicts between competing bureaucracies would be used to maintain morale of individual agencies but at the same time the president would be better informed.

While Gelb and Halperin present an overall perspective on the problems a president faces in attempting to maintain control over foreign policy, Richard Holbrooke's "The Machine That Fails" deals more specifically with the dangers inherent in the size of the foreign-policy apparatus. Holbrooke shows us the dangers and problems of a foreign policy pursued by process rather than design in a bureaucracy grown too large for its own good, one in which a variety of agencies (e.g., State, Commerce, Agriculture, CIA, National Security Council) may all be simultaneously involved in the same foreign-policy issue.

In "How Could Vietnam Happen? An Autopsy," James Thomson, Jr., presents the most notorious American case of the application of bureaucratic methods to a particular area of foreign policy. Vietnam was the result of a variety of cultural and political misconceptions, as well as policy errors; but it is possible to argue that the Vietnam debacle might have been averted had not the bureaucratic procedures which were supposed to produce careful consideration of all possible options become highly convoluted. Thomson, who was personally involved in the early stages of the Vietnam imbroglio under both Kennedy and Johnson, attempts to show how Vietnam did happen, presenting us with an extraordinary case history of a government making incremental decisions based on misleading information and false conceptions. The perils of the bureaucratic crisis in the American government, the risks of bureaucratic entanglement for all governments, and the threat to world order created by bureaucratic procedures are thus graphically presented.

In the past, conditions of turmoil or crisis have sometimes resulted in the emergence of dramatic individuals who have become rallying points for those who sought radical change. As Lincoln and Churchill did, such leaders have brought their countries through great crises and led them to a new era. A "great man" usually emerges in a crisis (often a war) and is renowned beyond his political acumen and achievements for a philosophy of life or ideology which he represents. He is often a scholar or even a literary figure. In the last section of Part III, we examine the achievements of two of the most controversial but intriguing figures of our time, Mao Tse-tung and Charles de Gaulle. Stuart Schram is generally respectful of Mao's achievements; David Singer is highly critical of de Gaulle. Each reader will have to determine for himself the place such leaders deserve in history.

Schram's and Singer's articles provide a useful balance to our previous examination of the crisis of institutions, for they make clear that it is not only bureaucracies which control governments and the course of international affairs. The personal values, objectives, style, and effectiveness of a determined and vigorous leader at the pinnacle of a governmental hierarchy may in certain circumstances powerfully affect both that government's policies and the international order. It may be that the directions taken by international and domestic institutions will be the primary determinants of the global system of the future, but the role of individual leaders placed in strategic positions cannot be ignored.

Internationalism: The Crisis of International Institutions and Unity Movements

20

European Unification in the Seventies

MIRIAM CAMPS

. . . In thinking about the future of the European Community today—whether one is thinking about institutional reform, the extent of the integration to be sought among the members of the Community, or the relationship of the Community with the rest of the world—there is an obvious danger that problems will be looked at in the context of the late fifties and early sixties rather than in the context of the seventies. . . .

One of the unfortunate, if understandable, by-products of the long struggle between General de Gaulle and the 'Europeans' of the Monnet and Hallstein persuasions (which were, of course, not quite the same) has been the tendency of the 'Europeans' to become conservative and overly doctrinaire. At a time when they were trying above all to save and protect what they had built, it was natural enough to resist change and experimentation for fear that any tampering with their construction would open the path to its complete destruction. . . .

The European experiment, when it began in 1950 with the announcement of the Schuman Plan, was bold, daring and innovative. It was a brilliant response to the needs of the times: it brought the French and the Germans together in a new creative relationship and it caught the imagination of a battered continent in need of new goals. A 'European Community' could be a catalyst for needed change in the seventies, but if it is to play that role there must be as much willingness to think new thoughts, experiment with new forms and focus on forging new relationships as there was in the earlier, golden, period of the European movement.

At the risk of reciting the obvious, it is perhaps worth noting some of the things that have changed since the drive for European unity lost its momentum about a decade ago, some of the new factors to which any European Community will have to be responsive if it is again to be both relevant to the problems of the period and a pioneer in the long process of building a more rational global society. Although the dividing lines are inevitably somewhat abitrary, it is perhaps useful to group these changes under three broad headings: first, changes in the character of the political-security setting; second, changes in the nature of relationships among states and in attitudes within states; and third, changes in the nature of the agenda confronting the enlarged Community.

Perhaps the four outstanding changes in the political-security setting—if one compares the situation today with that of the late fifties or early sixties—are:

1. the recognition of, and acceptance of, strategic parity between the United States and the Soviet Union, and, related to that change, the opening and continuation of the talks between the two powers on the limitation of strategic arms (SALT);
2. the new triangular relationship between the United States, the Soviet Union and the People's Republic of China;
3. the *de facto* acceptance of the *status quo* in Central Europe as evidenced, for example, by the Western reaction to the Soviet invasion of Czechoslovakia in 1968, by the German pursuit of *Ostpolitik,* and by the character of the arrangements for Berlin which have recently been negotiated by the four responsible powers;
4. the emergence of Japan as the third (or fourth, if the European Community is counted as one rather than six) industrial power which some futurologists predict will overtake the Soviet Union by the end of the decade.

Thus, as compared with the picture a decade ago, the situation today is one of greater fluidity, of five main powers—the United States, the Soviet Union, China, Japan and, potentially, Western Europe— with rather greater freedom of movement for each of the five; it is no longer the essentially bipolar world that characterized the fifties and still dominated thought in the early sixties.

Turning, next, to the changes in the nature of the relationships among states, I suppose the outstanding change is the rate at which the time and space dimensions of the world are shrinking as a result of scientific and technological progress, a change that was most dramatically demonstrated, not only by the fact of the landing on the moon in the summer of 1969, but also by the fact that this extraordinary event was watched and listened to by millions of people everywhere. Connected with the rate at which modern communications are making the world one, but also an important development in its own right, is the growth in the economic interdependence of countries, especially among the highly developed countries with market economies. This trend was, of course, visible a decade ago, but it is so much more marked today that it is worth emphasising. Another development—and one which is closely related to the first two and again not totally new but more pronounced and more obvious today than it was a decade ago—is the blurring of the line between internal and external problems, between matters traditionally thought to be of purely domestic concern and those considered to be of foreign or international concern. Again, this is particularly apparent in the relationships among the developed countries; such things as interest rates come immediately to mind. The emergence of new problems—pollution and other aspects of environmental deterioration today, perhaps weather control and genetic manipulation tomorrow—seem bound to accentuate these three trends, thereby shrinking further the time-space dimensions of the globe, intensifying the interactions between countries and smudging further the traditional lines between domestic and foreign concerns.

Then, there is the change within societies, again particularly in the societies of the developed countries: the disenchantment of youth with affluence, its distrust of all forms of organisation and its faith in a kind of humanistic anarchism. And related to this, but less identified with youth and most noticeable in the United States, there is a shift in priorities: a growing concern with the quality of domestic life and a growing resistance to overseas involvements.

Finally, when one looks at the internal problems that the enlarged Community will need to tackle in the years ahead—the agenda for the seventies—one is struck by two things: first, that the decisions that will soon have to be taken about the tasks needing to be done will confront the member countries with large new choices: there is very little hard guidance in the existing agreements. The injunctions in the Treaties of Rome and Paris have either been largely carried out, as is the case with the formation of the customs union; or they have been outlived, as is the case with some of the provisions of the coal and steel treaty; or the attempts to implement them have so clearly run into the sand that they can probably be given new life only by basic new decisions, as is the case with some of the provisions of the Euratom treaty; or they are so general in character that the decisions yet to be taken on how these precepts are to be implemented will constitute the key decisions, as is the case with monetary union and the other statements of intent in the Hague Communiqué of December 1969. Thus there is, inescapably, a critical period of large and very basic decision-making ahead if the Community is not simply to remain on its present plateau.

The second thing that strikes one is that there is very little clear guidance in what might be called the imperatives of the European situation. Today Western Europe is prosperous beyond its wildest post-war dreams; relationships among the Western European countries are sometimes strained, but there is no longer any serious prospect of armed conflict between the ancient rival great powers; and there is little fear of military attack from the East. Even the consequences of the steps towards union already taken, the spill-over effect that for a time seemed likely to give a continuing momentum to the process of integration, although still a factor, is a much less irresistible force than it seemed to be at one time. It is easy enough to enumerate tasks that an enlarged Community *might* now undertake; but it is difficult to list many that either the objective facts of the European situation, or the results of past actions, or the obligations of commitments already entered into *require* it to undertake. British membership is in a very real sense unfinished business. But once that has been achieved, the slate is remarkably clean. This is very different from the situation in the fifties, or even that of a decade ago when the Community had the timetable laid down in the Treaty of Rome for the transitional period as a clear guide to action. Some convinced 'Europeans' will doubtless rejoin that there are all the imperatives one could wish for in the frequently declared objective of 'uniting Europe.' But this would only be true if the governments concerned had, in effect, bound themselves to a precise form of union which, of course, none of them has done. The rhetoric of European unity is, today, no guide to specific action.

However, if as suggested above, changes in the third category permit an extraordinary amount of freedom for thinking about the future tasks of the Community, the changes that have taken place in the other two categories—in the political-security setting and in the general character of relationships among states and within societies—do suggest certain guidelines for the new thinking that is now called for. Thus the changes noted in the first category suggest that Western Europe has a substantial role to play as a power in the fluid international system that seems in prospect, if it can organise itself to speak collectively. One can go even further. In a curious way, in the realm of geo-political discourse, Western Europe—not France, Germany or the United Kingdom—is already the 'actor'; the question is not whether there is a fifth great power, or more accurately power-grouping, but whether it will organise itself to be an effective 'actor.' [1]

The second group of changes suggests a somewhat different concept of, and role for, a 'uniting Europe.' These changes tend to set, I think, clear limits to the usefulness of thinking about 'Europe' simply as the fifth great power and point to the need to think of 'Europe' as a level between that of the European nation-state on the one hand and more inclusive groupings of states on the other. In other words, certain functions should now be performed at the 'European level' rather than the national level because that is the level that corresponds to the dimension of the problem and not because of some compulsion to push to the European level anything and everything that the concept of 'Europe as a power' might seem to imply. This point is worth some elaboration; for what I am here suggesting is that there will be constraints—both from above and from below—on the kind of functions or tasks that are appropriate for handling at the 'European' level.

The growing interdependence, or inter-relatedness, of the advanced industrialised countries and the growth of trans-national phenomena, like the multinational corporation, that escape national control and treat the world as an incipient single economy, are posing problems with which existing global international institutions built, essentially, on the concept of the autonomy of individual nation states cannot cope. Increasingly, many problems will either have to be looked at by the advanced industrialised countries, at least, as common problems requiring common action, or the network of economic relationships will deliberately have to be loosened.[2] The recent American action imposing unilaterally and with no prior consultation a 10 per cent surcharge on imports and renouncing its obligation to sell gold (thus, in effect, floating the dollar contrary to the Articles of Agreement of the IMF) was, of course, a move to loosen international economic linkages; it was a big step towards a more national, less international, management of the network of economic relationships in which all the advanced countries are today enmeshed. This was only the first move, however, in what promises to be a long process of modifying the existing rules. As this is being written, the eventual reshaping of the international rules could still be towards closer co-ordination of policies and more common action among the advanced industrialised countries or towards a deliberate loosening of linkages with more scope for national management and for national protective action. But, whichever way the argument goes in this round, it is difficult to believe that, in the long term, the kind of intimate consultation that has developed in the Group of Ten[3] and Working Party Three of the OECD will not be continued and intensified. If this is so, greater co-operation among the West European countries extending, perhaps, to the point of a monetary union would seem to have advantages for its members, principally perhaps because it would increase the West European voice in the management of the international system as a whole. But in the long term, European action could not be a substitute for a wider system or for closer co-ordination of policies among the key members of that wider system.

The general point being made here is this. If one looks ahead, many of the things which today it makes sense for the European countries to treat as common problems and to act on collectively can no longer be handled effectively even by large units like the United States or Western Europe acting alone. Thus although a 'European' approach will frequently be more in accord with the dimensions of today's problems than a purely national approach, there will increasingly be need for co-operation that extends well beyond the European complex and for co-operation that is so close, so continuous and so intimate that it will erode some of the functions of 'Europe as a power' even as it will erode some of the functions of the 'United States as a power.' A forward-looking European Community should, therefore, shun the temptation to clothe itself with those attributes of sovereignty that reason suggests are already threadbare and should soon be cast off.

There are also constraints of a different order on the transfer of functions to the 'European level'—what I have called constraints from below—which also suggest that it would be out of tune with the times simply to take some federal system such as that of the United States as a model and to act by analogy in considering what should be done by 'Europe.' Today, at all levels of society, a pervasive organisational problem is how to combine efficiency with an adequate sense of participation. Alienation and anomy are today particularly marked in the United States, although they are apparent in most highly developed societies. As power has shifted to the federal government and as the government has become larger and more remote and less personal (and with the advent of the computer less personal in a new sense) any effective participation by the individual has become, in fact, extremely difficult. And the situation tends to feed on itself: as the individual loses the feeling that he can affect what happens he loses his sense of responsibility, or opts out, and a bad situation is made worse. Regardless of one's view of the details of the plan, President Nixon's recent proposals for pushing various powers back down to the state and local level is a welcome recognition of the need to re-engage the individual in the process of government through a deliberate decentralisation of power and decision-making. There will be a similar need in Europe. And, as functions that can now be handled more appropriately at the European, rather than national, level are transferred upwards, there should be a deliberate process of decentralisation and a strengthening of local regional governments within the Community.[4]

Can these two roles be combined? Can 'Europe' be both a world power and a 'layer' or a 'level' in the continuum of organised society? I see no reason why it cannot. And to think about it in these terms, in this dual perspective, seems to me to be in accord with the real needs of the times. But it is a lot harder to break new ground than it is to reproduce known patterns. Moreover, to think adequately about the functions that a European Community will have to perform if it is to play these two quite different roles requires both a conception of the kind of international order one wants to move towards and some minimum level of consensus about the values in domestic society one wants to preserve and to strengthen. These are large issues and not the kind of questions that make an instant appeal to pragmatic politicians. But I think it unlikely that the 'Europe of the Seventies' will generate the kind of enthusiasm that was evoked by the 'Europe of the Fifties' unless today's 'Europe of the Sixties' can break out of the uneasy compromise between the 'Europe of Monnet' and the 'Europe of de Gaulle' with which it has been condemned to live, can forget the quarrels of the past and can become again a living experiment in creating new relationships among states and between peoples.

NOTES

1 See, for example, the frequent use of the expression 'Western Europe' in President Nixon's second report to the Congress on U.S. Foreign Policy (*U.S. Foreign Policy for the 1970s,* February 25, 1971) and the paucity of references in this document to the individual countries of Western Europe.

2 Richard Cooper has written extensively on this theme. William Diebold has

rightly pointed out that the phenomenon Cooper is discussing is usually not strictly one of interdependence but, rather, of interaction.

3 The Group of Ten is an informal gathering, under the general aegis of the IMF, of Ministers of Finance and Central Bank Governors (or, more usually, their deputies) from the following countries: Belgium, Canada, France, Germany, Italy, Japan, the Netherlands, Sweden, the United Kingdom and the United States (Switzerland, although not originally a member, now normally meets with the Group).

4 If this were done it might well contribute to the easing of various regional ethnic problems that now bedevil some of the individual member states, e.g. Bretons, Welsh, Flemings.

21

Can We Revive the U.N.?

HARLAN CLEVELAND

We are, it seems, at another of those moments of history when, as Churchill wrote of the days before a Great War, "every man had only to do his duty to wreck the world." The Secretary General of the United Nations, in a short speech ending the General Assembly "debate" on the U.N.'s 25th Anniversary, harked back to an earlier Englishman, Edmund Burke, and a similar sentiment: "The only thing necessary for the triumph of evil is for good men to do nothing." And commenting on the worldwide environmental crisis, U Thant captured a mood of desperation which only served to dramatize how far mankind still is behind its declared aspirations:

"As we watch the sun go down evening after evening through the smog across the poisoned waters of our native earth, we must ask ourselves whether we really wish some future universal historian on another plane to say, 'With all their genius and their skill, they ran out of foresight and air and food and water and ideas'; or, 'They went on playing politics until their world collapsed around them'; or 'When they looked up, it was already too late.' If the United Nations does nothing else, it can at least serve a vital purpose in sounding the alarm."

But the United Nations under new leadership will have to serve a more vital purpose than crying havoc. It is not man's last best hope, because if we cannot revive the U.N. we will have to do something else. But the other options all require us to start from scratch in building an international order to avoid the scourge of war, so we had better start from where we are.

Where we are is not on the brink of disaster; there is still some elbow room. The caution induced by possession of thermonuclear weapons has almost ruled out war among the major world powers; military stalemate of the NATO-Warsaw Pact variety is not the most attractive kind of peace, but it is proving a durable kind. "Little" wars are likely to continue, more in the developing world than among industrialized nations. And it is precisely in "little" war peacekeeping that we the members of the United Nations have some relevant experience. How are we going to build on that experience? Let me first suggest a good red-blooded American reason for doing so.

I

The trouble with the United Nations is that it became indispensable before it became possible. Our problem now is to make it a practical proposition. Because the U.N., or some facsimile thereof, is paradoxically the best chance to develop an *American* foreign policy that works.

The war in Vietnam has been our longest, and our bitterest experience with what must now be counted the first principle of world politics—that unilateral action, even by the strongest powers, is increasingly likely to be inconclusive abroad and unpopular at home. Peacekeeping, peaceful settlement of disputes, aid-giving and the control of global technologies—the lesson of experience since the Second World War is that, with few exceptions each is better tackled through international organizations than unilaterally, better legitimated by international consensus than by domestic decision-making, better symbolized by an international flag than by the Stars and Stripes. And this is so despite the rigidities, inefficiencies, and hesitancies of international organizations in general and the United Nations variety in particular.

The lesson of this lesson is that it is heavily in the U.S. national interest to invent, nourish and lend our power to international organizations, buying specialized results by burying general rivalries, trading some of our discretion for legitimacy, attracting partners by swallowing our pride and prejudice.

The technological imperative to world-wide organizations gets more obvious as each new proud technical achievement turns out to be also an ecological threat. Perhaps it was natural that a nation like ours, which has the capacity to act on the world stage and to affect by its own decisions that world environment, should be slow to think transnationally—just as the smoker in a roomful of non-smokers does not think of himself as a polluter while others do.

But everybody knows now that the air we breathe is an international resource. How much the content of carbon dioxide in the atmosphere is being increased by the burning of fossil fuels, or what foreign particles are being introduced into the air we share, cannot even be estimated, let alone controlled, by nations acting alone. Oil dumping and waste disposal in the oceans are choice current examples of issues that will be sorted out internationally or not at all. And the power to modify other people's weather, redirecting the winds and changing the pattern of precipitation at human command—that would certainly be an outrageous form of power for one or a few scientifically advanced countries to arrogate to themselves.

The internationalizing imperative is equally evident in development aid, the transfer of resources and technique from rich countries to poor countries. We have been through it all in the twenty-five years since the first relief and rehabilitation programs after World War II, and we know that national "foreign aid" does not—as most people used to think—provide more control, elicit more gratitude, or produce better results than aid administered through the World Bank and the U.N. Development Program. They are not very efficient, but neither are the unilateral aid programs. And in terms of domestic political support, unilateral "foreign aid" is consistently in hotter water than U.S. support for international organizations. If there is not a lot to choose between them for effectiveness, why take the political fallout abroad and the annual political trauma in Washington, that "American-flag" operations seem to entail? . . .

When it comes to peacekeeping the lesson of experience is even more striking. We were able to withdraw from the Congo because the "we" that were engaged was the United Nations. Deeply enmeshed though we are in the Middle East, the presence for a time of U.N. observers and until now of a U.N. mediator has enabled us to avoid taking a unilateral responsibility for keeping an uneasy truce and making an almost impossible peace. In the Cuba missile crisis, we managed to engage two international agencies, the Organization of American States to sponsor our blockade and bless our overflights, and the U.N. Secretary General to urge a Soviet pullback and propose international inspection in Cuba. (The published histories of this crisis have missed how multilateral was the diplomacy that legitimated the threat to use our military power to get rid of those missiles; for example, Castro's refusal to consider U Thant's inspection proposals provided the justification for continued aerial surveillance of Cuba by the United States acting for the OAS.)

Even in the Dominican Republic intervention, when President Johnson acted unilaterally, the peacekeeping operation was converted in time to OAS sponsorship, which certainly helped us get out in about a year instead of staying around to become involved in the local aftermath. And where United States forces have had to stay for protracted defense—in NATO Europe and in South Korea—international consultation and command have helped protect American involvement from ineffectiveness abroad and unpopularity at home.

The contrasting case is of course Vietnam. Our effort in the 1960s to tackle that peacekeeping job unilaterally has to be counted a major strategic error. Taken together with the early American belief in conventional military force as a counter to unconventional attack, and the later illusion that escalation by imported armies and bombing by American planes could lead to a negotiated peace, the unilateralism of our approach guaranteed an inconclusive outcome. This has been the most unilateral, the most unsuccessful, and the most unpopular war in American history; there is clearly a correlation among these superlatives.

In his address to the U.N. General Assembly last Fall, Andrei Gromyko said of Vietnam that "by its aims and its nature the war is still an American war." The irony of our involvement is that most Americans, both those who have supported the war and those who have opposed it, would have to agree with Gromyko.

If operating unilaterally is the worst foot forward in international politics, and equally a dead-end street in U.S. domestic politics, it is quite natural that the Vietnam experience has produced a widespread yen to cut back on U.S. commitments and ambitions, indeed a turning away from foreign policy in favor of concentration on domestic issues—race, poverty, the cities and the environment. The danger in this sudden shift of priorities is that future peace-and-security crises will find us no longer willing to face unilateral involvement and not yet able to work through effective international peacekeeping machinery—because it doesn't yet exist.

During recent "peace games," in which possible future crises are played out by responsible officials or their surrogates, the players representing the United States Government have been much inclined, when the crunch comes, to rule out the use of U.S. military power on the ground that, after Vietnam, the American people could not be brought to support of another overseas adventure. They are probably right; the slogan "No More Vietnams" has very wide support today across the American political spectrum. If the option is unilateral adventure or none, the mood of America in the 1970s might well dictate a kind of isolationism. But if the options also include U.S. support to a multilateral operation, legitimated by some reputable international organization and shared in by a number of other countries, Americans are likely to reject both lonely withdrawal and Lone Ranger activism, and join an international patrol instead. And one result of acting multilaterally is to require us to consult internationally before acting; in some cases this might have the effect of substituting a political settlement process for military intervention. Again, the Vietnam experience teaches us how important it is to keep that option open.

II

If in order to make sense of American foreign policy we need multilateral options so badly, can we revive the U.N.? That it needs a major injection of both strength and adrenalin, there can be no doubt.

I will not rehearse the multiple sclerosis which has overtaken the United Nations in its less than three decades. The detachment from reality of much General Assembly debate, the frozen procedures of the Security Council, the underfinancing and over-bureaucratization of the Specialized Agencies, the demoralization of the U.N. executive and the growing timidity of its aging leadership—these are the familiar complaints, no less justified for being familiar.

A House of Representatives subcommittee was surprisingly gentle in referring to the U.N. as "ill-equipped" for its future, "impotent" in the face of threats to the peace, "cumbersome" in its structure and "peculiarly inefficient" in its method of operation—and even gentler in its summary finding that "the overall record of United States' participation in the United Nations has been less than satisfactory." Gromyko, in the U.N. speech already mentioned, was equally circumspect: ". . . we feel it can safely be concluded that the task of keeping and strengthening the peace has been growing increasingly more complicated, but the requirements for successfully coping with this task have been developing even more rapidly and to a greater extent."

The circumspection illustrated by these two quotations may itself be part of the problem. The almost universal stake in pro-U.N. rhetoric discourages frank analysis of the Organization's reparable deficiencies. Thus, for example, it is often said that there is no nourishment in reviewing the United Nations Charter to look for ways of changing it. "If we renegotiated the Charter, we would not come out with as good a document as we have already." You have heard it said many times; I used to say it myself when I had some responsibility for U.S. participation in the U.N. The judgment is probably true of the Preamble and the first two Articles; they still stand as eloquent statements of universal human aspirations. But is it equally true of the fifty pages of procedure that follow the Charter's five pages of philosophy? Is the mind of man incapable of inventing processes that move more quickly to consensus about action instead of disagreement about words?

The Charter is essentially an expression of Western democratic philosophy. In consequence the machinery it establishes reflects a devotion to two-sided parliamentary procedures which just may be out of place in dealing with the "increasingly more complicated" tasks of peacekeeping and peacemaking, which almost never have just two sides. Certainly the emphasis in U.N. bodies on choosing up sides, and on voting, has often reduced the Organization to absurdity, forcing nations to record rather than negotiate their differences, and producing outcomes which merely harden in their intransigeance the holders of minority views.

The North Atlantic Council, by contrast, rarely takes a formal vote—because it is obvious that there is no point in outvoting the Scandinavians on how to defend Scandinavia or outvoting the Germans on how much money they will contribute, or outvoting the United States on how many troops it will retain in Europe, or outvoting the French on whether France will cooperate in NATO defense. These are real-world decisions, and everybody involved knows by instinct that if they cannot achieve a consensus by persuasion, dramatizing the disagreement by a vote doesn't help—and many even hinder a further effort to achieve consensus later on.

The U.N. way, at least in the General Assembly, is more often the opposite: the majority outvotes the nations whose policies are at issue (the colonial powers on colonial issues, the rich countries on money questions, the Communist countries on questions of Communist behavior). This fails to persuade the dissenters, and may even harden them in their dissent. The only thing it clearly accomplishes is to dramatize the impotence of the General Assembly to affect the real world by voting. In the Security Council, smaller numbers, more urgent issues and the veto threat combine to produce negotiations that better reflect the facts of power; when a vote is finally taken after long nights of bargaining, it sometimes reflects real *quid pro quo* accommodations among the member nations.

It would be foolish to suggest that the only trouble with the U.N. as peacekeeper and peacemaker is its formal machinery for making decisions by voting. At least one of its chief executives, Secretary General Dag Hammarskjöld, found ways to get executive action launched that jollied or shamed national governments into following his lead. The record of U.N. agencies in promoting economic and social development provides some evidence that the awkwardnesses of parliamentary diplomacy need not inhibit major executive actions by international organizations, if there is a will to action on the part of the relevant national governments. Other less-than-global organizations, notably the North Atlantic Treaty Organization and the European Economic Community, have also demonstrated the capacity for large scale executive activity.

But what are the common factors in these comparative successes? Without reviewing here the evidence for my conclusion, I would say that the most effective international organizations are those which have (a) eschewed votes in their governing bodies, operating as much as possible by consensus procedure, and (b) placed the major responsibility for initiative in their international executives.

The promise of the United Nations was always, and still is, its capacity to act—as a mediatory force in the politics of nations, and as the source of law and the organizer of its enforcement. Yet the structure of the Organization requires such an overwhelming concentration on hearing the nation's differences aired (and therefore widened) in public, that the leadership is not available to plan and administer even the executive actions that all nations would acknowledge to be in the general interest. It is certainly dysfunctional for the Secretary General to sit on the General Assembly dais, listening to predictable sentiments in five languages, when he could be developing from his unique vantage point some executive initiative to deal with the multiple crises of our time.

III

Less irrelevant voting and more executive leadership—what would these two principles of growth imply for changes in the United Nations? Here is a checklist—each item is worth a full article by itself.

1. *Streamline the General Assembly.* It is arguable that the General Assembly is now too far gone to be useful for anything but blowing off steam. But the amount of diplomats' time it requires can certainly be reduced by permitting statements for the record (as in the U.S. Congress), exercising birth control on new membership by micro-states, doing more of the work in expert groups, and encouraging the Secretary General to take more of the leadership in organizing the debate and posing the questions that can usefully be addressed by such a body. The notion of expert groups is especially constructive; apart from the General Assembly, no parliamentary body in the world does nearly all its committee work in Committees of the Whole.

2. *Make the Security Council work.* The key to international legitimacy for peacekeeping operations is the Security Council. The U.N.'s experience shows that it works best when the Secretary General is taking the initiative—as in the Congo, Cyprus, and pre-1967 Mideast operations. A special place should be made for powerful but nonnuclear powers—such as Argentina and Brazil from Latin America, Australia, India and Japan from the Asian region, Nigeria and Egypt from Africa, Poland, Sweden and Germany (when admitted) from Europe, and Canada and Mexico from North America. There are ten nonpermanent members on the Security Council now; five or six seats might well be reserved for those which—as the Charter contemplated—could make a greater contribution to the maintenance of international peace and security. . . .

3. *Encourage the Secretary General to engage in fact-finding* in peace-and-security disputes, without waiting to be told by some legislative body to do so. New observation technologies may make this a far more important power than heretofore: for example, we are just around the corner from reconnaissance satellites which can monitor a visible happening on earth (say, launching of a missile), and televise it in real time to whoever controls the satellite. But quite apart from modern technology, the U.N. executive's ability to send a competent fact-finder or mediator into a complicated situation is still one of his main powers—if it isn't used in too gingerly a manner.

Moreover, the United Nations provides a sponsor for peaceful settlement which combines the pressure of latent big-power intervention with the facilities for keeping it latent. If most "little" wars are likely to be fought or threatened in non-Western regions, we need local and regional machinery for settling disputes in which Westerners Russians as well as Americans) do not have to be involved. The initiative of the U.N. executive, however, can be an "outside" factor that is politically acceptable to peoples which can't settle their own disputes yet don't want to turn their problems over to external Big Brothers to settle for them. The U.N. has hardly begun to realize its potential as sponsor of regional conciliation machinery.

4. *Establish a real standby force.* So far, the earmarking of national forces for U.N. employment has been good symbolism but has not provided the U.N. executive with any real discretion in emergencies. A modern force actually available, equipped and with at least

a minimum airlift capability of its own, has become an indispensable part of the Secretary General's "third man" role in international disputes. A permanent international peacekeeping staff, with the capacity to plan, train for, and execute peacekeeping missions, should be located in the Secretary General's office; it might be supplemented with a special group of Undersecretaries who, whatever called, would be effectively in touch with the permanent members of the Security Council to maximize the Secretary General's freedom of action.

How big a standby force? Twenty or thirty thousand well-trained men, with the requisite airlift to get around in a hurry and the arrangements to call forward further national forces promised by member nations, would be large enough to ensure that the U.N.'s mediatory role is taken seriously—and not so much as to threaten the security of the nations whose military restraint is ultimately the key to peace in every region. To the cynical question, "How many divisions has the U.N. executive?" the answer should be "One for sure, and it can be there the day after tomorrow."

Much smaller peacekeeping responsibilities brought the U.N. to a condition of financial crisis during the 1960s. Can a major peacekeeping force be financed internationally? The answer, as always, is in the will of the nations to pay—or to contribute forces, equipment, and airlift in kind. The cost is certainly small by the grotesque standard of current military budgets; even a billion dollars for international peacekeeping would be a fraction of one per cent of world defense spending. New U.N. leadership and a new system for command and control, backed by an unprecedented American willingness to pay for a force which would be subject to some U.S. influence but not to U.S. control, might make a voluntary peacekeeping fund possible —especially since most of the expenses for troop pay, material and airlift could probably be contributed in kind and thus count as national security spending rather than as eleemosynary contributions. We can readily abandon the notion of paying for standby forces through everymember assessments; the General Assembly has already demonstrated that it is not willing to back its taxing authority with two-thirds of its votes.

5. *Develop a consortium of the concerned.* There is a growing body of opinion to support the notion that the United States should take the lead in developing a working community of those nations which would be willing to go farther than others in building up an international executive to keep the peace and mediate disputes of less than global magnitude. Such a consortium, constituted within the framework of the Charter's purposes but outside its established machinery, with its own arrangements for fact-finding, mediation, and quick mobilization of peacekeeping forces, might well be a useful pressure on the U.N. executive and the Security Council to act, for then the alternative to U.N. intervention would not be inaction but action by a smaller number of members in the Charter's name. The same group of nations might develop among themselves procedures for settlement and adjudication which would provide a quicker reference to the

World Court or to conciliation processes of disputes among the members of the self-constituted inner circle.

6. *Sponsor a formal review of the Charter.* The Charter cannot be changed without U.S. consent. It is worth a year or two of intensive multilateral diplomacy to see if the procedures of parliamentary diplomacy cannot be streamlined and the U.N. executive given more discretion to act in, or avert, emergencies.

7. *Fill . . . . vacancies carefully. . . .*

. . . . We would also do well to have a new look at the concept of U.N. careers. A generation ago, the need to protect U.N. staff from undue national influence produced the notion of an international civil service. We can see now that lifetime employment in an international bureaucracy produces the same Parkinsonian tendencies, and the same cautious time-serving, that are so evident in national career services. For many categories of position, and especially in the policy-making roles, the member nations might well be better served by a reasonably frequent turnover of U.N. functionaries. At a minimum, future appointments to middle level and higher positions should be limited to term contracts lasting not more than five or six years.

8. *Give the U.N. major jobs to do.* Throughout the life of the Organization, nations (including ours) have justified unilateral action by saying the U.N. was too fragile for major peace-and-security tasks, and would collapse under the strain of a Berlin or a Vietnam. But institutions grow in strength and relevance because they must—and not until they must. And in Southeast Asia especially, an international solution, internationally monitored and enforced, seems the only alternative to an American commitment indefinitely prolonged.

As long as we are not nationally responsible for the outcome, there is a wide range of outcomes possible in Southeast Asia. Any of them will probably mean some sharing of authority and territory between Communists and non-Communists, and the many shades in between. Our interest lies in turning back to the Southeast Asians the bickering and politicking and governance for which we have unilaterally assumed too much responsibility these past few years. It is hard to imagine an outcome worked out under U.N. sponsorship that would be worse from the point of view of the American interest than a continued massive commitment in Vietnam, Laos and Cambodia.

Preceding a new "Geneva conference," it might well be possible to induce a number of countries, representing an acceptably wide spectrum of political orientation, to take on the peacekeeping task after a settlement is reached. The Russians would have to agree, of course; but they may have some interest in keeping the foot in the Southeast Asian door which we have made possible by our involvement there. The mainland Chinese would also have to agree. . . . The Chinese and Russians both agreed to the Laos settlement of 1962; of course it wasn't a very good deal from our standpoint, but we have not won the war in Vietnam and we won't be able to have the peace all our own way either.

Given the projected American withdrawal and a willingness on our part to share the burden of masterminding Southeast Asia's future with the widest possible community of nations, the natural venue for the question "after Vietnam, what?" is the Security Council of the United Nations. The aftermath will go on for a decade or more; any settlement will be ragged. If the results of U.N. involvement are not then to our taste, we still have to ask ourselves—would we have done better taking on the post-war settlement as an American responsibility? Experience in the Congo, Cyprus and the Middle East is instructive: multilateralism is often messy, but still, better than direct confrontations of major powers.

In his 25th Anniversary speech to the General Assembly last October 23rd [1970], President Nixon gave assurances that we want neither a Pax Americana nor an American Century. But the alternative he there described is equally undesirable—"a structure of stability and progress that will enable each nation to chart its own course and make its own way without outside interference, without intimidation, without domination by ourselves or by any other power." The world of independent sovereignties, from which words like these have been handed down from Administration to Administration, was never a good description of the probable, and is now a description of anarchy. What we need is a structure of stability and progress which rests on the close, organized cooperation of nations who know they are interdependent, and have learned to stop talking about independence. U Thant, criticizing the tendency of nations to use the United Nations "to promote their own national policies," was closer to the mark when he went on to advocate "a new kind of organization in which the nations of the world in cooperation could forge *and execute* (the italics are mine) solutions to world problems. . . ."

22

The Multinational Corporation and the Nation-State

ROBERT L. HEILBRONER

Of all the problems we call "economic," few have so baffled the expert and the nonexpert alike as those that involve the relations between nation-states. Indeed, one might even go so far as to say that economics, as a "science," got its start from efforts to explain how gold and goods traveled from nation to nation, working their various effects on the countries they left and those they entered. In particular, that ill-associated group of seventeenth- and early eighteenth-century pamphleteers we call the mercantilists deserve their place in the history of economic thought if only because they annoyed people like Hume and Adam Smith (among others) sufficiently to get economic inquiry started along its present lines.

The basic theme of mercantilist doctrine had, at first glance, a certain logic. The mercantilists believed that a nation's self-interest lay in the accumulation of a national treasure—gold. Gold was to be gained by selling goods to foreigners and was lost by buying goods from them. Therefore the pursuit of national self-interest resided in policies that would encourage exports and discourage imports, thereby increasing the stock of precious bullion by which the national wealth has to be measured.

To describe this underlying belief is enough to reveal that the philosophy of mercantilism is by no means dead. But at least in its original crude form, the mercantilist theory of international economic relations received its *coup de grâce* from the cool analysis of the classical economists. For the central message of Smith's *Wealth of Nations* (1776) was that the proper measure of national wealth was not its stock of gold bullion but its annual flow of production. The road to maximizing wealth lay therefore in the pursuit of policies that would encourage the increase in that annual flow—in particular, policies that would augment production by encouraging the division of labor.

Smith, accordingly, envisaged the basic objective of international economic relations as one of bringing about a world-wide division of labor, a point of view that clearly required a willingness to buy abroad as well as an eagerness to sell abroad. Under his great successor, David Ricardo, this doctrine received its first keen analytical treatment, as Ricardo demonstrated that one nation, such as England, would benefit by trading with another, such as Portugal, even though England might be able to produce *both* cloth and wine more effectively than Portugal.[1]

From this genuinely stunning insight of the classical economists there followed an obvious prescription regarding the economic relationships between nations. That was that the well-being, not merely of one nation but of *all* nations, would be achieved by a willing surrender to the international division of labor, in which each did the work for which its climate, soil, skills, etc., best suited it. As a corollary, of course, each would thereafter trade its own products for the products of other nations, with no effort to block this exchange by tariffs or other impediments (except in very special cases, such as the infant industries of emerging nations). Thus emerged the doctrine of free trade, a doctrine under which most economists still march, fortified by a century of theoretical buttressing of Ricardo's work which culminates, in our own time, in contributions by such major figures as Paul Samuelson and others.

Alas for economics, from the beginning this grand and logically impeccable doctrine has ruled the theory of international economic relations rather than its reality. The reasons are not difficult to find. First, there was the fact that the flows of trade between nations often failed to "balance," giving rise to complicated problems that had to be resolved by an international settlement of accounts. But this in turn was rendered difficult by the stubborn refusal of nation-states to adopt a single universal money-of-account, so that monetary bottlenecks of all kinds constantly prevented the smooth settlement of international obligations. (These so-called balance of payments problems also arose—and still do arise—from the fact that international financial transactions are not limited to the payment for international flows of goods and services, but are also used to transfer capital from one nation to another, to wage war overseas, to find a haven in numbered bank accounts in Switzerland, etc.) As a result, some nations have had trouble "financing" the imports they would have otherwise been willing to buy, while other nations have had trouble "selling" goods they were eager to get rid of because they were not willing to accept payment in another country's currency.

Second, the doctrine of free trade has from the beginning encountered the stubborn resistance of the very workmen and employers whose ultimate well-being it was supposed to promote. No doubt part of the appeal of Ricardo's theory lay in the fact that there were, in fact, no wine-makers in England who were being asked to shift to sheep-shearing. But the advice is more difficult to follow for the wine-makers of California who might be advised to take up automobile making, or for the French auto worker who is urged into champagne-bottling, so that the international output of both wine and automobiles might thus be maximized.

Last, the classical doctrine of the international specialization of labor and free trade has received its most crushing rejection from those nations on whom the theory was imposed most ruthlessly. Among the underdeveloped nations of the world a genuine specialization of labor did take place, accompanied by a more or less free importation of their products. But the emergence of banana-economies and coffee-economies and copper-economies did not bring with it the gradual convergence of living standards that was implicit in the theories of both Ricardo and Samuelson. Instead, the mono-economies discovered to their dismay that the ruling doctrine worked to widen rather than to narrow the disparity between themselves and their rich customers—a state of affairs for which standard theory had no explanation at all.[2]

II

I trust that the reader, especially if he or she is an economist, will forgive this capsule resumé of the theory of international economic relations. I offer it not to attack current theory, large portions of which are relevant to and indispensable for an understanding of these relations. My purpose, rather, is to set the stage for an exposition of the most important change in both the conception and practice of international economic affairs since Hume and Smith and Ricardo first promulgated the notion of international *trade* as the paradigm for the economic intercourse of nations. This change is the emergence of a new form of international economic relationship, based not so much on the exchange of goods as on the *internationalization of production itself*—an internationalization arising from the startlingly rapid growth of what are called multinational corporations.

Perhaps the best way to illustrate the nature of the change is to examine the multinational operation in action. Let me begin with a description of his own company offered by Donald M. Kendall, president of PepsiCo:

> PepsiCo [operates] in 114 countries. Its most familiar product is bottled in 512 plants outside the United States. Production and distribution facilities in almost every country are owned by nationals of those countries. Regional managers may come from the area in question—or from some other part of the world—Frenchmen, Englishmen, Latin Americans —not necessarily from the United States. In the Philippines, where PepsiCo is about the twelfth largest taxpayer, the whole operation has only two persons from the home office. The company is multinational as far as employment, operations, manufacturing and marketing are concerned, and a good part of the operating management and plant ownership abroad is also multinational.[3]

We will come back to certain aspects of this multinational operation—one suspects, for example, that the two Americans in the Philippine office are not office boys. But the essence of the matter is that PepsiCo no longer exports Pepsi-Cola to, say, Mexico. *It produces it there.* And precisely this same internationalization of production is to be found in IBM, General Motors, Ford, Standard Oil, and so on down the hierarchy of American corporate enterprise. I do not wish to imply that every big company is multinational. But we do know that sixty-two of the top one hundred firms have production facilities in at least six foreign countries, and Kenneth Simmonds has shown that seventy-one of the top 126 industrial corporations (for which data could be obtained) averaged one-third of their employment abroad.[4] This is probably a considerable *under*estimate of the extent of multinationality of the top industrials, but we will have to await the 1970 census data to be sure.

Meanwhile, on a broader canvas, there is little doubt about the importance of US international production taken as a whole. In 1966 (the last year for which we have all the data we need), the United States exported $43 billion of goods and services to various parts of the world. In that same year, the value of United States overseas production—that is, of goods and services made in US-owned factories or establishments abroad—came to $110 billion, or two and a half times as much.

Another way of establishing the importance of international production is to trace the rise in the value of US foreign "direct" investment (that is, investment in real assets rather than in securities). In 1950 the size of our foreign direct investment was roughly $11 billion. In 1969 it was something over $70 billion, or about one-fifth of the total assets (domestic as well as foreign) of the top 500 industrials. Moreover this figure for foreign direct investment represents only the value of the American dollars invested abroad, and not the additional value of foreign capital that is controlled by these American enterprises (for instance by their command over subsidiaries).[5] If we add these assets to the purely American ones, the value of the American business empire abroad comes to considerably more than $100 billion.[6]

This is still, however, only part of the changing picture of international economic relations. The expansion of American corporate production abroad, especially in Europe, has given rise to a general awareness of The American Challenge, best expressed in Servan-Schreiber's book of that name. But as economists Stephen Hymer and Robert Rowthorn point out, what seems to Europeans like an American challenge can be seen from another vantage point as a challenge *to* American corporations.[7] For whereas it is true that American companies in Europe have been expanding faster than their European rivals, thereby scaring the daylights out of many Europeans, it is also true that European corporations have been expanding their total production, in Europe and abroad, as fast as or faster than the growth in *total* sales (at home and abroad) of the US giants.[8] Thus while we challenge Europe in Europe, the Europeans challenge us elsewhere in the world, including within our own borders (think of the invasion of the American automobile market by European models).

The dynamics of this challenge and counterchallenge are complex, depending in part on the general tendency of larger companies to grow *less* rapidly than not-quite-so-large ones (hence the slower average rate of growth of the American giant); in part on the effect of the environment on corporate effort (the American companies in Europe were operating in a very fast-expanding market); and partly again on the relative technological capabilities of different countries and companies.

But Hymer and Rowthorn's critical point is that the change in international economic relations is not an American, but a truly multinational phenomenon. If we take the ten leading capital exporting nations together, for example, we find that for 1967 their combined exports came to over $130 billion, whereas their combined overseas production amounted to at least $240 billion. Estimates by Professor Sidney Rolfe, by Judd Polk of the International Chamber of Commerce, and by Professor Howard Perlmutter (among others) indicate that the rate of capital outflow from the industrialized European nations and from Japan bears roughly the same proportion to their GNPs as does our own.

On the basis of such data, one can estimate that the value of international production of all kinds is now roughly equal to about a fourth of world output of the commodities produced, and that if the rate of expansion of overseas production continues as it has in the recent past, the internationals will account for half or more of world industrial output by the year 2000. Indeed, Professor Perlmutter has argued that some 300 corporations (200 of them American) will soon dominate the world economy in much the way that the fifty or one hundred top American corporations dominate our economy.[9]

But enough of these figures. The essential point is that the rise of the multinational corporation signals a new era in international economic relationships, an era in which the international shipment of domestically produced goods is giving way to one in which nations affect one another by directly producing "foreign" goods within each other's economies.

III

It must be apparent that the rise of the multinationals poses a bewildering array of questions. Why did they come into being? What is likely to be the outcome of the struggle among them? How does the rise of the vast international company affect the underdeveloped nations? How can a corporation simultaneously abide by the often conflicting laws and policies of a dozen countries? Is the multinational company a new source of potential international friction or an embryonic form of a new world order?

One asks such questions more to introduce some semblance of order into a sprawling problem than in the hope of providing crisp answers. As we shall see, much concerning the future of the multinationals remains obscure and unpredictable. But we can at least begin with some facts, for thanks to the work of Mira Wilkins, we now have a picture of the evolution of the overseas thrust of corporations, comparable to their domestic evolution from single-plant, single-product firms to multidivisional enterprises.[10] For the reason why a corporation should *produce* abroad is, on reflection, not self-evident. It is expensive for a corporation to run facilities overseas. Inevitably, it leads to the kinds of economic and political tangles that our initial set of questions suggests. If the profit drive is the impelling force behind corporate expansion, as most economists and businessmen tell us it is, we must explain why at one stage a corporation is perfectly content to export its wares, at another point to license their production overseas, and then finally to assume the responsibility for their actual foreign production.

As Miss Wilkins points out, the involvement of American business with foreign production has a considerable history. Samuel Colt, the inventor and successful producer of automatic pistols on an "assembly line" basis in America, transplanted his equipment and key workmen to London in the mid-1850s, and promptly failed. On the other hand, in those same years a group of American capitalists and engineers pushed the first railway across the Panama isthmus; and by the 1870s, Singer Sewing Machine was successfully producing abroad (in Scotland) and was in fact selling half its total output overseas. Moreover the degree of penetration (by export as well as production) continued until by 1914 a British writer could already speak on an "American challenge" in these terms:

> The most serious aspect of the American industrial invasion lies in the fact that these newcomers have acquired control of almost every new industry created during the past fifteen years. . . . What are the chief new features of London life? They are, I take it, the telephone, the portable camera, the phonograph, the electric street car, the automobile, the typewriter, passenger lifts in houses, and the multiplication of machine tools. In every one of these, save the petroleum automobile, the American maker is supreme; in several, he is the monopolist.[11]

Miss Wilkins's work allows us to see a certain organizational logic behind the quantum leaps overseas. It lies (if I may read certain conclusions into her work) in the existence of critical thresholds of size, domestic market saturation, and technology—thresholds that may differ from industry to industry, but that provide for each one, at some stage in its development, a point at which it is "natural" (i.e., more profitable) to take the leap.[12]

What is it, then, that marks the recent surge of international investment? If my speculations are justified, the answer must lie in the arrival of more and more industries at their critical thresholds, powerfully aided in our day by the development of a new technology for transferring information that makes it not markedly more difficult to supervise a plant in Hong Kong than one in Indianapolis. In a general way we can trace the influence of the improvement in the technology of supervision by noting the long-term shift of investment away from "next door" to more distant areas. In 1897, 56 percent of our direct foreign investment was in Canada and Mexico; in 1914 it had fallen to 46 percent; in 1968 to 32 percent.[13]

A second part of the difference (I am here again speculating beyond the bounds of Miss Wilkins's work) can be traced to the gradual shift of corporate interest toward "high technology," as contrasted with heavy capital, products, and activities. In 1897, 59 percent of American foreign direct investment was in agriculture (plantations), mining, or railways; by 1969 this figure had dropped to 11 percent. Conversely, in 1897 only 15 percent of our overseas direct investment was in manufacturing; this has jumped to over 40 percent today.

This shift to high technology has redirected the marketing concentration of international direct investment. In 1897, 54 percent of our overseas direct investment was in the underdeveloped parts of the world, the remainder in the European-Canadian developed areas. Today the balance has swung the other way. Sixty-four percent of our foreign direct investment is now in Canada, Europe, and Oceania and only 36 percent in Asia, Africa, and Latin America. More striking, of the increase in American foreign direct investment during the last decade, almost three-quarters was located in the developed world.

Thus behind the rise of the interlocking, interpenetrating webs of overseas production there lies a certain logic of technology and organization—a logic that no doubt applies in much the same fashion to the expansion of European or Japanese investment as it does to our own. The gradual "saturation" of national markets (which occurred, needless to say, earlier in the small European nations than in our continental-sized one) provided the initial stimulus for a shift from mere export-orientation to true international production, and accounts for the fact that in 1914 European foreign investments (both direct and portfolio) were ten times larger than American; whereas in 1966 American direct investments were a third larger than European.[14]

Simultaneously, the explosion of high technology vastly altered the character of international enterprise in a direction favorable to American-dominated industries: the annual growth rate of IBM alone at home and abroad for the past decade has been sufficiently great so that, if it continues uninterrupted for another generation, IBM will be the largest single economic entity in the world, including the entities of nation-states. This proliferation of high technology in turn has redirected the areas in which international investment was profitable, turning it away from the banana groves of Honduras, whose market was relatively slow-growing, to the developed world where the demand for high technology products was expanding with extraordinary speed.

IV

What is apt to be the outcome of this shift in the nature of international economic relations? Here we move from the domain of fact, however shadowy, to that of findings, however speculative. Let us postpone the most tenuous of these to the end and deal initially with a few things that we know.

The first of these is that—despite the claim made on behalf of PepsiCo by Mr. Kendall—the great international producers are not "truly" multinational. With very few exceptions (one thinks of Unilever or Shell, whose ownership is genuinely divided between different national interests) most of the multi-corps, PepsiCo included, are essentially extensions of national enterprises, controlled by a single national center, in so far as the location of investment and (more important) the international remission of profits are concerned.

To be sure, the multinationals have learned to break away from what Howard Perlmutter calls an ethnocentric attitude, in which the number of calls made per day by a salesman in Hoboken becomes the standard for operations in Brazzaville or Buenos Aires, toward a more "polycentric" and even geocentric (world-oriented) perspective.[15] Moreover a few harbingers of true internationalism are visible in the presence of a Canadian as president of Standard Oil of New Jersey, a Venezuelan on its board, and a Frenchman as president of the IBM World Trade Corporation.[16]

But these are, I think it can safely be said, exceptions to the general rule of the tight retention of *national control* over the operations of the international corporation. As Kenneth Simmonds has pointed out (in the study we previously cited), foreigners constituted only 1.6 percent of the 1,851 top managers in those US companies with substantial employment overseas. Simmonds has not matched his findings with similar studies of Belgian, British, Swiss, Swedish, Japanese, etc., firms, but one has the strong suspicion that a similar conclusion would emerge. Simmonds, with his eye on the rise of American economic power in Europe, fears that an American "master race" of executives will come to control much of the international production of the globe, unless American corporations allow other nationals into the top echelons of power. On the other hand, if Hymer and Rowthorn are correct in stressing the genuinely multinational character of international production, we are more apt to have a master "race" of executives of different nationalities.

Whichever view is right, the problem brings us to the next question: What of the relationship between these corporations, which, whatever their "nationalities," are organized for private ends, and the nation-states within whose territories they operate? Here we begin to arrive at the critical areas in which politics and economics collide or coincide, and in which the "logic" of this new kind of international economic relations must make its peace with the "logic" of national interests as they now exist.

On one side of this complex issue is the fact that the multinational corporations are often in the same position in dealing with governments as were the railroad builders of the West in dealing with the various municipalities that competed for their services. A considerable competition exists among European nations for the location of high technology investment within their national borders, a competition that takes the form of capital grants, tax privileges, and, not least, an "acquiescence" in a growing American presence. As Kenneth Waltz points out, in 1962 the French government refused to permit General Electric to buy 20 percent of the ownership of Machines Bull, a large manufacturer of computers and other electronic products. By 1964, unable to find another buyer and unhappily aware that Machines Bull could not begin to develop the R & D needed to stay abreast in its field (IBM spends more on R & D than the sales of its largest English competitor), the government capitulated to a 50 percent GE ownership.[17]

To an even greater degree, the multinationals can dictate to the governments of the underdeveloped nations. For all the talk (and the reality) of imperialist domination, most of the underdeveloped nations want domestic foreign investment, European and/or American, for a variety of reasons. The multinationals pay higher wages, keep more honest books, pay more taxes, and provide more managerial know-how and training than do local industries. Moreover, they usually provide better social services for their workers, and certainly provide fancy career opportunities for a favored few of the elite. They are, in addition, a main channel through which technology, developed in the West, can filter into the backward nations. To be sure, the corporations typically send home more profits than the capital that they originally introduce into the "host" country; but meanwhile that capital grows, providing jobs, improving productivity, and often contributing to export earnings.[18]

This is, however, only one side of the story—the side that stresses the ability of the multinationals to drive hard bargains, to win strategic geographic positions, and to exercise a powerful voice in the economic policy of the countries in which they deign to operate. There is another side as well. For if the multinationals are bases for the exercise of economic power, they are also hostages within the nations in which they have settled. In the backward nations, the threat—and, more and more, the practice—of nationalization hangs over the heads of the multinational corporations, partly as an act of revenge against an often grossly exploitative past history, but more and more, simply because countries that are beginning to plan for development cannot allow critical decision-making powers to escape their control. As George Ball, in an essay highly sympathetic to the "cosmocorp," candidly puts it: "How can a national government make an economic plan with any confidence if a board of directors meeting 5,000 miles away can by altering its pattern of purchasing and production affect in a major way the country's economic life?" [19]

Ball and others think that the answer lies in the gradual "denationalization" of the international company, a view to which we will revert at the end of this essay. But let me first emphasize that the balance of power between the corporation's ability to allocate its technical expertise and its production, and the nation's ability to force a plant, once located, to abide by its will, is by no means one-sided in Europe or the developed areas, any more than it is in the underdeveloped countries. Here too, the economic benefits provided by foreign capital are often overwhelmed by the sentiments of nationalism to which the plusses and minuses of the balance sheet simply do not apply.

For example, the Canadians may be grateful in their moments of economic reflection for the enormous boost to productivity that has resulted from the inflow of American investments, but in their political moments they are bitterly resentful of a situation in which US residents own at least 44 percent of *all* capital invested in Canada, and in which foreigners (mainly Americans) own 54 percent of all Canadian manufacturing, 64 percent of all Canadian oil, and virtually 100 percent of its auto industry. Hence, in Canada, France, and elsewhere, the multinationals face actual or prospective legislation limiting the degree to which they can invade or dominate the domestic economy. As a case in point in 1969 France refused to allow Westinghouse Electric Corporation to buy a controlling interest in the Jeumont-Schneider group (producers of heavy electrical equipment), insisting that the company remain French.

In this tension between the corporate drive for logistical coherence and the national drive for economic independence, the "proper" role for the multinational is far from clear. Even if we assume that the directing management is of "neutral" national composition, what should be its guiding policy with respect to the international location of research and development facilities, the expansion or contraction of production in plants located in different countries, the remission of profits from one unit to another? It is not enough to say that the rule of profitability must hold sway, for in obeying that rule the multinationals are also affecting the growth rates, the employment, and the balance of payments problems of nation-states who put *their* national well-being far ahead of the profits of any international enterprise.

There is, in fact or theory, no answer to such questions, for they pose problems entirely outside the present legal and juridical arrangements of nation-states and international organizations. Henry de Vries notes for example that no consistent pattern can even be discerned for such a basic question as where the "home office" of a corporation exists. In the United States and the United Kingdom, it is the place of incorporation. In Morocco, it is the location of the registered head office.

In France, Belgium, and Germany it is the center of management. In Italy and Egypt it is the locus of principal business activity. This and innumerable other legal problems bestrew the path of international production and are far from being close to solution.[20]

V

What, then, are the ultimate implications of this new form of international economic relationship? If the question leaves us groping, the reason lies in the fact that we have not yet developed a coherent picture in our minds—a "model"—with which to organize the confusions and conflicts introduced by the rise of the multinational company. We lack, in other words, a theory of international production (even a wrong theory) that would introduce into the disarray of facts the possibility for systematic analysis that the theory of free trade gave us for an earlier epoch.

Already, however, we can see some of the elements with which such a model will have to come to grips. First, a theory of international production must explain whether or not the interpenetration of national territories by foreign producers will lead to a stable "division of the market" or not. If, as Perlmutter and others hypothesize, the industrial core of world production and trade is moving in the direction of global oligopoly, will the outcome be a more or less peaceful coexistence of giants, such as we see in the American automobile or steel or electrical equipment industries, or a struggle *à outrance*, such as characterized the cut-throat competitive race of the late nineteenth century?

The answer to this question lies partly in the habits and attitudes of business managers, who are now mainly accustomed to the non-price-cutting "competition" of gadgetry and style. But it will also be powerfully influenced by the national elements that are inextricably intermingled with the economic ones. That is, the degree of ferocity and effectiveness of the "European" response to *le défi americain* depends to a large extent on whether European governments overcome their parochial nationalisms enough to allow the formation of truly Pan-European corporations whose strength and penetrative power could then be matched against American enterprise *on American soil*.

Thus, unlike the theory of international trade, which rested its case solely on the economic consequences of the division of labor, there is no theory of "the division of the market" unless we introduce political variables into the picture. Lacking a knowledge of this political element, we cannot yet place limits on the degree of interpenetration that will occur, or on the probability of an "equilibrium" being reached on a global scale.

Second, there arises the question of whether the rise of international production can be viewed as a force making for world integration and betterment, or for world divisiveness and disruption. The classical theory of international trade promised that the international division of labor would in fact unify the world, both with regard to living standards and (implicitly) with regard to political stability because of the increased interdependence of nation-states. That noble image proved to be delusive. But what image does the rise of international production project?

Two views are currently propounded. One, advanced by George Ball, sees in the emergence of the "denationalized" multinational corporation the first appearance of a supranational world order—an order in which the terrible and violent rule of competitive nationalism would gradually be superseded by an international organization of production, regulated by the impersonal constraints of profit (which even the socialist countries concede is the single best indicator of efficiency). What is envisaged is a "businessman's peace" in which pragmatism and production take precedence over national pride and vainglory.

The proponents of this view have very little trouble demonstrating that the multinationals are much less interested in the cold war than are the members of the political elites; that "co-production" between capitalist and socialist countries is already in existence; and that, all stereotypes (and some examples) to the contrary, businessmen usually have preferred to do business with governments, even revolutionary governments, than to call in the Marines.[21]

There is undoubtedly an element of truth in this view: one thinks of Henry Ford seeking to build tractor plants for the Soviets; of the recent Fiat contract to build Russian autos; of the chafing of American companies at the idiocy of State Department constraints on their investment in communist countries, etc. It is one thing, however, to point to the presumably less bellicose disposition of businessmen (a point that was first made by Herbert Spencer) and another to ask what sort of "world order" the multinationals could create.

Ball's view assumes that the internationalization of production would bring about a more rational world than that in which we now live. But such a view begs the question as to whether a world order that is rational for the multinational corporation is necessarily also rational for a backward nation seeking to escape from the shackles of its heritage. For the assumption that the multinational company can become a major vehicle for development ignores a major aspect of underdevelopment itself—the gulf between the "Western" metropolises of the backward world and their "Eastern" countrysides. This is a gulf that the presence of the multinationals is more likely to widen than to bridge. Ball's view overlooks as well the certainty that the multinationals will powerfully oppose the kinds of revolutionary upheavals that in many backward areas are probably the essential precondition for a genuine modernization.

This conflict between the demands of the nation-state and those of the corporation forms the core of the Hymer-Rowthorn view, which stands opposed to that of Ball and his like-minded business internationalists. Hymer and Rowthorn do not doubt that the momentum behind the internationalization of enterprise is very strong, but they see this as leading to an exacerbation of world conflict rather than to a resolution of it. For they do not see the economic imperative asserting itself easily over that of the national entity, either in the developed world or in its backward regions. "Nation-states are powerful and are not likely to die easily," they write. "Merely to ask which institution one expects to be around 100 years from now, France or General Motors, shows the nature of the problem." [22]

I should say, rather, that this question reveals the tensions of the problem but does not fully analyze its outcome. There are some things that nation-states can do that international corporations cannot, but there are other things, of increasing importance, in which the corporation is the more effective instrument of social action. If Hymer and Rowthorn had posed the question of long-term survival as between Costa Rica and IBM, another answer might have suggested itself; and if they had asked which was likely to be here a century hence, the French national state or some transnational production unit that had evolved from IBM, the answer would not be so unambiguously clear; it is probable that both will be here.

Thus what we seem to be witnessing at the moment is a conflict between two modes of organizing human affairs—a "vertical" mode that finds its ultimate expression in the pan-national flows of production of the giant international corporation, and a "horizontal" mode expressed in the jealously guarded boundaries of the nation-state.

Hymer and Rowthorn conceptualize this conflict in two "ideal-types"—a capitalist ideal-type in which the global production of a single commodity is organized under the unified direction of a single corporation; and a socialist ideal-type in which the production of all commodities in a single state is organized under the control of a single planning agency. In a word, they see the trend of capitalism toward the vertical unification of production and the trend of socialism toward its horizontal unification. In this conflict of ideals, they clearly believe that the socialist mode of organization will, in the end, prove the more resilient and enduring.

Perhaps. And perhaps not. At least in my belief, their dichotomy underestimates the adaptive capabilities of both systems. Hymer and Rowthorn do not ask what might be the role of a vertical organization of production among *socialist* states—whether, for example, a Russian ministry of computers might not play the same role, within a bloc of planned economies, as IBM might play within the bloc of capitalist economies. Nor do they inquire into the possibilities of capitalist economies adopting "socialist" modes of control through the agencies of conglomerate corporations.

In the mid 1960s, for example, at the very time that the Ford Motor Company was investing American dollars in the purchase of Ford in England, a British syndicate was investing pounds in the Pan Am Building. Why did not Ford build Pan Am and the British investors put their money into cars? If the full-blown conglomerate corporation comes into existence, where the top management serves only as a (private) planning board for the allocation of capital, precisely this sort of thing may take place. Indeed it already has: International Telephone now bakes bread, rents cars, runs hotels, builds houses, lends money, and manages a mutual fund, in addition to providing communication service. At this level of organization, the "fundamental" conflict between the ideal-types of socialist and capitalist planning begins to melt away.

Indeed, to my way of thinking, it is quite the wrong way of seeking to understand the problem of the nation-state and the multinational corporation. Both nation-states and corporations are crude instrumentalities by which we deal with the state of humankind today. Governments, no matter how socialist, still depend on patriotism which remains the last refuge of scoundrels; and international corporations, no matter how purified of national taint, are still run by motives that glorify propensities of mankind that should be, at most, tolerated. Both forms are ill-suited to the long-run development of humanist societies. It is only because we do not know how else to organize large masses of people to perform those tasks essential for society that we have to depend on the nation-state with its vicious force and shameful irrationality, and the corporation with its bureaucratic hierarchies and its reliance on greed and carefully inculcated dissatisfaction.

This is emphatically not to claim that other organizational means do not exist. From the study of primitive societies we know that people can order their lives without the commands and incentives of modern society, by building them around the great supportive principle of tradition. What we have not learned is how to reintroduce this mode of societal organization in a civilization dedicated to the accumulation of knowledge, to experiment, to change, to accumulation. Perhaps it is impossible, at least until the period of accumulation has come to an end.

In our present-day conflict between the organizational capabilities of the state and the corporation, it is difficult to state with certitude on which side "progress" lies, when both modes of social control are freighted with the capacity for human degradation and even destruction. All that one can say is that at this moment in history both seem necessary. I suspect that the interaction of the international corporation and the nation-state is less comprehensible as a conflict between "capitalism" (Sweden? Japan? South Africa? The US?) and "socialism" (USSR? Yugoslavia? Cuba? China?) than as part of the ignorant and often desperate processes by which we seek to contain the demon of technology and to organize the collective endeavors of men at a time when the level of human understanding is still pitiably low, even in the most "advanced" countries.

NOTES

1 The point of this doctrine of comparative advantage can be summed up in the homely analogy of the banker who is also the best carpenter in town. Will it pay him to build his own house? Clearly not, for he will make more money by devoting all his hours to banking, even though he has to pay for a carpenter less skillful than himself. In the same manner, the classicists explained that one country will gain from another if it devotes all its resources to those activities in which it is relatively advantaged, allowing less well-endowed or less skilled nations to supply those goods which it has relinquished in order (like the banker) to concentrate its efforts where their productivity is greatest.

2 It should be mentioned that in recent years the idea of the benign effect of an international specialization of labor has come under increasingly critical scrutiny, stemming mainly from the work of Gunnar Myrdal. Myrdal pointed out that in international relations (as also in the interregional relationships within a given country), free trade does not always lead to an equalization of wages, etc. Rather, an initial center of industrial strength attracts supporting skills and services, public as well as private, whereas an initial center of weakness loses them. (E.g., an industrialized center has a rich tax base that provides schools, roads, etc., while a rural backwater stagnates.)

These so-called "spread" and "backwash" effects can override the pull of market forces that supposedly act as a great equalizer between the high-priced city and the low-priced country. Instead, as Myrdal has shown, the advantages of developed areas or countries attract skills and resources away from the hinterland, with the result that strong nations or regions grow stronger, and weak ones weaker. See his *Rich Lands and Poor* (Harpers, 1957).

3 In *World Business*, edited by Courtney Brown, pp. 258–9.

4 *Interplay* (November, 1968), p. 17; Simmonds in *World Business*, p. 49.

5 Much of these assets may also be grossly undervalued. The entire book value of the US private investment in Middle Eastern petroleum for 1969 is carried at $1.65 billion. Earnings from petroleum from that area amount to over $1.1 billion for the same year. (*Survey of Current Business*, October, 1970, pp. 28–9.)

6 Kenneth Waltz in *The International Corporation*, edited by Kindleberger, p. 219.

7 In Kindleberger, *The International Corporation*, pp. 57–91.

8 In Kindleberger, *The International Corporation*, p. 72.

9 *Interplay* (November, 1968); also Louis Turner, *Invisible Empires*, p. 191.

10 Wilkins, *The Emergence of Multinational Enterprise*. For the most impressive exposition of the changing structure of domestic enterprise, see Alfred Chandler, *Strategy and Structures* (MIT, 1962).

11 Wilkins, pp. 216–7.

12 It is interesting to note that the degree of international production (as contrasted with export) varies widely from one industry to another. There is a considerable amount of international production in glass and very little in steel; a huge amount in computers but virtually none in machine tools; a great deal in automobiles but not (so far as I am aware) in shipbuilding. The reasons for this variation are not altogether clear. The answer may lie in specifics affecting the technologies of different industries, or in the characteristics of the markets they serve, or simply in their "outlooks," for I believe there is a discernible variation in the "character" of industries, much as there is in that of nations.

13 See Wilkins, p. 110; *Survey of Current Business* (October, 1970), pp. 28–9.

14 Wilkins, p. 201; *Interplay* (November, 1968), p. 16.

The destruction or forced sale of European foreign assets during World War II was also an immense factor in this striking turnabout. But the shift since the war seems to indicate that the US has reached a domestic "saturation threshold" comparable to that which England or Germany experienced long before.

15 In Brown, pp. 66–82.

16 Kindleberger, *American Business Abroad*, p. 208.

17 In Kindleberger, *The International Corporation*, p. 216.

18 See essays by Emile Benoit in Brown, p. 22; and by Carlos Alejandro, in Kindleberger, *The International Corporation*, p. 329.

19 In Brown, p. 334.

20 In Brown, pp. 281–303.

21 Wilkins, pp. 154–72; Brown, pp. 6–7, 122.

22 In Kindleberger, *The International Corporation*, pp. 88–9.

The United States:
The Crisis of Government

23

The Ten Commandments of the Foreign Affairs Bureaucracy

LESLIE H. GELB and
MORTON H. HALPERIN

The average reader of *The New York Times* in the 1950s must have asked: why don't we take some of our troops out of Europe? Ike himself said we didn't need them all there. Later, in 1961, after the tragi-comic Bay of Pigs invasion, the reader asked: how did President Kennedy ever decide to do such a damn fool thing? Or later about Vietnam: why does President Johnson keep on bombing North Vietnam when the bombing prevents negotiations and doesn't get Hanoi to stop the fighting?

Sometimes the answer to these questions is simple. It can be attributed squarely to the President. He thinks it's right. Or he believes he has no choice. As often as not, though, the answer lies elsewhere—in the special interests and procedures of the bureaucracy and the convictions of the bureaucrats.

If you look at foreign policy as a largely rational process of gathering information, setting the alternatives, defining the national interest, and making decisions, then much of what the President does will not make sense. But if you look at foreign policy as bureaucrats pursuing organizational, personal, and domestic political interests, as well as their own beliefs about what is right, you can explain much of the inexplicable.

In pursuing these interests and beliefs, bureaucrats (and that means everyone from Cabinet officials to political appointees to career civil servants) usually follow their own version of the Ten Commandments:

I

On May 11, 1948, President Harry Truman held a meeting in the White House to discuss recognition of the new state of Israel. Secretary of State George Marshall and State Undersecretary Robert Lovett spoke first. They were against it. It would unnecessarily alienate forty million Arabs. Truman next asked Clark Clifford, then Special Counsel to the President, to speak. Arguing for the moral element of U.S. policy and the need to contain Communism in the Middle East, Clifford favored recognition. As related By Dan Kurzman in *Genesis 1948,* Marshall exploded: "Mr. President, this is not a matter to be determined on the basis of politics. Unless politics were involved, Mr. Clifford would not even be at this conference. This is a serious matter of foreign policy determination . . ." Clifford remained at the meeting, and after some hesitation, the U.S. recognized Israel.

The moral merits of U.S. support of Israel notwithstanding, no one doubts Jewish influence on Washington's policy toward the Middle East. And yet, years later, in their memoirs, both Truman and Dean Acheson denied at great length that the decision to recognize the state of Israel was in any way affected by U.S. domestic politics.

A powerful myth is at work here. It holds that national security is too important, too sacred, to be tainted by crass domestic political considerations. It is a matter of lives and the safety of the nation. Votes and influence at home should count for nothing. Right? Wrong. National security and domestic reactions are inseparable. What could be clearer than the fact that President Nixon's Vietnam troop reductions are geared more to American public opinion than to the readiness of the Saigon forces to defend themselves? Yet the myth makes it bad form for government officials to talk about domestic politics (except to friends and to reporters off the record) or even to write about politics later in their memoirs.

And what is bad form on the inside would be politically disastrous if it were leaked to the outside. Imagine the press getting hold of a secret government document that said: "President Nixon has decided to visit China to capture the peace issue for the '72 elections. He does not intend or expect anything of substance to be achieved by his trip— except to scare the Russians a little." Few things are more serious than the charge of playing politics with security.

Nevertheless, the President pays a price for the silence imposed by the myth. One cost is that the President's assumptions about what public opinion will and will not support are never questioned. No official, for example, ever dared to write a scenario for President Johnson showing him how to forestall the right-wing McCarthyite reaction he feared if the U.S. pulled out of Vietnam. Another cost is that bureaucrats, in their ignorance of Presidential views, will use their own notions of domestic politics to screen information from the President or to eliminate options from his consideration.

II

In the early months of the Kennedy Administration, CIA officials responsible for covert operations faced a difficult challenge. President Eisenhower had permitted them to begin training a group of Cuban refugees for an American-supported invasion of Castro's Cuba. In order to carry out the plan, they then had to win approval from a skeptical new President whose entourage included some "liberals" likely to oppose it. The CIA director, Allen Dulles, and his assistant, Richard Bissell, both veteran bureaucrats, moved effectively to isolate the opposition. By highlighting the extreme sensitivity of the operation, they persuaded Kennedy to exclude from deliberations most of the experts in State and the CIA itself, and many of the Kennedy men in the White House. They reduced the effectiveness of others by refusing to leave any papers behind to be analyzed; they swept in, presented their case, and swept out, taking everything with them. But there remained the problem of the skeptical President. Kennedy feared that if the operation was a complete failure he would look very bad. Dulles and Bissell assured him that complete failure was impossible. If the invasion force could not establish a beachhead, the refugees, well-trained in guerrilla warfare, would head for the nearby mountains. The assurances were persuasive, the only difficulty being that they were false. Less than a third of the force had had any guerrilla training; the nearby mountains were separated from the landing beach by an almost impenetrable swamp: and none of the invasion leaders was instructed to head for the hills if the invasion failed (the CIA had promised them American intervention).

Kennedy was told what would persuade him, not the truth or even what the CIA believed to be true. Bureaucrats like Dulles and Bissell are confident that they know what the national security requires. The problem is to convince an uninformed and busy President. To do that you do not carefully explain the reasoning that leads to your position, nor do you reveal any doubts you may have. Rather you seek to figure out what the President's problem is as he sees it and to convince him that what you want to do will solve it.

III

Vietnam policy under President Johnson exemplified the concept of Option B. The papers to the President went something like this: Option A—Use maximum force (bomb Hanoi and Haiphong and invade North Vietnam, Laos, and Cambodia). Recommend rejection on the ground that the Soviets and the Chinese might respond. Option C— Immediate unilateral American withdrawal. Recommend rejection because it will lead to a Communist victory in Vietnam. Option B—Bomb a little more each time and seek negotiations (even though the bombing was preventing negotiations). Turn more of the fighting over to the Saigon forces and send more U.S. troops (even though the American buildup obviated the need for the South Vietnamese to shoulder more of the burden). Press Saigon for reforms and give them all they want for the war effort (even though aid without conditions gave Saigon no incentive to reform). Option B triumphed.

Option B solves a lot of problems for the bureaucrat. Bureaucrats do not like to fight with each other. Option B makes everybody a winner (by letting everyone do the essence of what he wants), preserves the policy consensus, and provides ultimate comfort to the bureaucrat—deference to his expertise and direct responsibility. Very few will be so dissatisfied as to take their case to the public.

Unfortunately, while this process allows the President to keep his house happy, it also robs him of choice. The alternatives he is given are often phony, two ridiculous extremes and a jumbled, inconsistent "middle course." Unless a President knows enough and has the time to peel off the real alternatives from within Option B, he ends up being trapped by the unanimity of advice.

IV

Former Secretary of State Dean Acheson, summoned by President Kennedy to join the Executive Committee of the National Security Council debate on Soviet missiles in Cuba, favored a "surgical strike," a limited air attack designed simply to destroy the missiles before they could become operational. Each time the military was asked to come in with a plan for a surgical strike, they asserted that a limited air strike could not destroy all the missiles—despite their having the capability to do so. Instead, they produced a plan for their favored option—an all-out air assault on Cuba climaxed by a ground invasion. Their plan had something in it for each service—the Air Force and Navy would pound the island by sea and air, the Marines would storm ashore as the Army paratroopers descended—and the military would be left free to act as they chose. The military insisted that a surgical strike was "infeasible" in part because they assumed that Soviet missiles were "mobile" (i.e., capable of being moved in a few hours) rather than "movable" (i.e., their actual capability of being moved in a few days). Kennedy was intrigued by the surgical-strike option and met with the commander of the Tactical Air Command. When the commander solemnly assured the President face-to-face that the option was "infeasible," Kennedy with great reluctance abandoned it.

"Infeasibility" is one technique to disqualify an option; demanding full authority is another. Early in his administration, Kennedy confronted a deteriorating situation in Laos. He was reluctant to commit any American forces, but neither was he prepared to have Laos overrun. At a critical White House meeting he asked the military what could be done with various levels of force. The Joint Chiefs' answer was clear. They would not recommend any landing of American forces and could guarantee nothing unless the President was prepared to authorize the use of nuclear weapons whenever, in their judgment, that use was required. Kennedy reluctantly decided not to send any forces to Laos.

V

With the Chinese Communist guns firing at the tiny island of Quemoy three miles from the mainland and an invasion expected momentarily, President Eisenhower's principal advisers met to frame a recommendation. The problem, as they saw it, was to formulate an argument that would persuade the President that the U.S. must defend Quemoy. The advisers resorted to the prediction of dire consequences, recognizing that only if the alternative could be shown to be very adverse to American interests would Eisenhower agree to the use of force. They warned the President that in their unanimous judgment, if he permitted Quemoy to be captured, "the consequences in the Far East would be more far-reaching and catastrophic than those which followed when the United States allowed the Chinese mainland to be taken over by the Chinese Communists."

Did Eisenhower reject this prediction as absurd? On the contrary, he accepted it and defended Quemoy.

The uncertainties of international politics are so great that it is difficult to disprove any prediction. This put the President in a bind. If he fails to act and things go badly, the overruled advisers are likely to leak their warnings. In fact, much of the dialogue within the government is in terms of worst cases. An advocate who does not warn of extreme consequences is often viewed as not seriously supporting his prediction.

VI

Although the advocates of the Bay of Pigs landing had convinced President Kennedy that the invasion of Cuba was worth a try, they recognized that they were not yet in the clear: they still had to persuade the President to act immediately. Presidents are, in the eyes of bureaucrats, notorious for putting off decisions or changing their minds. They have enough decisions to make without looking for additional ones. In many cases, all the options look bad and they prefer to wait. The Bay of Pigs plan called for an effective "now or never" argument, and the CIA rose to the occasion. The agency told Kennedy that the invasion force was at the peak of its effectiveness; any delay, and it would decline in morale and capability. More important, it warned the President that a vast shipment of Soviet arms was on the way to Cuba; the Castro forces would soon have such superior weapons that substantial American combat involvement would be necessary to bail out the anti-Castro Cuban invaders. Faced with these arguments, Kennedy gave the order to proceed.

Conversely, when a President wants to act, bureaucrats can stymie him by arguing that "now is not the time." President Eisenhower reported in his memoirs that he came into office believing, after having served as commander of the allied forces in Europe, that the United States should withdraw most of its forces there; he left office eight years later still believing that the U.S. had far too many troops assigned to NATO. Secretary of State John Foster Dulles knew better than to argue with the military substance of General Eisenhower's position. Instead he argued timing. Each time Eisenhower raised the issue, Dulles pointed to some current NATO difficulty. This was, he would argue, a critical moment in the life of the alliance in which one or another NATO country was experiencing a domestic crisis. For the U.S. to withdraw troops would be to risk political disintegration. The moment for troop withdrawals never arrived. To this day, pressures for some American withdrawals from Europe have been headed off by the same ploy.

VII

We had a glimpse of this phenomenon with the publication of the Anderson Papers, in which we read about Henry Kissinger warning his State, Defense, and CIA colleagues: "The President does not believe we are carrying out his wishes. He wants to tilt in favor of Pakistan. He feels everything we do comes out otherwise." And, "The President is under the 'illusion' that he is giving instructions; not that he is merely being kept apprised of affairs as they progress." The President's subordinates disagreed with the President's policy toward the India-Pakistan crisis. They were undermining him by resisting his orders and then by leaking his policy. He knew it and did not like it; but apparently could not do much about it.

Although leaking the texts of many documents, à la Pentagon and Anderson papers, is relatively rare, much classified information regularly makes its way into the press. Presidents are surprised not when something leaks but rather when any hot item remains out of the press for even a few days. Providing information to the press—whether in press conferences, backgrounders, or leaks—is the main route by which officials within the executive branch bring their supporters in the Congress and the interested public into action. Only bureaucrats with potential outside support are tempted to leak. In some cases, it is sufficient to leak the fact that an issue is up for decision: in others, what is leaked is information on the positions of key participants. In many instances sufficient factual material must be leaked to convince Congressmen and others to join the fray.

Presidents don't like leaks by others and complain about them whenever they occur, often asking the FBI to run down the culprit. Such efforts almost always fail.

VIII

On March 20, 1948, President Harry Truman rose from bed early, as was his custom, and began scanning the morning newspapers. He was astonished to read that his ambassador to the United Nations, Warren Austin, had told the Security Council the previous day that "there seems to be general agreement that the plan [for the partition of Palestine] cannot now be implemented by peaceful means." Truman had agreed to no such thing. He was firmly committed to partition and on the previous day had reiterated his support in a private meeting with Chaim Weizmann, the leader of worldwide Zionism. Austin and the

Arabists in the State Department did not know about the meeting with Weizmann, but they knew that the President wanted partition and believed that it could be carried out peacefully. Austin and his associates had no doubts about what the President wanted; they simply felt no obligation to do what he wanted them to do.

At the end of his term in office, Truman was acutely conscious of the limited ability of Presidents to have their orders obeyed, and he worried about his successor. "Poor Ike," he was heard to muse, "he'll sit here and say do this and do that and nothing will happen." And so it continues.

During the first week of the Cuban missile crisis, in October 1962, an adviser warned Kennedy that the Russians were likely to demand that the United States withdraw its missiles from Turkey in return for the Soviet withdrawal of its missiles from Cuba. Kennedy was astonished. Months before, he had ordered the missiles removed from Turkey and could not believe they were still there.

Most students of the Cuban missile crisis have emphasized the degree to which Kennedy controlled every detail of what the American Government did. However, a closer look by Graham Allison, in his book on the crisis, *Essence of Decision,* has shown that the bureaucracy was behaving otherwise, choosing to obey the orders it liked and ignore or stretch others. Thus, after a tense argument with the Navy, Kennedy ordered the blockade line moved closer to Cuba so that the Russians might have more time to draw back. Having lost the argument with the President, the Navy simply ignored his order. Unbeknownst to Kennedy, the Navy was also at work forcing Soviet submarines to surface long before Kennedy authorized any contact with Soviet ships. And despite the President's order to halt all provocative intelligence, an American U-2 plane entered Soviet airspace at the height of the crisis. When Kennedy began to realize that he was not in full control, he asked his Secretary of Defense to see if he could find out just what the Navy was doing. McNamara then made his first visit to the Navy command post in the Pentagon. In a heated exchange, the Chief of Naval Operations suggested that McNamara return to his office and let the Navy run the blockade.

Bureaucrats know that the President and his principal associates do not have the time or the information to monitor compliance with all Presidential orders. Often, the bureaucrats can simply delay or do nothing, and no one will notice. If the President is actively involved, they may find it necessary to obey the letter, but not the spirit, of his orders. As Henry Kissinger observed to a journalist recently, the problem is not to know what to do, but rather to figure out how to get the bureaucracy to do it.

IX

The commandments discussed thus far have all dealt with relations between the Departments and the White House. When issues get that far, one of the fundamental rules has already been violated: keep issues away from the President. Bureaucrats prefer to be left alone to do their own thing. They will not voluntarily bring issues to the attention of the President (or senior officials) unless they conclude that he is likely to rule in their favor in a conflict with another agency. Consider the case of surplus and long supply arms transfers to other countries.

One of Secretary McNamara's goals in the Pentagon was to reduce the level of military assistance, particularly to countries that did not need the weapons and could afford to pay for what they needed. A prime objective was Taiwan. McNamara and his office of International Security Affairs engaged in a yearly battle with the State Department and the military over the level of aid to Taiwan. The White House was drawn in because a number of influential Congressmen were strong supporters of aid to Taiwan. One year in the late 1960s a battle raged over whether Taiwan would get $30 million or $40 million in military assistance. During the same year, the military quietly shipped to Taiwan more than $40 million worth of military equipment, which the Pentagon had labeled "excess or long supply." No senior civilian official was aware of the fact that these transfers were taking place, and no junior official aware of what was going on felt obliged to report up. Thus while senior officials argued over irrelevant ceilings on expenditures, Taiwan got more aid than anyone realized.

Observers sometimes assume that the bureaucracy bucks the hard choices to the President. Nothing could be further from the truth. Left alone, the bureaucracy will settle as many issues as it can by leaving each organization free to act as it chooses. When and if the President learns of an issue, bureaucrats will try to incorporate current behavior into "Option B."

X

If an official strongly disagrees with a consensus or dislikes a key man behind the consensus, he might chance a leak to the press. But frontal assaults on a consensus happen only rarely. In the summer of 1965, Undersecretary of State George Ball was among the first to confirm this fact with respect to the policy of bombing North Vietnam. Ball thought U.S. bombing of the North was folly—and worse than that, would only stiffen Hanoi's will. But he did not propose a unilateral cessation. In a TV interview last year, Ball explained himself as follows: "What I was proposing was something which I thought had a fair chance of being persuasive . . . if I had said let's pull out overnight or do something of this kind, I obviously wouldn't have been persuasive at all. They'd have said 'the man's mad.' "

Ball's remarks express at once the futility of resisting agreed policy and the bureaucrat's concern for his personal effectiveness. Ball knew he could not convince anyone if he revealed his true beliefs. He knew he would have been dismissed as "mad" and would not have been in a position to argue another day. So, he tempered his arguments and went along. Like all other bureaucrats, he hoped to preserve his effectiveness.

As it turned out, Ball's more moderate arguments were not persuasive either, but he did not resign over Vietnam and did not take his case to the public. No one resigned over Vietnam policy. Indeed, there seems to be no evidence that any civilian official has resigned over any foreign-policy matter since World War II.

The only officials with a record for resigning are the professional military. Generals Ridgway, Taylor, and Powers are notable examples. What is more, they tour the hustings, write books, and complain out loud. Military officers feel strongly about the interests of their military organization and often believe that if the people of the country only knew "the truth," they would support the military's position. With this record on resigning and going to the public, it is no wonder the military has been so influential in Presidential decisions.

But again, it is the President and the nation who ultimately suffer. If the President remains confident that none of his civilian advisers will resign and take their case to the public, he has little incentive ever to question his own assumptions.

The Ten Commandments pose a serious problem for a President, who is after all the one who got elected and has the responsibility. Truman understood the problem but feared that Eisenhower would not. But evidence abounds that President Eisenhower, precisely because of his background in Army politics and international military negotiations, was far from a novice. President Kennedy was quite expert and attuned to the ways of the bureaucracy—especially after the Bay of Pigs fiasco. His famous calls to State Department desk officials made the point well. President Johnson was a master of such maneuvering. Even as he stepped up the bombing of North Vietnam he would say, "I won't let those Air Force generals bomb the smallest outhouse north of the 17th parallel without checking with me. The generals know only two words—spend and bomb."

The Nixon-Kissinger team is second to none in its sensitivity to bureaucratic behavior. The elaborate National Security Council decision-making apparatus they established is predicated on tight White House control of the bureaucracy. Their system is designed to neutralize narrow organizational interests (meaning the viewpoints of State and Defense), force the bureaucracy to suggest real alternatives and provide more accurate information (meaning, as has been done, to centralize the intelligence functions around Kissinger).

While this new system has been an improvement in some respects over the past, it has decisive costs and limitations. It has totally demoralized the State Department. The Department's expertise has been for naught, and its exclusion had led to a rash of pointless leaks from disgruntled Foreign Service Officers. With all its reins on the bureaucrat, the new system did not prevent part of the bureaucracy from tilting the "wrong way" (meaning against the President, as revealed in the Anderson papers) in the recent India-Pakistan crisis.

The problem, then, boils down to this: given the fact that the President cannot either chain the system or entirely work around it without serious costs, and given the judgment that a President strong enough to collar the bureaucracy would be too strong for the good of the nation, is there a better way to make foreign policy?

The answer is yes—probably. The President, we think, should make a determined effort to use the system. The personal and organizational interests of the bureaucrat are a reality. So are the different viewpoints on what is good policy. The President's main theme of operation should be to force bureaucratic differences out into the open. Pick strong and able men to lead State and Defense. Let them use their judgment and be advocates for their organizations. Encourage debate and contention rather than asking for agreed upon recommendations. Such tactics may be the only way for the President to ferret out hidden or conflicting information and to leave himself with real choices.

Perhaps, in the end, neither this suggested system nor any system will produce better decisions. Perhaps better decisions really depend on beliefs and events and guesses. But a fuller, more honest and open treatment of the bureaucracy might make for more honest and open treatment of the American people. Presidents might be less inclined to spend a good deal of their time denying differences and hiding policy. This would mean less deception and less manipulation. What better reason for trying it?

24

The Machine That Fails

RICHARD HOLBROOKE

In the realm of policy some changes have been made, others promised. But the massive foreign affairs machine built up during the postwar era rumbles on, as ornate and unwieldy as ever. If meaning is attached to the President's promise of a new foreign policy for the seventies, then the shape of our massive bureaucracies must be changed, and those changes must be substantial.

"If we were to establish a new foreign policy for the era to come," Mr. Nixon went on to declare, "we had to begin with a basic restructuring of the process by which policy is made." But the restructuring has not yet met the problem—the accumulation of more than two decades of institutions, procedures and personnel, existing unchanged in a changing situation. Can we create an apparatus which will, in fact, "respond to the requirements of leadership in the 1970's"?

As a member of the bureaucracy myself, I feel its shortcomings with a special keenness. It is hard to decide whether to play the drama as tragedy, comedy, or simply theater of the absurd.

> After several years' absence in private life, an elder statesman is recalled by the President to temporary duty in the State Department. He notices that there are twice as many Assistant Secretaries and "deputies" as he had remembered from his last stint of public service a decade before. "I have three people on my staff," he says, "who spend all their time attending meetings so they can come back and 'brief' me about what was said at the meetings. The funny thing is," he adds, "I don't give a damn about what's said at any of those meetings."

Size—sheer, unmanageable size—is the root problem in Washington and overseas today. Most studies and recommendations discuss in detail valid but secondary issues: reorganizations, personnel policy, more managerial skills, the need for youth and new ideas, and so on. All these are important factors, but they are primarily unrecognized spin-offs of the central and dominant problem—*size*. There are two distinct but related ways that the apparatus is too big—in numbers of people (or, as we bureaucrats say, "warm bodies") and the multiplicy of chains of command. Of the two, the latter is by far the more serious:

> An officer arrives at a consulate in an area where a minor guerrilla war has been going on for years. The United States is officially uninvolved, but the officer discovers that another agency of the U.S. government is giving limited covert assistance to the guerrilla movement. Rather than send a coded message (the code clerks work for cia), he dispatches a letter via the diplomatic pouch to his Ambassador and the Washington desk officer to ask how this was authorized and why. Neither man, it turns out, knew what was going on. After some interagency wrangling, the policy is changed—to the best of the officer's knowledge.

In order to appreciate how fragile and jerry-built the foreign affairs machine really is, with its five major engines and countless minor ones, it is only necessary to remember how it was built. The present structure was the result of compromises made in time of emergency, as America reacted after World War II to the newly perceived threat of the cold war. Senior officials often disagreed over the need for new agencies even while agreeing that the function needed to be performed. Dean Acheson, for example, opposed the formation of a separate Central Intelligence Agency (cia) in 1946. But for reasons which Presidents Truman and Eisenhower felt were valid, as each new front in the cold war was perceived in Washington, a new agency or organization was formed to fight it: for "the battle for men's minds," the United States Information Agency (usia); for technical assistance and economic development, a series of foreign aid agencies leading up to the present Agency for International Development (aid); for covert operations, as well as independent analysis, the cia; for the building up of armed forces of friends and allies, a massive military assistance and advisory effort in more than

80 countries, under the control of the Pentagon; and, of course, a large U.S. military presence deployed around the globe.

To pull everything together back in Washington, a National Security Council (NSC) was created in 1947. It has gradually acquired a staff of more than 100 officials and grown to its present position of preeminence within the foreign affairs establishment. Other new agencies have also been created, among them the Peace Corps and the Arms Control and Disarmament Agency, while existing departments including Commerce, Labor and Agriculture, sent specialists overseas.

Despite the NSC, Washington's foreign policy apparatus has remained extremely cumbersome. Critics have usually focused on the State Department as the culprit, charging that it has failed to be the strong "coordinator" which several Presidents, most notably Kennedy and Johnson, expected. Richard Neustadt, for example, testifying before Senator Jackson's subcommittee in 1963 observed: "The State Department has not yet found means to take the *proffered role* and play it vigorously across the board" (emphasis added). Other critics have been harsher, and the strongest attacks have come from former high-ranking officials of State and the White House staff, people who were in an unusually good position to observe the problem.

They have accused the State Department of being overly cautious, unimaginative, filled with career officers thinking only of their own promotions, incapable of producing coherent recommendations or carrying out policy once the President has decided what that policy should be. In book after book of memoirs and analysis, the career Foreign Service has been found incapable and unwilling to serve the President, regardless of party, with the effectiveness, brilliance, and courage which is expected of it. In particular, State has been taxed for failing to "take charge" in 1966 when President Johnson set up a Senior Interdepartmental Group (SIG) under the Under Secretary of State.

The critics generally suggest that if the State Department had the right sort of creative, courageous, and effective people (whatever that means), then everything would be fine, and State would assume its rightful place at the center of American foreign policy, or as Arthur Schlesinger put it in *A Thousand Days*, as the "Presidential 'agent' of coordination."

All these criticisms have validity. But the critics of the Department, in understandable frustration and bafflement, have nonetheless been blaming the Foreign Service for a situation which has long been out of its—or anyone's—control. They have repeatedly suggested remedies which are beyond the power of the Foreign Service and the State Department to administer. The critics fail to see the significance of the fact that every other agency involved in foreign affairs jealously guards its prerogatives and fights back whenever State makes the slightest movement to broaden its role; that Presidential exceptions frequently have weakened the theoretical hegemony of the American ambassador over all other official Americans; that several other major agencies have their own independent and private channels of communication back to their own headquarters in Washington; that the funds available to several other agencies for their overseas operations exceed those available to State; that the White House has not always given State the necessary support. Those who hold high hopes for a resurgent State Department are, in short, victims of wishful thinking. They have failed to recognize how unlikely it is that any other agency will ever voluntarily relinquish its policy-making prerogatives, or release its grip on the levers that really matter—personnel assignments, promotions, recruitment, and the budget.

> A desk officer in State has recently calculated that while in theory he is the focal point of all Washington efforts concerning "his" country, in fact there are 16 people working on the country in Washington, in different chains of command. They are receiving information directly from the Americans in the country through up to nine different channels. No one sees all the communications in every channel. Through great effort the desk officer has come to know all the other officers, but, he points out, they change regularly (himself included); someone is always out of town or sick; and most importantly, each one has his own boss, who can determine his future career; each one has his own set of priority projects and problems. "All I can do is try to stay on top of the really important problems," he says.

In fact, at its present size and with its present structure, the foreign affairs community cannot be pulled together under any central agency —not even the White House. Larger coordinating staffs are always possible, and perhaps inevitable; within the last year alone both State and the NSC have added or enlarged offices designed to fill a central coordinating role. But coordinating levels of government do not solve the problem, nor do they eliminate the risks that we face from large bureaucracies. In time, as former Secretary of State Dean Rusk once pointed out, most new levels become additional layers, and only slow down further the movement of policy recommendations or action through the machine. Thus, many "routine" matters—problems of importance not necessarily requiring close attention from Presidential appointees— become immobilized by the requirement for "interagency coordination." Inertia takes over. Someone whose signature is required is off on a trip or too busy with something else; papers sit in in-boxes; no one ever says no but action is somehow not taken. The process has been brilliantly and precisely described by Professor Parkinson, and his Law seems to govern with inexorable force.

> A junior member of the White House staff gets involved in a subject not normally of interest at the White House—routine training programs for overseas assignments. He finds that each agency runs its own training programs, emphasizing different points of view and in effect training its personnel for the bureaucratic battles ahead. Hearing this, a high Presidential assistant now decides to support a unification of the training programs for Vietnam. Every agency gives lip service to this concept, everyone says it is necessary—but every agency offers technical reasons why it must continue its own separate training programs. Finally—and only because of high-level White House intervention—a unified training program for Vietnam is set up. The unusual White House involvement

has resulted in a temporary combined training program, but there is little chance that it will be duplicated—as it should be—for other areas of the world.

Over time, each agency has acquired certain "pet projects" which its senior officials promote. These are often carried out by one agency despite concern and even mid-level opposition from others, as part of a tacit trade-off: "We'll let you do your thing, and you let us do ours." Such deals, or "non-aggression treaties," are almost never explicit, but are nonetheless well understood by the participants. The results from such arrangements obviously vary. Sometimes programs are in direct conflict. Waste and duplication are frequent; lack of information about what one's colleagues are doing is common. These are all direct costs of the multi-agency system, which is too large and scattered to come under one driver.

> A new Under Secretary of State discovers that a routine cable—the kind that Under Secretaries are not supposed to see—on the Food for Peace Program has received 27 clearances before being sent out. No one is able to convince him that 27 different people needed to agree to the dispatch of such a message.

The size of each of the five major agencies leads to additional problems. The distance and number of layers through which information must travel creates difficulties and misunderstandings. From the Secretary of State (to say nothing of the White House) to his country directors and desk officers is a long way. For many officers charged with responsibility for a specific country, the route to the *four* top policy-makers of the State Department may include the "alternate" country director,[1] the country directors, a deputy assistant secretary of state, an assistant secretary of state, and the executive secretariat. And on the way up, any policy recommendation must receive clearance with all concerned horizontal layers. Sixteen bureau chiefs of assistant-secretary rank, with 2,500 personnel below them, report to the Secretary of State on policy matters. (On routine business, or during the Secretary's absence, they may report to one of his three top deputies or 336 staff members.) A separate set of officials in State, with more than 3,000 employees beneath them, handle "administration."

> In producing a draft for the President's "State of the World" message, every State Department country desk was asked to submit a paragraph or two on its area. These paragraphs wended their way upward, were collected and sent to the White House along with a covering summary in a "huge bundle." "They didn't use a word of it—not a word," recalls an official who worked on the message.

On matters of an immediate and pressing nature, the President and his senior aides can usually decide, after the normal give-and-take, on a policy. If it involves few enough agencies and few enough people, the government can even carry it out with precision. But the number of issues that can be handled in this personalized way is very small, and is necessarily restricted to those matters of the greatest importance, and usually the greatest immediacy. If the press knows about a problem, big or small, that problem is far more likely to receive the personal attention of senior policy-makers than if it remains a well-kept secret. A former official of State puts it this way: "The amount of high-level interest in an issue varies with potential press interest."

On matters of long-range concern, the President and his senior aides can and do try to lay out a rational "long-range-policy." But between the generalities of a vague policy document and its implementation by hundreds of people—*most of whom will never have read the policy document*—lie many places for miscalculation or derailment. With each agency deciding for itself what a policy means in terms of specific programs, there is more than enough room for disaster or, at the very least, confusion. Stalemate is one danger of the structure: the possibility that routine matters will not be dealt with until they become well-publicized problems.

> A modest corollary to Parkinson's Law: The chances of catastrophe grow as organizations grow in number and in size, and as internal communications become more time-consuming and less intelligible.

Can the new era of shrinking commitments be one in which our huge bureaucracies also shrink in size? The odds, as every serious student of Professor Parkinson knows, are against it. Bureaucracies cling to their office space, their secretaries, their official cars, and their every allocated dollar and personnel position with a tenacity that drowning men might well envy. (The analogy may be apt in more ways than one.)

The person who has the most to gain from a massive reform of the foreign affairs machine—besides the American taxpayer—is the President himself. If a manageable and responsive apparatus is a true Presidential priority, then he personally must order major changes. Each President must decide whether or not he will attempt major changes, or instead choose to build small, personally loyal, bypass mechanisms with which to carry out policy on those matters of overwhelming high-level interest. Increasingly in recent years, the White House has chosen the latter route.

Since it would cut personnel and budget levels, major reform should be a popular move politically. Who except the bureaucratic losers themselves would voice serious opposition? Except for the military, the bureaucracies do not have much congressional support to fall back on. But the President must want reform and make it his personal priority if it is to succeed. For a man with far greater worries facing him daily, it is tempting to defer action on such an issue. In the absence of White House pressure, minor reforms and reorganizations can always take place, but they are unlikely to be more than small adjustments, part of the self-protective coloration in which bureaucracies wrap themselves.

The test is not yet at hand. The plans, the discussions, the criticism of recent years do not go far enough. The White House—regardless of its occupant—will not be measurably better served in the future than

it has been in the past unless major changes take place in every agency
—unless, in fact, some agencies disappear. Fundamental questions, long
submerged under the imperatives of the "postwar era," must be examined by people who are neither indebted nor subservient to the bureaucracies.

This is not a plea for the hegemony of the Foreign Service or the
State Department as we know it today. It is clear to most people who
have worked in Washington that State is presently unequipped to run
U.S. foreign policy. Indeed, *no one* is equipped to run the foreign affairs
machine today—a machine that fails. It requires a complete remodeling,
by people who are not predisposed in advance to one particular solution, but who are committed in advance to the search for a model
which can be driven by the only man in it elected by the people—the
President.

Such remodeling requires study. We have been surfeited with task
forces in recent years, but—with the notable exception of the 1949
Hoover Commission report—the studies have had their vision restricted,
their mandate limited. If there is another task force, it must be able
to deal with the entire foreign affairs/national security apparatus. But
how the President gets his answers—whether from a task force or from
an individual who has his confidence—is not important. It is important
that the President be personally committed to action. If he is not, then
the bureaucracies, sensing indecision or ambivalence, will evade, and
avoid, and survive.

Hard questions must be asked. Some of them have been raised in
the press and in Congress. But they are rarely asked within the executive branch. Samples of such questions:

The United States Information Agency: Should we still maintain a
world-wide information service with its own personnel, priorities, problems, programs, and promotion system? Do we need it?

The foreign aid program: Should AID remain in its present confused
status? The Peterson Report of last February made some thoughtful
recommendations, looking to the abolition of AID. But it also suggested
a proliferation of new agencies. Could these proposals be reworked to
fit the broader needs of a coherent foreign policy?

The Pentagon: Privately, almost every senior official of the past two administrations has lamented the power and bureaucratic strength of the
Armed Forces. The recent Fitzhugh Report made some intriguing suggestions for cutting this power down. But, again, can Pentagon reforms
be folded into a more inclusive scheme which encompasses *all* foreign
affairs bureaucracies? And—in this case—will there be sufficient political
strength to overcome the military and its allies?

The State Department: How can anyone reduce the layers between the
"experts" and the policy-makers? How can the Department play its
proper role of adviser to the Secretary of State and the President?

The Foreign Service: Should the FSO spend almost half his career in
Washington, where he seems so ill-suited to the requirements? Should
the Foreign Service continue to insist on a "well-rounded" officer, which
results in men who know little about any specific area or functional

field—but who are experts on surviving bureaucracies? How can the Foreign Service attract specialists—or, if it cannot, how can the State Department attract them from outside the Foreign Service? What is wrong with our professional diplomacy? ("Kennedy was angry because he thought the Foreign Service was too conservative. Nixon thinks they are too liberal," says a man who worked in both Administrations. "They are both wrong. The Foreign Service is just the Foreign Service.")

The Central Intelligence Agency: Is the CIA out of control, an "invisible government"? Why do so many ambassadors claim little or no knowledge of covert CIA operations in their countries? Should the CIA be allowed to conduct its business with little State Department involvement? Should State desk officers know exactly what the CIA is doing?

Career vs. Political: How can we reconcile the legitimate need for a professional career structure in foreign affairs—a corps of professionals —and the overriding need for more Presidential control?

Who is in charge? Who, finally, is to be put in charge of running the foreign affairs machine? Who will see that the policy, once decided, is carried out? Will it be the State Department, with its faults glaring at us from the pages of every memoir and almost every memo? Or the NSC structure, growing stronger every day? Or the Pentagon, finally taking charge through sheer bureaucratic strength and longer hours of work and better briefing charts than anyone else? Or will we continue the inefficient system that now exists—with bureaucratic stalemates and compromises, with Presidential decisions carried out (sometimes) but lesser matters usually deferred, with agencies either going their own way or becoming stalemated by "inter-agency coordination"?

I do not pretend to have the definitive answers. But my own conclusion is that a major reduction in the number of organizations and chains of command must take place, or else the bureaucratic chaos will get worse, and more bypass mechanisms will be created, and more layers will spring up, and . . .

If this vital premise is accepted, then institutional change could follow one of several possible paths. Ideally, the organization that is called the State Department could become the central point of the foreign affairs administrative structure. The balance of powers in our government is such that it would be a mistake to put central coordinating power into the hands of the NSC staff, which is immune to the legitimate and constitutional desire of Congress to play a role in policy through the appropriations process and through confirmation of Presidential appointees, and hearings on policy. And much evidence piled up over the last decade shows that overreliance on a White House staff isolates the President from the great departments of government and leads to costly mistakes.

But only an *ideal* State Department, not today's State Department, could play the central role. Only a reformed organization, residing perhaps in the same physical shell but altogether different in internal structure, can do what must be done. Here, indeed, is where the greatest reforms, the most drastic surgery, must occur. More political appointees are surely needed, men on whom the President and the Secretary can rely; fewer FSO's on short Washington tours; a larger number of permanent Washington-based career officials who understand both the Washington bureaucratic game and their regional specialty; much closer relationships between the other agencies (in whatever form they survive) and State; more authority to the desk officers and country directors, who should be aware of *everything* affecting U.S. relations with their country; and fewer layers between the desk officer and the Secretary of State.

> During one recent discussion of this endless subject, an academic observer who is a devout student of bureaucracies scoffed at the chances of ever seeing the kinds of major reform which are proposed above: "Why even the Russian Revolution never produced anything that revolutionary."

Maybe he is right. Certainly there are many people in the government who do not believe that it is too big, or too cumbersome. In some recent studies, expansion of the foreign affairs apparatus has been advocated. But if a President wishes to get the machine under his control, he can—provided he is willing to upset a few established applecarts along the way. The price would not be as high as many people think, and the return, to the President and to the people, would be substantial. Only the bureaucracies would be the losers.

> It's a famous story, but it bears retelling. Ellis Briggs, diplomat of much experience, was Ambassador in Prague in the late 1940's when the Czechs expelled all but 12 members of the swollen U.S. mission. If the Communists thought they were hurting the United States, Briggs recounts, they could not have been more wrong. They had, in fact, accomplished what Briggs had always wanted to do, but couldn't because of opposition from Washington: to reduce the size of the U.S. mission in Czechoslovakia. "It was probably the most efficient embassy I ever headed," Briggs says.

· NOTE

1 The alternate country director is really a deputy. But when the present system was proposed to Dean Rusk, then Secretary, he said he did not want additional layers. Thus, the semantic solution: the Secretary is satisfied; the bureaucracy still creates a new layer.

25

How Could Vietnam Happen?
An Autopsy

JAMES C. THOMSON, JR.

As a case study in the making of foreign policy, the Vietnam War will fascinate historians and social scientists for many decades to come. One question that will certainly be asked: How did men of superior ability, sound training, and high ideals—American policy-makers of the 1960s —create such costly and divisive policy?

As one who watched the decision-making process in Washington from 1961 to 1966 under Presidents Kennedy and Johnson, I can suggest a preliminary answer. I can do so by briefly listing some of the factors that seemed to me to shape our Vietnam policy during my years as an East Asia specialist at the State Department and the White House. I shall deal largely with Washington as I saw or sensed it, and not with Saigon, where I have spent but a scant three days, in the entourage of the Vice President, or with other decision centers, the capitals of interested parties. Nor will I deal with other important parts of the record: Vietnam's history prior to 1961, for instance, or the overall course of America's relations with Vietnam.

Yet a first and central ingredient in these years of Vietnam decisions does involve history. The ingredient was *the legacy of the 1950s* —by which I mean the so-called "loss of China," the Korean War, and the Far East policy of Secretary of State Dulles.

This legacy had an institutional by-product for the Kennedy Administration: in 1961 the U.S. government's East Asian establishment was undoubtedly the most rigid and doctrinaire of Washington's regional divisions in foreign affairs. This was especially true at the Department of State, where the incoming Administration found the Bureau of Far Eastern Affairs the hardest nut to crack. It was a bureau that had been purged of its best China expertise, and of farsighted, dispassionate men, as a result of McCarthyism. Its members were generally committed to one policy line: the close containment and isolation of mainland China, the harassment of "neutralist" nations which sought to avoid alignment with either Washington or Peking, and the maintenance of a network of alliances with anti-Communist client states on China's periphery.

Another aspect of the legacy was the special vulnerability and sensitivity of the new Democratic Administration on Far East policy issues. The memory of the McCarthy era was still very sharp, and Kennedy's margin of victory was too thin. The 1960 Offshore Islands TV debate between Kennedy and Nixon had shown the President-elect the perils of "fresh thinking." The Administration was inherently leery of moving too fast on Asia. As a result, the Far East Bureau (now the Bureau of East Asian and Pacific Affairs) was the last one to be overhauled. Not until Averell Harriman was brought in as Assistant Secretary in December, 1961, were significant personnel changes attempted, and it took Harriman several months to make a deep imprint on the bureau because of his necessary preoccupation with the Laos settlement. Once he did so, there was virtually no effort to bring back the purged or exiled East Asia experts.

There were other important by-products of this "legacy of the fifties":

The new Administration inherited and somewhat shared *a general perception of China-on-the-march*—a sense of China's vastness, its numbers, its belligerence; a revived sense, perhaps, of the Golden Horde. This was a perception fed by Chinese intervention in the Korean War (an intervention actually based on appallingly bad communications and mutual miscalculation on the part of Washington and Peking; but the careful unraveling of that tragedy, which scholars have accomplished, had not yet become part of the conventional wisdom).

The new Administration inherited and briefly accepted *a monolithic conception of the Communist bloc*. Despite much earlier predictions and reports by outside analysts, policy-makers did not begin to accept the reality and possible finality of the Sino-Soviet split until the first weeks of 1962. The inevitably corrosive impact of competing nationalisms on Communism was largely ignored.

The new Administration inherited and to some extent shared *the "domino theory" about Asia*. This theory resulted from profound ignorance of Asian history and hence ignorance of the radical differences among Asian nations and societies. It resulted from a blindness to the power and resilience of Asian nationalisms. (It may also have resulted from a subconscious sense that, since "all Asians look alike," all Asian nations will act alike.) As a theory, the domino fallacy was not merely inaccurate but also insulting to Asian nations; yet it has continued to this day to beguile men who should know better.

Finally, the legacy of the fifties was apparently compounded by an uneasy sense of a worldwide Communist challenge to the new Administration after the Bay of Pigs fiasco. A first manifestation was the President's traumatic Vienna meeting with Khrushchev in June, 1961; then came the Berlin crisis of the summer. All this created an atmosphere in which President Kennedy undoubtedly felt under special pressure to show his nation's mettle in Vietnam—if the Vietnamese, unlike the people of Laos, were willing to fight.

In general, the legacy of the fifties shaped such early moves of the new Administration as the decisions to maintain a high-visibility SEATO (by sending the Secretary of State himself instead of some underling to its first meeting in 1961), to back away from diplomatic recognition of Mongolia in the summer of 1961, and most important, to expand U.S. military assistance to South Vietnam that winter on the basis of the much more tentative Eisenhower commitment. It should be added that the increased commitment to Vietnam was also fueled by a new breed of military strategists and academic social scientists (some of whom had entered the new Administration) who had developed theories of counterguerrilla warfare and were eager to see them put to the test. To some, "counterinsurgency" seemed a new panacea for coping with the world's instability.

So much for the legacy and the history. Any new Administration inherits both complicated problems and simplistic views of the world. But surely among the policy-makers of the Kennedy and Johnson Administrations there were men who would warn of the dangers of an open-ended commitment to the Vietnam quagmire?

This raises a central question, at the heart of the policy process: Where were the experts, the doubters, and the dissenters? Were they there at all, and if so, what happened to them?

The answer is complex but instructive.

In the first place, the American government was sorely *lacking in real Vietnam or Indochina expertise.* Originally treated as an adjunct of Embassy Paris, our Saigon embassy and the Vietnam Desk at State were largely staffed from 1954 onward by French-speaking Foreign Service personnel of narrowly European experience. Such diplomats were even more closely restricted than the normal embassy officer—by cast of mind as well as language—to contacts with Vietnam's French-speaking urban elites. For instance, Foreign Service linguists in Portugal are able to speak with the peasantry if they get out of Lisbon and choose to do so; not so the French speakers of Embassy Saigon.

In addition, the *shadow of the "loss of China"* distorted Vietnam reporting. Career officers in the Department, and especially those in the field, had not forgotten the fate of their World War II colleagues who wrote in frankness from China and were later pilloried by Senate committees for critical comments on the Chinese Nationalists. Candid reporting on the strengths of the Viet Cong and the weaknesses of the Diem government was inhibited by the memory. It was also inhibited by some higher officials, notably Ambassador Nolting in Saigon, who refused to sign off on such cables.

In due course, to be sure, some Vietnam talent was discovered or developed. But a recurrent and increasingly important factor in the decision-making process was *the banishment of real expertise.* Here the underlying cause was the "closed politics" of policy-making as issues become hot: the more sensitive the issue, and the higher it rises in the bureaucracy, the more completely the experts are excluded while the harassed senior generalists take over (that is, the Secretaries, Undersecretaries, and Presidential Assistants). The frantic skimming of briefing papers in the back seats of limousines is no substitute for the presence of specialists; furthermore, in times of crisis such papers are deemed "too sensitive" even for review by the specialists. Another underlying cause of this banishment, as Vietnam became more critical, was the replacement of the experts, who were generally and increasingly pessimistic, by men described as "can-do guys," loyal and energetic fixers unsoured by expertise. In early 1965, when I confided my growing policy doubts to an older colleague on the NSC staff, he assured me that the smartest thing both of us could do was to "steer clear of the whole Vietnam mess"; the gentleman in question had the misfortune to be a "can-do guy," however, and is now highly placed in Vietnam, under orders to solve the mess.

Despite the banishment of the experts, internal doubters and dissenters did indeed appear and persist. Yet as I watched the process, such men were effectively neutralized by a subtle dynamic: *the domestication of dissenters.* Such "domestication" arose out of a twofold clubbish need: on the one hand, the dissenter's desire to stay aboard; and on the other hand, the nondissenter's conscience. Simply stated, dissent, when recognized, was made to feel at home. On the lowest possible scale of importance, I must confess my own considerable sense of dignity and acceptance (both vital) when my senior White House employer would refer to me as his "favorite dove." Far more significant was the case of the former Undersecretary of State, George Ball. Once Mr. Ball began to express doubts, he was warmly institutionalized: he was encouraged to become the inhouse devil's advocate on Vietnam. The upshot was inevitable: the process of escalation allowed for periodic requests to Mr. Ball to speak his piece; Ball felt good, I asume (he had fought for righteousness); the others felt good (they had given a full hearing to the dovish option); and there was minimal unpleasantness. The club remained intact; and it is of course possible that matters would have gotten worse faster if Mr. Ball had kept silent, or left before his final departure in the fall of 1966. There was also, of course, the case of the last institutionalized doubter, Bill Moyers. The President is said to have greeted his arrival at meetings with an affectionate; "Well, here comes Mr. Stop-the-Bombing . . ." Here again the dynamics of domesticated dissent sustained the relationship for a while.

A related point—and crucial, I suppose, to government at all times —was *the "effective" trap,* the trap that keeps men from speaking out, as clearly or often as they might, within the government. And it is the trap that keeps men from resigning in protest and airing their dissent outside the government. The most important asset that a man brings to bureaucratic life is his "effectiveness," a mysterious combination of training, style, and connections. The most ominous complaint that can be whispered of a bureaucrat is: "I'm afraid Charlie's beginning to lose his effectiveness." To preserve your effectiveness, you must decide where and when to fight the mainstream of policy; the opportunities range from pillow talk with your wife, to private drinks with your friends, to meetings with the Secretary of State or the President. The inclination to remain silent or to acquiesce in the presence of the great men

—to live to fight another day, to give on this issue so that you can be "effective" on later issues—is overwhelming. Nor is it the tendency of youth alone; some of our most senior officials, men of wealth and fame, whose place in history is secure, have remained silent lest their connection with power be terminated. As for the disinclination to resign in protest: while not necessarily a Washington or even American specialty, it seems more true of a government in which ministers have no parliamentary backbench to which to retreat. In the absence of such a refuge, it is easy to rationalize the decision to stay aboard. By doing so, one may be able to prevent a few bad things from happening and perhaps even make a few good things happen. To exit is to lose even those marginal chances for "effectiveness."

Another factor must be noted: as the Vietnam controversy escalated at home, there developed *a preoccupation with Vietnam public relations as opposed to Vietnam policy-making.* And here, ironically, internal doubters and dissenters were heavily employed. For such men, by virtue of their own doubts, were often deemed best able to "massage" the doubting intelligentsia. My senior East Asia colleague at the White House, a brilliant and humane doubter who had dealt with Indochina since 1954, spent three quarters of his working days on Vietnam public relations: drafting presidential responses to letters from important critics, writing conciliatory language for presidential speeches, and meeting quite interminably with delegations of outraged Quakers, clergymen, academics, and housewives. His regular callers were the late A. J. Muste and Norman Thomas; mine were members of the Women's Strike for Peace. Our orders from above: keep them off the backs of busy policymakers (who usually happened to be nondoubters). Incidentally, my most discouraging assignment in the realm of public relations was the preparation of a White House pamphlet entitled *Why Vietnam,* in September, 1965; in a gesture toward my conscience, I fought—and lost— a battle to have the title followed by a question mark.

Through a variety of procedures, both institutional and personal, doubt, dissent, and expertise were effectively neutralized in the making of policy. But what can be said of the men "in charge"? It is patently absurd to suggest that they produced such tragedy by intention and calculation. But it is neither absurd nor difficult to discern certain forces at work that caused decent and honorable men to do great harm.

Here I would stress the paramount role of *executive fatigue.* No factor seems to me more crucial and underrated in the making of foreign policy. The physical and emotional toll of executive responsibility in State, the Pentagon, the White House, and other executive agencies is enormous; that toll is of course compounded by extended service. Many of today's Vietnam policy-makers have been on the job for from four to seven years. Complaints may be few, and physical health may remain unimpaired, though emotional health is far harder to gauge. But what is most seriously eroded in the deadening process of fatigue is freshness of thought, imagination, a sense of possibility, a sense of priorities and perspective—those rare assets of a new Administration in its first year or two of office. The tired policy-maker becomes a prisoner of his own narrowed view of the world and his own clichéd rhetoric. He becomes irritable and defensive—short on sleep, short on family ties, short on patience. Such men make bad policy and then compound it. They have neither the time nor the temperament for new ideas or preventive diplomacy.

Below the level of the fatigued executives in the making of Vietnam policy was a widespread phenomenon: *the curator mentality* in the Department of State. By this I mean the collective inertia produced by the bureaucrat's view of his job. At State, the average "desk officer" inherits from his predecessor our policy toward Country X; he regards it as his function to keep that policy intact—under glass, untampered with, and dusted—so that he may pass it on in two to four years to his successor. And such curatorial service generally merits promotion within the system. (Maintain the status quo, and you will stay out of trouble.) In some circumstances, the inertia bred by such an outlook can act as a brake against rash innovation. But on many issues, this inertia sustains the momentum of bad policy and unwise commitments—momentum that might otherwise have been resisted within the ranks. Clearly, Vietnam is such an issue.

To fatigue and inertia must be added the factor of internal confusion. Even among the "architects" of our Vietnam commitment, there has been persistent *confusion as to what type of war we were fighting* and, as a direct consequence, *confusion as to how to end that war.* (The "credibility gap" is, in part, a reflection of such internal confusion.) Was it, for instance, a civil war, in which case counterinsurgency might suffice? Or was it a war of international aggression? (This might invoke SEATO or UN commitment.) Who was the aggressor—and the "real enemy"? The Viet Cong? Hanoi? Peking? Moscow? International Communism? Or maybe "Asian Communism"? Differing enemies dictated differing strategies and tactics. And confused throughout, in like fashion, was the question of American objectives; your objectives depended on whom you were fighting and why. I shall not forget my assignment from an Assistant Secretary of State in March, 1964: to draft a speech for Secretary McNamara which would, *inter alia*, once and for all dispose of the canard that the Vietnam conflict was a civil war. "But in some ways, of course," I mused, "it *is* a civil war." "Don't play word games with me!" snapped the Assistant Secretary.

Similar confusion beset the concept of "negotiations"—anathema to much of official Washington from 1961 to 1965. Not until April, 1965, did "unconditional discussions" become respectable, via a presidential speech; even then the Secretary of State stressed privately to newsmen that nothing had changed, since "discussions" were by no means the same as "negotiations." Months later that issue was resolved. But it took even longer to obtain a fragile internal agreement that negotiations might include the Viet Cong as something other than an appendage to Hanoi's delegation. Given such confusion as to the whos and whys of our Vietnam commitment, it is not surprising, as Theodore Draper has written, that policy-makers find it so difficult to agree on how to end the war.

Of course, one force—a constant in the vortex of commitment—was that of *wishful thinking*. I partook of it myself at many times. I did so especially during Washington's struggle with Diem in the autumn of 1963 when some of us at State believed that for once, in dealing with a difficult client state, the U.S. government could use the leverage of our economic and military assistance to make good things happen, instead of being led around by the nose by men like Chiang Kai-shek and Syngman Rhee (and, in that particular instance, by Diem). If we could prove that point, I thought, and move into a new day, with or without Diem, then Vietnam was well worth the effort. Later came the wishful thinking of the air-strike planners in the late autumn of 1964; there were those who actually thought that after six weeks of air strikes, the North Vietnamese would come crawling to us to ask for peace talks. And what, someone asked in one of the meetings of the time, if they don't? The answer was that we would bomb for another four weeks, and that would do the trick. And a few weeks later came one instance of wishful thinking that was symptomatic of good men misled: in January, 1965, I encountered one of the very highest figures in the Administration at a dinner, drew him aside, and told him of my worries about the air-strike option. He told me that I really shouldn't worry; it was his conviction that before any such plans could be put into effect, a neutralist government would come to power in Saigon that would politely invite us out. And finally, there was the recurrent wishful thinking that sustained many of us through the trying months of 1965–1966 after the air strikes had begun: that surely, somehow, one way or another, we would "be in a conference in six months," and the escalatory spiral would be suspended. The basis of our hope: "It simply can't go on."

As a further influence on policy-matters I would cite the factor of *bureaucratic detachment*. By this I mean what at best might be termed the professional callousness of the surgeon (and indeed, medical lingo— the "surgical strike" for instance—seemed to crop up in the euphemisms of the time). In Washington the semantics of the military muted the reality of war for the civilian policy-makers. In quiet, air-conditioned, thick-carpeted rooms, such terms as "systematic pressure," "armed reconnaissance," "targets of opportunity," and even "body count" seemed to breed a sort of games-theory detachment. Most memorable to me was a moment in the late 1964 target planning when the question under discussion was how heavy our bombing should be, and how extensive our strafing, at some midpoint in the projected pattern of systematic pressure. An Assistant Secretary of State resolved the point in the following words: "It seems to me that our orchestration should be mainly violins, but with periodic touches of brass." Perhaps the biggest shock of my return to Cambridge, Massachusetts, was the realization that the young men, the flesh and blood I taught and saw on these university streets, were potentially some of the numbers on the charts of those faraway planners. In a curious sense, Cambridge is closer to this war than Washington.

There is an unprovable factor that relates to bureaucratic detachment: the ingredient of *cryptoracism*. I do not mean to imply any conscious contempt for Asian loss of life on the part of Washington officials. But I do mean to imply that bureaucratic detachment may well be compounded by a traditional Western sense that there are so many Asians, after all; that Asians have a fatalism about life and a disregard for its loss; that they are cruel and barbaric to their own people; and that they are very different from us (and all look alike?). And I *do* mean to imply that the upshot of such subliminal views is a subliminal question whether Asians, and particularly Asian peasants, and most particularly Asian Communists, are really people—like you and me. To put the matter another way: would we have pursued quite such policies—and quite such military tactics—if the Vietnamese were white?

It is impossible to write of Vietnam decision-making without writing about language. Throughout the conflict, words have been of paramount importance. I refer here to the impact of *rhetorical escalation* and to the *problem of oversell*. In an important sense, Vietnam has become of crucial significance to us *because we have said that it is of crucial significance*. (The issue obviously relates to the public relations preoccupation described earlier.)

The key here is domestic politics: the need to sell the American people, press, and Congress on support for an unpopular and costly war in which the objectives themselves have been in flux. To sell means to persuade, and to persuade means rhetoric. As the difficulties and costs have mounted, so has the definition of the stakes. This is not to say that rhetorical escalation is an orderly process; executive prose is the product of many writers, and some concepts—North Vietnamese infiltration, America's "national honor," Red China as the chief enemy—have entered the rhetoric only gradually and even sporadically. But there is an upward spiral nonetheless. And once you have *said* that the American Experiment itself stands or falls on the Vietnam outcome, you have thereby created a national stake far beyond any earlier stakes.

Crucial throughout the process of Vietnam decision-making was a conviction among many policy-makers: that Vietnam posed a *fundamental test of America's national will*. Time and again I was told by men reared in the tradition of Henry L. Stimson that all we needed was the will, and we would then prevail. Implicit in such a view, it seemed to me, was a curious assumption that Asians lacked will, or at least that in a contest between Asian and Anglo-Saxon wills, the non-Asians must prevail. A corollary to the persistent belief in will was a *fascination with power* and an awe in the face of the power America possessed as no nation or civilization ever before. Those who doubted our role in Vietnam were said to shrink from the burdens of power, the obligations of power, the uses of power, the responsibility of power. By implication, such men were soft-headed and effete.

Finally, no discussion of the factors and forces at work on Vietnam policy-makers can ignore the central fact of *human ego investment*. Men who have participated in a decision develop a stake in that decision. As they participate in further, related decisions, their stake increases. It might have been possible to dissuade a man of strong self-confidence at an early stage of the ladder of decision; but it is infinitely harder at later stages since a change of mind there usually involves implicit or explicit repudiation of a chain of previous decisions.

To put it bluntly: at the heart of the Vietnam calamity is a group of able, dedicated men who have been regularly and repeatedly wrong—and whose standing with their contemporaries, and more important, with history, depends, as they see it, on being proven right. These are not men who can be asked to extricate themselves from error.

The various ingredients I have cited in the making of Vietnam policy have created a variety of results, most of them fairly obvious. Here are some that seem to me most central:

Throughout the conflict, there has been *persistent and repeated miscalculation* by virtually all the actors, in high echelons and low, whether dove, hawk, or something else. To cite one simple example among many: in late 1964 and early 1965, some peace-seeking planners at State who strongly opposed the projected bombing of the North urged that, instead, American ground forces be sent to South Vietnam; this would, they said, increase our bargaining leverage against the North—our "chips"—and would give us something to negotiate about (the withdrawal of our forces) at an early peace conference. Simultaneously, the air-strike option was urged by many in the military who were dead set against American participation in "another land war in Asia"; they were joined by other civilian peace-seekers who wanted to bomb Hanoi into early negotiations. By late 1965, we had ended up with the worst of all worlds: ineffective and costly air strikes against the North, spiraling ground forces in the South, and no negotiations in sight.

Throughout the conflict as well, there has been *a steady give-in to pressures for a military solution* and only minimal and sporadic efforts at a diplomatic and political solution. In part this resulted from the confusion (earlier cited) among the civilians—confusion regarding objectives and strategy. And in part this resulted from the self-enlarging nature of military investment. Once air strikes and particularly ground forces were introduced, our investment itself had transformed the original stakes. More air power was needed to protect the ground forces; and then more ground forces to protect the ground forces. And needless to say, the military mind develops its own momentum in the absence of clear guidelines from the civilians. Once asked to save South Vietnam, rather than to "advise" it, the American military could not but press for escalation. In addition, sad to report, assorted military constituencies, once involved in Vietnam, have had a series of cases to prove: for instance, the utility not only of air power (the Air Force) but of supercarrier-based air power (the Navy). Also, Vietnam policy has suffered from one ironic by-product of Secretary McNamara's establishment of civilian control at the Pentagon: in the face of such control, interservice rivalry has given way to a united front among the military—reflected in the new but recurrent phenomenon of JCS unanimity. In conjunction with traditional congressional allies (mostly Southern senators and representatives) such a united front would pose a formidable problem for any President.

Throughout the conflict, there have been *missed opportunities,*

*large and small, to disengage ourselves from Vietnam on increasingly
unpleasant but still acceptable terms.* Of the many moments from 1961
onward, I shall cite only one, the last and most important opportunity
that was lost: in the summer of 1964 the President instructed his chief
advisers to prepare for him as wide a range of Vietnam options as possible for postelection consideration and decision. He explicitly asked that
all options be laid out. What happened next was, in effect, Lyndon
Johnson's slow-motion Bay of Pigs. For the advisers so effectively con-
verged on one single option—juxtaposed against two other, phony options (in effect, blowing up the world, or scuttle-and-run)—that the
President was confronted with unanimity for bombing the North from
all his trusted counselors. Had he been more confident in foreign affairs,
had he been deeply informed on Vietnam and Southeast Asia, and had
he raised some hard questions that unanimity had submerged, this
President could have used the largest electoral mandate in history to
de-escalate in Vietnam, in the clear expectation that at the worst a
neutralist government would come to power in Saigon and politely
invite us out. Today, many lives and dollars later, such an alternative
has become an elusive and infinitely more expensive possibility.

In the course of these years, another result of Vietnam decision-
making has been *the abuse and distortion of history.* Vietnamese, Southeast Asian, and Far Eastern history has been rewritten by our policy-
makers, and their spokesmen, to conform with the alleged necessity of
our presence in Vietnam. Highly dubious analogies from our experience
elsewhere—the "Munich" sellout and "containment" from Europe, the
Malayan insurgency and the Korean War from Asia—have been imported in order to justify our actions. And more recent events have
been fitted to the Procrustean bed of Vietnam. Most notably, the change
of power in Indonesia in 1965–1966 has been ascribed to our Vietnam
presence; and virtually all progress in the Pacific region—the rise of
regionalism, new forms of cooperation, and mounting growth rates—
has been similarly explained. The Indonesian allegation is undoubtedly
false (I tried to prove it, during six months of careful investigation at
the White House, and had to confess failure); the regional allegation is
patently unprovable in either direction (except, of course, for the clear
fact that the economies of both Japan and Korea have profited enormously from our Vietnam-related procurement in these countries; but
that is a costly and highly dubious form of foreign aid).

There is a final result of Vietnam policy I would cite that holds
potential danger for the future of American foreign policy: *the rise of
a new breed of American ideologues who see Vietnam as the ultimate
test of their doctrine.* I have in mind those men in Washington who
have given a new life to the missionary impulse in American foreign
relations: who believe that this nation, in this era, has received a threefold endowment that can transform the world. As they see it, that
endowment is composed of, first, our unsurpassed military might;
second, our clear technological supremacy; and third, our allegedly
invincible benevolence (our "altruism," our affluence, our lack of territorial aspirations). Together, it is argued, this threefold endowment

provides us with the opportunity and the obligation to ease the nations of the earth toward modernization and stability: toward a full-fledged *Pax Americana Technocratica*. In reaching toward this goal, Vietnam is viewed as the last and crucial test. Once we have succeeded there, the road ahead is clear. In a sense, these men are our counterpart to the visionaries of Communism's radical left: they are technocracy's own Maoists. They do not govern Washington today. But their doctrine rides high.

Long before I went into government, I was told a story about Henry L. Stimson that seemed to me pertinent during the years that I watched the Vietnam tragedy unfold—and participated in that tragedy. It seems to me more pertinent than ever as we move toward the election of 1968.

In his waning years Stimson was asked by an anxious questioner, "Mr. Secretary, how on earth can we ever bring peace to the world?" Stimson is said to have answered: "You begin by bringing to Washington a small handful of able men who believe that the achievement of peace is possible.

"You work them to the bone until they no longer believe that it is possible.

"And then you throw them out—and bring in a new bunch who believe that it is possible."

The Great Men:
Are They a Dying Breed?

26

What Makes Mao a Maoist

STUART R. SCHRAM

In May, 1853, a correspondent for *The New York Tribune* by the name of Karl Marx, who regularly wrote for that newspaper on the European workers' movement, contributed an article called "Revolution in China and in Europe." In it he discussed the possible impact of "rebellion" in China on England—then the leading world power—and through England on the European order as a whole, venturing the "very paradoxical assertion" that events in China might well prove to be the most important single cause of revolutionary change in Europe. He found in this a striking illustration of the views of that "most profound yet fantastic speculator," Georg Friedrich Hegel, who was "wont to extol as one of the ruling secrets of nature what he called the law of the contact of extremes."

"It would," wrote Marx, "be a curious spectacle, that of China sending disorder into the Western world while the Western powers, by English, French and American war-steamers, are conveying 'order' to Shanghai, Nanking and the mouths of the Great Canal." Of such a curious spectacle we are today the witnesses—but the details of the picture diverge substantially from those foretold by Marx. America now comes first rather than last in the list of the "European" powers intervening in the Far East, weapons more modern than "war-steamers" are employed, and the action takes place well to the south of Shanghai. But these are merely external and superficial differences compared to the change in the nature of the Chinese "disorder," and the way it is transmitted to the West. If there was one thing Marx thought Asians were incapable of producing, it was ideas relevant to the modern world.

In his view, China would contribute to revolution in Europe only by disrupting British commerce. And yet today the Little Red Book, containing the words of a peasant from Hunan Province, is read and quoted by students from Berkeley to the Sorbonne. What is the explanation for this "contact of extremes?"

The response that Mao's ideas have found in the West must be understood in the context of developments within our own society, but the ideas themselves have been shaped by half a century's experience of the Chinese revolution. It would be exceedingly rash to assert that Mao's contribution to the theory and practice of revolution has now been finally and definitively spelled out, and that he has no more surprises in store for us. Nevertheless, the Ninth Congress of the Chinese Communist party in April, 1969, marked, if not the end of the cultural revolution, at least the end of one major phase, and in the intervening months the broad contours of the pattern that Mao is endeavoring to establish have become increasingly clear. It is therefore an appropriate moment to sum up his life's work.

The inhabitants of Mao's native province have long been renowned in China for their military and political talents. When Mao was born in 1893, Hunan was already in the forefront of the strivings toward intellectual and political renewal that were to lead to the Reform Movement of 1898. This attempt to modernize the political system was soon crushed by the reactionary Empress Dowager, but the problems it had raised remained. China was in danger, not merely from the incursions of the foreigners, Western and Japanese, who had been trampling on the country and carving out spheres of influence ever since the Opium War of 1840, but above all from her own weakness and failure to adapt to the modern world. Only if a remedy could be found for the lack of political and economic dynamism that lay at the root of Chinese military inferiority would there be a future for Mao Tse-tung's generation at all, or in any case a future worthy of their ambitions for their country and themselves.

Mao has recounted that he first began to have "a certain amount of political consciousness" when, as an adolescent, he read a pamphlet beginning: "Alas, China will be subjugated." He has spent a lifetime endeavoring to transform the Chinese people in such a way as to defeat this prophecy—and in his own eyes the task is not yet done.

Mao Tse-tung grew to manhood in the first and second decades of the 20th century, at a time when the most progressive Chinese revolutionaries or reformists were seeking in the West the secrets of the strength which would make it possible to resist the West. It was characteristic of Hunan, however, that the older generation of scholars, who were Mao's teachers and models, did not restrict themselves to the "new learning" from abroad, but at the same time promoted the study of China's own tradition, and especially of the philosophers who, at the time of the Manchu conquest three centuries earlier, had exhorted the Chinese to revive the pragmatism and martial spirit of their ancestors. Such ideas were more immediately accessible to Mao than those of foreign origin. His first published article, written in 1917 when he was 23, is filled with references to the "heroes, martyrs and warriors" of old, and quotes admiringly from a poem attributed to the unsuccessful rival of the founder of the Han Dynasty: "My strength uprooted mountains, my energy dominated the world." Thus, while preaching the need to influence people's "subjective attitudes" in order to promote "self-awareness," Mao was still concerned at this time above all with the self-discipline and strength of will that should be cultivated by an élite.

Already Mao had been exposed, both through reading and the instruction of his teachers, to the basic ideas of Western liberalism, and for two or three fleeting years he came to share its ideals. "Wherever there is repression of the individual," he wrote in 1918, "there can be no greater crime." The traditional social order, with its ingrained respect for authority, both political and parental, must therefore be destroyed, together with the Confucian philosophy that buttressed it, in order that individual freedom might prevail.

By 1920 Mao had been converted to Communism, under the impact of the Russian revolution. Henceforth, he was persuaded that the liberation of every Chinese could only be a collective liberation resulting from victory over the foreign oppressors and the domestic reactionaries. Nevertheless, he retained the conviction that men themselves and their attitudes had to be transformed if society was effectively to be changed. A genuine revolutionary movement had to be made up of individuals consciously carrying out tasks accepted of their own free will. This enterprise could only appear to skeptics like squaring the circle, but the cultural revolution demonstrates that Mao has still not given up trying.

Mao Tse-tung and his comrades now regarded themselves as Marxists, and they did their best to learn how to be "Marxist-Leninists" as well (though the term had not yet been coined). In other words, they set about assimilating the modifications in Marxist theory that Lenin had made in order to adapt it to conditions in Asiatic Russia and in the even more backward lands to the east. There, Lenin had proclaimed, the patriotic capitalists were not necessarily (at least in the first instance) the enemies of the Communist revolutionaries, but could even be their allies for a time in the struggle for national liberation and independent economic development. Moreover, the peasants and not the workers would provide the main strength of the revolutionary movement, though they would, of course, require the leadership of the workers' party—i.e. of the Communists—not to mention the "international proletariat," as incarnate in the representatives of the Comintern.

Even with these modifications, Marxism (or Marxism-Leninism) remained a fundamentally urban-centered philosophy. Progress and enlightenment would radiate outward from the cities to the backward countryside. Mao Tse-tung himself had become thoroughly impregnated during his student days with the traditional contempt of the Chinese intellectuals for physical labor. And though as a Communist he could no longer retain an attitude of superiority toward manual workers in general, his early experience as a trade-union organizer fostered in him the snobbish disdain for the dirty and ignorant peasants that has characterized Marxist thinking since Marx himself first stigmatized "the class that represents barbarism in the midst of civilization."

Then, almost accidentally, while resting in his native village, Mao suddenly found himself confronted with an extremely militant peasant movement which had sprung up in the Chinese countryside in the wake of the nationalist outburst provoked by the massacre of a number of Chinese by the foreign police in Shanghai on May 30, 1925. At one stroke, the urban intellectual turned back to the countryside, and grasped that there China's fate would be decided. The peasants were (as he put it in early 1927) "like a tornado or tempest—a force so extraordinarily swift and violent that no power, however great, will be able to suppress it." Mao set out to organize that power. He was forced to desist momentarily in the spring of 1927, when Stalin ordered the Chinese Communists to refrain from actions that might jeopardize the alliance with the Kuomintang, and thereby menace the security of his Siberian frontier. But soon this policy led to bloody catastrophe and the utter destruction of the urban workers' movement in China. Mao took refuge in the mountain range known as the Chingkangshan, and there began a long search for revolutionary methods better adapted to the realities of the Chinese countryside.

In these gropings Mao endeavored to take as a guide the principles of Marxism as he understood them, including the dogma of working-class leadership; but inevitably, being thus plunged once more into the peasant world of his youth, he thought again of the legends that had been the companions of his youth. The organ of the Chinese Communist party was soon accusing him of emulating the Robin Hood-like bandit heroes of "Water Margin" (translated by Pearl Buck under the title "All Men are Brothers"), and a few years later he was ridiculed for deriving his military tactics from the famous novel of war and statecraft, "The Romance of the Three Kingdoms." [1]

It would, of course, be absurd to suggest that Mao had simply fallen back into the intellectual universe of his adolescence. He already had, when he went to the Chingkangshan, some knowledge of Marxist theory, and considerable experience with and mastery of the organizational principles of Leninism. A decade later, when more Soviet books had been translated into Chinese, and he had the leisure in his headquarters in Yenan to engage in reading and study, he greatly deepened and extended his knowledge of Marxism. Nevertheless, both Mao and the revolution he led remained most profoundly marked by the rural environment in which the revolutionary process was taking place.

Much has been written about the originality (or lack of originality) of the Chinese revolution, and the crucial points have long since been identified: a revolution from the bottom up rather than from the top down; protracted warfare in the countryside rather than a rapidly victorious urban insurrection; the Red Army rather than the armed workers as the spearhead. In all of these respects, the Soviet pattern, with its stress on the workers and the cities, was far more in conformity with the basic precepts of Marxism than was the Chinese pattern. But perhaps the most un-Marxist thing that Mao did was to reject the need for Soviet guidance. Marx regarded Asia as hopelessly backward and stagnant until prodded into action by the impact of the West. Such backward societies and cultures were quite incapable, in his view, of modernizing in their own way; the only salvation for them lay in "Europeanization." Moreover, they would require the Europeans to tell them "how it is done." Soviet insistence that the revolution in the agrarian lands of the East, where there was hardly any indigenous working class, must be carried out under the guidance of a "proletarian" International dominated by the Europeans, was thus solidly rooted in Marx's own thinking about Asia. (The fact that the most influential of these Europeans turned out to be Russians would have been less satisfying to Marx, since he regarded Russia herself as an Oriental despotism.)

Mao had seen in 1927 the fruits of such guidance—and therefore, while endeavoring to keep in the good graces of Stalin in order to forestall Russian intervention on the side of his rivals, he progressively asserted the right and the ability of the Chinese to solve their own problems without European tutelage. Asked by Edgar Snow in 1936 whether, if the Chinese revolution were victorious, there would be "some kind of actual merger of governments" with the Soviet Union, Mao replied abruptly, "We are certainly not fighting for an emancipated China in order to turn the country over to Moscow!" And in 1943, hailing the dissolution of the Comintern, he declared that, although the International had not meddled in the affairs of the Chinese Communist party since 1935, that party had "done its work very well, throughout the whole anti-Japanese war of national liberation."

Mao himself recognized, in 1949, that his road to power was an unorthodox one, but he declared that henceforth these tendencies would be reversed:

"From 1927 to the present the center of gravity of our work has been in the villages—gathering strength in the villages, using the villages in order to surround the cities and then taking the cities. The period for this method of work has now ended. The period of 'from the city to the village' and of the city leading the village has now begun. The center of gravity of the party's work has shifted from the village to the city."

In the first few years of the existence of the Chinese People's Republic, an effort was indeed made to follow the Soviet pattern. Large numbers of urban workers were recruited into the Chinese Communist party—which had functioned for two decades primarily as a soul or parasite in the body of Mao's peasant army in the countryside—in order to make of it a "proletarian" party not only in theory but in fact. Simultaneously, a beginning was made toward planned economic development on the Soviet model, with the active participation of Soviet advisers. But these attempts at following the orthodox path soon clashed head-on with Mao's conception of what revolution was all about.

Chinese society in 1949 was overwhelmingly rural. Perhaps the most important single question presenting itself to Mao as he assumed control of the nation's destiny was whether the key to the transformation of the Chinese countryside lay within the villages themselves or without. The answers to this question dictated by Marxist theory and Soviet practice were diametrically opposed to those drawn from his own experience.

Marx had regarded the peasants as totally incapable of independent political action, and this view had dictated the approach of his Soviet disciples to collectivization and agricultural development.

Stalin had dispatched élite workers from Moscow and Leningrad at the beginning of the collectivization drive of 1929–30 to provide the political consciousness, organizing capacity and technical knowledge that the peasants were, in his view, incapable of generating themselves. And today, 40 years later, a patronizing attitude toward people in the countryside still prevails in the Soviet Union.

Mao's experience, on the other hand, was that of a revolution which not only took place in the countryside, but which (despite the lip service paid to Marxist slogans about "proletarian hegemony") derived its leadership largely from the countryside, and its strength from the fact that it genuinely reflected the aspirations of the peasantry. To be sure, Mao and his comrades cherished ultimate goals, such as collectivization and the introduction of modern technology, which did not correspond to what the peasants themselves spontaneously wanted. But the 20 years of symbiosis between Mao's guerrilla forces in the countryside and the peasants who provided the "ocean" in which the "fish" of the revolutionary army could swim, had laid the basis for a relationship between the Communists and the peasants totally different from that in the Soviet Union.

Instead of ordering the rural people—from without and from above —to accept a complete upheaval in their way of life, the Chinese Communists were in a position to communicate with them through men within the villages enjoying their confidence, and to obtain their adhesion to a much greater degree than had been possible in Russia. This was, of course, partly the result of the unbelievable degree of exploitation to which the Chinese peasantry had been exposed at the hands of the landlords—exploitation which for centuries had lent to their revolts, whenever they finally burst out, the "violence of a hurricane" noted by Mao in 1927. But the ability of the Chinese Communists to communicate with the peasants and to channel their bitterness to revolutionary ends was greatly increased by their political methods, and by their physical and moral presence in the countryside over a long period.

Although Mao and his comrades have, on the whole, been closer to the peasants than Lenin or his successors ever were, there have been significant fluctuations in this respect. In the early nineteen-fifties, when the Chinese were making a conscious effort to learn from the Soviet example (the more so as the Russians considered such conformity to be only the normal price of continued economic aid), Mao himself appeared to accept the principle that the really fundamental developments were taking place in the cities, where the heavy industry necessary to further economic growth was being created. But such an emphasis in fact contradicted his most cherished beliefs: that revolution was above all a matter of changing the patterns of thought and behavior of human beings, and that ideological indoctrination and social mobilization were more important than technical factors in bringing about such changes.

Mao's speech of July, 1955, advocating a speed-up in the formation of rural cooperatives marked the first decisive step toward reversing the order of priorities that characterized not only the Soviet model, but the logic of Marxism itself. Discussing the relationship between collectivization and mechanization, Mao declared: "The country's economic conditions being what they are, the technical transformation will take somewhat longer than the social." In other words, the potential for reshaping the Chinese peasantry was to be found in the revolutionary virtue of the peasants themselves, and not in mere material instruments produced by a minority of technical specialists and skilled workers.

These tendencies had their culmination in the Great Leap Forward of 1958. The foundations of Socialism, and even of Communism, were to be laid in the countryside, where the "people's communes" provided the best form for the transition to the future ideal society. Progress toward social and moral transformation would be somewhat slower in the cities, where "bourgeois ideology" was still prevalent.

Not surprisingly, the Great Leap Forward, with its emphasis on the revolutionary capacity of the "poor and blank" Chinese people, was accompanied by a growing skepticism regarding the utility either of the Soviet example or of Soviet assistance. In a speech of June, 1958, Mao declared that, while it was necessary to obtain Soviet aid, the main thing was for China to develop her economy by her own efforts. Nor should the Chinese blindly copy Soviet methods, either economic or military.

"Some people have suggested that if our comrades, the Soviet advisers, see we are not copying from them, they will complain or be discontented. Well, I might ask these [Soviet] comrades, 'Are you copying from China?' If they say they are not copying from us, then I could say, 'If you don't copy from us, we won't copy from you either.' "

Summing up the problem of learning from the Soviet Union, Mao declared that the slogan for internal use should be "Study critically," while the slogan for public consumption put it somewhat more tactfully as "Study selectively."

The Great Leap policies led to grave economic difficulties, not only because Mao had overestimated the technical capacity of the rural population at that particular stage, but also because he deliberately flouted the need for effective coordination of the economy. This much Mao admitted himself in a speech delivered in July, 1959, in which he assumed responsibility for the failure of the planners to attend to the plans:

"What I mean by saying that they didn't attend to planning is that they rejected comprehensive balances—they completely failed to calculate the amounts of coal, iron and transport required. Coal and iron cannot walk by themselves. They must be transported in carriages. This point I had not foreseen. . . . Prior to August of last year I devoted most of my energy to the revolutionary side of things. I am fundamentally incompetent on economic construction, and I do not understand industrial planning."

The pendulum therefore swung back toward an emphasis on technical factors and the role of the manager and the expert. This was clearly most distasteful to Mao, but he was forced to bow to circumstances and to the opinions of the "capitalist roaders" in the Chinese Communist party. At the same time, he had learned from the experience of the Great Leap. Therefore, when, beginning in 1963, he made a new attempt to change the temper of society, he did not limit himself, as in 1955-58, primarily to the rural sector. This time, on the contrary, he attached greater importance to remolding urban intellectuals, as well as the party and state bureaucrats in the cities, so as to make use of them in modernizing the countryside.

The cultural revolution has been, as everyone now knows, to a very considerable extent a struggle for power between Mao and his partisans on the one hand, and the proponents of a more orthodox brand of Communism, such as Liu Shao-ch'i and Teng Hsiao-p'ing, on the other. But it has also been a great and wide-ranging debate about the nature of revolution, and at the center of this debate has been the problem of the role to be played by "intellectuals" in society.

The Chinese, like the Soviets, use this term in a far wider sense than is commonly imparted to it in the West, to designate any literate person with a modicum of specialized knowledge who makes use of this training in his work. In China, however, the word has resonances quite different from those in Russia, because of the traditionally high social status of the intellectuals and the fact that in the past many of them actually exercised political power as scholar-officials. This offered a unique opportunity for the Chinese Communists to fill the void left by the collapse of the old imperial bureaucracy, (as the Kuomintang had tried and failed to do), but it also concealed a most dangerous snare in the temptation to imitate the arrogance and contempt for the common people that often characterized the old imperial officials.

It is because he had become convinced, by 1964 at the latest, that party cadres in general (and not merely a corrupt minority) were all too prone to succumb to this temptation, that Mao proceeded to discipline the party from without, with the support of the army, rather than undertaking another "rectification" campaign within the party, as he had done in the past.

Such campaigns had long been a characteristic feature of Mao's leadership style. The greatest and most memorable of them had taken place during World War II, in 1942 and 1943. When the United States Army mission came to Yenan in August, 1944, Mao described rectification as a manifestation of the democratic spirit of the Chinese Communists, declaring to John S. Service:

"Of course, we do not pretend that we are perfect. We still face problems of bureaucracy and corruption. But we do face them. And we are beating them. We welcome observation and criticism—by the

Americans, by the K.M.T. or by anyone else. We are constantly criticizing ourselves and revising our policies toward greater efficiency and
effectiveness."

The results of these and other policies, Mao continued, were visible
in the areas then ruled by the Communists: "You can see the difference
in our areas—the people are alive, interested, friendly. They have a
human outlet. They are free from deadening repression."

Even at the time this was something of an idealization—though the
reports of many visitors to Yenan during the war years attest that there
was much truth in it. But Mao did express in simple language, in these
remarks to an American diplomat, the two basic aims of this and all
subsequent rectification movements: to combat the bureaucratic tendencies of the party cadres by subjecting them to mass criticism, thus
developing at the same time a sentiment of participation and therefore
of freedom among the people.

Similar campaigns were conducted in the early nineteen-fifties, and
again in 1957, after the outcome of the "Hundred Flowers" experiment,
in which all citizens were invited freely to criticize the party and the
Government, had revealed to Mao that the Chinese had not yet been
as thoroughly re-educated as he imagined. Although they involved mass
criticism sessions that were often highly traumatic for the individuals
concerned, all such campaigns prior to the cultural revolution remained
clearly under the control of the Chinese Communist party, which was
expected to reform itself from within, under the stimulus of outside
criticism.

Although the bureaucratic tendencies of those enjoying even a small
parcel of authority are a particular source of concern to Mao, the problem with which he has been grappling in recent years is, as already
suggested, much broader, involving not merely that small fraction of
"intellectuals" who constitute the party apparatus, but the relation between all those who possess modern skills and the other members of
society.

In the long run, of course, Mao is persuaded that the gulf between
the educated and the uneducated will disappear, with the progressive
effacement of differences between town and countryside and between
mental and manual labor. But for the time being it persists, and nour-
ishes attitudes on the part of those who do have some "book learning" of which Mao is all the more wary, since he once entertained them
himself. "I began as a student and acquired the habits of a student,"
he declared in 1942. "Surrounded by students who could neither fetch
nor carry for themselves, I used to consider it undignified to do any
manual labor, such as shouldering my own luggage. At that time it
seemed to me that the intellectuals were the only clean persons in the
world; next to them the workers and peasants seemed rather dirty." It
was only after becoming a revolutionary, Mao continued, and living
together with the workers and peasants of the revolutionary army, that
he divested himself of the "bourgeois and *petit bourgeois* feelings" im-
planted in him by the bourgeois schools, and came to feel that "it was

those unreconstructed intellectuals who were unclean . . . , while the workers and peasants were after all the cleanest persons . . . , even though their hands are soiled and their feet smeared with cow dung."

No doubt it is a mixture of guilt resulting from his own past feelings, and resentment by a man partly self-taught who never took a proper university degree (though he has an excellent grounding in traditional Chinese history and philosophy) that has led Mao to adopt an increasingly hostile and patronizing attitude toward the intellectuals. "Throughout history," he declared in 1964, "no highest graduate of the Hanlin Academy has been outstanding. . . . The reading of too many books is harmful, and one with too much education cannot be a good emperor. . . . We must read Marxist books, but we should not read too many of them either. It will be enough to read a few dozen of them."

The culmination of Mao's suspicions regarding both the uselessness and the inherently narrow and selfish outlook of the intellectuals was first of all the assault by the young students constituting the Red Guards on the "reactionary bourgeois academic authorities," who had hitherto regarded themselves as indispensable, and ruled the universities according to their own pleasure. Mao himself, though he had launched the movement, was startled by the violence of the first outburst in the autumn of 1966. At the end of October he declared, "I did not foresee that as soon as the big-character poster from Peking University was broadcast [on Mao's orders], the whole country would be in an uproar. . . . Red Guards in the whole country were mobilized, and charged with such force as to throw you into dismay. I myself had stirred up this big trouble, and I can hardly blame you if you have complaints against me."

But if he had not realized that events would take quite this turn, Mao set out deliberately to accomplish the end which was in fact accomplished, namely to make sure that henceforth no one in China (except himself) would dare to demand unquestioning obedience by virtue of either official status or specialized knowledge. His chosen instrument for this purpose was a highly ambiguous one. Seen in relation to the party, the Red Guards appeared as "masses," attacking the ruling élite from outside. But at the same time, in relation to the real masses of the Chinese people, they themselves were very much élite. And so, once the students had accomplished their function of humiliating the "authorities" in the cities, they were packed off to the countryside, there to learn humility by listening to the tales of the peasants about the hardships and oppression of former days, and to discover thus how little they knew of real life.

The ambiguous role of the Red Guards is, of course, only one facet of the ambiguous and contradictory nature of the cultural revolution as a whole. On the one hand, it has involved opening wide the floodgates of criticism, and turning what was, four years ago, a tightly organized political system entirely in the hands of party leaders into the world's biggest experiment in direct democracy, where at any moment those theoretically in charge of a certain sector—be it a school, a factory, or a government department—might find things taken out of their hands by a mass meeting or a group of Red Guards or "revolutionary rebels." On the other hand, the whole movement originated not spontaneously, but at Mao's command, and under the guidance of the army—even though, as Mao later said, the results surprised even him. Subsequently, these anarchistic tendencies were brought under control by the network of "Revolutionary Committees" which are (despite the lip service paid to party leadership since the Ninth Congress) effectively dominated by the army. And above the whole scene towers the figure of the Great Leader, Chairman Mao, who decides in accordance with his infallible historical vision which groups, movements and ideas are genuinely proletarian and revolutionary.

This ambiguity of Mao's own personality and of the revolution he leads explain the singularly disparate nature of the groups that have rallied around his name in today's "contact of extremes" between China and the West. The first phase of the cultural revolution, when young people shouting the slogan "To rebel is justified!" attacked all received opinions and all established authority, called forth a profound echo among students in Europe and America in search of new political and social forms whereby small groups can shape their own lives. At the same time, Mao's defense of Stalin against "modern revisionism," and his vigilance in unmasking one after the other as counter-revolutionaries all those who venture to oppose his "correct proletarian line," have drawn to the pro-Chinese splinter parties in the West a number of unrepentant and unregenerate Stalinist bureaucrats and hacks filled with nostalgia for the reassuring certainties of a world dominated by the "Father of the Peoples."

The picture just sketched—two halves of Mao's personality, corresponding to two categories among his supporters—is of course an oversimplified one, for anarchist and authoritarian tendencies are linked, both in Mao and in his disciples. The thirst for absolute purity that characterizes much of the New Left today inclines one to view all those who differ as evil men who must be prevented from leading others astray. And the denial of the collective authority of the party, on the grounds that any organization whose members automatically enjoy power over others is by definition a bureaucracy, leads necessarily to the exaltation of the personal authority of chairman Mao as the only instrument for deciding who is evil and must be suppressed.

In a speech of January, 1958, Mao claimed that one day China would teach the West the true meaning of democracy:

"If we are to exert our utmost efforts, if we are to leave the West behind us, must we not rectify and get rid of bourgeois thinking? No one knows how long it will take the West to get rid of bourgeois thinking. If Dulles wanted to get rid of his bourgeois style, he too would have to ask us to be his teacher."

It would be all too easy to dismiss these pretensions, in the light of Mao's doubtful success in rooting out selfishness and creating a new humanity in China herself. But there may be something to be learned from the experience of the cultural revolution, precisely because it has taken place in a pre-industrial society. In the last analysis, Mao's aim is to prevent the emergence in China of tendencies that he calls "capitalist," and which characterize, in fact, advanced industrial societies: the progressive alienation of the individual in an economic system that has become a vast impersonal machine, and in which it is hard to find out who is responsible for the decisions affecting people's lives; increasing functional specialization and economic inequality; and, as a result of all this, the tendency for people to bury themselves in the pursuit of self-interest and personal satisfaction.

Mao's declared aim is to prevent such a society from taking shape in China (as, in his view, it has already done in the Soviet Union—hence the term "capitalist restoration"). Read literally, such fears are groundless, or at least premature, for China has not yet reached the economic and technological level where she could begin to be threatened by phenomena of this kind. There is servitude enough in China, but it is of a different type, rooted less in technology and more in the arbitrariness of human beings. But Mao, who has always shown the strongest interest in laying the economic foundations for China's status as a great power, is, as he has repeatedly stated, looking to the future —to the fate of the Chinese revolution in the decades and centuries to come. He sees his fellow countrymen, from the highly paid bureaucrats and technicians to the moderately well-off peasants, all too preoccupied with their own material well-being, and asks himself whether things would not become much worse if there were more wealth to covet.

However inadequate are Mao's answers to these questions (as already pointed out, his utopia is in fact run by the army), he is the first major political leader to have raised them with such urgency. This in itself is enough to explain the sympathy he has aroused among many students in the West, who find in his statements and policies an echo of their own most fundamental conviction: that the principal concern of men should be with the quality of human life, rather than with the accumulation of things as an end in itself. On the other hand, though the experience of a nation on the verge of large-scale industrialization can provide a stimulus to self-examination, the real solution to the problem of the human use of technology and of the material wealth it produces can only be devised by those who are themselves the victims of technology.

Marx would, of course, have found outrageous the suggestion that Europeans could learn anything from Asians at all. In any case, he was persuaded that detachment from material possessions could flourish only in highly industrialized societies where an abundance of products was available to all. The experience of the U.S.S.R. and of other "Socialist" countries in Europe does not provide evidence of any such tendency, but this does not mean that salvation must come from the East. Mao's project for regenerating the West by the example of Chinese virtue is no more viable in the 20th century than was Marx's project for the Europeanization of Asia in the 19th. The "contact of extremes" must remain a two-way street.

NOTE

1 Mao himself mentioned this book in a speech in December, 1965, as one of the few works touching on military tactics with which he was familiar, but said he forgot all about it when he went into battle. (This and other references to Mao's statements during the past decade are from previously secret materials compiled by the Red Guards and similar organizations. The "Mao papers" referred to in *Time,* Dec. 12, 1969, pages 32–33, are only one such collection. Incidentally, these documents were not "released to some top Western scholars," but put on sale to anyone who wanted to buy them. That was two years ago; they "became available to *Time*" when an English translation was published recently in a widely distributed magazine.)

27

Charles de Gaulle: Death of a Legendary Hero

DANIEL SINGER

The verdict of history is the one that really mattered to Charles de Gaulle and we obviously shall not get it amid the current chorus of genuine and hypocritical praise. Had the General departed, say, three years ago, it would have been easier for his admirers to make of his second reign a saga of unmitigated success: the miracle worker switching his country from chaos to stability, from the brink of civil war to unity, from near bankruptcy to prosperity. And, having thus consolidated his base, successfully defying the American giant. But this image was shattered by the political crisis and social upheaval of May 1968, which showed the divisions, the depth of discontent, hidden beneath the glittering surface. Indirectly, they also revealed the limited means of Gaullist foreign policy. Instinctively, the General must have felt that the days of grandeur were gone. His official exit—in April of last year, after a lost referendum—had all the elements of political suicide. Nevertheless, he managed to use even this retreat to boost his image: Cincinnatus was returning to the plough—in his case, to the writing table at Colombey.

Nothing is more sickening than the sudden outpouring of love on funeral occasions. With de Gaulle now closely following Nasser, we have had our ration. Let me, then, state quite bluntly that, whatever my occasional sneaking admiration for the General as a performer, I have never, as a Socialist, shared his nationalist outlook or his political conceptions. Even when in sympathy with some of his struggles—not just against the Nazis but also against French colonels in Algeria or the American war in Vietnam—I always remained suspicious of his motives. This openly admitted, I see only more reason to try to understand why it fell upon a conservative military man to extricate France from its colonial ventures; or why a man, who at home was a pillar of the capitalist Establishment, was hailed abroad as a champion of the anti-imperialist struggle. One should not minimize de Gaulle's stature for polemical purposes. The only duty is to seek a proper balance and historical perspective; to disentangle, if one can, fact from fiction and reality from myth. But in the case of Gaullism, the task is difficult because the legend itself was vital for the General and he himself was its artful keeper. Mastery of the spoken and the written word were among his key weapons.

One of the legends will stand the test of time. It is the original one, presenting him as a symbol of French resistance, which was born on June 18, 1940 when, from a London studio, he urged the French people to carry on the fight. He was an acting brigadier and a junior minister, nearly 50 at the time. He found the courage to dissociate himself from his fellow officers, most of whom were rallying around Pétain, and to break with his class—the bulk of the French bourgeoisie having chosen collaboration with the Germans. The London episode, as recorded in his *Memoirs,* hovers perilously between the sublime and the ridiculous. De Gaulle, in those first days in England, had few forces at his disposal and probably more conflicts with his allies than with the enemy. His very weakness dictated a policy of intransigence and, for once, the man was really destined for his role. In the end, he achieved his objective: France was one of the victors and, officially, one of the big powers.

But however genuine, the original legend lies at the root of many subsequent troubles and misunderstandings. To present France as an ally, it was necessary to describe collaboration as an exception and resistance as the rule. Far from being a traitor to his class, de Gaulle proved its savior. He limited the scope of reforms to what was unavoidable and prevented a more radical transformation of society—a vision which had inspired many a fighter in the underground. Altogether, the fiction of national unity, transcending all class conflicts, suited General de Gaulle better than it did the French Left that dominated the resistance. Contemptuous of parties and "intermediaries," the General was not going to settle for less than his own concept of the divine right of elected monarchy. A clash seemed inevitable. De Gaulle's departure in 1946 was a miscalculation. He expected to be called back with enhanced powers. When that failed to happen, he had to form a party—the Gaullist Rally or RPF—and launch it against the regime. The Fourth Republic, however, showed an unexpected capacity for passive resistance. After the assault, Gaullism seemed a spent force and the General doomed to exile. He might have stayed at Colombey but for the inability of the French bourgeoisie to extricate itself from the colonial war and for the *Putsch* of military commanders in Algeria.

That the General used the *Putsch* seems undeniable. On one side, he was encouraging the rebels to step up their threats; on the other, he was pressing the regime to call him in as a savior. A couple of weeks was enough to force the cowardly rulers of the Fourth Republic to surrender. Despite the legal trappings, it was a shotgun transfer of power. *Vae Victis*, retort the Gaullists, and besides the transition was legalized by an overwhelming vote. The argument sounds rather strange coming from men who are, by now, Agnew-like upholders of law and order. Still, it is wiser to assess the Fifth Republic on its record rather than on its original sin.

Like the General in his last book, one may best start with institutions. After years of merry-go-round, when the average government lasted about six months, the stability of the Fifth Republic is impressive. Two governments in a decade and really only one ruler. But how much was it due to constitutional change? A system of "direct democracy," based on the master's "communion" with his subjects and occasional referenda, requires a charismatic figure at the top. De Gaulle himself was to discover that it yielded diminishing returns as his support dwindled from the initial 80 per cent. A heavy price also had to be paid: parliament was reduced to a rubber-stamp institution, the television to a government tool, while official propaganda and pressure reached unprecedented proportions. The absence of safety valves and warning signals may have had something to do with the May explosion.

Political stability was indispensable to economic recovery; so runs the Gaullist argument, and it has some validity when not overplayed. The empty vaults of the Bank of France were refilled with gold; trade expanded and production grew. But Gaullist France carried out no major structural reforms; it merely widened the gap between rich and poor. The outcome was the biggest general strike the country had ever known.

The failure of France to introduce more radical reforms than did its neighbors should put an end to a once fashionable theory that Gaullism is a superior form of capitalist rule, liberal democracy being no longer able to cope with monopolistic competition. The theory was linked with the dream of French technocrats that the regime would allow them to speed up the process of economic concentration and rationalization. The dream did not come true. De Gaulle had to gather votes for his referenda from somewhere, and a great deal of his support came from the very people, such as small farmers and shopkeepers, who were supposed to be squeezed out. Gaullism was a response to a specific situation, in a country faced with colonial complications and a militant working class. Indeed, the French experiment confirms that parliamentary democracy is a more effective defense mechanism, whenever capitalism can afford it. After de Gaulle comes a Guizot, with his slogan, "enrich yourselves," though whether neo-Gaullism can provide the safety valves and avoid an explosion remains to be seen.

Are the external achievements more solid? The fact that Algeria, once a cancer on the French political body, can now be treated as an external matter must be cited as an achievement. Here, again, however, the critics have their points. It is true that the war lasted as long—four years—under each Republic. It is equally true that the delay under the Fifth Republic was due not only to de Gaulle's need to come to terms with the French military commanders, with the barons who had made him king. For a time, he also clung to the illusion that he could force the FLN to accept his conditions. Yet when all this is said, he did make peace in the end, unlike his allegedly Socialist predecessors, and his experience is relevant for America. France, after all, had half a million men in Algeria; it also had native troops and a better control of the military situation than Americans have in Vietnam. It took General de Gaulle quite a time to realize that this was not enough, that war against a determined liberation movement was pointless. His strictures against American policy in Vietnam were no less valid because they were the fruit of bitter experience.

Foreign policy proper was the General's favorite field and here the vedict is difficult. To dispel some ambiguity, one must recall that the now classical image of de Gaulle as the champion of détente with the Russians and the darling of the Third World really arises from the second half of his reign. In the first four or five years, admittedly handicapped by the Algerian War, he pursued quite a different policy. He was trying to gain the leadership of a continental coalition, based on the Paris-Bonn axis, which was to put him on a par with the super-powers. Adenauer, the cold warrior, was then his chief ally. The scheme had logic. The snag was its basic premise—the assumption that Germany could be forced into a junior partnership, particularly in an enterprise aimed at the United States. Yet by about 1963, when his edifice was obviously in ruins, de Gaulle showed his extraordinary capacity for recovery and his skill in performance. Within a short period he was opening lines to Eastern Europe and challenging "American hegemony," to applause echoing from Asia to Latin America.

Performance, nothing but performance, claimed the critics, but they were only half right. To take France out of NATO, to keep Britain, the "Trojan Horse," out of the Common Market, to slow down the process of European integration were themselves achievements of a negative kind. The strength and weakness of Gaullist foreign policy were connected with the role of the nation-state in our time. Having grasped how strong the state still was, the General defied the United States, putting to shame his European colleagues who had never dared say No to Washington. But the nation-state, particularly one of medium size, can no longer transcend the imperatives of internationalism. His was, thus, an anachronistic realism. To say that de Gaulle did not have the means to match his ends does not mean simply that France was too small. Internally, he did not have the instruments ready to resist the American invasion; externally, he could not turn to the people of Europe, offering them a different life, a society radically different from the American model. You cannot expect a General, however skillful and bold, to propose the foundation of the United Socialist States of Europe.

As heads of state filed into Notre Dame for a last tribute, many thoughts crossed one's mind. These included strange reflections on the role of the individual in history, remembering that de Gaulle, having so dominated his country for a decade, then vanished almost without a ripple. One recalled his stature, if only by contrast with surrounding dwarfs. His foreign policy, for what it was worth, showed up the failure of the European Left, the bankruptcy of social democracy. Finally, with the last of the old heroes gone, one also felt that the postwar period was at last over. The General's own reign had really come to an end in May 1968, when the master tactician seemed utterly bewildered for a while by new political and social forces. That was not yet a change of the guard, but for Europe, at least, it marked the beginning of a new age of conflict in which we shall need not the deceptive protection of a legend but the more potent weapon of political consciousness.

PART IV

The Problems of the Future

It has become commonplace today to consider and evaluate the problems of the future. Discussions of the year 2000, of "future shock," of the "energy crisis," and of the "population bomb" have become prevalent. Many view what has been called the post-industrial society as an emerging scientific utopia in which many of the serious physical problems of modern social systems will have been solved. Others see the new society as one plagued by the poisonous fruits of science and technology themselves. Pessimism about the results of scientific progress and economic growth has intensified among intellectual and professional elites. Indeed, to many, preoccupation with such policy problems as the balance of power seems trivial at a time when peril to our future physical existence appears to arise more directly from environmental conditions than from any threatened atomic Armageddon.

In the two articles in Part IV, Paul Ehrlich and Zbigniew Brzezinski deal with these problems from different perspectives. Ehrlich is most concerned that our domestic and foreign policies be oriented to the consequences of growing population. He is not a total pessimist, for he believes that actions, however drastic, can be taken to solve the problems he has identified. Indeed DDT, about which Ehrlich was so concerned when he wrote in 1968, has now been banned in the United States, though it continues to be used in many countries abroad. Ehrlich presents the image of a stark future but argues that its effects can be ameliorated by resort to dramatic and controversial political acts.

Zbigniew Brzezinski deals more broadly with the nature of the new society in its social and technological implications. Basically more optimistic about these novel conditions than Ehrlich, Brzezinski projects a future which is already partially upon us, one in which domestic and international problems are transformed but not resolved. Brzezinski examines the types of progress science will provide, but he also depicts the growing differentiation of the world which the new science will encourage and the possibility of intensified conflict as the gaps widen between rich and poor, scientifically advanced and technologically backward. He shows how this stratification will also be reflected in domestic societies in both the developed and developing worlds.

The two articles suggest a world which is focused less on military devices of competition and more on economic, technological, and scientific developments. They also show that becoming accustomed to this world may be even more traumatic than the adjustment to the atomic era which occurred in the past generation. Indeed, the technetronic age may make the thermonuclear era appear tranquil by comparison.

Edmund Burke once wrote,

> Society is indeed a contract. . . . It is a partnership in all science; a partnership in all art; a partnership in every virtue, and in all perfection. As the ends of such a partnership cannot be obtained in many generations, it becomes a partnership not only between those who are living, but between those who are living, those who are dead, and those who are to be born.

In a new scientific society the links between generations may seem broken as technology makes it increasingly difficult for us to identify with the ways in which people have lived before us. Perhaps the greatest challenge of all in this future environment will be to maintain our links with tradition, to preserve the best of human values, even as society continues to change. In the world arena a search for links to the past may become central to the quest for a form of order that will maintain what Burke called "the great primeval contract of eternal society."

28

Population, Food, and Environment: Is the Battle Lost?

PAUL R. EHRLICH

The facts of human population growth are simple. The people of the earth make up a closed population, one to which there is no immigration and from which there is no emigration. It can be readily shown that the earth's human population will remain essentially closed—that no substantial movement of people to other planets is likely and that no substantial movement to other solar systems is possible. Now, a closed population will grow if the birth rate exceeds the death rate, and will shrink in size if the death rate is greater than the birth rate. Over the past half-century or so a massive increase in man's understanding and utilization of death control has resulted in a rapid rise in the rate of growth of the human population (a rate which is equal to the birth rate minus the death rate). So, we have a closed, growing population. And, intriguing as the prospect may be to certain irresponsible politicians, economists, and religious leaders, we will not achieve an infinite population size. Sooner or later the growth of the human population must stop.

On the "later" side it has been possible to compute when physical limitations, notably the problem of dissipating the heat produced by human metabolic processes, will put an end to growth in the solar system. We are forever barred from exporting a significant part of our population to the stars, so the theoretical maximum for the solar system coincides closely with the extreme possible numerical peak for *Homo sapiens*. This peak would be reached, at the current growth rate, in far under 1500 years. Indeed, if we are confined in large part to the planet earth (and there is every reason to believe we will be), the end will be reached in less than 1000 years. For those interested in such long-range thinking there is one more cheery datum—the rate of increase of the population is itself accelerating!

On the "sooner" side we must face considerably less certainty. A fantastic world effort over the next decade at changing the attitude of people towards family size and developing, promoting, and distributing birth control technology might conceivably arrest population growth at two to three times its present level—if nothing untoward intervenes. On the other hand, it is quite within our power to reduce the population size to zero tomorrow, should we opt for thermonuclear war. But, later or sooner, one thing is certain. The human population *will* stop growing. This halt must come through either a decrease in the birth rate, or an increase in the death rate, or a combination of the two. A corollary of this is that anyone or any organization opposing reduction in the birth rate is automatically an agent for eventually increasing the death rate.

Since we need have only an academic interest in theoretical limits on the size of the human population, I am going to address my remarks to the very real crisis we face this instant. In particular I want to examine the relationship of our current population growth to food resources and the quality of our environment. Finally, I want to examine what, if anything, can be done to give our descendants a world to live in.

At the moment it is shockingly apparent that in the battle to feed humanity our side has been routed. In 1966 the population of the world increased by some seventy million people, and there was no compensatory increase in food production. Indeed, in areas such as Africa and Latin America there has actually been a decrease in food production over the past two years. According to the United Nations Food and Agriculture Organization advances in food production made in developing nations between 1955 and 1965 have been wiped out by agriculture disasters in 1965 and 1966. All this means that last year, on the average, each person on earth had 2 per cent less to eat. The reduction is, of course, not uniformly distributed. Starvation already is a fact in many countries. Only ten countries, including the United States, grew more food than they consumed—all other populous countries, including Russia, China, and India, imported more than they exported. Last year the United States shipped one quarter of its wheat crop, nine million tons, to India. In spite of this aid, serious famines still threaten the Indian population. And, what is worse, our aid has retarded the development of grain production in that country. Our wheat reserves are now so low that they can no longer serve as anti-starvation insurance for the Indian subcontinent. Every month there are some one and a half million more Indians. Should India's present population growth continue for another ten years it would take the *entire* grain production of the United States to relieve the Indian food shortage.

Agricultural experts state that a tripling of the food supply of the world will be necessary in the next thirty years or so, if the six or seven billion people who may be alive in the year 2000 are to be adequately fed. Theoretically such an increase might be possible, but it is becoming increasingly clear that it is totally impossible in practice. A few months ago I would have told you that *if* we had ideal conditions of research, development, and international cooperation we might triple our food production by then—if we started immediately. I would then have examined the possibility of meeting such assumptions. You would have been treated to the history of the unsuccessful attempts of the International Whaling Commission to control the hunting of whales, as a sample of the kind of international cooperation we can anticipate. I would have explained why the idea that our food supply can be dramatically increased by harvesting the sea is a gigantic hoax. Then I would have told you about some of the unhappy physical and social barriers in the way of attempting to produce much more food on the land.

All of this, however, now seems to me to be beside the point. There is not going to be any massive tooling up to meet the food crisis. There is not going to be any sudden increase in international cooperation. Even if there were a miraculous change in human attitudes and behavior in this area, *it is already too late to prevent a drastic rise in the death rate through starvation.* In a massively documented book, *Famine 1975!*, William and Paul Paddock recently stated:

> A locomotive is roaring full throttle down the track. Just around the bend an impenetrable mudslide has oozed across the track. There it lies, inert, static, deadly. Nothing can stop the locomotive in time. Collision is inevitable. Catastrophe is foredoomed. Miles back up the track the locomotive could have been warned and stopped. Years ago the mud-soaked hill could have been shored up to forestall the landslide. Now it is too late.
>
> The locomotive roaring straight at us is the population explosion. The unmovable landslide across the tracks is the stagnant production of food in the undeveloped nations, the nations where the population increases are greatest. The collision is inevitable. The famines are inevitable.

The Paddocks predict that the time of famines will be upon us full-scale in 1975. The U.S. Department of Agriculture estimates that America can continue to feed the developing countries until 1984. Which estimate is more correct will depend in part on the validity of the assumptions on which they are based, and in part on such things as the weather. My guess is that the Paddocks are more likely correct, but in the long run it makes no difference. A great many people are going to starve to death, and soon. There is nothing that can be done to prevent it.

Much of the Paddocks' book deals with the problem of how the United States should behave in the time of crisis. We are the only country which will be in a position to *give* food to starving countries, and the amount of food which we will be able to donate will fall far short of world-wide needs. We will be forced to choose who will live and who will die. The Paddocks suggest that we place each country in one of three categories based on the method used to classify wounded entering a military hospital:

1. Those who will die regardless of treatment.
2. Those who will survive regardless of treatment and regardless of the agony they may suffer.
3. Those who can be saved if given prompt treatment.

India, where population growth is colossal, agriculture hopelessly antiquated, and the government incompetent, will be one of those we must allow to slip down the drain. This year C. Subramaniam, former Minister for Food and Agriculture of India, speaking at Stanford University blamed the United States for not giving his country enough food to get her through the last couple of years. He blamed drought for India's problems, and predicted a massive increase in Indian agriculture which would "save the day" by yielding nineteen million more tons of grain a year. This from an ex-official of a government which itself *officially* predicted in 1959 that a serious gap would appear in 1965–66 between demand and available food in India. This man is trying to tell us that in the next eight years India is going to find a way to produce enough food to support some 120 million more people than they cannot feed today—a challenge which would tax a highly efficient agricultural system. Millions of Indians will die because of governmental attitudes exemplified by Subramaniam. They will die because some religious organizations have blocked attempts over the years to get governmental and United Nations action under way to control human birth rates. They will die because scientists have managed to persuade many influential people that a technological rabbit can always be pulled out of the hat to save mankind at the last moment. They will die because many people, like myself, who recognized the essential role of overpopulation in the increasing woes of *Homo sapiens* could not bring themselves to leave the comforts of their daily routine to do something about it. Their blood will be distributed over many hands.

But then, what good can a partitioning of guilt do? Perhaps some people will recognize their culpability and mend their ways—too late. What's done is done, to coin a phrase. We must look to the survivors, if there are to be any. We must assume that the "time of famines" will not lead to thermonuclear Armageddon, and that man will get another chance, no matter how ill-deserved. What I'd like to consider now is what we can do today that would improve the probability of man's making the most of a second chance, should he be lucky enough to get one.

Of course, the most important thing that we must do is to educate people and change many of their attitudes. We must, for example, alert people to the possible environmental consequences of attempting continually to increase food production. They must be made aware of subtle biological properties of our environment which, if ignored, may lead to very unsubtle future calamities. For instance, one of the basic facts of population biology is that the simpler an ecological system (or ecosystem) is, the more unstable it is. A complex forest, consisting of a great variety of plants and animals, will persist year in and year out with no interference from man. The system contains many elements, and changes in different ones often cancel one another out. Suppose one kind of predator eating small rodents, say foxes, suffers a population decline. Its role in the forest may be assumed by another predator, perhaps owls. Such compensation may not be possible in a simpler system. Similarly, no plant-eating animal feeds on all kinds of plants, and the chance of a population explosion of a herbivore completely defoliating a mixed woodland is virtually nil.

Man, however, is a simplifier of complex ecosystems, and a creator of simple ecosystems. For instance, he persists in creating systems which consist almost entirely of uniform stands of a single grass—wheatfields and cornfields are familiar examples. Any farmer can testify to the instability of these ecosystems. Without human protection such an ecosystem rapidly disappears.

Plans for increasing food production invariably involve large-scale efforts at environmental modification. Land must be cleared, water must be provided, fertilizers must enrich soils, and pesticides must be used against organisms which compete with us by eating our crops. It seems unlikely that, if we should choose to push ahead with increasing world food production on a monumental scale, this push will be accompanied by an upsurge in the level of ecological sophistication of those responsible for directing the effort. We can expect more bad land management, such as caused the American dust bowl and, indeed, is ruining soils in many parts of the world today. Farming practices are often followed which lead to the loss of topsoil or the rapid conversion of soil into unmanageable compacted material. Soil is often "mined" by grazing or single-crop farming. Minerals taken up by plants are not returned to the soil when crops or cattle are marketed. Careless irrigation also ruins soils, by permitting the building up of salts. Another factor, often unappreciated, is poisoning of the soil. If we attempt to greatly increase the agricultural yield of the earth it seems certain that the use of synthetic pesticides, already massive, will be increased. And, synthetic pesticides are one of man's most potent tools for simplifying ecosystems. They not only reduce the diversity of life above ground, but long-term applications almost certainly reduce the diversity in the soil. Remember that soil is not just crushed rock. It contains a rich flora and fauna which are essential for its fertility.

Do we want to embark on a program which would involve a great increase in the usage of synthetic pesticides? In spite of massive publicity the intimate relationship between pesticides and environmental deterioration is not widely recognized. Unfortunately, the entire issue has been clouded by the efforts of health nuts on one side and paid industrial propagandists on the other. One group urges a return to nature which, even if it were desirable, is now clearly impossible. The other would have us believe that food did not exist until synthetic organic pesticides provided it for us, and that these chemicals are the only way in which our health can be maintained. Both sides tend to concentrate on consideration of direct toxic effects on man, rather than looking at the entire ecological picture. I think this is a serious mistake.

Of all the synthetic organic pesticides, we probably know the most about DDT, the oldest and most widely used chlorinated hydrocarbon insecticide. Virtually all populations of animals the world over are contaminated with it. Concentrations in the fat bodies of Americans average 11 parts per million, and Israelis have been found to have as much as 19.2 parts per million. More significant in some ways has been the discovery of DDT residues in such unlikely places as the fat bodies of Eskimos, antarctic penguins, and antarctic seals. Pesticide pollution is truly a world-wide problem.

DDT breaks down only very slowly, and will last for decades in soils. A recent study of a Long Island marsh which has been sprayed for twenty years for mosquito control revealed up to thirty-two pounds per acre of DDT in the upper layer of mud. Unhappily, the way DDT circulates in the ecosystem leads to a concentration in carnivores. The danger to life and reproductive capacity of meat-eating birds may be approaching the critical now, and the outlook for man if current trends continue does not seem healthy. The day may soon be upon us when the obese people of the world must give up diets, since metabolizing their fat deposits will lead to DDT poisoning. But, on the bright side, it is clear that fewer and fewer people in the future will be obese. We must remember that DDT has been in use for only about a quarter of a century. It is difficult to predict the results of another fifty years of application of DDT and similar compounds, especially if those years are to be filled with frantic attempts to feed more and more people. Of course, DDT is just one of many synthetic substances with which we are dosing our environment. In addition to their direct toxic threat to man, these compounds all have the effect of simplifying ecosystems and thus aggravating the instability created by man's agricultural and other activities.

Pest organisms ordinarily have large populations—that, indeed, is why they are pests. The large size of their populations makes them much more likely to have the kind of reserve genetic variability which leads most easily to the development of resistant strains. Therefore, extermination of a pest by use of synthetic pesticides is unlikely—and, in fact, is almost unknown. The usual picture is one in which the pesticides decimates the natural enemies of the pest, while the pest develops resistant strains. These problems of pesticides are just one example of a trend which has accompanied the expansion of the human population. The more we have manipulated our environment, the more we have been required to manipulate it. The more we have done with synthetic pesticides, the less we have been able to do without them. The more we have deforested the more flood control dams we have had to build. The more farmland we have subdivided the more pressure we have created to increase the yield on the land remaining under cultivation and to farm marginal land. This trend has been enhanced by an unhappy historical factor. The earth has come largely under the

control of a culture which traditionally sees man's proper role as dominating nature, rather than living in harmony with it. It is a culture
which equates "growth" and "progress" and considers both as self-
evidently desirable. It is a culture which all too often considers "undeveloped" land to be "wasted" land. Unquestionably people's attitudes
toward their physical environment need changing if we are to make
the grade—attitudes which unfortunately are among the most basic
in Western culture. And, unfortunately, the state of our physical environment is just part of the problem.

Perhaps more important than recent changes in our physical environment are those in our psychic environment. Unhappily, we cannot be sure of the significance of these latter changes—although riots,
the hippie movement, and increased drug usage are hardly cheery signs.
We can't even be sure of how much of an individual's reaction to these
environmental changes will be hereditarily conditioned, and how
much it will be a function of his culture. Let me quote part of what
three biologists recently have written on the subject:

"Unique as we may think we are, we are nevertheless as likely to be
genetically programmed to a natural habitat of clean air and a varied
green landscape as any other mammal. To be relaxed and feel healthy
usually means simply allowing our bodies to react in the way for which
100 millions of years of evolution has equipped us. Physically and
genetically we appear best adapted to a tropical savanna, but as a
cultural animal we utilize learned adaptations to cities and towns.
For thousands of years we have tried in our houses to imitate not only
the climate, but the setting of our evolutionary past: warm, humid,
air, green plants and even animal companions. Today, if we can afford
it, we may even build a greenhouse or swimming pool next to our
living room, buy a place in the country, or at least take our children
vacationing on the seashore. The specific physiological reactions to
natural beauty and diversity, to the shapes and colors of nature (especially to green), to the motions and sounds of other animals, such as
birds, we as yet do not comprehend. But, it is evident that nature in
our daily life should be thought of as a part of the biological need. It
cannot be neglected in the discussions of resource policy for man."
(H. H. Iltis, P. Andrews, and O. L. Loucks. "Criteria for an Optimum
Human Environment." Manuscript, 1967).

Man clearly has gone a long way toward adapting to urban en-
vironments and despoiled landscapes We badly need to understand
the effects of this adjustment, especially in terms of group behavior,
and to be able to predict the effects of further changes in man's perceptual environment. It is important to note that our perceptual
systems have evolved primarily to react to stimuli representing a sudden
change in our environment—a lion's charge, a flaring fire, a child's
cry. Long-term changes often are not noticed. We tend not to perceive
a friend's aging, or the slowing of our reflexes. If the transition from
the Los Angeles of 1927 to that of 1967 had occurred overnight Ange-
lenos surely would have rebelled. But a gradual forty-year transition
has permitted southern Californians actually to convince themselves

that the Los Angeles basin of 1967 is a suitable habitat for *Homo sapiens*.

It is clear that man's present physical and psychic environment is far from optimum, and that permitting today's trends to continue is likely to lead to further rapid deterioration. We also know that we will have a dramatic increase in the death rate in the near future, an increase we can do nothing about. What then should be our course of action?

I think our first move must be to convince all those whom we can that the planet Earth must be viewed as a space ship of limited carrying capacity. It must be made crystal clear that population growth must stop, and we must arrive at a consensus as to what the ideal size of the human crew of the Earth should be. When we have determined the size of the crew, then we can attempt to design an environment in which that crew will be maintained in some sort of optimum state. The socio-political problems raised by such an approach are, of course, colossal. People within cultures have different ideas on how close they want to live to their neighbors, and cross-cultural differences in feelings about crowding are obvious. The only way I can think of for achieving a consensus is for people to start voicing opinions. So here goes.

I think that 150 million people would be an optimum number to live comfortably in the United States. Such a number is clearly enough to maintain our highly technological society. It is also a small enough number that, when properly distributed and accommodated, it should be possible for individuals to find as much solitude and breathing space as they desire. With a population stabilized at such a level we could concentrate on improving the quality of human life at home and abroad. And, what a pleasure it would be to work toward an attainable goal instead of fighting the miserable rear guard action to which runaway population condemns us.

After all, what do we gain from packing more and more people into the United States? Those encouraging population growth in the hope of keeping our economy expanding must realize the consequences of such advocacy. Some men would doubtless accumulate considerable wealth, and would be able to retreat from riot-torn cities to the increasingly smoggy countryside in order to live. If thermonuclear war does not solve their children's problems permanently, what kind of a world will those children inherit? Will their heritage include social disorder and unemployment on an unprecedented scale? Will they have to wear smog masks as a matter of routine? Will they enjoy mock steaks made from processed grass or seaweed? Will they have to be satisfied with camping under plastic trees planted in concrete? Will they accept regimentation and governmental control at a level previously unheard of? Will they fight willingly in small wars and prepare diligently for the big one? Above all, will they be able to retain their sanity in a world gone mad?

Let's suppose that we decide to limit the population of the United States and of the world. How can such limitation be accomplished? Some biologists feel that compulsory family regulation will be necessary to retard population growth. It is a dismal prospect—except when viewed as an alternative to Armageddon. I would like to suggest four less drastic steps which might do the job in the United States. I suggest them in the full knowledge that they are socially unpalatable and politically unrealistic.

The first step would be to establish a Federal Population Commission with a large budget for propaganda which supports reproductive responsibility. This Commission would be charged with making clear the connection between rising population and lowering quality of life. It would also be charged with the evaluation of environmental tinkering by other government agencies—with protecting us from projects such as the FAA's supersonic transports or from the results of the Army Engineer's well-known "beaver complex" (which some predict will only be satiated when every gutter in the country has a dam thrown across it). Commission members should be distinguished citizens, as free as possible from political or bureaucratic meddling.

The second step would be to change our tax laws so that they discourage rather than encourage reproduction. Those who impose the burden of children on society should, whenever they are able, be made to pay for the privilege. Our income tax system should eliminate all deductions for children, and replace them with a graduated scale of increases. Luxury taxes should be placed on diapers, baby bottles, and baby foods. It must be clear to our population that it is socially irresponsible to have large families. Creation of such a climate of opinion has played a large role in Japan's successful dealing with her population problem.

Third, we should pass federal laws which make instruction in birth control methods mandatory in all public schools. Federal legislation should also forbid state laws which limit the right of any woman to have an abortion which is approved by her physician.

Fourth, we should change the pattern of federal support of biomedical research so that the majority of it goes into the broad areas of population regulation, environmental sciences, behavioral sciences, and related areas, rather than into short-sighted programs on death control. It is absurd to be preoccupied with the medical quality of life until and unless the problem of the quantity of life is solved. In this context we must do away with nonsense about how important it is for "smart" people to have large families in order to keep *Homo sapiens* from being selected for stupidity. It is far from established that the less intelligent portion of our population is outreproducing the more intelligent. Even if a reproductive disparity did exist, the worst consequence over a period of a few generations only would be a slight lowering of average intelligence—a slight and *reversible* lowering. And, the consequences of such a lowering, if any, would be a small price to pay for the survival of mankind. Besides, who is going to determine how to measure intelligence and who will decide which people can be permitted to breed? There surely won't be voluntary abstention on the part of the less intelligent—I've never even met anyone who thought he was in the stupid half of the population! *Quantity is the first problem.* If we can lick that one perhaps we will buy the time for scientists in fields such as biochemical genetics to solve some of the problems of quality. If we don't solve the quantity problem, the quality problem will no longer bother us.

All of these steps might produce the desired result of a reversal of today's population growth trend. If they should fail, however, we would then be faced with some form of compulsory birth regulation. We might, for instance, institute a system which would make *positive* action necessary before reproduction is possible. This might be the addition of a temporary sterilant to staple food, or to the water supply. An antidote would have to be taken to permit reproduction. Even with the antidote freely available, the result of such a program would be a drastic reduction in birth rates. If this reduction were not sufficient, the government could dole out the antidote in the proper quantities. If we wished to stabilize the American population at its present level, each married couple could be permitted enough antidote to produce two offspring. Then each couple who wished could be given a chance in a lottery for enough antidote for a third child—the odds carefully computed to produce the desired constancy of population size. At the moment the chances of winning would have to be adjusted to about two out of five, assuming that all couples wanted to play the game!

An attempt to institute such a system is interesting to contemplate, especially when one considers the attitude of the general public towards fluoridation. I would not like to be the first elected official seriously to suggest that a sterility agent be added to our reservoirs! Perhaps it might seem that we can start such a program by treating the wheat we ship to India, or fish meal we ship to South America. Or can we? As you doubtless realize, the solution does not lie in that direction. For one thing, saying that the population explosion is a problem of underdeveloped countries is like telling a fellow passenger "your end of the boat is sinking." For another, it is naive to think that Indians or Brazilians are any more anxious to be fed fertility-destroying chemicals with their daily bread than are Americans. Other people already are suspicious of our motives. Consider what their attitude would be towards an attempt to sterilize them en masse.

If we can solve the population problem at home then we will be in a position to make an all-out effort to halt the growth of the world's population. Perhaps we can shorten the time of famines and lay the groundwork for avoiding a second round of population-food crises. Our program should be tough-minded. We should remember that seemingly charitable gestures such as our grain exports to India have actually harmed rather than helped Indians in the long run. I think that we should:

1. Announce that we will no longer ship food to countries where dispassionate analysis indicates that the food-population unbalance is hopeless.
2. Announce that we will no longer give aid to any country with an increasing population until that country convinces us that it is doing everything within its power to limit its population.

3. Make available to all interested countries massive aid in the technology of birth control.
4. Make available to all interested countries massive aid for increasing yield on land already under cultivation. The most important export in this area should be trained technicians, not fertilizer. We need to establish centers in the country where technicians can be trained not only in agronomy, but also in ecology and sociology. Many of the barriers to increased yields are sociological, and all increase should be made in a manner which minimizes environmental deterioration.
5. Accept the fact that if we can use our power to further military goals then it can also be used for the good of mankind as well. Extreme political and economic pressure should be brought on any country impeding a solution to the world's most pressing problem. A good way to start would be to urge the Vatican to bring its policies into line with the desires of the majority of American Catholics. Much of the world would be horrified at our stand, but as a nation we're clearly willing to go against world opinion on other issues—why not on the most important issue?

Well, perhaps if we get on the ball and set a good example the United States can lead the way in focusing the world's attention on the cause of its major sickness rather than upon the symptoms. Perhaps we can shift our efforts from the long-term pain-depressing activities to the excising of the cancer. The operation will require many brutal and callous decisions. The pain will be intense, but the disease is so far advanced that only with radical surgery does the patient have any chance of survival.

29

America in the Technetronic Age

ZBIGNIEW BRZEZINSKI

Ours is no longer the conventional revolutionary era; we are entering a novel metamorphic phase in human history. The world is on the eve of a transformation more dramatic in its historic and human consequences than that wrought either by the French or the Bolshevik revolutions. Viewed from a long perspective, these famous revolutions merely scratched the surface of the human condition. The changes they precipitated involved alterations in the distribution of power and property within society; they did not affect the essence of individual and social existence. Life—personal and organised—continued much as before, even though some of its external forms (primarily political) were substantially altered. Shocking though it may sound to their acolytes, by the year 2000 it will be accepted that Robespierre and Lenin were mild reformers.

Unlike the revolutions of the past, the developing metamorphosis will have no charismatic leaders with strident doctrines, but its impact will be far more profound. Most of the change that has so far taken place in human history has been gradual—with the great "revolutions" being mere punctuation marks to a slow, eludible process. In contrast, the approaching transformation will come more rapidly and will have deeper consequences for the way and even perhaps for the meaning of human life than anything experienced by the generations that preceded us.

America is already beginning to experience these changes and in the course of so doing it is becoming a "technetronic" society: a society that is shaped culturally, psychologically, socially and economically by the impact of technology and electronics, particularly computers and communications. The industrial process no longer is the principal determinant of social change, altering the mores, the social structure, and the values of society. This change is separating the United States from the rest of the world, prompting a further fragmentation among an increasingly differentiated mankind, and imposing upon Americans a special obligation to ease the pains of the resulting confrontation.

The far-reaching innovations we are about to experience will be the result primarily of the impact of science and technology on man and his society, especially in the developed world. Recent years have seen a proliferation of exciting and challenging literature on the future. Much of it is serious, and not mere science-fiction.[1] Moreover, both in the United States and, to a lesser degree, in Western Europe a number of systematic, scholarly efforts have been designed to project, predict, and possess what the future holds for us. Curiously, very little has been heard on this theme from the Communist World, even though Communist doctrinarians are the first to claim their 19th-century ideology holds a special pass-key to the 21st century.

The work in progress indicates that men living in the developed world will undergo during the next several decades a mutation potentially as basic as that experienced through the slow process of evolution from animal to human experience. The difference, however, is that the process will be telescoped in time—and hence the shock effect of the change may be quite profound. Human conduct will become less spontaneous and less mysterious—more predetermined and subject to deliberate "programming." Man will increasingly possess the capacity to determine the sex of his children, to affect through drugs the extent of their intelligence and to modify and control their personalities. The human brain will acquire expanded powers, with computers becoming as routine an extension of man's reasoning as automobiles have been of man's mobility. The human body will be improved and its durability extended: some estimate that during the next century the average life-span could reach approximately 120 years.

These developments will have major social impact. The prolongation of life will alter our values, our career patterns, and our social relationships. New forms of social control may be needed to limit the indiscriminate exercise by individuals of their new powers. The possibility of extensive chemical mind-control, the danger of loss of individuality inherent in extensive transplantation, and the feasibility of manipulation of the genetic structure will call for a social definition of common criteria of restraint as well as of utilisation. Scientists predict with some confidence that by the end of this century, computers will reason as well as man, and will be able to engage in "creative" thought; wedded to robots or to "laboratory beings," they could act like humans. The makings of a most complex—and perhaps bitter—philosophical and political dialogue about the nature of man are self-evident in these developments.

Other discoveries and refinements will further alter society as we now know it. The information revolution, including extensive information storage, instant retrieval, and eventually push-button visual and sound availability of needed data in almost any private home, will transform the character of institutionalised collective education. The same techniques could serve to impose well-nigh total political surveillance on every citizen, putting into much sharper relief than is the case today the question of privacy. Cybernetics and automation will revolutionise working habits, with leisure becoming the practice and active work the exception—and a privilege reserved for the most talented. The achievement-oriented society might give way to the amusement-focused society, with essentially spectator spectacles (mass sports, TV) providing an opiate for increasingly purposeless masses.

But while for the masses life will grow longer and time will seem to expand, for the activist élite time will become a rare commodity. Indeed, even the élite's sense of time will alter. Already now speed dictates the pace of our lives—instead of the other way around. As the speed of transportation increases, largely by its own technological momentum, man discovers that he has no choice but to avail himself of that acceleration, either to keep up with others or because he thinks he can thus accomplish more. This will be especially true of the élite, for whom an expansion in leisure time does not seem to be in the cards. Thus as speed expands, time contracts—and the pressures on the élite increase.

By the end of this century the citizens of the more developed countries will live predominantly in cities—hence almost surrounded by man-made environment. Confronting nature could be to them what facing the elements was to our forefathers: meeting the unknown and not necessarily liking it. Enjoying a personal standard of living that (in some countries) may reach almost $10,000 per head, eating artificial food, speedily commuting from one corner of the country to work in another, in continual visual contact with their employer, government, or family, consulting their annual calendars to establish on which day it will rain or shine, our descendants will be shaped almost entirely by what they themselves create and control.

But even short of these far-reaching changes, the transformation that is now taking place is already creating a society increasingly unlike its industrial predecessor.[2] In the industrial society, technical knowledge was applied primarily to one specific end: the acceleration and improvement of production techniques. Social consequences were a later by-product of this paramount concern. In the technetronic society, scientific and technological knowledge, in addition to enhancing productive capabilities, quickly spills over to affect directly almost all aspects of life.

This is particularly evident in the case of the impact of communications and computers. Communications create an extraordinarily interwoven society, in continuous visual, audial, and increasingly close contact among almost all its members—electronically interacting, sharing instantly most intense social experiences, prompting far greater personal involvement, with their consciousnesses shaped in a sporadic manner fundamentally different (as McLuhan has noted) from the literate (or pamphleteering) mode of transmitting information, characteristic of the industrial age. The growing capacity for calculating instantly most complex interactions and the increasing availability of bio-chemical means of human control increase the potential scope of self-conscious direction, and thereby also the pressures to direct, to choose, and to change.

The consequence is a society that differs from the industrial one in a variety of economic, political and social aspects. The following examples may be briefly cited to summarise some of the contrasts:

1. In an industrial society, the mode of production shifts from agriculture to industry, with the use of muscle and animals supplanted by machine-operation. In the technetronic society, industrial employment yields to services, with automation and cybernetics replacing individual operation of machines.

2. Problems of employment and unemployment—not to speak of the earlier stage of the urban socialisation of the post-rural labour force —dominate the relationship between employers, labour, and the market in the industrial society; assuring minimum welfare to the new industrial masses is a source of major concern. In the emerging new society, questions relating to skill-obsolescence, security, vacations, leisure, and profit-sharing dominate the relationship; the matter of psychic well-being of millions of relatively secure but potentially aimless lower-middle class blue collar workers becomes a growing problem.

3. Breaking down traditional barriers to education, thus creating the basic point of departure for social advancement, is a major goal of social reformers in the industrial society. Education, available for limited and specific periods of time, is initially concerned with overcoming illiteracy, and subsequently with technical training, largely based on written, sequential reasoning. In the technetronic society, not only has education become universal but advanced training is

available to almost all who have the basic talents. Quantity-training is reinforced by far greater emphasis on quality-selection. The basic problem is to discover the most effective techniques for the rational exploitation of social talent. Latest communication and calculating techniques are applied to that end. The educational process, relying much more on visual and audial devices, becomes extended in time, while the flow of new knowledge necessitates more and more frequent refresher studies.

4. In the industrial society social leadership shifts from the traditional rural-aristocratic to an urban "plutocratic" élite. Newly acquired wealth is its foundation, and intense competition the outlet—as well as the stimulus—for its energy. In the post-industrial technetronic society plutocratic pre-eminence comes under a sustained challenge from the political leadership which itself is increasingly permeated by individuals possessing special skills and intellectual talents. Knowledge becomes a tool of power, and the effective mobilisation of talent an important way for acquiring power.

5. The university in an industrial society—rather in contrast to the medieval times—is an aloof ivory-tower, the repository of irrelevant, even if respected wisdom, and, for only a brief time, the watering fountain for budding members of the established social élite. In the technetronic society, the university becomes an intensely involved *think-tank*, the source of much sustained political planning and social innovation.

6. The turmoil inherent in the shift from the rigidly traditional rural to urban existence engenders an inclination to seek total answers to social dilemmas, thus causing ideologies to thrive in the industrial society.[3] In the technetronic society, increasing ability to reduce social conflicts to quantifiable and measurable dimensions reinforces the trend towards a more pragmatic problem-solving approach to social issues.

7. The activisation of hitherto passive masses makes for intense political conflicts in the industrial society over such matters as disenfranchisement and the right to vote. The issue of political participation is a crucial one. In the technetronic age, the question increasingly is one of ensuring real participation in decisions that seem too complex and too far-removed from the average citizen. Political alienation becomes a problem. Similarly, the issue of political equality of the sexes gives way to a struggle for the sexual equality of women. In the industrial society, woman—the operator of machines—ceases to be physically inferior to the male, a consideration of some importance in rural life, and she begins to demand her political rights. In the emerging society, automation discriminates equally against males and females; intellectual talent is computable; the pill encourages sexual equality.

8. The newly enfranchised masses are coordinated in the industrial society through trade unions and political parties, and integrated by relatively simple and somewhat ideological programmes. Moreover, political attitudes are influenced by appeals to nationalist sentiments, communicated through the massive growth of newspapers, relying, naturally, on native tongues. In the technetronic society, the trend would seem to be towards the aggregation of the individual support of millions of uncoordinated citizens, easily within the reach of magnetic and attractive personalities effectively exploiting the latest communication techniques to manipulate emotions and control reason. Reliance on TV—and hence the tendency to replace language with

imagery, with the latter unlimited by national confines (and also including coverage for such matters as hunger in India or war scenes)—tends to create a somewhat more cosmopolitan, though highly impressionistic, involvement in global affairs.

9. Economic power in the industrial society tends to be personalised, either in the shape of great *entrepreneurs* like Henry Ford or bureaucratic industrialisers like Kaganovich in Russia, or Minc in Poland. The tendency towards de-personalisation of economic power is stimulated in the next stage by the appearance of a highly complex interdependence between governmental institutions (including the military), scientific establishments, and industrial organisations. As economic power becomes inseparably linked with political power, it becomes more invisible and the sense of individual futility increases.

10. Relaxation and escapism in the industrial society, in its more intense forms, is a carry-over from the rural drinking bout, in which intimate friends and family would join. Bars and saloons—or fraternities—strive to recreate the atmosphere of intimacy. In the technetronic society social life tends to be so atomised, even though communications (especially TV) make for unprecedented immediacy of social experience, that group intimacy cannot be recreated through the artificial stimulation of externally convivial group behaviour. The new interest in drugs seeks to create intimacy through introspection, allegedly by expanding consciousness.

Eventually, these changes and many others, including the ones that affect much more directly the personality and quality of the human being itself, will make the technetronic society as different from the industrial as the industrial became from the agrarian.

America is today in the midst of a transition. U.S. society is leaving the phase of spontaneity and is entering a more self-conscious stage; ceasing to be an industrial society, it is becoming the first technetronic one. This is at least in part the cause for much of the current tensions and violence.

Spontaneity made for an almost automatic optimism about the future, about the "American miracle," about justice and happiness for all. This myth prompted social blinders to the various aspects of American life that did not fit the optimistic mould, particularly the treatment of the Negro and the persistence of pockets of deprivation. Spontaneity involved a faith in the inherent goodness of the American socio-economic dynamic: as America developed, grew, became richer, problems that persisted or appeared would be solved.

This phase is ending. Today, American society is troubled and some parts of it are even tormented. The social blinders are being ripped off—and a sense of inadequacy is becoming more widespread. The spread of literacy, and particularly the access to college and universities of about 40% of the youth, has created a new stratum—one which reinforces the formerly isolated urban intellectuals—a stratum not willing to tolerate either social blinders nor sharing the complacent belief in the spontaneous goodness of American social change.

Yet it is easier to know what is wrong than to indicate what ought to be done. The difficulty is not only revealed by the inability of the new social rebels to develop a concrete and meaningful programme. It is magnified by the novelty of America's problem. Turning to 19th-century ideologies is not the answer—and it is symptomatic that the "New Left" has found it most difficult to apply the available, particularly Marxist, doctrines to the new reality. Indeed, its emphasis on human rights, the evils of depersonalisation, the dangers inherent in big government—so responsive to the felt psychological needs—contain strong parallels to more conservative notions about the place and sanctity of the individual in society.

In some ways, there is an analogy here between the "New Left" and the searching attitude of various disaffected groups in early 19th-century Europe, reacting to the first strains of the industrial age. Not fully comprehending its meaning, not quite certain where it was heading—yet sensitive to the miseries and opportunities it was bringing—many Europeans strove desperately to adapt earlier, 18th-century doctrines to the new reality. It was finally Marx who achieved what appeared to many millions a meaningful synthesis, combining utopian idealism about the future of the industrial age with a scorching critique of its present.

The search for meaning is characteristic of the present American scene. It could portend most divisive and bitter ideological conflicts —especially as intellectual disaffection becomes linked with the increasing bitterness of the deprived Negro masses. If carried to its extreme, this could bring to America a phase of violent, intolerant, and destructive civil strife, combining ideological and racial intolerance.

However, it seems unlikely that a unifying ideology of political action, capable of mobilising large-scale loyalty, can emerge in the manner that Marxism arose in response to the industrial era. Unlike even Western Europe or Japan—not to speak of Soviet Russia—where the consequences and the impact of the industrial process are still reshaping political, social, and economic life, in America science and technology (particularly as socially applied through communications and increasing computerisation, both offsprings of the industrial age) are already more important in influencing the social behaviour of a society that has moved past its industrial phase. Science and technology are notoriously unsympathetic to simple, absolute formulas. In the technetronic society there may be room for pragmatic, even impatient, idealism, but hardly for doctrinal utopianism.

At the same time, it is already evident that a resolution of some of the unfinished business of the industrial era will be rendered more acute. For example, the Negro should have been integrated into U.S. society *during* the American industrial revolution. Yet that revolution came before America, even if not the Negro, was ready for full integration. If the Negro had been only an economic legacy of the pre-industrial age, perhaps he could have integrated more effectively. To-day, the more advanced urban-industrial regions of America, precisely because they are moving into a new and more complex phase, requiring even more developed social skills, are finding it very difficult to integrate the Negro, both a racial minority and America's only "feudal legacy." Paradoxically, it can be argued that the American South today stands a better long-range chance of fully integrating the Negro: American consciousness is changing, the Negro has stirred, and the South is beginning to move into the industrial age. The odds are that it may take the Negro along with it.

Whatever the outcome, American society is the one in which the great questions of our time will be first tested through practice. Can the individual and science co-exist, or will the dynamic momentum of the latter fundamentally alter the former? Can man, living in the scientific age, grow in intellectual depth and philosophical meaning, and thus in his personal liberty too? Can the institutions of political democracy be adapted to the new conditions sufficiently quickly to meet the crises, yet without debasing their democratic character?

The challenge in its essence involves the twin-dangers of fragmentation and excessive control. A few examples. Symptoms of alienation and depersonalisation are already easy to find in American society. Many Americans feel "less free"; this feeling seems to be connected with their loss of "purpose"; freedom implies choice of action, and action requires an awareness of goals. If the present transition of America to the technetronic age achieves no personally satisfying fruits, the next phase may be one of sullen withdrawal from social and political involvement, a flight from social and political responsibility through "inner-emigration." Political frustration could increase the difficulty of absorbing and internalising rapid environmental changes, thereby prompting increasing psychic instability.

At the same time, the capacity to assert social and political control over the individual will vastly increase. As I have already noted, it will soon be possible to assert almost continuous surveillance over every citizen and to maintain up-to-date, complete files, containing even most personal information about the health or personal behaviour of the citizen, in addition to more customary data. These files will be subject to instantaneous retrieval by the authorities.

Moreover, the rapid pace of change will put a premium on anticipating events and planning for them. Power will gravitate into the hands of those who control the information, and can correlate it most rapidly. Our existing *post*-crisis management institutions will probably be increasingly supplanted by *pre*-crisis management institutions, the task of which will be to identify in advance likely social crises and to develop programmes to cope with them. This could encourage tendencies during the next several decades towards a technocratic dictatorship, leaving less and less room for political procedures as we now know them.

Finally, looking ahead to the end of this century, the possibility of bio-chemical mind-control and genetic tinkering with man, including eventually the creation of beings that will function like men —and reason like them as well—could give rise to the most difficult questions. According to what criteria can such controls be applied? What is the distribution of power between the individual and society with regard to means that can altogether alter man? What is the social and political status of artificial beings, if they begin to approach man in their performance and creative capacities? (One dares not ask, what if they begin to "outstrip man"—something not beyond the pale of possibility during the next century?)

Yet it would be highly misleading to construct a one-sided picture, a new Orwellian piece of science-fiction. Many of the changes transforming American society augur well for the future and allow at least some optimism about this society's capacity to adapt to the requirements of the metamorphic age.

Thus, in the political sphere, the increased flow of information and more efficient techniques of co-ordination need not necessarily prompt greater concentration of power within some ominous control agency located at the governmental apex. Paradoxically, these developments also make possible greater devolution of authority and responsibility to the lower levels of government and society. The division of power has traditionally posed the problems of inefficiency, co-ordination, and dispersal of authority; but today the new communications and computer techniques make possible both increased authority at the lower levels and almost instant national co-ordination. It is very likely that state and local government will be strengthened in the next ten years, and many functions currently the responsibility of the Federal government will be assumed by them.[4]

The devolution of financial responsibility to lower echelons may encourage both the flow of better talent and greater local participation in more important local decision-making. National co-ordination and local participation could thus be wedded by the new systems of co-ordination. This has already been tried successfully by some large businesses. This development would also have the desirable effect of undermining the appeal of any new integrating ideologies that may arise; for ideologies thrive only as long as there is an acute need for abstract responses to large and remote problems.

It is also a hopeful sign that improved governmental performance, and its increased sensitivity to social needs is being stimulated by the growing involvement in national affairs of what Kenneth Boulding has called the Educational and Scientific Establishment (EASE). The university at one time, during the Middle Ages, was a key social institution. Political leaders leaned heavily on it for literate confidants and privy counsellors, a rare commodity in those days. Later divorced from reality, academia in recent years has made a grand re-entry into the world of action.

Today, the university is the creative eye of the massive communications complex, the source of much strategic planning, domestic and international. Its engagement in the world is encouraging the appearance of a new breed of politicians-intellectuals, men who make it a point to mobilise and draw on the most expert, scientific and academic advice in the development of their political programmes. This, in turn, stimulates public awareness of the value of expertise—and, again in turn, greater political competition in exploiting it.

A profound change in the intellectual community itself is inherent

in this development. The largely humanist-oriented, occasionally ideo-
logically-minded intellectual-dissenter, who saw his role largely in terms
of proffering social critiques, is rapidly being displaced either by experts and specialists, who become involved in special governmental
undertakings, or by the generalists-integrators, who become in effect
house-ideologues for those in power, providing overall intellectual integration for disparate actions. A community of organisation-oriented,
application-minded intellectuals, relating itself more effectively to the
political system than their predecessors, serves to introduce into the
political system concerns broader than those likely to be generated
by that system itself and perhaps more relevant than those articulated
by outside critics.[5]

The expansion of knowledge, and the entry into socio-political life
of the intellectual community, has the further effect of making education an almost continuous process. By 1980, not only will approximately
two-thirds of U.S. urban dwellers be college-trained, but it is almost
certain that systematic "élite-retraining" will be standard in the political system. It will be normal for every high official both to be engaged in almost continuous absorption of new techniques and knowledge, and to take periodic retraining. The adoption of compulsory
elementary education was a revolution brought on by the industrial
age. In the new technetronic society, it will be equally necessary to
require everyone at a sufficiently responsible post to take, say, two years
of retraining every ten years. (Perhaps there will even be a constitutional amendment, requiring a President-elect to spend at least a year
getting himself educationally up-to-date.) Otherwise, it will not be
possible either to keep up with, or absorb, the new knowledge.

Given diverse needs, it is likely that the educational system will
undergo a fundamental change in structure. Television-computer con-
soles, capable of bringing most advanced education to the home, will
permit extensive and continuous adult re-education. On the more advanced levels, it is likely that government agencies and corporations
will develop—and some have already begun to do so—their own advanced educational systems, shaped to their special needs. As education becomes both a continuum, and even more application-oriented,
its organisational framework will be re-designed to tie it directly to
social and political action.

It is quite possible that a society increasingly geared to learning
will be able to absorb more resiliently the expected changes in social
and individual life. Mechanisation of labour and the introduction of
robots will reduce the chores that keep millions busy doing things
that they dislike doing. The increasing GNP (which could reach approximately $10,000 per capita per year), linked with educational ad-
vance, could prompt among those less involved in social management
and less interested in scientific development a wave of interest in the
cultural and humanistic aspects of life, in addition to purely hedonistic
preoccupations. But even the latter would serve as a social valve, reducing tensions and political frustration. Greater control over external
environment could make for easier, less uncertain existence.

But the key to successful adaptation to the new conditions is in effective selection, distribution and utilisation of social talent. If the industrial society can be said to have developed through a struggle for survival of the fittest, the technetronic society—in order to prosper—requires the effective mobilisation of the ablest. Objective and systematic criteria for the selection of those with the greatest gifts will have to be developed, and the maximum opportunity for their training and advancement provided. The new society will require enormous talents —as well as a measure of philosophical wisdom—to manage and integrate effectively the expected changes. Otherwise, the dynamic of change could chaotically dictate the patterns of social change.

Fortunately, American society is becoming more conscious not only of the principle of equal opportunity for all but of special opportunity for the singularly talented few. Never truly an aristocratic state (except for some pockets such as the South and New England), never really subject to ideological or charismatic leadership, gradually ceasing to be a plutocratic-oligarchic society, the U.S.A. is becoming something which may be labelled the "meritocratic democracy." It combines continued respect for the popular will with an increasing role in the key decision-making institutions of individuals with special intellectual and scientific attainments. The educational and social systems are making it increasingly attractive and easy for those meritocratic few to develop to the fullest their special potential. The recruitment and advancement of social talent is yet to extend to the poorest and the most underprivileged, but that too is coming. No one can tell whether this will suffice to meet the unfolding challenge, but the increasingly cultivated and programmed American society, led by a meritocratic democracy, may stand a better chance.

For the world at large, the appearance of the new technetronic society could have the paradoxical effect of creating more distinct worlds on a planet that is continuously shrinking because of the communications revolution. While the scientific-technological change will inevitably have some spill-over, not only will the gap between the developed and the underdeveloped worlds become wider—especially in the more measurable terms of economic indices—but a *new one* may be developing *within* the industrialised and urban world.

The fact is that America, having left the industrial phase, is today entering a distinct historical era: and one different from that of Western Europe and Japan. This is prompting subtle and still indefinable changes in the American psyche, providing the psycho-cultural bases for the more evident political disagreements between the two sides of the Atlantic. To be sure, there are pockets of innovation or retardation on both sides. Sweden shares with America the problems of leisure, psychic well-being, purposelessness; while Mississippi is experiencing the confrontation with the industrial age in a way not unlike some parts of South-Western Europe. But I believe the broad generalisation still holds true: Europe and America are no longer in the same historical era.

What makes America unique in our time is that it is the first society to experience the future. The confrontation with the new—which will soon include much of what I have outlined—is part of the daily American experience. For better or for worse, the rest of the world learns what is in store for it by observing what happens in the U.S.A.: in the latest scientific discoveries in space, in medicine, or the electric toothbrush in the bathroom; in pop art or LSD, air conditioning or air pollution, old-age problems or juvenile delinquency. The evidence is more elusive in such matters as music, style, values, social mores; but there, too, the term "Americanisation" obviously defines the source. Today, America is *the* creative society; the others, consciously and unconsciously, are emulative.

American scientific leadership is particularly strong in the so-called "frontier" industries, involving the most advanced fields of science. It has been estimated that approximately 80% of all scientific and technical discoveries made during the last few decades originated in the United States. About 75% of the world's computers operate in the United States; the American lead in lasers is even more marked; examples of American scientific lead are abundant.

There is reason to assume that this leadership will continue. America has four times as many scientists and research workers as the countries of the European Economic Community combined; three-and-a-half times as many as the Soviet Union. The brain-drain is almost entirely one-way. The United States is also spending more on research: seven times as much as the E.E.C. countries, three-and-a-half times as much as the Soviet Union. Given the fact that scientific development is a dynamic process, it is likely that the gap will widen.[6]

On the social level, American innovation is most strikingly seen in the manner in which the new meritocratic élite is taking over American life, utilising the universities, exploiting the latest techniques of communications, harnessing as rapidly as possible the most recent technological devices. Technetronics dominate American life, but so far nobody else's. This is bound to have social and political—and therefore also psychological—consequences, stimulating a psycho-cultural gap in the developed world.

At the same time, the backward regions of the world are becoming more, rather than less, poor in relation to the developed world. It can be roughly estimated that the per capita income of the underdeveloped world is approximately ten times lower than of America and Europe (and twenty-five times of America itself). By the end of the century, the ratio may be about fifteen-to-one (or possibly thirty-to-one in the case of the U.S.), with the backward nations *at best* approaching the present standard of the very poor European nations but in many cases (*e.g.*, India) probably not even attaining that modest level.

The social élites of these regions, however, will quite naturally tend to assimilate and emulate, as much as their means and power permit, the life-styles of the most advanced world, with which they are, and increasingly will be, in close vicarious contact through global television, movies, travel, education, and international magazines. The international gap will thus have a domestic reflection, with the masses, given the availability even in most backward regions of transistorised radios (and soon television), becoming more and more intensely aware of their deprivation.

It is difficult to conceive how in that context democratic institutions (derived largely from Western experience—but typical only of the more stable and wealthy Western nations) will endure in a country like India, or develop elsewhere. The foreseeable future is more likely to see a turn towards personal dictatorships and some unifying doctrines, in the hope that the combination of the two may preserve the minimum stability necessary for social-economic development. The problem, however, is that whereas in the past ideologies of change gravitated from the developed world to the less, in a way stimulating imitation of the developed world (as was the case with Communism), today the differences between the two worlds are so pronounced that it is difficult to conceive a new ideological wave originating from the developed world, where the tradition of utopian thinking is generally declining.

With the widening gap dooming any hope of imitation, the more likely development is an ideology of rejection of the developed world. Racial hatred could provide the necessary emotional force, exploited by xenophobic and romantic leaders. The writings of Frantz Fanon —violent and racist—are a good example. Such ideologies of rejection, combining racialism with nationalism, would further reduce the chances of meaningful regional co-operation, so essential if technology and science are to be effectively applied. They would certainly widen the existing psychological and emotional gaps. Indeed, one might ask at that point: who is the truer repository of that indefinable quality we call human? The technologically dominant and conditioned technetron, increasingly trained to adjust to leisure, or the more "natural" and backward agrarian, more and more dominated by racial passions and continuously exhorted to work harder, even as his goal of the good life becomes more elusive?

The result could be a modern version on a global scale of the old rural-urban dichotomy. In the past, the strains produced by the shift from an essentially agricultural economy to a more urban one contributed much of the impetus for revolutionary violence.[7] Applied on a global scale, this division could give substance to Lin Piao's bold thesis that:

> Taking the entire globe, if North America and Western Europe can be called "the cities of the world," then Asia, Africa and Latin America constitute "the rural areas of the world." . . . In a sense, the contemporary world revolution also presents a picture of the encirclement of cities by the rural areas.

In any case, even without envisaging such a dichotomic confrontation, it is fair to say that the underdeveloped regions will be facing increasingly grave problems of political stability and social survival. Indeed (to use a capsule formula), in the developed world, the nature of man as man is threatened; in the underdeveloped, society is. The interaction of the two could produce chaos.

To be sure, the most advanced states will possess ever more deadly means of destruction, possibly even capable of nullifying the consequences of the nuclear proliferation that appears increasingly inevitable. Chemical and biological weapons, death rays, neutron bombs, nerve gases, and a host of other devices, possessed in all their sophisticated variety (as seems likely) only by the two super-states, may impose on the world a measure of stability. Nonetheless, it seems unlikely, given the rivalry between the two principal powers, that a full-proof system against international violence can be established. Some local wars between the weaker, nationalistically more aroused, poorer nations may occasionally erupt—resulting perhaps even in the total nuclear extinction of one or several smaller nations?—before greater international control is imposed in the wake of the universal moral shock thereby generated.

The underlying problem, however, will be to find a way of avoiding somehow the widening of the cultural and psycho-social gap inherent in the growing differentiation of the world. Even with gradual differentiation throughout human history, it was not until the industrial revolution that sharp differences between societies began to appear. Today, some nations still live in conditions not unlike pre-Christian times; many no different than in the medieval age. Yet soon a few will live in ways so new that it is now difficult to imagine their social and individual ramifications. If the developed world takes a leap—as seems inescapably the case—into a reality that is even more different from ours today than ours is from an Indian village, the gap and its accompanying strains will not narrow.

On the contrary, the instantaneous electronic intermeshing of mankind will make for an intense confrontation, straining social and international peace. In the past, differences were "livable" because of time and distance that separated them. Today, these differences are actually widening while technetronics are eliminating the two insulants of time and distance. The resulting trauma could create almost entirely different perspectives on life, with insecurity, envy, and hostility becoming the dominant emotions for increasingly large numbers of people. A three-way split into rural-backward, urban-industrial, and technetronic ways of life can only further divide man, intensify the existing difficulties to global understanding, and give added vitality to latent or existing conflicts.

The pace of American development both widens the split within mankind and contains the seeds for a constructive response. However, neither military power nor material wealth, both of which America possesses in abundance, can be used directly in responding to the onrushing division in man's thinking, norms, and character. Power, at best, can assure only a relatively stable external environment: the tempering or containing of the potential global civil war; wealth can grease points of socio-economic friction, thereby facilitating development. But

as man—especially in the most advanced societies—moves increasingly
into the phase of controlling and even creating his environment, increasing attention will have to be given to giving man meaningful content—to improving the quality of life for man *as man*.

> Man has never really tried to use science in the realm of his value systems.
> Ethical thinking is hard to change, but history demonstrates that it does
> change. . . . Man does, in limited ways, direct his very important and
> much more rapid psycho-social education. The evolution of such things
> as automobiles, airplanes, weapons, legal institutions, corporations,
> universities, and democratic governments are examples of progressive
> evolution in the course of time. We have, however, never really tried
> deliberately to create a better society for man *qua* man. . . .[8]

The urgent need to do just that may compel America to redefine
its global posture. During the remainder of this century, given the perspective on the future I have outlined here, America is likely to become less concerned with "fighting communism" or creating "a world
safe for diversity" than with helping to develop a common response
with the rest of mankind to the implications of a truly new era. This
will mean making the massive diffusion of scientific-technological knowledge a principal focus of American involvement in world affairs.

To some extent, the U.S. performs that role already—simply by
being what it is. The impact of its reality and its global involvement
prompts emulation. The emergence of vast international corporations,
mostly originating in the United States, makes for easier transfer of
skills, management techniques, marketing procedures, and scientific-
technological innovations. The appearance of these corporations in the
European market has done much to stimulate Europeans to consider
more urgently the need to integrate their resources and to accelerate
the pace of their own research and development.

Similarly, returning graduates from American universities have
prompted an organisational and intellectual revolution in the academic
life of their countries. Changes in the academic life of Britain, Germany,
Japan, more recently France, and (to even a greater extent) in the less
developed countries, can be traced to the influence of U.S. educational
institutions. Indeed, the leading technological institute in Turkey con-
ducts its lectures in "American" and is deliberately imitating, not only
in approach but in student-professor relationships, U.S. patterns. Given
developments in modern communications, is it not only a matter of
time before students at Columbia University and, say, the University
of Teheran will be watching, *simultaneously*, the same lecturer?

The appearance of a universal intellectual élite, one that shares
certain common values and aspirations, will somewhat compensate for
the widening differentiation among men and societies. But it will not
resolve the problem posed by that differentiation. In many backward
nations tension between what is and what can be will be intensified.
Moreover, as Kenneth Boulding observed:

> The network of electronic communication is inevitably producing a world
> super-culture, and the relations between this super-culture and the more

traditional national and regional cultures of the past remains the great question mark of the next fifty years.[9]

That "super-culture," strongly influenced by American life, with its own universal electronic-computer language, will find it difficult to relate itself to "the more traditional and regional cultures," especially if the basic gap continues to widen.

To cope with that gap, a gradual change in diplomatic style and emphasis may have to follow the redefined emphasis of America's involvement in world affairs. Professional diplomacy will have to yield to intellectual leadership. With government negotiating directly—or quickly dispatching the negotiators—there will be less need for ambassadors who are resident diplomats and more for ambassadors who are capable of serving as creative interpreters of the new age, willing to engage in a meaningful dialogue with the host intellectual community and concerned with promoting the widest possible dissemination of available knowledge. Theirs will be the task to stimulate and to develop scientific-technological programmes of co-operation.

International co-operation will be necessary in almost every facet of life: to reform and to develop more modern educational systems, to promote new sources of food supply, to accelerate economic development, to stimulate technological growth, to control climate, to disseminate new medical knowledge. However, because the new élites have a vested interest in their new nation-states and because of the growing xenophobia among the masses in the third world, the nation-state will remain for a long time the primary focus of loyalty, especially for newly liberated and economically backward peoples. To predict loudly its death, and to act often as if it were dead, could prompt (as it did partially in Europe) an adverse reaction from those whom one would wish to influence. Hence, regionalism will have to be promoted with due deference to the symbolic meaning of national sovereignty—and preferably also by encouraging those concerned themselves to advocate regional approaches.

Even more important will be the stimulation, for the first time in history on a global scale, of the much needed dialogue on what it is about man's life that we wish to safeguard or to promote, and on the relevance of existing moral systems to an age that cannot be fitted into the narrow confines of fading doctrines. The search for new directions —going beyond the tangibles of economic development—could be an appropriate subject for a special world congress, devoted to the technetronic and philosophical problems of the coming age. To these issues no one society, however advanced, is in a position to provide an answer.

NOTES

[1] Perhaps the most useful single source is to be found in the Summer 1967 issue of *Daedalus,* devoted entirely to *"Toward the Year 2000: Work in Progress."* The introduction by Professor Daniel Bell, chairman of the American Academy's Commission on the Year 2000 (of which the present writer is also a member) summarises some of the principal literature on the subject.

2 See Daniel Bell's pioneering "Notes on the Post-Industrial Society," *The Public Interest*, Nos. 6 and 7, 1967.

3 The American exception to this rule was due to the absence of the feudal tradition, a point well developed by Louis Hartz in his work *The Liberal Tradition in America* (1955).

4 It is noteworthy that the U.S. Army has so developed its control-systems that it is not uncommon for sergeants to call in and co-ordinate massive air-strikes and artillery fire—a responsibility of colonels during World War II.

5 However, there is a danger in all this that ought not to be neglected. Intense involvement in applied knowledge could gradually prompt a waning of the tradition of learning for the sake of learning. The intellectual community, including the university, could become another "industry," meeting social needs as the market dictates, with the intellectuals reaching for the highest material and political rewards. Concern with power, prestige, and the good life could mean an end to the aristocratic ideal of intellectual detachment and the disinterested search for truth.

6 In the Soviet case, rigid compartmentalisation between secret military research and industrial research has had a particularly sterile effect of inhibiting spill-over from weapons research into industrial application.

7 See Barrington Moore's documentation of this in his pioneering study *Social Origins of Dictatorship and Democracy* (1967).

8 Hudson Hoagland, "Biology, Brains, and Insight," *Columbia University Forum*, Summer 1967.

9 Kenneth Boulding, "Expecting the Unexpected," *Prospective Changes in Society by 1980* (1960).